The Cambridge Companion to Tolstoy

Best known for his great novels, *War and Peace* and *Anna Karenina*, Tolstoy remains one the most important nineteenth-century writers; throughout his career, which spanned nearly three-quarters of a century, he wrote fiction, journalistic essays, and educational textbooks. The specially commissioned essays in *The Cambridge Companion to Tolstoy* do justice to the sheer volume of Tolstoy's writing. Key dimensions of his writing and life are explored in essays focusing on his relationship to popular writing, the issue of gender and sexuality in his fiction, and his aesthetics. The introduction provides a brief, unified account of the man, for whom art was only one activity among many. The volume is well supported by supplementary material including a detailed guide to further reading and a chronology of Tolstoy's life, the most comprehensive compiled in English to date. Altogether the volume provides an invaluable resource for students and scholars alike.

CAMBRIDGE COMPANIONS TO LITERATURE

CAMBRIDGE COMPANIONS TO CULTURE

THE CAMBRIDGE
COMPANION TO
TOLSTOY

EDITED BY
DONNA TUSSING ORWIN
University of Toronto

CAMBRIDGE
UNIVERSITY PRESS

PUBLISHED BY THE PRESS SYNDICATE OF THE UNIVERSITY OF CAMBRIDGE
The Pitt Building, Trumpington Street, Cambridge, United Kingdom

CAMBRIDGE UNIVERSITY PRESS
The Edinburgh Building, Cambridge CB2 2RU, UK
40 West 20th Street, New York, NY 10011-4211, USA
477 Williamstown Road, Port Melbourne, VIC 3207, Australia
Ruiz de Alarcón 13, 28014 Madrid, Spain
Dock House, The Waterfront, Cape Town 8001, South Africa

http://www.cambridge.org

First published 2002

Printed in the United Kingdom at the University Press, Cambridge

Typeface Sabon 10/13 pt   *System* LATEX 2$_\varepsilon$ [TB]

A catalogue record for this book is available from the British Library

ISBN 0 521 79271 1 hardback
ISBN 0 521 52000 2 paperback

CONTENTS

CONTRIBUTORS

GEORGE R. CLAY is a fiction writer, literary essayist, and reviewer whose work has appeared in *The New Yorker, The Best American Short Stories*, and *The International Fiction Review*, among other publications. In 1998, Northwestern University Press published his monograph: *Tolstoy's Phoenix: From Method to Meaning in "War and Peace."*

EDWINA CRUISE is Professor of Russian and Chair of the Department of Russian and Eurasian Studies at Mount Holyoke College. Her special teaching interests include elementary Russian language, the novel, Tolstoy, and Chekhov and the drama. Her current research, on the horse in Russian culture, with a special emphasis on Tolstoy, is reflected in her recent publications. Professor Cruise is Business Manager for the *Tolstoy Studies Journal*.

CARYL EMERSON is A. Watson Armour III University Professor of Slavic Languages and Literatures at Princeton University, with a co-appointment in Comparative Literature. She is a translator and critic of the Russian literary critic and philosopher, Mikhail Bakhtin, and has published widely on nineteenth-century Russian literature (Pushkin, Dostoevsky, Tolstoy, and Chekhov), the history of literary criticism, and Russian opera and vocal music. Most recently she is the author of *The First Hundred Years of Mikhail Bakhtin* and a biography of Modest Mussorgsky.

RICHARD FREEBORN is Professor Emeritus of Russian Literature, University of London. He is the author of monographs on Turgenev, Russian history, the Russian nineteenth-century novel, and the Russian revolutionary novel; a translator of Turgenev (*Sketches from a Hunter's Album, Rudin, Home of the Gentry, Fathers and Sons, First Love and Other Stories*, and others) and Dostoevsky (*An Accidental Family*). Professor Freeborn is also an editor and novelist.

GARY R. JAHN teaches Russian language and literature at the University of Minnesota. He is the author of numerous essays and papers on Tolstoy and other Russian writers and has written a critical monograph and edited an anthology of essays on *The Death of Ivan Ilich*. He has also developed three major computer-assisted language-learning projects, and more recently has been working on the development of a model for the implementation of electronically enhanced scholarly editions of Russian literary masterworks.

W. GARETH JONES is Professor Emeritus, the University of Wales, Bangor. He has written extensively on aspects of the Russian eighteenth-century enlightenment including *Nikolay Novikov: Enlightener of Russia*. Among his publications on nineteenth- and twentieth-century Russian literature are editions of Tolstoy's *What is Art?*, *I Cannot be Silent: Writings on Politics, Art and Religion by Leo Tolstoy* and the collection *Tolstoi and Britain*.

LIZA KNAPP teaches Russian literature at the University of California at Berkeley. She is the author of *The Annihilation of Inertia: Dostoevsky and Metaphysics*, the editor of Dostoevsky's *The Idiot: A Critical Companion*, and the co-editor, with Amy Mandelker, of *Approaches to Teaching Anna Karenina*, which is in preparation for the Modern Languages Association "Approaches to Teaching World Literature" series.

BARBARA LÖNNQVIST is Professor of Russian Language and Literature at Abo Akademi, the Swedish-language university in Turku (Abo), Finland. She has written extensively on Russian Modernism (Khlebnikov, Pasternak, Tsvetaeva, Akhmatova) but has lately devoted herself to a close reading of Tolstoy. Her special interest is the relationship between folklore and literature.

HUGH MCLEAN is Professor Emeritus at the University of California at Berkeley. He is the author of *Nikolai Leskov: The Man and His Art*. He edited the volume *In the Shade of the Giant: Essays on Tolstoy* and has also published articles on Pushkin, Gogol, Chekhov, and Mayakovsky as well as on Leskov and Tolstoy. He wrote the essay on "The Countryside" for the *Cambridge Companion to the Russian Novel*.

GARY SAUL MORSON is Frances Hooper Professor of the Arts and Humanities and McCormick Professor of Teaching Excellence at Northwestern University, Illinois. He won the Rene Wellek award for *Narrative and Freedom: The Shadows of Time*, and has published, under the pseudonym

Alicia Chudo, *And Quiet Flows the Vodka: The Curmudgeon's Guide to Russian Literature and Culture.*

DONNA TUSSING ORWIN teaches Russian literature at the University of Toronto. She is the author of *Tolstoy's Art and Thought, 1847–1880*, co-editor (with Robin Feuer Miller) of Kathryn Feuer's posthumously published *Tolstoy and the Genesis of "War and Peace"*, and the editor of *Tolstoy Studies Journal*.

ANDREW WACHTEL is Herman and Beulah Pearce Miller Research Professor in Literature, Chair of the Department of Slavic Languages and Literatures, and Director of the Program in Comparative Literary Studies at Northwestern University. His most recent book is *Making a Nation, Breaking a Nation: Literature and Cultural Politics in Yugoslavia*. Earlier books include *The Battle for Childhood: Creation of a Russian Myth, An Obsession with History: Russian Writers Confront the Past*, and *Petrushka: Sources and Contexts*. Professor Wachtel is editor of Northwestern University Press's acclaimed series "Writings from an Unbound Europe."

Leo Tolstoy presents special challenges to the editor of a single volume that seeks in any way to be comprehensive. He wrote steadily for six decades and for at least half that time he was acknowledged by almost everyone as the greatest living Russian writer. He was more than a writer of fiction. He was an indefatigable letter writer. His diaries alone take up many volumes of his collected works and constitute in themselves a unique product of his genius. In his old age he published a controversial book on aesthetics. He studied philosophy in his youth and wrote philosophical tracts in his old age. Later in life he became a social critic, a prophet of Old Testament intensity and doom, a creator of an influential if now largely forgotten social movement (Tolstoyanism), and even the founder of a new variety of Christianity. He rewrote the Gospels, and endorsed William Jennings Bryan in the 1904 American presidential elections. His life, exhaustively documented in his later years, was the stuff of daytime soaps.

Rather than mapping this entire vast terrain, the essays in *The Cambridge Companion to Tolstoy* focus on areas most accessible to the general reader while making brief excursions into more remote territory. Collectively the contributors do justice to the sheer number of works by Tolstoy and to the long time period over which they were written. They concentrate on the fiction, but provide some commentary on other kinds of writing as well. The widely divergent critical approaches of the individual essays help the reader break through the surface illusion of simplicity and "reality" to the complex and beautiful mysteries which dwell beneath the surface of Tolstoy's texts. Each essay stands on its own, of course, but using the index readers can also follow a work horizontally, across chapters. In other words, the aim of this Companion is not to explain Tolstoy in a textbook format, but to introduce him to readers who, having read some or all of the essays in it, will return to the primary texts ready to engage with them on a deeper level.

The subject of the introduction is Tolstoy himself, as author of those ninety volumes within which we devoted scholars toil. In my Introduction I discuss him from three different perspectives on human beings that intersect in his fiction: the psychological, the historico-cultural, and the philosophical. The volume also contains a chronology of Tolstoy's life that is longer and more detailed than any that has appeared before in English. Here the aim is not interpretation, but breadth, and as balanced a picture of the man as possible. Contradictions are allowed to stand and await explanation (or not) from others. Of course I am aware that any biographical material interprets, if only by what it leaves out. The chronology lists the most significant events in Tolstoy's life. It centres narrowly on Tolstoy himself – not, for instance, following the lives of even his closest relatives – but on a few occasions mentions an historical event which Tolstoy himself regarded as immensely important. The comments of or quotations from Tolstoy that supplement the events are characteristic or represent a pattern; throwaway remarks, of which there are very many in so well documented a life, are excluded. The chronology is intended to be comprehensive enough to provide background for the various chapters in this book, as well as starting points for discussion and more detailed investigations.

Donna Tussing Orwin

ACKNOWLEDGMENTS

It has been an honor and a pleasure to work with the contributors to this volume. I owe a special thanks to Edwina Cruise and Caryl Emerson, who edited the work of the editor. Linda Bree and Rachel De Wachter of Cambridge University Press have been supportive and understanding as various glitches in the making of the volume confirmed the truth of Tolstoy's theory of the unpredictability of history. Penny Wheeler has done an excellent job as copy editor. The Tolstoy Museum at Iasnaia Poliana provided slides for the cover of this book, and I want to thank both the Museum Director, Vladimir Tolstoy, and Head of the Research Department, Galina Alexeeva, for this. I am grateful to Megan Swift for her assistance in preparing the chronology, and Jennifer Olson for her work on the index. I am especially indebted to Edith Klein, Production Editor at *Tolstoy Studies Journal*, who has advised me on all matters relating to form in this project. Finally, I want to thank my husband, Clifford Orwin, for his support and encouragement.

NOTE ON EDITIONS, CITATIONS, AND TRANSLITERATIONS

There is no standard English edition of Tolstoy's works, so the contributors have been asked to refer, where possible, to editions in print and readily available. The standard Russian edition is the Academy, or Jubilee, in ninety volumes. Within each chapter of this Companion, contributors have keyed all references to Tolstoy's works, first to the specified English edition or editions and then to the Jubilee (abbreviated as *PSS*) by volume and page numbers. In a further complication, some English editions, especially of the long novels, alter chapter divisions. Chapter numbers, where indicated, refer to the specific English edition used by that contributor.

Throughout the volume we have used a modified version of the Library of Congress system to transliterate Russian from the Cyrillic into the Roman alphabet. Exceptions include established English spellings of Russian names (for instance, Tolstoy instead of Tolstoi, Herzen instead of Gertsen) and names like the Russian Marya (instead of Maria), where a "y" is used to indicate proper pronunciation. Where names occur in quotations from English sources, the spelling in the particular source is maintained.

Chronology[1]

1828   Born August 28, son of Count Nikolai Ilich Tolstoy and Princess Marya Nikolaevich Volkonskaia, at Iasnaia Poliana (Clear, or Ash Tree Glade), an estate inherited from maternal grandfather in Tula Province about 130 miles south of Moscow. As a child known as Lyova-Ryova (Crybaby Lev) because he is so sensitive and cries so easily.

1830   Mother dies, leaving four sons – Nikolai (b. 1823), Sergei (b. 1826), Dmitrii (b. 1827); and Lev (b. 1828) – and younger sister Marya (b. 1830).

1836   Tolstoy family moves to Moscow to prepare eldest son Nikolai for university.

1837   Father dies; Tolstoy children placed under guardianship of his very pious sister, Countess Aleksandra Ilinichna Osten-Saken. Distant relative, T. A. Ergolskaia, Tolstoy's beloved "Aunty," assumes major role in raising the children. Family lives mostly in Moscow, summers at Iasnaia Poliana.

1841   Aunt Aleksandra dies, and Tolstoy children move to Kazan (an ancient river port with Tatar as well as Russian cultural influences about 400 miles east of Moscow on the Volga) to live with her sister Pelageia, married to an influential Kazan landowner.

1844   Enters Kazan University to study oriental languages intending to become a diplomat. Transfers next year to the Faculty of Law.

1847   Begins Franklin journal with daily schedules and records of actual adherence (and most often, non-adherence) to them. Begins diary which, in various forms and with some significant breaks, he keeps for the rest of his life. Daily routine includes physical exercise – riding and gymnastics. Physically active, strong, agile, and good at all sports for his whole life. Hospitalized more than once for venereal disease. Fragments survive of a commentary on the discourses of Jean-Jacques Rousseau and a comparison of Tsarina

Catherine the Great's *Instruction* with Montesquieu's *De L'Esprit des Lois*. Around this time he reads all of Rousseau, "including the dictionary of music," as he later told one commentator. Rousseau is the thinker who most influenced T (see note 1 at the end of this chronology for a list of abbreviations used), who returns to him many times over his life and once said there were many pages in Rousseau that he felt he could have written himself.

May: withdraws from university without graduating and returns to Iasnaia Poliana. Philanthropic work among his peasants with mixed results.

1848 Moves to Moscow, where frequents high society and does little else.

1849 Moves to St. Petersburg, plans to enter civil service, then studies briefly in the Faculty of Law at the university there. Thinks of joining an élite guards unit. Returns to Iasnaia Poliana, where opens a school for peasant children. This year and the next spends much time thinking about music and playing piano. Fragmentary writings on music survive. Plays piano and loves music passionately his entire life. Favorite composers include Weber, Mozart, Haydn, Schubert, Schumann, Bach, Chopin, and early Beethoven; also folk and gypsy music. His Russian favorites are Glinka and then Tchaikovsky. Even in old age he never once speaks of abandoning music or music-making, although he claims at times that his tastes in music have changed. Applies to civil service and in 1850 is accepted at beginning rank in Tula province.

1851 More socializing in Moscow, and heavy gambling at cards. Various ideas for fiction recorded in diary. Writes the unfinished "History of Yesterday," first surviving artistic work.

April: returns with his artillery officer brother Nikolai to the Caucasus, Russia's southern frontier. Translates part of Laurence Sterne's *Sentimental Journey*, and begins to write *Childhood*.

July 3: conceives idea of never-completed novel called *Four Epochs of Life*. (The four stages are childhood, adolescence, youth, and young manhood.)

November: begins to read Plato's dialogues in French translation of Victor Cousin. Of these, *Symposium* and *Phaedo* are his favorites. He rereads these and other Platonic dialogues several times in his life.

1852 Hunting, gambling, and womanizing. Recurrent venereal disease. Reads Plato and various works by Rousseau, especially "The

Profession of Faith of the Savoyard Vicar" (from *Emile*). Finishes *Childhood* and works on *The Raid*. Conceives idea for *Novel of a Russian Landowner.*

January: takes an exam for the rank of cadet and joins the artillery as a "bombardier fourth class" stationed in the North Caucasus.

February: nearly killed in action by a shell that shatters the wheel of a cannon he is aiming.

August 3: "In my novel [*Novel of a Russian Landowner*] I will lay out the evil of the Russian government, and if I find that satisfactory, then I'll devote the rest of my life to the construction of a plan for an electoral monarchic and aristocratic government based on existing elections. This is truly a goal for a virtuous life. Thank you, Lord, give me strength" (d).

September 2: reading Dickens's *David Copperfield* for the second time, pronounces it "delightful" (d).

November 30: "Four epochs of life will be *my* novel up until Tiflis. I can write about it [that is, my own life], because it is far from me. And as the novel of an intelligent, sensitive and erring person, it will be instructive, though not dogmatic. The novel of a Russian landowner – that will be dogmatic" (d).

PUBLICATIONS: *Childhood*. Well received by both public and literati.

1853   Recommended for promotion to ensign. Sends in letter of resignation from army, but all leaves forbidden until the end of the Russo–Turkish War (declared on June 14). Gambles at cards and womanizes. Works intensively at times on *Novel of a Russian Landowner*, and comments frequently on writing by himself and others.

July 27: intimidated by Ivan Turgenev's *Sportsman's Sketches*: "It's somehow hard to be writing after him" (d).

August 28–30: works on "The Fugitive," the first, incomplete version of *The Cossacks.*

September 13–17: Writes and sends off story *Notes of a Billiard Marker* in a white heat, "so carried away that it's even hard for me: I feel faint" (d).

October 6: Applies for active service against the Turks.

October 18: "don't forget to look at it [each composition] from the point of view of the most narrow reader, who is seeking nothing in a book but entertainment" (n).

November 26: asks brother Sergei to send him *David Copperfield* in English.

December 1: "Literary success, satisfactory in and of itself, is achieved only by means of developing a subject from all angles. But the subject itself must be an elevated one if the labour is always to be pleasant" (d).

PUBLICATIONS: *The Raid*.

1854 Promoted to ensign for distinction in action in the Caucasus. Gambling and womanizing. Reads voraciously: Goethe, Schiller, Lermontov, Pushkin, Harriet Beecher Stowe, George Sand, contemporary Russian playwright Ostrovsky, and others. Reaches Bucharest in March, takes part in the siege of Silistria and the retreat, at the end of June, back to Bucharest.

July 11–12: reads Dickens's *Bleak House*, published in translation in *The Contemporary*.

September 6: promoted to second lieutenant. Arrives in Kishiniev on September 9, and applies for transfer to the Crimea where allied siege in the Crimean War is taking place.

September–October: sale of main house at Iasnaia Poliana – it is dismantled and carted away – for 5,000 roubles to raise money after heavy gambling losses.

November: transferred to the Crimean front, and arrives at Sevastopol November 7.

November 21: receives rejection by Tsar Nikolas I of proposal submitted by group of artillery officers to publish a popular journal for soldiers.

PUBLICATIONS: *Boyhood*.

1855 Takes part in defense of Sevastopol, sees action on the notorious fourth bastion (in April), fights at fall of Sevastopol in August. Reads Goethe, Thackeray (*Vanity Fair*, *Henry Esmond*, *Pendennis*), Balzac, and others. Works on *Youth*, the continuation of *Childhood* and *Boyhood*.

January: gambles away all 5,000 roubles received for sale of house.

January–February: works on several plans for military reform.

March 4: records plan to found new religion: "in accordance with the development of humanity, the religion of Christ, but cleansed of faith and mystery, a practical religion, not promising future bliss, but giving bliss on earth [...] To act *consciously* to unite people by means of religion – here is the foundation of a thought that will, I hope, captivate me" (d).

March 11: "A military career is not for me, and the sooner I get out of it to give myself utterly to literature, the better" (d).

Mid-November: arrives in St. Petersburg, moves in with Turgenev. Makes friends with leading literati, all anxious to meet L. N. T., celebrated author of enormously popular war stories. Generally regarded as best young Russian writer, especially admired for gifts of psychological analysis and moral power. Carouses, gambles, loves gypsies and gypsy music.

Later November: meets distant, somewhat older relative A. A. Tolstaia, a lady-in-waiting at the Court, who becomes a lifelong friend and confidante. By mid-December is fighting bitterly with Turgenev, loves to *épater* his new, cultured friends by claiming to despise such cultural icons as George Sand, Homer, and Shakespeare.

December: introduced by friends to poetry of F. I. Tiutchev. Along with Pushkin and A. A. Fet (with whom he became friends in early 1856), Tiutchev becomes his favorite Russian poet.

PUBLICATIONS: *Notes of a Billiard Marker, Sevastopol in December, Sevastopol in May,* and *The Wood-felling.*

1856 Participates in both Petersburg Westernizer and Moscow Slavophile circles. Quarrels and reconciles with Turgenev, whom he sees frequently. Under influence of Petersburg friends, especially aesthete V. P. Botkin, indulges and explores all forms of sensuality, from physiological to aesthetic and musical. Attends theatre, concerts, and operas. Keeps a mistress for a few months. Reads Shakespeare, Pushkin, Dickens (*The Pickwick Papers, Little Dorrit*), Thackeray (*The Newcomes*), Goethe, Molière, and Homer. In literary polemics, chooses the side of sympathetic portrayal, which he associates with Pushkin and Dickens, over that of satire, associated with Gogol. Briefly courts neighbor Valeriia Arsenieva. Works intensively on and completes part one of *Youth.* Begins two comedies, *A Noble Family* and *A Practical Man* (which remain unfinished), continues *Novel of a Russian Landowner* and *The Cossacks* and begins the novel *The Decembrists.* Remains interested his entire life in the 1825 Decembrist revolt of gentry army officers. Conceives and works on a story called "The Distant Field," never finished and related in subject matter to *War and Peace.*

February 2: hears of death from tuberculosis on January 18 of brother Dmitrii.

March: Poet N. Nekrasov, T's editor, intervenes to prevent a duel between T and one Longinov.

March 26: Promoted to lieutenant for "outstanding bravery and courage" at Sevastopol.

May–June: responding to political ferment under new tsar Alexander II, presents a plan to his serfs to free them.

Fall: sends in his resignation from the army, which becomes effective in the following year.

December 15: attends performance of Mozart's *Don Giovanni*.

PUBLICATIONS: *Sevastopol in August, 1855* (signing with his full name for the first time), *Meeting a Moscow Acquaintance in the Detachment (The Demoted Officer)*, *A Landowner's Morning* (the only part published from the unfinished *Novel of a Russian Landowner*), *Two Hussars, The Snowstorm*. Separate editions of *Childhood and Adolescence*, and *War Stories*.

1857 Mixed relations with Turgenev; close to Botkin. Reads Balzac, Tocqueville (*L'Ancien Régime*), Goethe, and *Don Quixote*.

January: Attends musical evenings, and especially enamored of Beethoven; meets an itinerant musician, Georg Kizevetter, gets idea for story *Albert*. Leaving in late January, travels to France, Switzerland, northern Italy, and Germany; returns at the end of July. While abroad writes *Lucerne* in the form of a letter to Botkin, works on *Albert*, part two of *Youth* (never completed), and *The Cossacks*.

March 25: witnesses a guillotining in Paris: "A strong impression that will leave its mark. I am not a political man. Morality and art. [These] I know, love, and can do" (d). On same day writes to Botkin that "Human law is nonsense! The truth is that government is a conspiracy not only to exploit, but mainly to corrupt citizens. [...] I will never serve *any* government anywhere."

April–May: idyllic two months in Switzerland: "I am gasping from love, both physical and ideal. [...] I am taking a very great interest in myself. And I even love myself for the fact that there is so much love of others in me" (d, May 12).

Friendship with AA intensifies.

July 12–20: loses heavily at roulette in Baden-Baden.

July 24: on way home, sees and admires Raphael's painting of the Madonna in Dresden. (AA later gives him a copy, which hangs first in his bedroom at Iasnaia Poliana and then in his study.)

August: having reread *Iliad*, vows to completely rewrite *The Cossacks*. Two weeks later rereads the Gospels "which I had not done for a long time."

Fall: distressed by declining reputation. In December or January 1858, drafts project to found a musical society in Moscow.

PUBLICATIONS: *Youth* and *From the Notes of Prince D. Nekhliudov. Lucerne*, both poorly received, the latter soon rejected by T himself.

1858 Continues to oppose satirical, politically motivated literature. Proposal to friends, eventually rejected but seriously discussed, for a new journal with one goal only: to make people weep and laugh.

January: begins friendship, close until 1861, with B. N. Chicherin, jurist and liberal philosopher.

March: reads Gospels, starts unfinished story "The Bright Resurrection of Christ."

March 21: "the political excludes the artistic, because the former, in order to prove [its point], must be one-sided" (d). Follows debates in his district about emancipation of serfs, with other landowners signs a manifesto declaring that peasants should be freed with land, and that landowners should be compensated for this. Finishes *Albert*, writes *Three Deaths*, works on *The Cossacks*, begins *Family Happiness*. Starting December, 1857, tentatively courts E. F. Tiutcheva, the poet's daughter. (Interest persists, with significant doubts and also other possible choices, through 1861.)

May: begins passionate affair with married peasant Aksinia Bazykina from Iasnaia Poliana: "I'm in love as never before." Spends summer on estate absorbed in Aksinia and farm life rather than literature. (The affair lasts until his marriage in 1862, and Aksinia bears T one son, Timofei, later a coachman on the estate.) In 1860 he wrote of this affair that "it's no longer the feelings of a stag, but those of a husband for a wife"(d).

August: reads published letters of Schellingian philosopher N. V. Stankevich from the 1830s. August 23: "Never has any other book made such an impression on me. I have never loved anyone as much as this man whom I have never seen" (letter to AA).

December 23: mauled and nearly killed by a she-bear on bear hunt.

PUBLICATIONS: *Albert*, poorly received.

1859 Relations with Turgenev worsen. Reads and admires George Eliot's *Scenes of Clerical Life* and *Adam Bede*. Works intensively on and finishes *Family Happiness*, mostly disliked by friends, and rejected by him after its publication. Subsequently – from April on – withdraws from literary life, writes little, lives at Iasnaia Poliana, farming and hunting.

February 4: first public address, given after joining the Society of Lovers of Russian Philology at Moscow University. Praises politically engaged "exposé" literature, but says that "the literature of a people is its full, many-sided consciousness, in which both the national love of the good and true and the national contemplation of beauty in a given epoch of development should be reflected."

Besides the "temporal interests of society," literature should reflect "eternal human interests, the ones that are most valuable and of greatest spiritual worth, in the consciousness of the nation."

October: starts another school for peasant children at Iasnaia Poliana.

PUBLICATIONS: *Three Deaths, Family Happiness.*

1860   Continues to declare himself no longer a professional writer, but an educator.

March 12: writes to brother of Minister of Education suggesting the foundation of a society to promote public education because "the most essential need of the Russian people is for public education," which as of now does not exist, and never will if it is left to the state.

In July goes abroad, returning to Russia only in April 1861, travels to Germany, France, Belgium, Italy, and England studying modern educational methods. In September brother Nikolai, who has accompanied him abroad, dies of tuberculosis.

A month later T writes: "It will soon be a month since Nikolenka died. It's horrifying how this event ripped me from life. Again the question: Why? It's not long before I go there. Where? Nowhere. I'm trying to write, I'm forcing myself, and it's not working only because I can't ascribe to my work that meaning that I must have to have the strength and patience to work. Right during the funeral services I had the idea of writing a materialist Gospel, a life of Christ as materialist [. . .] Nikolenka's death has been the strongest impression of my life" (d).

After Nikolai's death, a trickle of interest in writing turns into an underground river, works on *The Cossacks*, writes several chapters of *The Decembrists* (published in unfinished form only in 1884), and begins writing stories of peasant life, none finished, that draw upon his passion for Bazykina ("Idyll," "Tikhon and Malanya").

December: In Florence meets second cousin S. G. Volkonskii, a Decembrist recently pardoned by Alexander II after over thirty years' exile in Siberia.

1861   January: visits Naples and Rome, where feels "a return to art" (d).

February 18–March 5: in London, visits Alexander Herzen several times, and perhaps attends a lecture by Dickens on education. (Subsequently reads Herzen's journalism and corresponds with him about it.) Meets Matthew Arnold, who writes a letter of introduction for him asking London teachers to allow him to visit their schools.

March: in Brussels begins *Polikushka*.

Mid-March: writes Turgenev that he has returned to fiction, and is reading Goethe's *Faust*, which he highly praises.

March 16: writes that public education is the most important, unifying task of society (n).

March 31–April 6: in Weimar, visits Goethe's house, studies schools. Back in Russia on April 12, continues work on education. Now and throughout the 1860s spends much time hunting, sometimes going off for days with his friend D. D. Obolensky.

April 20: applies for permission from the Ministry of Education to publish a journal called *Iasnaia Poliana* on practical pedagogy.

May 16: over the objections of many neighboring landowners, is appointed Arbiter of the Peace to resolve disputes between peasants and their former masters. Landowners mistrust T because of his generous settlements with his own peasants both before and after the Emancipation Proclamation of February 19. (T resigns position in 1862, citing "sickness" as his reason.)

May: challenges Turgenev to a duel following a quarrel, and the two break off relations until 1878.

1862   Works intensely on pedagogy, and especially the journal *Iasnaia Poliana*. In response to this, many schools for peasants founded nearby. T follows reaction to journal and his publications in it, and worries about perceived lack of interest (letter to Katkov, April 11). His pedagogical theories evoke mixed reaction in the press, but the journal itself, as well as his efforts to promote literacy, are widely praised.

February: loses badly at cards (the last such episode), and finishes *The Cossacks* to pay debt. Reads and admires Dostoevsky's *Notes from a Dead House*.

May–June: goes to drink *kumys* (fermented mare's milk) for his health in Samara province.

July 6–7: in his absence secret police search Iasnaia Poliana looking for evidence of radical political agitation among the peasants by teachers at school. They find nothing, and T so infuriated that he considers immigration.

September 16: proposes to eighteen-year-old Sofya Andreevna Behrs, daughter of a former playmate only two years his senior, and a prominent Moscow doctor. Marries her on September 23. Before he does so, he shows her his early diaries. Although the marriage is tumultuous from the beginning, the couple is very happy for the first twenty years, until T's religious conversion takes him in a direction that his wife cannot follow. Even after they begin to quarrel, the bond between the two is deep and endures until T's death.

October 1: writes E. A. Behrs (SA's sister) that his pedagogical journal is beginning to seem a burden. "[I'm] drawn now to free work *de longe haleine* [on a grand scale] – a novel or something like it."

PUBLICATIONS: Commences monthly issues of *Iasnaia Poliana* (lasting into mid-1863) to which he contributes "Education for the People," "Methods for Learning Grammar," "The Spontaneous Founding and Development of Schools Among the People," "The Iasnaia Poliana School in the Months of November and December," "Project for a General Plan for the Construction of Public Schools," "Upbringing and Education," "Social Work in the Field of Popular Education," "Who Learns to Write from Whom: Peasant Children From Us or We from Them?," and "Progress and the Definition of Upbringing."

1863 In January announces cessation of *Iasnaia Poliana*. Works on *Strider* ("the story of a horse" first conceived in 1856) and begins comic drama *The Infected Family*. Rewrites a short story *The Dream*, and tries unsuccessfully to publish it. Begins *War and Peace*, which will occupy him for another six years. Selected comments related to novel from diary:

January 3: "The epic mode is becoming the only natural one for me."

January 23: "It's been a long time since I have felt such a strong and calmly self-conscious desire to write. I don't have subjects, that is, no one [subject] stands out urgently, but, whether I'm wrong or not, it seems to me I could do any one of them."

February 23: reads Victor Hugo's *Les Misérables* – "Powerful"; "I went through my papers – a swarm of thoughts and a return, or an attempt to return to lyricism. Lyricism is good. I cannot write, so it seems, without a set intention and enthusiasm."

June 2: "I'm reading Goethe, and thoughts swarm."

October 6: "I'm happy with her [SA], but terribly dissatisfied with myself. I'm sliding down toward death and I barely feel the strength in myself to stop. I don't want death, though, I want and love immortality. There's no use choosing. The choice was made long ago. Literature, art, pedagogy and family."

Forms close bond with SA's beloved lively and pretty younger sister Tatiana, who spends much time on estate. (Brother Sergei and Tatiana fall in love, but Sergei eventually does the "right thing" by marrying his long time live-in gypsy mistress Marya, who has borne him three children.)

June 28: Sergei, the first of thirteen children, is born.

PUBLICATIONS: *The Cossacks*, which receives mixed reviews in the press, but is greeted ecstatically by friends, including AA, and F. It remains Turgenev's favorite work by T. *Polikusha*, less well-received.

1864   During entire writing of *War and Peace*, keeps diary only sporadically, and except for hunting trips leaves home rarely and for short periods. Four children are born by the time he finishes novel. Marriage is happy and very close. Much hunting now and throughout the 1860s and 1870s. Visitors numerous in the summer, almost exclusively old friends and family. Only the Fets are exceptions. F is one of T's closest friends in the 1860s and 1870s, and their correspondence is as lively, playful, and poetic as the one with AA. Loves devising home entertainments, balls, and masquerades during which sings gypsy songs and accompanies himself on guitar. Exercises every day. Long walks, riding, hare-hunting with borzoi dogs, gymnastics – keeps barbells in study. Reads English and Russian novels, histories and memoirs from the Napoleonic wars. SA acts as copyist: by the time the novel finished she has copied it the equivalent of several times. Arranges to publish *The Year 1805* (as *War and Peace* called at this point) in Mikhail Katkov's journal *The Russian Herald*. During this period (up until 1870), busy with various projects to improve his farm. Plants an apple orchard, and takes up beekeeping. Works to improve his stock of cattle, pigs, and poultry, with his childhood friend and neighbor D. A. Diakov his main advisor. Looks after the estate of his sister, who lives abroad.

March 26: by chance sighting a hare while on the way to visit a neighbor, bolts after it, falls from his horse and seriously injures right arm. (It is incompetently set, and two operations are required to repair it.)

October 4: birth of daughter Tatiana.

December 9: in Moscow for operation on arm, reads part of novel to friends who praise it, writes SA that "I'm glad, and more cheerful about writing on. It's dangerous when people don't praise, or lie, but it's useful when you feel that you've made a strong impression."

PUBLICATIONS: two-volume set of collected works.

1865   Thinks sporadically about pedagogy. Sends out feelers to close friends about reception of novel. Asks F to report Turgenev's reaction: "He *will understand*." Rereads Goethe's *Faust*; reads Dickens's *Our Mutual Friend*, intimidated by Trollope's *The Bertrams*. Conceives idea of separate psychological novel about Alexander I and Napoleon.

"All the baseness, all the false phrases, all the madness, all the contradictions of the people around them and them themselves" (d).

Comments frequently on art of novel. *The Year 1805*, is "not a novel and not a long short story and does not have the kind of plot with a beginning and end in which, once it ends, so does [the reader's] interest" (unfinished introduction).

July–August: "The goals of art are disproportionate (as mathematicians would say) with social goals. The goal of the artist is not to indisputably resolve a question, but to force [people] to love life in all its innumerable and inexhaustible manifestations. If I were told that I could write a novel in which I could indisputably establish the viewpoint that seemed correct to me on all social questions, I would not devote two hours of labor to such a novel; but if someone told me that what I write now will be read by today's children twenty years hence, and that then they would cry and laugh over it and come to love life, then I would devote my whole life and all my powers to it" (Unsent letter to writer P. D. Boborykin). Writes F (in mid-December) that "Ars longa, vita brevis, I think this every day. If we could only get out one hundredth of what we understand, but only one ten thousandth comes out. Nonetheless this consciousness that I *can* constitutes the happiness of our fraternity. You know the feeling. This year I've felt it with special force."

August 13: Attacks notion of private property and defends peasant commune (n).

PUBLICATIONS: *The Year 1805* roughly corresponding to first book of *War and Peace* appears in two issues of *The Russian Herald*.

1866 Briefly takes up sculpture. Builds an addition to the house at Iasnaia Poliana and plants a birch forest. Reads *Don Quixote* and writings of Victor Hugo, whom he praises highly. Publishes continuation of *The Year 1805* with a subtitle "War." At this point decides to suspend serial publication, preferring to publish it all at once. Considers new title: *All's Well That Ends Well*. Learns indirectly of Turgenev's criticism of novel, agrees with him that there are too many psychological details, resolves to change (mid-May letter to F). Works on sources for novel in Rumiantsev Library (now the Lenin Library) in Moscow. Writes a comedy called *The Nihilist* for home performance.

May 22: birth of second son Ilia.

July–August: unsuccessfully defends soldier Shabunin, on trial for having struck an officer; Shabunin sentenced to death by shooting.

November 27: "The poet takes the best from his life and puts it in his writing. This is why his writing is fine and his life bad" (n).

PUBLICATIONS: part of *The Year 1805* roughly corresponding to book two of *War and Peace* appears in three issues of *The Russian Herald*. In June the part of the novel already published comes out separately in a small print run under title *1805*.

1867 March: title *War and Peace* first appears in a draft contract dated March 1867, in which T has crossed out title *1805* and inserted it.

Summer: suffers from ill health, revises *1805*, cutting it significantly. Still envisages the novel as only four volumes, three of which to appear at end of 1867, with a fourth promised.

June 28: writes F that "the reason that we love one another is that we both think with *the mind of the heart*, as you call it [...] The *mind's mind* and the *heart's mind* – that explained a lot to me [...] Without the power of love there is no poetry."

September 25–27: visits battlefield of Borodino as part of preparations to write novel.

1868 Works intensively on philosophical part of novel.

February 14–May 10: lives with family in Moscow apartment.

February 14: Turgenev, having read *1805*, praises it extravagantly in letter, but criticizes historical fatalism and excessive psychological detail.

March: T announces a fifth volume. In the same month publishes fourth volume and article "A Few Words about 'War and Peace'." By this time novel is a sensation, and the four-volume edition goes immediately into a second printing.

September: reads German philosopher Artur Schopenhauer (according to American consul Eugene Skyler, one of first prominent outsiders to make pilgrimage to Iasnaia Poliana), and "is ecstatic" over him. First mention of primer for peasant readers (n).

1869 Continues philosophical reflections as finishes volume 5 and writes volume 6. *War and Peace* published in a six-volume edition, goes into second printing almost immediately.

May 20: birth of third son, Lev. Consults philosophical friends in Moscow, and reads philosophy – Kant, and especially Schopenhauer – over the summer. Proposes a joint translation of Schopenhauer's *The World as Will and Idea* to F. (F does translate it, but without T's collaboration.) Much of T's philosophizing of the next decade (and indeed, the rest of his life) is a response to Schopenhauer.

September 2: on trip to Penza Province to inspect an estate for possible purchase, stops overnight at a hotel in Arzamas, where suffers an inexplicable attack of "anguish, fear, terror."

October 3: named a divisional justice of the peace for his district by the Senate.

Mid-October: turns down invitation to have portrait painted by leading portraitist I. N. Kramskoy for the Tretiakov Gallery in Moscow.

1870   Reads Molière, Shakespeare, Goethe, Pushkin, Gogol. With an eye to creating an ABC primer with readings for children, reads Russian folk tales and *byliny* (folk epics). During this and subsequent years takes a great interest in poetry, often discussing it in letters to F and in diary.

February: Experiments with writing comedy or drama. Briefly infatuated with Shakespeare – "enormous dramatic talent" (February, SA's diary) – and writes that comedy is possible today, "but tragedy, given the psychological development of our time, is extremely difficult" (n, February 2).

February 22: conceives idea for *Anna Karenina*. February 23: "Yesterday evening he [T] told me that the type of a married woman, from high society but having lost her reputation, had come into his head. He said that his task was to make this woman only pitiable, not guilty and that no sooner had this type come to him than all the other characters and male types who had occurred to him earlier found their places and grouped themselves around this woman" (SA's diary).

May: serves on a jury in Tula, and finds it "very interesting and instructive" (May 11, letter to F).

October 28: "Poetry is a flame burning in a person's soul. The flame burns, it warms and gives light... [some think that the purpose of art is to warm or give light, but this is not true]... A real poet suffers involuntarily as he himself burns and he burns others. And that is the crux of the matter" (n).

December: begins intensive study of Greek, within three months reads Xenophon, Homer, Plato, and others in original.

1871   Suffers from serious depression. Crisis passes, but this period also marks first sign of estrangement from SA. Builds large addition to house at Iasnaia Poliana. Works intensely on primer which includes his own stories and translations, and first part ready to be set in print by end of year.

February 12: birth of second daughter, Marya, after which SA is seriously ill, and afraid of another pregnancy.

June–July: at SA's urging spends two months on the steppes of Samara province living with Bashkirs, drinking *kumys*, reading Herodotus in Greek. Buys land in Samara. (Now and throughout the decade pursues interest in horse-breeding.)

Mid-August: N. N. Strakhov, the author of highly laudatory articles from 1869 and 1870 on *War and Peace*, visits T at his invitation, and quickly becomes his closest intellectual friend, with whom he especially likes to discuss issues of philosophy, science, and religion. S a favorite with both Tolstoys, visits them often until his death in 1896, and the correspondence between him and T is one of the most important sources of our knowledge of T's ideas. T also reads and responds to S's writings.

Approx. August 21: meets Tiutchev by chance on a train, and they have a long conversation. "A magnificent and simple and such a profound, truly intelligent old man" (letter to F).

December 26: at Christmas masquerade festivities, dresses as a goat.

1872　Revival of peasant school, at which T, SA, and older children all teach. Corresponds with F and S about issues of religion and philosophy. Works on novel about Peter the Great, and reads extensively in the period.

January 8: views the body of a woman, the mistress of a neighboring landowner, who has thrown herself under a train, and this gives him the ending for *Anna Karenina*.

January 12: "my proud hopes for the primer are these: that two generations of *all* Russian children, from those of the Tsar to those of the peasants, will learn using only this primer, and they will get their first poetic impressions from it, and that, having written this primer, it will be possible for me to die peacefully" (letter to AA).

April: gives A. A. Erlenvein, former teacher at his schools, permission to republish stories for children from journal *Iasnaia Poliana*, because no books for peasant children have come out in the ten years since the journal ceased publication. (The resulting book is republished seven times from 1873 to 1909.)

June: finishes primer which contains a complete curriculum for beginning students. S publishes the primer in the fall but negative reviews radically curtail sales of the first edition. T upset by bad reviews and sales, but still believes in project.

June 13: birth of fourth son, Piotr.

Late summer: on return from Samara, learns that a bull at Iasnaia Poliana has gored its young keeper to death. The investigating magistrate charges him with criminal negligence and orders him not to leave estate until the case settled. Indignant at this arbitrary exercise of power, T considers moving his family to England.

PUBLICATIONS: *The Prisoner of the Caucasus* and *God Sees the Truth But Waits* published separately and also in primer.

1873 With assistance of S reworks *War and Peace* for *Collected Works*. This time the novel is published in four rather than six volumes, with philosophical and historical digressions published together as appendixes and titled "Articles about the Campaign of 1812." Almost all the French is translated to Russian and other stylistic changes are made.

Works on novel about Peter the Great until March.

March: having reread Pushkin, begins *Anna Karenina*.

April 7: writing to S but not yet mentioning new novel, T says that "I am fulfilling a duty laid upon me by some most high command – I am in torment, and I find in this torment the whole, not joy, but goal of life."

Spends summer in Samara, where he has bought still more land, and becomes involved with famine relief work there. Writes open letter to Moscow newspaper with inventory of inhabitants and conditions in every tenth household (twenty-three in all) in the nearest village. Letter raises almost 2 million roubles and 375 tons of grain in donations.

September: Kramskoy paints famous portrait of T, and himself serves as model for painter Mikhailov in *Anna Karenina*.

November 6: "From youth I prematurely began to analyse everything and to destroy mercilessly. I have often feared and thought that nothing would be left whole, but here I am getting old, and there is much more whole and unharmed in me than in others [. . .] People my age who believed in everything while I was destroying don't have one hundredth as much" (d).

November 9: baby Piotr dies of croup – as T writes F, "the first death in our family in eleven years."

PUBLICATIONS: Collected works in four volumes, including revised *War and Peace*.

1874 Teaches, serves on district educational committees, thinks and writes about education. Too busy to make much progress on novel, but various journals offer very high rates to publish it. Is chosen a member of the Academy of Sciences.

January 15: lectures in Moscow at the official Committee for Literacy defending his theories about teaching Russian, and a six-week pilot project is set up to compare his method to the old one adopted from German pedagogy.

April 22: birth of fifth son, Nikolai.

June 20: death of beloved "Aunty" T. A. Ergolskaia.

August: pays a brief visit to Samara estate.

October 22: approaches F for a one year loan of 10,000 roubles to buy property elsewhere. (F declines.)

November 22: letter to clergyman Archimandrite Leonid, an expert in hagiography, asking him to compile a list of appropriate saints' lives which T proposes to publish in a book for a popular audience.

PUBLICATIONS: "On Popular Education," which generates much public discussion.

1875 At this point, with five children, the oldest of whom is twelve, the house is full of teachers of all sorts. Guests frequent, especially in summer, still mostly family and close friends. T works in public education, applying for permission to open a school for peasant teachers on his estate. (Request wends its way slowly through official bureaucracy, receiving cautiously positive responses. Permission granted in 1876, but there are no applicants in 1877 and drops idea.) Turgenev arranges for T's writings to begin to be published in France. In a foreword to a translation of *Two Hussars*, Turgenev introduces T to the French public as Russia's most popular writer. T meets philosopher Vladimir Soloviev. Starts philosophical treatise on the vanity of life and the need for religion, part of which goes into the first draft of *A Confession*. Works on two unfinished philosophical writings entitled "On the Afterlife outside Time and Space" and "On the Soul and its Life outside Life as it is Known to and Understood by Us." Spends two months on Samara estate with whole family and organizes a highly successful horse race for local tribesmen. Several deaths in family.

February 20: Baby Nikolai dies suddenly of meningitis.

Late October: SA dangerously ill with peritonitis, miscarries in the sixth month of pregnancy; the baby girl, named Varvara, lives less than two hours.

December 22: former guardian and member of household Aunt Pelageia dies.

PUBLICATIONS: First installments of *Anna Karenina* appear in Katkov's *Russian Herald*. Wildly popular, and also controversial because of its explicitly sexual material. Four children's readers based on the primer, and *New Primer*. The first volume of the four readers contains twelve new stories, and the rest are unchanged. The *New Primer* – shorter and cheaper – is published, recommended by the Ministry of People's Enlightenment and is already into its second printing by December. (All these books are very popular and widely used in schools. The so-called *New Primer* goes through twenty-eight editions in T's lifetime.)

1876 SA in poor health. S visits often and letters exchanged about philosophy and religion.

February: old friend S. S. Urusov visits, T reads him a religious–philosophic composition. In a letter dated October 26, Urusov chastises T for abandoning Russian Orthodoxy, and he burns letters from the 1870s in which T criticizes Orthodoxy.

Late March: reads the *Pensées* of Pascal, who becomes a favorite writer.

April 14: writes A. P. Bobrinskii that to live without faith, as he does now, is "terrible torment."

April 23: writes S famous letter about the "labyrinth" of different ideas, themselves not connected by thought, but by something else, of which his works are composed.

December: makes the acquaintance of composer P. I. Tchaikovsky, whose music he loves. Weeps upon hearing the Andante to his first quartet.

PUBLICATIONS: Parts Three, Four, and Five of *Anna Karenina* published serially in *The Russian Herald* to continued acclaim.

1877 As in earlier years of the decade, praises F's poems and writes about them in letters to him. Agonizes over religion. In fall complains repeatedly of depression and ill health, inability to work. Goes to church. Fasts. Works on religious philosophical composition, never finished, called "Interlocutors." Works furiously to finish *Anna Karenina*. Burns two (positive) reviews without reading them because fears negative criticism (letter to S, April 5). Especially in summer works intensely with S to prepare a separate edition of *Anna Karenina*. S marvels at T's attention – that of a "scrupulous poet" – to every word and phrase in the text. T tells SA that the idea of *War and Peace* had been the "nation," that of *Anna Karenina* the "family," now plans a novel about Russian expansion east (SA's diary).

July: Visits Optina Monastery with S to consult monks.

August 16: bored by *The Philosophical Beginnings of Whole Knowledge* by Soloviev, sends it back to S.

September 29: participates as secretary in district meetings of gentry, chosen for three-year term as a member of a committee on education.

December 6: birth of sixth son, Andrei.

December 24: writes F that he needs Kant's *Critique of Practical Reason*, which provides key elements in his later religious doctrine.

PUBLICATIONS: Parts Six and Seven of *Anna Karenina* appear, but editor Katkov refuses to publish the final part of the novel because he disagrees with T's attack on Russo–Turkish war.

1878   Religious quest continues. Returns to *The Decembrists* as a continuation of *War and Peace*, collects material, interviews surviving Decembrists and their relatives, researches behavior of Tsar Nicholas I toward Decembrists, and also resettlement of peasant populations in the 1820s. Resumes diary after almost no entries for thirteen years. Reads Dickens's *Life and Adventures of Martin Chuzzlewit* and *Dombey and Son*. Starts a memoir, *My Life*.

March 8: meets admirer and influential music and literary critic V. V. Stasov, and despite Stasov's avowed secularism, the two correspond until Stasov's death. (After S's death in 1896, Stasov, who also works in the Rumiantsev Library in Moscow, becomes T's main supplier of books on various topics.)

March 10: In Petersburg attends a lecture by Soloviev on "god-manhood," pronouncing it "childish nonsense" (letter to S, April 17).

April 6: writing Turgenev in Paris, initiates reconciliation after seventeen years.

April 9: writes S that the Zasulich affair (in which a jury acquits a revolutionary who attempted to assassinate the military governor of St. Petersburg) is a harbinger of revolution.

Summer: several weeks with family in Samara, where S also visits. Holds horse races with prizes for local Bashkis, and interviews local priest and sectarians on religion.

Early August: Turgenev visits, relations cordial but not intimate.

PUBLICATIONS: a separate edition of *Anna Karenina*, including the final part.

1879   Moves away from official church, and SA disapproves of this. Interest in sectarians intensifies. Friendship with F begins to cool because of T's changing ideas. Stops work on *The Decembrists* in February, and turns to novel on Peter the Great. Collects material, visits historical archives, and takes an interest in the lives of his own ancestors. Starts a large religious philosophical composition. Writes article "The Church and Government."

March 25: asks AA to exert influence at court to have three imprisoned old-believers released.

April 12: starts a special notebook for nature descriptions. (Keeps it until June 7, 1880. Also notes down many folk expressions and turns of phrase from conversations with peasants and especially religious pilgrims.)

June: visits churches and churchmen in Kiev, not impressed.

July: records stories and folk legends from oral poet who visits Iasnaia Poliana, and uses these subsequently as basis for stories *What People Live For, Two Old Men, Prayer, Kornei Vasiliev.*

August 31: writes F to recommend Ecclesiastes, which "has much in common with Schopenhauer."

October: first of series of visits to the Troitskii-Sergeev Monastery to discuss religion; starts *A Confession*, first called *An Introduction to an Unpublished Work*. It is mostly written this year, but not entirely finished until 1882.

October 30: looks to early Christianity, before third century, for true teaching of Christ, which rejects government (n).

December 20: birth of seventh son, Mikhail.

1880 January 12: in letter Turgenev reports the reaction of Flaubert on reading *War and Peace*: "what an artist and what a psychologist!"

January 22: in Petersburg quarrels with AA over anti-church views, and leaves town the next day. (They reconcile, although they continue to disagree about religion, and AA's memoirs about her later visits to Iasnaia Poliana provide an invaluable picture of the changed atmosphere there.) Soon after returning from Petersburg, works on *A Confession* and *A Critique of Dogmatic Theology*, which SA copies although she disapproves of it.

February: goes elk-hunting.

March: begins work on *A Translation and Harmony of the Four Gospels*. In afternoons reads *Pickwick Papers* for relaxation.

May: Turgenev visits and tries unsuccessfully to convince T to take part in the Pushkin celebrations scheduled for June.

July 8: writes F that the house is full of guests, the children are putting on funny theatricals (composed by T). "It's now summer, a captivating summer, and I, as usual, am going crazy with joy at physical life and forgetting my work. This year I struggled for a long time, but the beauty of the world conquered me. And I'm rejoicing at life and doing very little else."

October 7: makes acquaintance of painter I. E. Repin, who subsequently paints him several times, and with whom he maintains cordial relations to the end of his life.

November: rereads Dostoevsky's *Notes From a Dead House* and asks S to convey his admiration of it to Dostoevsky: "tell him that I love him."

October: an exchange of letters between him and F in which he explains his new religious views and F refutes these.

December 30: in letter to S calls Goethe's *Faust* "rubbish."

PUBLICATIONS: another *Collected Works* with *War and Peace* in 1873 version.

1881 Correspondence with F ends. Quarrels with SA. Works on *A Translation and Harmony of the Four Gospels*.

January 31: in her diary SA describes T at this time:

> as he puts it, he's become happy in his soul. He's recognized (in his expression) "the light." His entire world view has been illuminated by this light. His view of people has become such (as he himself put it), "that before, there was a certain circle of *our, close* people, but now millions of people have become brothers [...] Every day he sits at his work, surrounded by books and labors until dinner. His health has considerably declined, his head aches, he's gotten grey and thin this winter. He's obviously not at all as happy as I would wish, and he's become quiet, absorbed and silent. Almost never does that merry, lively state of soul burst out that used to animate all of us who surround him [...] The clarity and calmness of his own state of soul is indubitable, but suffering for misfortunes, for human injustice, for poverty, for the imprisoned, about human evil, persecution – all this acts on his impressionable soul and sears his existence.

Early February: on hearing of the death of Dostoevsky, realizes that "he was very, very close, dear [and] necessary for me" (letter to S).

March 1: responding to assassination of Tsar Alexander II, writes letter to new tsar requesting that he spare the six assassins as a demonstration of Christian love. The six are hanged on April 3, and T's sympathy for them alienates his family. Soon after this (around April 8), begins "Notes of a Christian," which will become the first part of *What I Believe*.

May 18: first record in diary of disagreements with family.

June: visits Optina Monastery on foot.

July: goes horse-buying in Samara – "An unbearable task. Idleness. Shameful" (d, July 17) – and visits with sectarians.

September: moves with family to Moscow to attend to the children's educational needs. Hates city life, but begins to explore it, and to record his negative impressions.

October 31: birth of eighth son, Alexei.

December: visits Liapin House, a shelter for the poor, which he subsequently describes in chapter 2 of *What Then Must We Do?*

PUBLICATIONS: *What Men Live By*, based on legend recorded from oral poet in 1879, published in children's journal, and first fiction to appear since the final installments of *Anna Karenina* in 1877.

1882 Police begin to spy on T because of links to religious sectarians in Samara Province.

January: participates in the three-day Moscow census. Out of this experience comes two works dealing with urban poverty: the article "On the Moscow Census," and the treatise *What Then Must We Do?*, written over the next four years. Begins friendship with artist N. N. Ge, who contacts him after reading "On the Moscow Census." Ge becomes a Tolstoyan, paints T many times, remains close friend of whole family until death in 1894. Around this time, makes first notes for *Death of Ivan Ilich*, and works on it in spring.

April 9: reports reading Balzac "with pleasure" (letter to SA).

May: reads Marcus Aurelius with great enthusiasm; *A Confession* under the title *Introduction to an Unpublished Work* banned from publication. (It begins to circulate illegally within Russia. It is first published in Geneva in 1884, and is published in Russia only in 1906.) During summer begins religious treatise *What I Believe*, intended as the fourth part of a large work consisting of *A Confession, An Investigation of Dogmatic Theology*, and *A Translation and Harmony of the Four Gospels*. Unhappy with city life, makes several short trips to Iasnaia Poliana. Complains of depression.

August 26: SA reports in her diary that he has shouted at her that he would like to leave the family. In fall sets up so-called post box in upstairs hall at Iasnaia Poliana. Anyone could contribute a note or composition, and the box was opened and read to the assembled household on Sundays. This practice continues, with breaks, until the mid 1880s. Buys Khamovniki, a house with large grounds in Moscow, and in the fall goes before the family to prepare it for occupancy. Until 1902, divides time between Khamovniki and Iasnaia Poliana.

October: reads Epictetus; engages a Moscow rabbi to teach him Hebrew.

December 16: elected to three-year term as district marshal of nobility in Tula province, declines to serve.

1883   Works intensively on *What I Believe*.

May 21: gives SA legal authority to conduct his business affairs; leaves for a month in Samara, where combines business with discussions with peasants about religious ideas and their political implications. These are reported as dangerous agitation, and authorities now sufficiently alarmed by T's new ideas that he is not allowed to read a public lecture on Turgenev after the latter's death in August.

May 29: reading Bible in Hebrew.

September 28: refuses jury duty for religious reasons.

Mid-October: meets V. G. Chertkov, the son of a wealthy nobleman, who has resigned from an élite guards unit to do charitable work among rural peasants. Ch soon becomes T's most dedicated disciple, who helps him puts his ideas into practice. On trip in fall to Iasnaia Poliana, T has trouble working (on *What I Believe*) and occupies himself with hunting and practical matters.

November: reads *Letters from the Countryside* by populist A. N. Engelhardt and in letter to SA pronounces them "captivating… a contrast of our life and the real life of mouzhiks" (November 11).

PUBLICATIONS: *Prologue to A Short Exposition of the Gospels*. French translation in the Paris journal *La Nouvelle Revue* – the first religious-philosophical writing of T to appear abroad.

1884   The publishing house Intermediary Press is established at Ch's suggestion and initiative. Its goal is the production of affordable literature for a popular audience. From this time on, T participates more or less intensively in translation and editorial work of Intermediary Press. He writes many stories for it in the first two years. Takes up shoe-making. In contact with revolutionaries, tries to help them. Sympathizes with their goals, but not their methods, blames the government for stifling dissent. Over this year relations with family and especially SA so bad that asks Ch, whose influence SA is already beginning to fear, to destroy his diary. (Ch does not do this.) Works on *Death of Ivan Ilich*. A new *Collected Works*, the fifth, is planned by SA, who now begins to publish the collected works herself (instead of selling them to a publisher) in order to raise more money sorely needed for life in Moscow.

January: publishes *What I Believe*, but already printed copies seized at press in February. Like *A Confession*, it circulates widely in manuscript in Russia, and is soon published abroad in several languages.

February: begins to study Chinese philosophy; reads a speech on publishing houses for the people to a group of experts in education at his Moscow house.

March 15: first mention of idea of a cycle of reading, which would include Epictetus, Marcus Aurelius, Lao-Tse, Buddha, Pascal, the Gospels (d).

May: reads and admires *On Reliance* by American transcendentalist Ralph Waldo Emerson.

June: threatens to leave home, and actually sets out for Tula, but returns in time for birth of third daughter, Aleksandra (June 18).

Summer: tries to stop smoking, give up wine, meat, tea.

Fall: gives up hunting.

December: part of *What Then Must We Do?* prepared for journal publication, but banned almost immediately.

PUBLICATIONS: fragments of *The Decembrists*. *A Confession* published in Geneva by Elpidin's Russian-language press. Elpidin subsequently publishes many of T's works that are banned in Russia.

1885 Participates in hay-mowing in the summer, and in Moscow in November provides water and wood for the household each day. Visits Iasnaia Poliana alone for short periods during winter season. Corresponds with Repin about various paintings. Works on *Death of Ivan Ilich*. After *What Then Must We Do?* has been banned, three short fragments from it are published in Russian journal. The unpublished manuscript begins to circulate illegally in Russia, but is published there in full, uncensored, only in 1906. On October 16 still writing it because "I've got to shove out everything that has settled in my throat" (letter to Ch).

January: using German and Russian translations, but checking these against the original ancient Greek, begins work on a translation of recently discovered *Teaching of the Twelve Apostles*. (T's translation published unsigned and revised to satisfy censors, and then revised and republished in 1905, as part of a *Cycle of Reading*.)

February 2: writes to SA that George Eliot's *Felix Holt* is "an outstanding work." Recommends it and other novels by Eliot for publication in rewritten form for the people by Intermediary Press. Also recommends all the novels of Dickens (late November).

April: meets and begins close collaboration with philosopher Nikolai Grot, who wants to unite science and philosophy through an inductive metaphysics based on psychological data; reads Matthew

Arnold's *Literature and Dogma*, declaring in a letter to Ch that it expresses many of his own opinions (April 26).

May and June: substantially rewrites a biography of Socrates prepared by A. M. Kalmykova for Intermediary Press, and in connection with this rereads the works of Plato and the Stoics.

June 5: "I would very much like to put together a cycle of reading, that is a series of books and selections from them which would all speak of that one thing most needful to a person, namely, what life and the good are for him" (letter to Ch).

Around June 8: recommends Rousseau's *Confession* and *Emile*, which had had an "enormous" influence on him in his youth (letter).

July: enthuses over manuscript entitled *Love of Labour and Parisitism, or the Triumph of the Landowner* sent to him by peasant–sectarian T. M. Bondarev, living in exile in Siberia. (In March 1888 Bondarev's article appears in Russian journal with a foreword by T.) Reads Henry George's *Progress and Prosperity*, approves of George's arguments against private ownership of land.

October 28: a story by sister-in-law Tatiana called *A Woman's Lot* "is not suitable for the people – it's too much like a photograph and almost without ideals, but it's very good for the likes of us" (letter to SA).

November: Succeeds (with SA's assistance) in having a conscientious objector transferred to a non-combat responsibility.

Fall and winter: depressed over disagreements with family.

December 18: again threatens to leave home (letter from SA to sister).

PUBLICATIONS: Difficulties with censorship contribute to an increased number of publications abroad. *Ma réligion*, a French translation of *What I Believe* by T's friend L. D. Urusov appears in Paris; later that year a shortened Russian version of the same work appears in the Russian émigré journal *General Affairs* in Geneva and in book form in Elpidin's press. (*What I Believe* did not appear in Russia until 1906.) The Swiss Russian émigré journal *General Affairs* also publishes *Letter to NN*, T's letter to M. A. Engelhart (written 1882) on his beliefs and his feelings of loneliness both in his family and in society. In London the book *Christ's Christianity* is published, which includes English translations of *A Confession*, the *Prologue to A Short Exposition of the Gospels* and *What I Believe*.

Often using traditional plots, writes a large number of stories for the people, published in 1885–86, almost all by Intermediary Press. These include: *Two Brothers and Gold* (based on an ancient legend and with illustrations by Repin); *Little Girls Wiser than their Elders*; *Evil Allures, But Good Endures*; *A Spark Neglected Burns the House*; *Where God is, Love is* (based on a translation of a French story published in 1884); *Ilias*; *Two Old Men*; *The Candle* (said to have been published unchanged by T as he heard it from a drunken peasant); *Three Hermits*; and *The Tale of Ivan the Fool*. Intermediary also republishes *Prisoner of the Caucasus*, *God Sees the Truth But Waits*, and a revised version of *What Men Live By*. SA puts out the fifth edition of the collected works, without, however, including either *A Confession* or *What I Believe*, which she is not allowed by the censor to publish. *Strider*, the story of a horse begun in 1863, is finished this year and included in volume 3. SA works on a sixth edition of the collected works.

1886 During this year writes article "Nikolai The Stick" (about his nemesis Tsar Nicholas I) and play *The Power of Darkness* (published in Intermediary Press in 1887). Around this time, writes *Walk in the Light While There is Light* (published first in English in 1890, and then in Russian by Elpidin in 1892).

January 17–18: four-year-old Alexei falls ill with croup and dies in thirty-six hours.

April: walks 130 miles from Moscow to Iasnaia Poliana.

August: injures himself and is bedridden for three months.

December: in response to a letter from graduates of a woman's gymnasium in Tiflis asking him how they can best serve the public, publishes open letter in Tiflis newspaper recommending that they help prepare popular books. (Responding to a similar letter in 1887, especially recommends reworkings of English novels. Letter, republished in 1887 in major journal, produces a flood of volunteers.)

PUBLICATIONS:[2] A portion of chapter ten of *A Confession* called *What is Happiness?* is allowed by the censor and appears in a journal. In addition to the stories written in 1885, writes and Intermediary Press publishes *The Grain as Big as a Hen's Egg*, *The Repentant Sinner*, *How Much Land Does A Man Need?*, and *The Imp and the Crust*. *Death of Ivan Ilich* and *War and Peace* in its 1868–69 version, before the "corrections" of 1873, come out in the SA's fifth edition of *Collected Works*. (This 1886 version maintains the division of the book into four instead of the original six volumes, however.)

1887 Discusses metaphysics with Grot. Writes *Notes of a Madman* (based on experience at Arzamas in 1869; published 1912); parable *Three*

Sons (published 1888); adapts *The Coffee House of Surat* by Bernardin de St. Pierre for Intermediary. Staging of *The Power of Darkness* banned (but performed in Paris in 1888). Begins work on *The Kreutzer Sonata*.

January 19–21: Writes Ch that Intermediary should publish popular editions of foreign authors. Recommends Voltaire, Rousseau, Bernadin de St. Pierre, Lessing's *Nathan the Wise*, Schiller's *Robbers*, Goldsmith's *The Vicar of Wakefield*, Swift's *Gulliver's Travels*, Cervantes's *Don Quixote*, Franklin's diary, Plutarch, and others.

March: discusses plan for publishing popular books on medicine in Intermediary Press with group of doctors. Intermediary also publishes anthology of folk tales, and a new short primer with passages from Gospels considered essential by T.

March 7: Ch announces publicly that all works or translations by T published by Intermediary Press are not bound by copyright.

March 14: at Moscow Psychological Society T reads a paper called "Life's Meaning," a draft of part of *On Life*, his major philosophical treatise, which he finishes this year.

In April and June respectively: admirer and fellow writer N. S. Leskov and famous jurist (and later, Senator) A. F. Koni visit Iasnaia Poliana for first time. Friendly with Leskov until his death in 1895. Koni gives him the subject for novel *Resurrection*, and T henceforth relies on him, as he does on AA, for access to high level of government.

Spring and summer: field work at Iasnaia Poliana; Repin visits, sketches T plowing.

September–October: reads Gogol's *Selected Passages From Correspondence With Friends* for third time – the first had been in 1851 – recommends that Intermediary Press publish selections.

Mid-October: Reads Kant's *Critique of Practical Reason*, starts a translation of which fragment survives. Struggles to give up smoking and drinking.

Around December 9: signs pledge to abstain from drink and invites others to do likewise. (As of 1890, 791 people had taken the pledge.)

December 27: disciple arrested for distributing copies of banned article "Nikolai The Stick."

1888 Physical labor at Iasnaia Poliana and in Moscow. Poor relations with SA. Troubles with church and state censorship grow, as does influence at home and abroad. Government reluctant to punish T directly, fearing bad publicity. Quits smoking for good, promotes temperance, and wants to translate book by American doctor Alice B. Stockham, *Tocology, A Book for Every Woman* (Chicago, 1888), which advocates chastity within marriage. (Writes introduction to Russian translation, which is published 1892.)

Correspondence with and visits from foreigners increasing. (Examples include Czech patriot Thomas Masaryk, at Iasnaia Poliana on April 27–29, and American translator, Isabel Hapgood, who visits the following year, and translates *On Life*.)

March 31: birth of thirteenth and last child, beloved son Vania (Ivan)

April: walks from Moscow to Iasnaia Poliana.

December: warmly welcomes birth of first grandchild, Anna (daughter of son Ilia).

1889　More connections with foreigners, including American writers, social reformers, and clergy. Relations with SA worsen amid tensions between her and his followers (especially Ch), whom she calls "dark ones." Criticizes, feels alienated from family with exception only of second daughter Marya, who joins his reformist activities. Relations distant with old friend F, whom he sees several times. Hard physical labor at both city and country houses. Preaches temperance to peasants, and also writes against the widespread use of rag pacifiers, responsible for many infant deaths. Takes active interest in schools for peasants run by his daughters. Discovers Shakers, Swedenbourgians, reads, and vows to translate *Christian Non-Resistance* (1846) by American abolitionist and pacifist writer Adin Ballou. Reads Walt Whitman, at first disliking, but soon warming to him. Several conversations with Soloviev. Discovers A. P. Chekhov and Guy de Maupassant.

Begins last novel *Resurrection* and writes *The Kreutzer Sonata* and *The Devil*. Works on *The Fruits of Enlightenment*. (*The Kreutzer Sonata* begins to circulate widely in unauthorized copies throughout Russia, and during this and the next year cause widespread debate. *The Devil* is published for the first time in the first posthumous collection of T's *Collected Works*. *The Fruits of Enlightenment* finished in 1890, permitted on the stage only in 1892 and not for general audiences until 1894.) Assists A. I. Orlov with popular biography of Pascal for Intermediary Press. More works published abroad: *On Life* appears French translation by SA. The full version of *What Then Must We Do?* published by Elpidin's Russian-language press in Geneva. Works intensely on aesthetics, and reads widely, including Plato, Schopenhauer, Arnold, and essays on art by John Ruskin. (Identifies especially strongly with Arnold's *Literature and Dogma*, which rereads in 1890.)

March 7: first sculpture of T – Tolstoy at the Plow – by K. A. Klodt.

March 17: "I've been reading Chekhov. No good – trite [...] I sat alone all evening, reading Chekhov. The ability to love to the point of artistic insight, but so far there's no point to it" (d).

March 28: visits textile factory, decries terrible labor conditions.

May: again walks from Moscow to Iasnaia Poliana.

September 12: writes S that he does not want to make money from *The Kreutzer Sonata*. In diary (September 15) names joy as first and inalienable principle of life; but elsewhere (November 18) writes that "I don't dare think about personal happiness – not even happiness but tranquillity. And I don't need to – it's better."

1890 Bad relations with family. Participates in protests against mistreatment of Jews. Ever increasing contact with foreigners. Praises true Christian spirit of Ge's painting entitled *What is Truth?* (depicting Christ before Pilate), banned from public exhibition in Russia. Praises novels of W. D. Howells, poetry of Whitman. In response to comments about *The Kreutzer Sonata*, circulating in manuscript, writes several drafts of afterword to it. Writes article "Why Do Men Stupify Themselves?" and begins *Father Sergius*. Recommends several stories by Maupassant for translation into Russian, and adapts a part of Maupassant's *Sur L'eau* in a story called *Expensive*. Writes and publishes short article "On Relations Between the Sexes." Writes many parts of what becomes *The Kingdom of God is Within You*. In connection with this project reads and subsequently promotes pacifist Christianity of Adin Ballou and American abolitionist William Lloyd Garrison.

February: visits monastery, disapproves of sequestered monastic life. Talks there to conservative Christian thinker K. N. Leontiev, who reports that T wishes the government would arrest and imprison him. T subsequently repeats this wish for martyrdom many times.

April 1–6: reads Russian translation of articles and aphorisms by Danish philosopher Søren Kierkegaard by Danish visitor P. Hansen.

August 8: writes George Kennan to thank him for his book on the Russian penal system, and to inform him of the recent execution by hanging of two peasants in Penza.

September 6: rereading Rousseau's *Emile*.

1891 Fame as spiritual leader and social critic grows in Russia and abroad, as authorities try unsuccessfully to counter influence through censorship. Gives up meat and alcohol. Continues shoe-making and hard labor. Chafes under luxurious living conditions and writes, "I want to suffer" (d, March 5). Exacerbating family tensions – SA threatens suicide – publicly renounces copyright for all of his works published after 1881. Reads books on aesthetics, and works on essay about art and science. Begins *The Kingdom of God is Within You* and works on *Father Sergius*. In connection with work on article "The First Step," advocating vegetarianism (published 1892), on June 7 visits slaughter house in Tula.

June: reads Montaigne.

June 29–July 16: Repin visits, does bust and several paintings. In his last years T is painted, sculpted, and photographed numerous times.

September 14: having read plays of Ibsen, writes translator P. Hansen that considers them "all artificial, false and even very poorly written in the sense that all the characters are unconvincing and inconsistent." In the same letter, praises writing of Kierkegaard as sincere, ardent, and serious.

Starting in late summer and into 1893, relief work for the famine ravaging Tula and Riazan. Family unites around issue, with SA collecting money for relief effort. Visits famine-stricken regions in Tula, Riazan, and Orlov, sets up cafeterias, and writes several articles about famine, chief among them "On Hunger," a strong indictment of the socio-political organisation of Russia. Personal letter on famine to Leskov is published in newspapers.

1892 Begins to find hard physical labor difficult. Government, concerned about T's power and sure of his ill will, persecutes disciples, but afraid to arrest him. Difficulties with censorship as further editions of *The Tale of Ivan the Fool* banned. "On Hunger" appears in English translation in The *Daily Telegraph* in January; later that month excerpts in reverse translation are published in *The Moscow Gazette* with editorial comments labelling the article as socialist propaganda. First biography of T, by Raphael Löwenfeld, published in Germany. Even after relief work on famine, T remains convinced that such aid is only palliative, and that solutions require complete social change (letter to S on April 24). As famine work ends, family problems return, and on July 7 T turns all his property over to his SA and heirs. Thinks again of leaving home.

November 15: reads poetry of French poet Baudelaire "to get an idea of the degree of depravity of the fin de siècle" (letter to SA).

1893   Reads Lao-Tze and other Chinese thinkers. Finishes *The Kingdom of God is Within You* (a denunciation of all government on the basis of his theory of all non-resistance) and sends it abroad for translation and publication. Reads letter by Al. Dumas on how love is only solution to class hatred (written as disapproving response to speech by Zola recommending life of science and work to youth), and writes article "Non-Acting" siding with Dumas. Writes "Religion and Morality" (a response to a letter) and works on "Christianity and Patriotism" (a condensation of *The Kingdom of God is Within You*, completed in 1894). Subsequently writes several articles in the form of letters. Having praised *Ward No. Six* in the previous year, expresses an interest in meeting Chekhov. Works on long preface to collection of stories by Maupassant (published in 1894). Considers Maupassant best nineteenth-century writer after Victor Hugo, because "he is the only writer who understood and recreated the negative side of the relations between a man and a woman" (memoirs of Iu. A. Veselovkii). Elsewhere, however, criticizes Maupassant for his "dirty" subject matter (March 2, 1894, letter).

November 5: in letter to Princess Iu. P. Khilkova begs her to return the minor children of her exiled Tolstoyan son Dmitrii. (On October 23, with the help of local authorities, Khilkova had seized the children, not properly christened, from their parents' home in the Caucasus. Despite T's efforts, including a direct appeal in early 1894 to Tsar Alexander III [which the tsar ignores], the children are never restored to their parents.)

1894   Ongoing complaints about family situation, feels trapped but does nothing because "I feel sorry for the spiders who have spun this web" (d, January 24). When T is photographed late in year with Ch and other disciples, SA obtains negative of photograph from photographer and destroys it. Mourns the death of Ge on June 1. Reads books sent to him by American economist Henry George, whose theories he had already embraced in early 1890s. Applies George's theories about land use to daughter Tatiana's neighboring estate. George's single tax theory and rejection of private ownership of land becomes the basis of T's subsequent economic and social recommendations for Russia. Begins *Master and Man*. Works on "Catechism," a short and clear statement of his religious beliefs (works on this intermittently until 1896). Elpidin publishes first volume of *Ripe Ears of Grain*, a series of books of thoughts and aphorisms drawn from T's private correspondence.

January 3: having written T several times, writer I. A. Bunin visits him at Iasnaia Poliana. (Bunin first contacts T in 1890, after reading *The Kreutzer Sonata*.)

January 11: sitting on the stage at a general session of a congress of natural scientists in Moscow, T receives ovation from audience.

January 27: Tolstoyan E. N. Drozhzhin dies of tuberculosis while in prison for refusing to serve in the military, and T soon starts writing preface to biography of Drozhzhin published following year in Germany.

February 17: visits Tretiakov Gallery, singles out as praiseworthy painting from peasant life by N. V. Orlov, who subsequently – from 1904 – becomes his favorite contemporary painter. (In 1908 writes an introduction to an album of his paintings.)

February 18: ten-year-old daughter Sasha in letter to sister Tatiana describes how the evening before T, Ge, and a visiting Englishman join the younger generation in dancing to music played by brother Sergei.

Mid-May: visit from American Ernest Howard Crosby, who becomes T's chief disciple in the United States.

June 14: "As I was approaching Ovsiannikovo, I looked at the lovely sunset. A shaft of light in the piled up clouds, and there, like a red irregular coal, the sun. All this above the forest, the rye. Joyful. And I thought to myself: No, this world is not a joke, not a vale of ordeal only and a passage to a better, eternal world, but one of the eternal worlds, which is good, joyful, and which we not only can, but must make finer and more joyful for those living with us, and for those who will live in it after us" (d).

Summer: Iasnaia Poliana filled with friends and younger generation of family. One friend (V. F. Lazurskii) reports T executing a mazurka step to general applause and laughter. Ch rents a nearby house, and T's letters begin to be routinely copied on press supplied by Ch to daughter Marya.

August 21: makes acquaintance of Slovenian doctor D. P. (Dushan) Makovitsky. (From 1904 on, M, a household favorite, became T's personal, live-in physician.) A dedicated Tolstoyan, M kept detailed notes, writing in a notebook in his pocket, of T's conversation, and these notes are among the best sources of life at Iasnaia Poliana at that time, and also cadences of T's speech.)

1895 Campaigns for sectarians called Doukhobors, who are being persecuted for refusing to serve in the military. Works hard on *Resurrection*. Publishes article "Shame," an indictment of flogging of peasants. Writes introduction to collected thoughts of Ruskin published by Intermediary.

Mid-January: refuses to sign a joint letter from writers asking the new tsar to abolish censorship, because according to T the tsar lacks all authority and should abdicate. Finishes *Master and Man*, of which he feels a bit ashamed (so he claims in a letter to S on January 14) just because it is a work of fiction.

February 6: in fit of anger and jealousy, SA runs in her nightclothes from the house over T's decision to publish *Master and Man* in journal whose editor is a woman. Eventually T agrees to publish it simultaneously in three places, one of them the collected edition belonging to SA.

February 21: declares in diary that not only Russia, but all states are illegitimate and should be rejected.

February 23: youngest son, Vania, dies suddenly from scarlet fever. Both parents devastated, and T finds it difficult to work for many weeks.

March: takes up bicycle riding. Rides for the next two years over the objections of some disciples, who regard it as undignified. (July 17, 1897: "I rode the bicycle to Iasenki. I like the motion a lot. But I feel guilty" [d].)

March 27: writes unofficial will in diary, asking SA, S, and Ch to dispose of his papers after his death.

April 28: explains three conditions necessary for relieving harsh working conditions and establishing brotherhood: don't force others to work for you; do difficult and dirty jobs for yourself (and others, if you can); and develop technologies that replace hard physical labor (d).

June 28: brotherhood of man (without separate nations) must be first priority, and both science and art must accommodate it, not the other way around (d).

August 8–9: Chekhov's first visit. T has him read part of *Resurrection* manuscript and listens carefully to his reaction. Over the years praises Chekhov's artistry, criticizes his reluctance to take moral stand.

September 4: letter to feminist N. V. Stasova criticizing "woman's work" as demeaning. This negative category does not include the bearing and raising of children.

October 28–November 3: rereads old diaries from 1888–95, crosses out all passages that SA considers offensive to her.

December: visited in Moscow by English disciple John Kenworthy.

1896   Agonizes over intensifying persecution of disciples while he remains untouched. SA throws herself into music after Vania's death, becomes infatuated with pianist and composer S. I. Taneev, Tchaikovsky's favorite student. He is twelve years her junior. T had known him since at least 1889, and often played duets and chess with him. Intense infatuation persists for at least the next four years. T restrains himself, but is jealous and angry, though he does not suspect SA of actual infidelity. Begins *What Is Art?*, writes draft of autobiographical drama *The Light Shines in the Darkness*, and begins *Hadji Murat*. (Worked on last two intermittently until 1904, but did not finish either.)

January 20: Meets concert pianist A. V. Goldenweizer, who becomes a disciple and has left detailed memoirs about T.

July 19: "I left the Chs on July 5. Evening, and beauty, happiness, blessings everywhere. But in the human world? Greed, spite, envy, cruelty, lust, depravity [a few words scratched out] . . . When will it be among people as it is in nature? There is struggle there, but it is honorable, simple, beautiful. While here it is base. I know this world and hate it, because I too am a human being" (d).

August 10–15: with SA visits sister Marya, who lives as nun in convent.

September 26: visit from two Japanese journalists.

1897   Home life difficult, especially with children grown. SA's infatuation with Taneev peaks during this year and next, and T once again contemplates leaving home.

July 8: writes long farewell letter to SA and hides it inside upholstery of armchair in study. (In 1901–2, seriously ill, gives letter to daughter Marya, with instructions to write on it: "To be opened fifty years after my death, if this episode of my biography is of interest to anyone." When he recovers, Marya does not follow his instructions. In 1907, when SA has furniture in study recovered, T entrusts letter to son-in-law, with instructions to give it to SA after his death. When this was done, according to the son-in-law, the envelope contains two letters, one of which SA, having read it, immediately tears up.) Government removes minor children from Molokans (a religious sect), and T agitates, eventually successfully, to have them returned. Ch exiled abroad for involvement in sectarian movement, and two other disciples are sent into internal exile for the same reason. (Ch takes up residence in England, where in 1898 he founds press called Free Word (*Svobodnoe slovo*), which subsequently publishes many of T's banned or censored writings, and also compilations of his thoughts.) T enjoys concerts, and plays four-handed pieces on the piano. Works intensely on *What Is Art?*. Reads books on aesthetics, and especially pursues the topic of aesthetics and ethics.

March 17: meets Aylmer Maude, who becomes his most important English translator and biographer.

Mid-April: sees an exhibit of Impressionist paintings in Moscow, criticizes them for their lack of an "idea." Around the same time, says to a memoirist that Chekhov "writes like a decadent, like an impressionist in the broad sense of the word." During summer plays lawn tennis.

1898   Finishes *What Is Art?*, which is published simultaneously in Russian and in English translation by Maude. Book widely praised, including by so-called "decadent" writers. Works for last time on *Father Sergius* (published only posthumously). More famine relief work. Writes "Hunger or No Hunger" describing the situation of the Russian peasantry, and "Carthago delenda est" (in the form of an answer to questions about war and militarism sent to him by two publishing houses in Milan and Paris). Works on *Resurrection* which decides to publish for profit to help the Doukhobors resettle in Canada. During the second half of the year, absorbed in the novel, which he calls "a joint letter – to many" (in a letter to P. Biriukov on December 16), he stops writing his diary almost entirely. At T's invitation, artist L. O. Pasternak (poet's father) illustrates *Resurrection*.

January: Composer N. A. Rimsky-Korsakov visits, and the two men disagree totally about music and art. T buys weights for gymnastic exercises.

February 14: assigns poetry of Heinrich Heine to category of bad art because too pessimistic and cynical, but adds that "not long ago he had reread Heine's poetry and had loved it, although he explained this was because he himself had been spoiled by our distorted views of art" (diary of V. F. Lazurskii).

February 16: rereads Schiller's *Robbers* and, as always, praises and recommends it (d).

March 28: "There is no woman question. There is the question of the freedom, the equality of all human beings" (d,n).

May 6: while setting up famine relief, writes SA that "I rode back through the forest of Turgenev's Spasskoe at sunset: the fresh green in the woods and underfoot, the stars in the sky, the smells of the flowering willow and the drooping birch leaf, the sounds of the nightingale, the drone of the maybeetles, the cuckoo and the solitude, and the cheerful, pleasant motion of the horse under you, and physical, and spiritual health. And I thought, as I do constantly, about death. It became clear to me that it will be as fine on the other side of death as it is on this side, only different, and I understood why the Jews describe paradise as a garden. The purest joy – the joy of nature. It became clear to me that there it will be just as fine – no, better. I tried to summon up the doubt in that life that had been there before. I couldn't, just as before I couldn't summon up belief."

July 17: considers leaving home for Finland (letter to Finnish writer and disciple).

July 28: after a long inconclusive talk with SA, writes down whole conversation in form of letter to sister-in-law Tatiana entitled "A Dialogue." Tells disciple (L. P. Nikiforov) that he does not leave SA because he fears she would commit suicide if he did.

1899 SA's obsession with Taneev continues, daughter Tatiana marries (Marya had married in 1897), and this is blow to T. Works hard on *Resurrection* during first part of year, very few diary entries, and comments by him about his – to him embarrassing – irresistible need to write fiction. (Novel is published serially, heavily censored, in Russian journal, and simultaneously uncut in Russian and in English translation abroad. An American edition – published by *The Cosmopolitan Magazine* – abridged because editors consider parts of novel immoral.)

January: asked by correspondent to be godfather to his child, T responds: "I consider it impossible to take any part in one of the cruellest and most vulgar deceptions perpetrated against people, which is called the christening of infants."

April: sympathizes with student protests in Petersburg, but will not endorse violence, calling instead for refusal to attend classes.

April 22: loves Chekhov's *The Darling*, takes extraordinary step of visiting young writer in his rooms. Also praises writing of A. M. Gorky, although criticizes his psychology as "made-up" at times. Chekhov writes to Gorky (April 25) that T says, "You can think up anything you like, but not psychology, and in Gorky there are some psychological inventions, he describes what he has not felt."

May 5: writes Ch that for him as a writer "the main thing is the inner life expressed in scenes."

August 8: in letter to Ch calls Herzen a model journalist, and in early September, rereads *Letters to An Old Comrade*. (During his last years, T reads and praises Herzen repeatedly.)

November: rereading poetry of Tiutchev, calls it "true art" – "I cannot read it without tears."

1900　Condemns Boer War, and struggles with impulse to take the side of the underdog Boers. Also criticizes suppression of Boxer rebellion in China, and the Philippine insurrection. Reads Confucius, Ruskin, and George Eliot. Writes a number of polemical articles against these imperialist wars, the most important of which is "The Slavery of Our Times": "I'm still correcting it and I'm making it more and more venomous" (letter to daughter Marya, July 11). Writes shorter works on similar themes: "Thou Shalt Not Kill," on occasion of assassination of King Humbert of Italy, and "Patriotism and Government."

January 24: attends Chekhov's *Uncle Vanya*. He finds that it lacks drama, his general criticism of Chekhov's plays. Partly motivated by dissatisfaction with *Uncle Vanya*, works on unfinished play *The Living Corpse* (published posthumously).

April 29: claims to have read all of Goethe and Shakespeare three times "and could never understand their charm." By contrast, loves all of Schiller's plays (G).

June 21: in response to American journalist Edward Garnet, who asks him for a "message to the American people," writes (in English), that he is grateful for the help he received from American writers of the 1850s, including William Lloyd Garrison, Theodore Parker, Ralph Waldo Emerson, Adin Ballou, and Henry Thoreau. Also mentions the "brilliant pleiad" of William Ellery Channing, John Greenleaf Whittier, James Russell Lowell, and Walt Whitman; and ends his letter with remark that he would like to ask the American people why they pay attention to (capitalists) Gould, Rockefeller, and Carnegie instead of the writers T so admires.

June 23: "I want terribly to write something artistic, and not dramatic, but epic – a continuation of *Resurrection*: the peasant life of Nekhliudov" (d). From the same diary entry: "Nature moves me to the point of tenderness: the meadows, the forests, the crops, the ploughed fields, the mowing. I think, is this my last summer that I am living through? Fine; all to the good. I'm thankful for everything – I have been endlessly blessed. How possible and how joyful it is always to be thankful."

July 3: regretting persecution of his disciples, says that he hopes his articles will lead to his own arrest (G).

July 12: "I cannot rejoice at the birth of children of the wealthy classes – they're breeding parasites" (d).

August 21: with SA still seeing Taneev, feels "old temptation" to leave home (d).

September 1: tells disciple P. A. Sergeenko that his drama *The Light Shineth in the Darkness* may be the most important thing he writes because "before I thought only about success, about glory, now none of that is any longer necessary for me, and I want to speak out my most sincere and intimate thoughts."

October 21: says that he has loved Giuseppe Verdi's music "from earliest youth" (letter).

Fall: plays chess frequently, and starts to study Dutch by reading the Gospels in Dutch translation. (By February 1, 1901, G reports that "already reads it fairly easily.") In October plans a letter to the Chinese people, but does not complete it.

December 29: having read Friedrich Nietzsche's *Thus Spake Zarathustra*, says that when Nietzsche wrote it he was truly insane, and ends diary entry about it with "What kind of a society is it that recognizes such a madman, and an evil madman, as a teacher?" (d). He also criticizes Nietzsche for the "disconnectedness" of his style, and his repudiation of all metaphysical laws in order to assert his own superhuman status. T attacks Nietzsche several times, but he read him carefully. Maude quotes him as saying in 1903 that "I was absolutely charmed by his language when I first read him. What vigor and what beauty! I was so carried away that I forgot myself. Then I came to and began to digest it all. Great God, what savagery! It is terrible to drag down Christianity like this!"

1901 Sympathetic to demonstrators roughed up by authorities in Petersburg. Helps free Gorky, arrested in connection with the disturbances. Writes articles on Christians and military service ("A Soldier's Leaflet" and "An Officer's Leaflet") and according to his disciple Boulanger is very upset that these are distributed by revolutionaries with manuals on how to kill.

February: turns over all negotiations with foreign publishers and translators of his work to Ch.

Late February: excommunicated from the Russian Orthodox Church. In response he publishes "A Reply to the Holy Synod's Edict." The reaction to the excommunication is worldwide and negative.

Late June: falls seriously ill with malaria, and for a while near death. Messages of support pour in from around the world.

September: goes to Crimea to recuperate at Gaspri, the luxurious estate of S. V. Panina. Government takes measures to keep secret, first T's possible impending death and then his trip south. T loves the Crimea, and is delighted by its beauty. Visited there by Chekhov, Gorky, V. G. Korolenko, decadent poet K. D. Balmont, and others.

1902   January: finishes most careful treatment of religion *What is Religion and Wherein Lies its Essence?* (published in England, 1902).

January 16: sends letter to Nicholas II criticizing autocracy and recommending freedom of religion, movement, and education, as well as abolition of private property.

In February near death from pneumonia, and remains in Crimea until late June. Despite weakness, follows political events closely, comments, and even writes on them. Gorky writes in a July letter to K. P. Piatnitskii: "Lev Nikolaevich is definitely back on his feet and already at Iasnaia Poliana. Genius is stronger than death. He's writing an article on the land question, hm? What enormous force, what an astonishing grasp of the issues of the day!" Disciple and biographer P. I. Biriukov sends him a list of questions. (Biriukov continues to question him, the first volume of his biography comes out in 1906.)

May 19: at first T "feared the lack of frankness characteristic of every autobiography, but now I seem to have found a form in which I can fulfill your wish by indicating the main character of succeeding periods of my life in childhood, youth and adulthood" (letter to Biuiukov).

July: finishes "Address to the Working People," published in Ch's London press. Back home during the summer, works intensely on fiction, chiefly *Hadji Murat*. Revisits *The Light Shines in the Darkness*, starts *The False Coupon*, and works on *The Restoration of Hell*, a fictional narrative first conceived as an illustration of his article "Address to the Clergy." In agreement with T's own wishes, doctors say that he must winter at Iasnaia Poliana, and from this time on, he no longer lives in Moscow. As soon as possible resumes his active life, with walks and horseback riding. Receives numerous congratulations on occasion of his fiftieth anniversary as a writer.

September 15: listening to Chekhov's *The Darling* read aloud, T "laughed until he cried, infecting everyone else with his laughter" (letter from eyewitness).

September 23: approvingly recites a poem by F from memory, and praises Homer. "I reread him not long ago, and I will read him again. The Greeks combine realism with poetry" (Sergeenko's memoirs).

November: very impressed by P. A. Kropotkin's *Notes of a Revolutionary*. Health remains fragile, and in December falls seriously ill from flu.

November 11: "I decided that I could write [my biography], because I understood that it could be interesting and useful to tell people the vileness of my life until my awakening and, speaking without false modesty, all the goodness (if only in intentions that were not always realized because of weakness) after the awakening. It's in this sense that I would like to write for you" (letter to Biuiukov).

November 30: "Often a clear representation of how I should and could narrate my entire soul will come to me. But this happens only momentarily, and then an instant later I don't even remember how" (d).

1903 Protests Jewish pogroms in Kishiniev, and writes three stories – *Esarhaddon, Three Questions,* and *Work, Death and Illness* – for inclusion (translated into Yiddish) in an anthology published in Warsaw to aid the pogrom victims. Writes *After the Ball* (only published posthumously), and begins *The Divine and the Human* (completed 1906). Collects historical material about the reign of Nicholas I for *Hadji Murat,* and works on chapter about tsar. During the last twenty years of his life, diary contains many lists of possible topics for fiction and non-fictional writing. As T grows feebler, his production, especially of artistic works, declines, but his ideas for them keep coming. Conceives what he regards as an important new literary form, the so-called *Cycles of Reading* – inspirational calendars with wise sayings and also stories, original and borrowed, for meditation each day and week. (Several are compiled and published in T's last years.) Occasionally chastises self for working on fiction (and especially *Hadji Murat*). Starts "Shakespeare and the Drama" (finished 1904). Responding to Biriukov's request for biographical material, begins *Memoirs* which he works on until 1906. In connection with this, rereads diaries of 1840s and 1850s, in which he finds "much of interest" (June 4, d).

March 7: writes to Japanese translator of *Anna Karenina*.

July 10–11: completes a definition of life in diary. It is recopied with title "On Consciousness" and sent to Ch to publish in England.

September 5–6: decadent poet and religious thinker A. M. Dobroli-ubov visits.

December 5: William Jennings Bryan visits and makes a good impression.

December: last exchange of letters with AA. On December 22, T, knowing that she is very ill, writes to thank her "for all the good" she has done for him during their "half-century-long friendship." He speaks of her "goodness and love," thanks to which "he himself has become better." She responds a few days later, thanking him for his love and saying that in his letter she hears "that same, very sincere note that had always sounded" between them when they were young. She dies in March 1904.

1904 To keep them from Ch, SA sends T's manuscripts to the Historical Museum in Moscow. In response to outbreak of Russo–Japanese war, T publishes enormously influential anti-war tract "Bethink Yourselves." Follows war closely, at times unable to suppress his Russian patriotism as it goes badly. Works with Biriukov on biography, and SA starts her own autobiography.

August 23: beloved brother Sergei dies.

December 12: reads aloud from Dickens's *Pickwick Papers* and "laughs heartily" (SA's diary).

1905 Deplores violence of both sides as Russo–Japanese war ends and revolution breaks out, with a brutally suppressed general strike in Petersburg and the mutiny of the battleship *Potemkin*. Considers the revolution to have been inevitable. Writes a number of articles applying his theories of non-resistance and social reform to the political situation (such as pamphlets "The One Thing Needed" and "The End of An Age"). Although courted by all sides of the conflict, does not back any of them. Rereads almost all of Dickens. Whole family occupied in compiling a cycle of reading. T writes *Alesha the Pot*, *Kornei Vasilyev*, *Strawberries*, and *Prayer*, the last three of which are published by Intermediary in 1906 in a new *Cycle of Reading*.

August 25: praises Haydn's music for its "joy of life" (G).

October 19: welcomes tsar's manifesto of October 17, which calls for a constitution, freedom of assembly, and abolition of censorship (M), but reading it on October 23, T writes that "there is nothing in it for the people"(d). Last evidence of work on *Hadji Murat* (published posthumously in 1912).

December 1: having read two letters from George Bernard Shaw critical of "Shakespeare and the Drama," directs Ch to make necessary changes himself rather than sending the manuscript back to him.

December 4: warns first Chinese correspondent that China should not modernize by simply importing Western models: "Changes must grow by themselves from the attributes of a people and be completely new, not like the forms of other peoples."

1906   In this and subsequent year spends much time instructing peasant children on the estate, and also writing for children and preparing readings for them (a *Children's Cycle of Reading*). On several different occasions, expresses his contempt for constitutional democracy as practiced abroad and as being attempted in Russia. Increasingly concerned about the intentions of reformers and revolutionaries, writes and publishes three articles on his solution to Russia's political crisis: "A Letter to a Chinese," "The Significance of the Russian Revolution," and "An Address to the Russian People: to the Government, to the Revolutionaries, and to the Masses." Argues in these against the suitability of industrialization and Western democracy for Russia. The last article criticizes revolutionaries so severely (for their violence) that Ch, with great difficulty, convinces T to modify it.

January: a letter in two Russian newspapers informs editors who want to publish T's previously forbidden or censored works in Russia that they can get authentic and complete copies from Ch in London.

January 16: having received letter from Kharkov landowner about how he had turned his land over to his peasants, keeping only one allotment for himself, T publishes an open response to him urging all property owners to follow suit.

January–February: composes and publishes story *For What?*.

February 24: "I've always wanted to write…a Russian Robinson [Crusoe]: to describe a community that would migrate from Tambov Province across the steppe to the borders of China. To characterize its most outstanding members." Goes on to say that *Robinson Crusoe* is the best book for children (M).

March 10: a note written on a separate sheet: "A dull depressed mood the whole day. Toward evening this mood turned into tenderness – a desire for a caress – for love. I wanted, as in childhood, to cling to a loving, pitying being and to weep and to be comforted. But who is that being to whom I could cling that way? I run through all the people I love – not one will do. Who to cling to? To become little and cling to mother as I picture her to myself. Yes, yes, Mommy, whom I never called by that name, not being yet able to speak. Yes, she, my highest image of pure love, not cold, divine, but earthly, warm, motherly. My best, tired soul is drawn to this. You, Mommy, caress me. – This is all insane, but it is all the truth."

April 12: writes Ernest Crosby that the revolution in Russia is a harbinger of a worldwide revolution that, not soon, but within a few decades, will destroy the power of states everywhere.

July 12: argues with sons Lev and Andrei against capital punishment, which they support, and writes daughter Marya that is beside himself for two days afterwards. Later that month, SA has two peasants prosecuted for cutting down oaks on estate, and although she relents after they are tried, they have to serve their sentences anyway. These two incidents revive his desire to leave home (G).

Late August: SA falls seriously ill. The tenderness of the couple for one another, severely tested though it has been, quickly surfaces. T cannot concentrate on his work, and admires his SA's stoicism. Too weak to be moved, she is operated on at home for a large uterine tumor.

November 26: beloved daughter Marya, visiting with her husband, falls ill of pneumonia and quickly dies.

December: reads Upton Sinclair's *The Jungle* and praises it highly.

1907 Much music-making. Ongoing interest in Eastern thought. Disparages the Duma (Russian Parliament) and constitutional government: for instance, responding to a question from a Petersburg newspaper, writes that "No Duma can promote the common good" (January 26). Begins to read Shaw, mostly does not like his writing. (In 1908, tells Shaw himself in a letter [August 17] that his writing is too satirical, and draws too much attention to the brilliance of the author.) Works on cycles of reading for children as well as adults, and also a children's version of the Gospels (*The Teaching of Christ Told For Children*, published 1908).

May 19: Brother-in-law Viacheslav Behrs, a transportation engineer, murdered during a strike in Petersburg.

September: very upset when SA and son Andrei ask authorities to prosecute peasants stealing from estate garden.

July: interview with T by correspondent published July 7 in *The New York Times*.

July 26: sends letter to influential liberal statesman P. A. Stolypin, urging him to promote the abolition of private property. Replying, Stolypin defends his policy of replacing communes with small private farms.

Late September: Repin visits and sketches T with SA listening intently to him. Of this T remarks on October 1 to M. S. Sukhotin that "For the last 45 years I've been waiting for SA to listen to me, and I haven't been able to make this happen."

October 26: "It's strange that it is my lot to be silent with the people living around me and to speak only with those who are far away in time and space, who will listen to me" (d).

1908 Begins to suffer from fainting spells. Having returned permanently to Russia, Ch settles near Iasnaia Poliana. SA increasingly out of control. Many concerts, and many comments on musical performances reported by G. T works on story *There Are No Guilty People in The World* (unfinished, reworked in 1909 and 1910). Publishes, among other things, "I Cannot Be Silent," directed against the death penalty. Receives a flood of letters, pro and con, in response. On July 10, Repin publishes letter in newspaper praising T for saying openly what Repin claims that millions of Russians privately believe. Government tries to censor this and other works of T that are in print or circulating, and sentences a disciple to prison for distributing T's banned writings.

January 4: receives dictaphone from American inventor Thomas Edison. Records various comments and stories on it, some of which survive, including a recitation of *The Wolf*, a story composed for grandchildren.

January 28: another letter to Stolypin deploring the strategy of fighting violence with violence, and calling once again for the abolition of private property.

March 6: an idea for a story – "I'll take the first trial of revolutionaries that comes along, and I'll describe what [the revolutionary] experienced when he decided to kill the agent provocateur, what this provocateur experienced when he was being killed, what the judge who sentenced him experienced, what the executioner who hung him experienced" (Gusev's diary). (As health declines, has many such ideas for fiction, most not realized.)

April 8: criticizes an article about punishments of revolutionaries as too sensational: "He expounds these terrible facts with his own epithets, explanations, conclusions... These only weaken the impression. It must be left to the reader himself to make these conclusions" (Gusev's diary).

June: Rereads Pushkin. Especially struck by long novel in verse *Eugene Onegin*, but singles out prose pieces as well.

July: writes a "secret diary" from July 2–18. In it expresses wish to leave or even to die to get away from unpleasantness at home; worries that he might leave for personal, not principled reasons. This diary is soon discovered, and when T is ill in August, he allows Ch to copy it.

August 11: dictates will to Gusev asking to be buried, without religious rites, in the woods where he and his brothers played the game of the "green stick," which supposedly had written on it the secret of universal brotherhood; also expresses the wish that his heirs allow all his writings to be in the public domain.

August 28: turns eighty years old. In February discourages plans for celebration of his eightieth birthday.

March 13: records on dictaphone that best birthday present would be to be put in jail. Government also tries to control public response to the birthday, but congratulations flow in from around the world. In just one example, the head of the British Museum brings him a message from England signed by more than 800 well-known cultural figures.

1909 Many concerts at Iasnaia Poliana, with performances by famous musicians such as Polish pianist Wanda Landowska (who played three times for T). For the most part praises the performances, and is often very affected by them. One of the musicians (violinist M. G. Erdenko) reports in October that listening to a mazurka, T "danced around the room." Persecution of disciples intensifies, and T tries unsuccessfully to make the government prosecute him rather than them. Advocates for abolition of private property according to the methods of Henry George. Reads Kant's *Religion Within the Limits of Reason Alone* twice. Writes a series of short dialogues called *A Child's Wisdom*. Rereads all of Gogol, and on March 5 declares short story *The Carriage* his best artistic work (n). Writes and publishes *Conversation With a Passerby* and *Songs in the Village*, both recording incidents that he witnesses. Corresponds with Gandhi, who praises *The Kingdom of God is Within You* as the work that has most inspired him. Publishes "The Inevitable Revolution" and "The Sole Commandment."

January 30: in letter gives Ch permission to publish any of his personal letters in an edition of his works.

February 14: "Executions in our day are good, because they obviously show that the leaders are bad people who have gone astray, and that therefore to obey them is as harmful and shameful as to obey the ataman of a robber gang" (d).

August 10: in conversation about a fellow writer (Saltykov-Shchedrin), remarks that "Le secret d'être ennuyeux, c'est tout dire" (The secret of being boring is to say everything; G).

August 22: "I went walking in the Forest Preserve, a marvelous morning. Like a little cloud with indistinct edges on one side, the moon is high in the bright blue sky over the green ocean of the forest. Very nice" (d).

September: Maude makes his last visit and remarks on how vigorous and passionately interested in life T still is despite the fact that at the time he was in a wheelchair.

September 3: on way to visit Ch in Moscow Province, recites a poem by F from memory (*Autumn Rose*), praises and comments on it. On return trip, thousands gather at train station in Moscow to cheer him and SA. Fainting spells connected to exertions of journey.

November 1: writes will giving control of all his works, including artistic ones, to daughter Aleksandra after his death. Aleksandra, age twenty-five, on bad terms with mother and sides with Ch. T also toys with the idea of finally giving up his property. SA exacerbates the situation with frequent hysterical outbursts and unreasonable demands.

December 23: T reads a book by Valentin Bulgakov on the Tolstoyan world view and comments: "In general it's poor – not his, but my work" (d).

December 24: having reread Sterne's *Sentimental Journey* twice with great enjoyment – "it's amazing how funny it is" – wants to reread *Tristram Shandy* as well (M).

Also compiles a collection of sayings called *The Path of Life*, this one organized by theme; and writes moralizing two-act play for peasants called *The Cause of It All*. Both are published in 1911.

1910 Works on compiling another calendar called *For Every Day*. SA prepares the twelfth edition of collected works, in twenty volumes. As Ch schemes from his nearby residence, SA accuses T of homosexual relations with Ch. T pities and defends her, but his disciples and youngest daughter do not.

October 28: having threatened to do so for so many years, leaves home in secrecy intending not to return. Goes first to sister in convent and then leaves when family discovers whereabouts.

October 31: on train develops a high fever, and stops at Astapovo railway station, where he is carried into house of station master.

November 7: dies of pneumonia. Unbeknownst to him, crowds of reporters have gathered at the station. His final agony and the suffering of SA, kept from his bedside until the very end, when he is already unconscious, become one of the first worldwide media events. He is buried according to his wishes, in the woods at Iasnaia Poliana.

NOTES

1 This chronology has been compiled with the help of Megan Swift. It is taken primarily from the two-volume N. N. Gusev, *Letopis' zhizni i tvorchestva L'va Nikolaevicha Tolstogo* (Moscow: Gosudarstvennoe izdatel'stvo khudozhestvennoi literatury, 1958; Gotlitizdat, 1960), but draws on many other sources as well. The purpose of the chronology is to give readers a general sense of the course of Tolstoy's life. It is not comprehensive even in listing all of Tolstoy's artistic works, and readers should not use it to establish exact dates of publication or events, which are often contentious in Tolstoy scholarship. In each entry, general items are listed before those with exact dates. Dates, unless otherwise noted, are given according to the old style Julian calendar in effect during Tolstoy's life. This calendar was twelve days behind the Western (Gregorian) one in the nineteenth century and thirteen days behind it in the twentieth. The translations are my own.

The following abbreviations apply throughout:

AA A. A. Tolstaia
Ch V. G. Chertkov
d Tolstoy's diary
F A. A. Fet
G A. B. Goldenweizer
M D. P. Makovitsky
n Tolstoy's notebook
S N. N. Strakhov
SA Sofya Andreevna Tolstaia
T Lev Tolstoy

2 From here on, the chronology does not list publications as a separate category because the publication history of T's writings becomes ever more complicated.

DONNA TUSSING ORWIN

Introduction: Tolstoy as artist and public figure

Count Lev Nikolaevich Tolstoy, one of the world's greatest novelists, came to fiction after toying with other vocations, and even after becoming a successful writer, he kept trying other things. In 1852 he entered the army and contemplated a military career. At various times in his life he paid more attention to agriculture, pedagogy, and various social reforms than he did to literature which, moreover, he more than once abandoned for more important activities. As he said proudly on one occasion, unlike Pushkin and Turgenev, he and the poet Lermontov were *not* literati.[1] He regarded the motives of writers with suspicion and once declared that his brother Nikolai had been more talented as a writer than he but had lacked the requisite vices.

When Tolstoy referred (in late unfinished memoirs) to the vices necessary for becoming an author, he meant the desire to influence others and to be loved by them. Unlike his very private brother Nikolai, he felt this keenly. He told his wife that when he read a favorable review of *Childhood* while on a hunting trip in 1852, he choked back "tears of joy."[2] As he mentioned many times in his early diaries and drafts of early works, he regarded his reader as potentially a close friend. While this is a convention of sentimentalist prose, Tolstoy adopted it for personal as well as professional reasons. (Many critics associate his need for intimacy with the loss of his mother before he was three, and his father when he was nine.) Even in his old age, in 1890, he told a disciple (P. A. Sergeenko) that because he no longer cared for glory, in his drama *The Light Shines in The Darkness* he now wanted "to speak out my most sincere and intimate thoughts."[3]

Inasmuch as Tolstoy's personal reasons for writing fiction were partly confessional, he resisted such writing (often unsuccessfully) as undignified. He had another purely personal reason for writing fiction as well. Like many people, he fantasized about life as a means of understanding and controlling it. Very often, therefore, his works are counterpoints to his life at the time he wrote them, and represent imagined solutions to real life problems. So, for instance, he wrote *Anna Karenina* with its happy ending (for the Levins) while he was going through a protracted crisis that began just after he finished *War and Peace* in 1869, and led eventually to *A Confession* with its avowed rejection of his earlier life. As Tolstoy grew older, the gap between his art and life in this respect began to narrow. Always prone to radical experimentation, he tried more and more to live the solutions that he was advocating in his books. Contradictions between his life and his theories led eventually to a final real life crisis. At age eighty-two, on October 28, 1910, after having threatened to do so intermittently for more than twenty-five years, Tolstoy finally left home to begin a new life more consistent with his ideas. Perhaps it was lucky for him that he died a little over a week later at the railroad station of Astapovo. His death provided one of those tidy endings that he abjured in fiction because "life isn't like that." Had he lived on, it would have meant a return to struggle and paradox. Just one of these paradoxes was pointed out to me by Tolstoy's biographer Lidiia Dmitrievna Gromova-Opulskaia in private conversation: it was only because of her loving care of him that Tolstoy was alive in 1910 finally to leave his wife. No sooner did he leave her than he died.

It is significant that according to Tolstoy the specific vice of poets is vanity, the lowest manifestation of the political passion of love of glory. The notorious anarchist and pacifist who believed that politics was by its very nature corrupting and corrupt was himself at bottom a political man who at age twenty-three conceived himself as born "to have great influence over the happiness and well-being of others" (diary, March 29, 1852). Tolstoy scholar Boris Eikhenbaum compared him to Napoleon, both in ambition and in his brilliant and successful maneuvering to remain relevant for over fifty years within an evolving literary and cultural milieu.[4] His greatest political achievement, in which he joins Homer, Dante, Shakespeare, Goethe, and Pushkin, was as a founding poet of his nation. He came to manhood in the 1840s and 1850s, just as Russians were struggling to define themselves as a modern people, and his works contributed to that project of national identity. From the time it appeared, *War and Peace* was immediately perceived as a founding epic, a Russian *Iliad*.

Both Tolstoy's personal circumstances and the time in which he lived shaped his political beliefs. His father, an officer in the Napoleonic wars, was captured and then freed in 1814 during the occupation of Paris. After five years of service in government, he retired to his wife's estate of Iasnaia Poliana, where Tolstoy was born. The Tolstoys, with 800 serfs, were independently wealthy, but members of an aristocracy whose political power had been steadily eroded under the Romanov tsars. Tolstoy grew up under Nicholas I, who came to power after a failed putsch by the aristocracy and as much as possible concentrated power in his own hands. Nicholas wanted soldiers, not advisors, and for him the aristocracy was a military caste only. Tolstoy once commented to his friend and biographer Aylmer Maude that Russians were freer than Englishmen, who had to occupy themselves with politics. From the other side of the fence, Maude speculated that their isolation from the hard practical tasks of governing made Russians prone to "extremely radical solutions."[5] Of Tolstoy himself he said that "Tolstoy had no adequate sense of being a responsible member of a complex community with the opinions and wishes of which it is necessary to reckon. On the contrary, his tendency was to recognize with extraordinary vividness a personal duty revealed by the working of his own conscience and intellect, apart from any systematic study of the social state of which he was a member."[6]

Tolstoy drew upon his own biography when he described young Dmitrii Olenin, the hero of *The Cossacks*, on the eve of his departure to the Caucasus.

> At the age of eighteen he was free – as only rich young Russians in the Forties who had lost their parents at an early age could be. Neither physical or moral fetters of any kind existed for him; he could do as he liked, lacking nothing and bound by nothing. Neither relatives, nor fatherland, nor religion, nor wants existed for him.

The Cossacks, begun as early as 1852 but published only in 1863, reveals the state of mind of the young Tolstoy in another way as well. Olenin is careful not to commit himself to anything or anyone that would diminish this freedom, but he is also consciously searching for a goal, "an aspiration or an idea" for which he could sacrifice himself and his freedom. This sense of personal freedom on the one hand and idealism on the other was typical of Russian gentry youth on the eve of the emancipation of the serfs in 1861.

As a hereditary aristocrat, Tolstoy was interested in politics: as a university student he started a commentary on Catherine the Great's *Instruction*, and in 1849 he even considered a career in the civil service. He joined the army in 1852. An artillery officer, he served on the front lines during the Crimean War, and witnessed the corruption and favoritism that, in his mind, undermined the heroic efforts of Russian soldiers on the battlefield. Like Prince Andrei in *War and Peace*, he suggested reforms to his superiors, but got nowhere. Tolstoy's later political anarchism derives in part from such disillusionments. His experience suggested to him that a meaningful, free life was possible only outside politics, and this became his lifetime opinion. In his fiction, his characters undergo educations that turn them away from politics, just as he turned away. Moral education is more important for him than political education, and he connects political or social change with individual change wrought by education. Yet inasmuch as Tolstoy's writings almost all concern the relation of the individual to society, they inevitably have a political dimension. He sought, paradoxically for us, a social organization outside of representative government, in which he did not believe. But why should he have believed in it? No matter how many reforms the Romanov tsars introduced to modernize Russia during Tolstoy's lifetime starting after the defeat of the Crimean War, none of them willingly gave away one iota of power. Every one of them reserved for himself the right to override the law, and by so doing made it impotent. Is it surprising that Tolstoy regarded political organizations as unjust attempts by the strong to oppress the weak? This is mostly what they were in the Russia of his lifetime.

Many Russians hoped that the abolition of serfdom would generate a new social cohesiveness. It is no accident that *War and Peace* was written in the decade immediately after the emancipation. In it, Tolstoy depicts the whole Russian people acting in concert as a model for a future, harmonious nation. He deliberately minimizes the tensions among the classes during the Napoleonic period, and he insists that the gentry, the main actors in the novel, are members of the Russian people along with peasant soldiers and merchants who all support the war. In fact, however, the emancipation and its aftermath exacerbated social problems in Russia rather than alleviated them. It destroyed the economic foundations of gentry life but – in a futile effort to avoid this result – ruined the peasants by freeing them without land. Migration to the cities swelled an urban proletariat which eventually became the focus of revolutionary agitation. From the late 1870s, determined persecution by the government of radical groups (who first agitated in the countryside, and only in the 1890s concentrated on cities) heightened discord.

Tolstoy's personal crisis depicted in *A Confession* (1881) had political as well as personal causes, and is organically linked to the political radicalism that he began to espouse soon after he wrote it. Starting in the early 1880s, he called for the dissolution of the state and the establishment in its place of a universal Christian brotherhood in which loosely organized small communities supported themselves and no one tyrannized over his fellows. In *What Then Must We Do?* (1882–86) he claimed that governments with their armies and police help the rich and powerful to oppress the poor. The privileged claim to have freed themselves from the necessity of working so as to be of use to others. But Tolstoy argues that "there is not one government or societal activity which would not be considered by many people to be harmful"; and therefore, the so-called usefulness of the privileged is always imposed by force on the people it is supposed to help. There is no such thing as a government to which every individual has given consent, and only such a government would be just. All rulers, democratic or otherwise, should admit that "their main motivation is their own personal advantage" (ch. 27).

What Then Must We Do? was written during a period of political crisis: Pan-Slavists were extremely critical of the Treaty ending the Russo–Turkish War; in 1877, the government in the late 1870s was determined to crush the populist movement; and Alexander II was assassinated by radical populists in 1881. Tolstoy warned that revolution was not only imminent, but had been averted only by guile for the last thirty years, that is, since the death of Nicholas I and defeat in the Crimean War (ch. 39).

By 1900 (fifteen or so years later), in "The Slavery of Our Times," Tolstoy's indictment of existing Russian society had been extended to all modern solutions to societal ills, including Marxism, which became important in Russia only in the 1890s. He argued bluntly that so long as people, rich and poor, insisted on living at the present standard of prosperity, slavery would be necessary to maintain it. The problem, according to him, was not as easy as improving the conditions of workers, themselves corrupted by city living. What was needed was a return to a rural life in which people did meaningful work in natural surroundings. Whatever cooperation such communities required would be supplied locally and agreed upon by all.

For Tolstoy in his later years, political instincts became the evil that must be overcome in order for the Kingdom of God to be established on earth. Practically, the least believable part of his political program is his claim that if individuals only considered their own self-interest, then we would all moderate our passions and live in harmony. Thousands of years of evidence to the contrary do not sway Tolstoy from this "simple" idea. He blames all past injustices on the crimes of the rich and powerful, but he seems to think that in the future these same spoilers can be talked into mending their ways. He presents the rewards of this past behavior as all connected to physical, material existence. The powerful want to rule the weak so that they need not work themselves, and so that they can indulge bodily passions. But, although he does not emphasize it, he has not forgotten the love of glory which Prince Andrei defines in *War and Peace* as the desire that others, even those he despises, love him. This passion requires the cooperation of others, and hence, politics. In *What I Believe*, Tolstoy asserts that the striving for "earthly happiness," which, although he does not mention it, includes at its pinnacle the love of glory, arises out of fear of death. We indulge our passions and seek to extend our existence by controlling others in an effort to forget and even avoid death; but since death is inevitable, we would be wise to give up these unjust activities and to live within the boundaries of material necessity.

Although Tolstoy thought that people almost always acted in accordance with their feelings rather than their thoughts, he never gave up attempting to appeal to reason in himself and others. (In fact he became more, not less of a rationalist in his old age, and therefore more of an enlightenment thinker.) During his short stint at Kazan University in 1847, he studied philosophy and kept a diary. As a thinker, however, Tolstoy was always more moralist than metaphysician: he always had a practical, moral reason for philosophizing. This didactic side made him a natural teacher. Pedagogy, in various forms of which he engaged throughout his life, was no sideline for him; in his mind, in fact, it was a less personal and therefore more justifiable reason for writing. The surviving philosophical fragments from Tolstoy's student days stand in relation to the diaries as theory to practice. The diaries set rules based on philosophical generalizations, and record Tolstoy's moral progress (or, more often, his backsliding). Reading these early unpublished writings in the 1920s, Eikhenbaum established that Tolstoy's fiction grew originally out of the diaries,[7] but the philosophical fragments are equally important. His shift from philosophy to fiction was as much strategic as temperamental. In his mind the purpose of both was didactic, to lead his reader to virtue and freedom through education.[8] The failure of his early attempts to control and shape his own life (and the consequences of his own Rousseauist philosophical orientation) taught him that education had to take place not through reason and philosophy, but through the sentiments and, therefore, art.

In the art that grew from his twin fascinations with details and philosophical generalization, the young Tolstoy may be said to have had two goals: to recreate reality and to order it according to higher moral truth. All of Tolstoy's fiction is autobiographical in some way. He believed that truth resides in individual experience, and hence that what he learned from self-observation could be applied to humankind in general. This premise underlies all his art, starting with his first great work, the trilogy *Childhood–Adolescence–Youth*, in which he attempted to recapitulate the first three stages of life. The fourth stage is described in the other masterpiece of Tolstoy's youth, *The Cossacks*, which was originally entitled *Young Manhood*.

Tolstoy's belief in the necessity of grounding all knowledge in personal experience also influenced his poetics. He worked on a style that would place the reader within a scene or character by appealing first to the reader's own sense perceptions and memories. The success of this technique is responsible for Tolstoy's reputation, already established in the nineteenth century, as the greatest realist writer. To structure his vivid realism, Tolstoy developed an authoritative narrative voice, a voice first heard thundering in the Sevastopol stories written as a response to different stages of the siege of Sevastopol during the Crimean War. Impersonal though it may sound, it would be a mistake to call this voice objective, or merely logical. It is Tolstoy himself speaking directly and lyrically to his readers, in tones reminiscent of his mentor Jean-Jacques Rousseau. In Tolstoy's fictional works, this voice does not dominate; in his non-fiction it does; but in both the intention of the author is the same: to infect the reader with his ideas and feelings. Already in 1853 he declared that the "main interest" of any literary work was "the character of the author" as expressed in it: "the most pleasant [works] are those in which the author seems to hide his personal viewpoint but remains consistent in it wherever it appears" (November 1, 1853). Once located imaginatively within the perspective of a given character or narrator, the reader will identify with his thoughts as well. In non-fictional works, the author steps out from behind his vividly imagined narratives, but he still relies on numerous parables and interpolated narratives to make his points. In other words, even in these, appealing as he does more to feeling rather than to reason, for philosophical reasons he still is more poet than philosopher.

Tolstoy's philosophy was anchored in a complex model of human psychology developed in his student days. He explained it in 1857, in drafts for the never finished second half of *Youth*:

> I remember that the basis of the new philosophy consisted in the fact that man consists of body, feelings, reason and will, but the essence of the human soul is will, and not reason; that Descartes, whom I had not read then, was wrong to say *Cogito, ergo sum*, because he thought only because he wished to think, consequently, one should say: *volo, ergo sum*. On this basis, the faculties of man can be divided into the will of the mind, the will of the feelings and the will of the body.[9]

Even though will is the essence of human nature, will itself is not a unified force in this psychological model. The moral goal that Tolstoy set himself in his first diaries was to organize his soul so that the various parts were in harmony with one another. For this to happen, the "will of the mind" had to govern the other "wills." As Tolstoy soon discovered, however, the mind itself could go astray. Especially troublesome was the "big brain" that left to its own devices indulged in dangerous mental gymnastics that destroyed unselfconscious moral instincts and tradition without providing anything conscious to replace them. In the early 1850s, Tolstoy read the "Profession of Faith of the Savoyard Vicar" in Rousseau's *Emile*, and adopted the Vicar's resolution to eschew all metaphysics except what was necessary to objectively ground moral freedom and law. He abandoned forever any attempt to directly connect with God or metaphysical truth, and became instead a kind of transcendentalist, which he remained, although in differing degrees and in different ways, his entire life.

In the early 1880s, Tolstoy began to see himself as more a sage and moral leader than an artist. Unlike artists, gurus depend upon an articulated moral teaching, and Tolstoy spent the first half of this decade developing one. In parallel and contrast to the autobiographical project of the 1850s, he planned and largely executed a large work consisting of *A Confession* (1879–82), *An Investigation of Dogmatic Theology* (1879–81, 1884), *A Translation and Harmony of the Four Gospels*, and *What I Believe* (1882–84). The four parts would move from a description of Tolstoy's crisis of faith (*A Confession*), through an examination and dismantling of contemporary Christianity (the two middle works), to a statement of faith as practiced by Tolstoy himself and recommended to others (*What I Believe*).

Tolstoy's Christianity was ethical and anti-metaphysical. God was inaccessible except through "knowledge of the meaning of human life" (*What I Believe*, ch. 9). This knowledge is progressive and ethical: only when one rejects, through experience and the power of reason, the "illusoriness of the finite" does one then turn to and believe in the "infinite." In practical terms, this meant a moral evolution from the natural life of the body centered around self and family to life centered around the well-being of others. Tolstoy's social theories, developed at the same time, depended on this central premise. He began to spend winters in Moscow in 1881, and for the first time encountered urban poverty. In response to it he wrote, first a powerful description of what he saw entitled "On the Moscow Census," and then *So What Then Must We Do?*. In this latter work, he says that philanthropy for the poor is not the solution to societal injustices. Instead the rich must abandon their idle way of life and model a good life for the poor and for society. This "solution" was also to apply to the artist. In the 1880s, Tolstoy tried very hard to change his life to make it conform to his new ideas, and his wife's opposition to this led to their estrangement. Already in 1884 he made his first attempt to leave home.

Tolstoy insisted that personal moral reform was more important than social action, which by itself, without the proper moral attitude, would not have lasting results. In any case, a properly organized society would not require large-scale or institutionalized social action, because everyone would be able to feed and clothe himself. In 1891–92, despite this official position, which he continued to advocate even in articles on the famine, Tolstoy and his family organized famine relief in his own and neighboring provinces. When it first began, the tsarist government denied the seriousness and even the existence of the famine, for which its economic policies were partly responsible. Tolstoy's article "On Hunger" was banned, whereupon Tolstoy arranged for it to be translated and published in several foreign countries. Partly as a result of the publicity generated by this and other articles by Tolstoy, aid flowed into the stricken areas from Russian and foreign contributors.

Already famous as Russia's greatest living author and moral authority, Tolstoy now became a social activist and a lightning rod for political dissent. By the early 1890s, he was being widely read abroad: in fact, since all his controversial tracts and some of his fiction were banned at home but immediately translated and distributed elsewhere, foreign readers had easier access to them than did Russians. Readers all over the world as well as at home responded to his *cris de coeur*, which promoted a new religious faith based on reason and ethics rather than dogma. In 1891, Ernest Howard Crosby (1856–1907), an American diplomat from a prominent New York family stationed in Alexandria, Egypt, read a French translation of *On Life*, Tolstoy's philosophical explanation of his new ideas. He immediately wrote Tolstoy to tell him of its impact on him: "Altho' brought up in Christian surroundings, I never saw and felt before the real secret of Christ's teaching and the real grounds of our faith and hope. All that you say finds an echo in my own heart and it is all so beautifully simple and self-evident."[10] This one work changed Crosby's life. He left his job, embarked on a life of public service based on his new ideals, and became Tolstoy's main advocate and disciple in the United States. Another American, Jane Addams, just out of college, read *My Religion* (or *What I Believe*) and, a little while later, *What To Do* (or *What Then Must We Do?*).[11] Addams, who went on to found Hull House and the settlement house movement, credited Tolstoy with inspiring her life's work, and visited him in 1896. In the 1890s, during a period of imperialist wars, Tolstoy became involved in the pacifist movement. He used his immense prestige as a writer to champion various causes in Russia and around the world, and many of his artistic works from this thirty-year period were written in their service. His teachings influenced Gandhi in India, and the kibbutz movement in Palestine, and at home his moral authority rivalled and often exceeded that of the tsar and church. At home too the older Tolstoy was a hero of resistance. It is something of an historical irony that we read Tolstoy today for his positive portrayals of gentry life, rather than for his later, satirical works. In a sense, these writings, so famous in their own time, are victims of their own success: in some small measure because of them, the regime and world they attacked have disappeared.

Tolstoy himself proclaimed loud and clear that he changed course in 1880, so much so that the writings of the following decade, both fictional and polemical, can be understood as an attempt to reinvent himself as another psychological being. There were personal reasons for this, the main ones being his own ageing and various deaths in his family.[12] He himself thought that these "biological" events had brought him to his senses, and to a right understanding of the world at last. When he was writing *War and Peace*, he had believed that nature was moral, and needed only to be fully expressed in an art which at its core was mimetic rather than didactic. The later Tolstoy believed less in the fusing of nature and morality, and used art to convey a moral lesson from his narrator, who now becomes the persona of an author bent on directly infecting his readers.[13]

Another way that he himself explained his evolution is that in later life he ceased to believe in the natural coupling of aesthetics and ethics.[14] The consequences of this change in thought are artistically expressed in a metaphor that develops through four appearances in A Confession. In chapter three, Tolstoy compares himself as a youth, with his early uncritical acceptance of "perfectification" [sovershenstvovanie] and progress as worthy goals of life, to a feckless passenger "carried in a boat through wind and waves," who answers the natural question "Where are we heading?" with the answer: "somewhere." Toward the end of chapter four, he repeats that "outside life carried me along on its waves while I believed that life has sense, although I could not express it." In chapter ten, he identifies the common people as those who will teach him the meaning of life and who "carry the likes of me and the Solomons [from Ecclesiastes] along the waves of life." Chapter twelve ends with a metaphor extended to Homeric length to poetically encapsulate Tolstoy's early life and conversion. Having embarked on the boat first mentioned in chapter three, having been given oars and directed to the other shore, he rowed out into the current. He worked conscientiously at first, but was influenced by others to drop his oars and drift with the current. Only when disaster loomed ahead did he look back, see the peasant rowers behind still headed for the other shore, and joining them, saved himself.

Tolstoy's readers, following this trope to its triumphant climax in chapter twelve, would inevitably be reminded of the comparison of history to a great ocean in the first epilogue of War and Peace and the explanation of its author that each individual, while going about his own business, unconsciously plays a role in currents and upheavals in the ocean which reflect the unknown will of God in history.[15] Hundreds of pages earlier, in book two, chapter seven (chapter four in Maude's translation), soldiers crossing a bridge are portrayed through the eyes of Nesvitskii, an officer–observer, as waves of a great river. In his great novel of expansive optimism, Tolstoy allows us to go with the flow so long as we don't abandon our humanity, and he assimilates the political and historical life of peoples into nature. In A Confession, the metaphor of the river represents not only human history, but a mix of physical life, passion, and outside, corrupt opinion – all the things, so it seemed to Tolstoy by then, that human beings are born to resist. In Resurrection, the river metaphor recurs in the wild spring break-up of the ice that accompanies the hero Nekhliudov's seduction of Maslova. The use of water imagery is complicated in the novel, which begins with a rejuvenating spring rainfall and elsewhere compares water and pity, but at the most we can say that nature by itself keeps us free – every spring the ice breaks in the river and the imprisoned torrent flows again – but not moral.

As I suggest above, the sea change in Tolstoy's ideas affected his attitude toward art. In *A Confession* he explains that in his early, mistaken period (when he wrote both *War and Peace* and *Anna Karenina*), he had conceived of art as strictly mimetic: "the expression of life of every sort in poetry and the arts made me happy, I enjoyed looking at life in the mirror of art . . . this play of lights and shadows – of the comic, the tragic, the touching, the fine, the terrible in life – comforted me" (ch. 4). When he realized that his life did not in fact make sense, his idea of art did not change, but mimesis becomes "either unnecessary, superfluous and funny, or torture." What is unsaid but implied in this passage is that earlier, Tolstoy had equated life and its ethical meaning, and art as a "mirror" was the perfect vehicle to express both the true and the good. Later, when he comes to believe that morality requires the rejection of the "play of lights and shadows" that Stiva Oblonsky so eloquently defends in *Anna Karenina*, his art, no longer reigning supreme, is officially subordinated wholly to the task of self-conquest and for the most part becomes "torture" for Tolstoy himself and his readers. His most typical later fiction was therefore both more naturalistic and more moralistic at the same time. On one end of the spectrum of these later didactic works are realistic stories with clear-cut morals like *The False Coupon* and on the other are modern parables like *Esarhaddon* and *The Restoration of Hell* which shade into Bunyanesque allegory or medieval morality plays as they illustrate moral points.

In keeping with these new ideas, the novel *Resurrection* differs significantly in structure from his two previous ones. No good love story balances a bad one here: instead the reader must follow the main character, Dmitrii Nekhliudov, as he gradually gives up personal happiness for love for others. As a Rousseauist, Tolstoy had always hated excess and social organization beyond that practiced in small communities, but he now went further to denounce the body itself as an unruly force that had to be tamed in order for life to be happy and virtuous. He debunks passions by carrying their consequences to negative extremes. In *The Kreutzer Sonata*, for instance, we are expected to admit that we all have, if only momentarily, hated our spouses and wanted to kill them. If such an impulse has ever crossed our minds as it apparently had Tolstoy's, then, as the epigraph to *The Power of Darkness* goes: "When the claw is caught, the whole bird is lost." We cannot resist playing out the whole scenario with Pozdnyshev, from lust to murder; and then Pozdnyshev, backed up by Tolstoy, turns to us and says, you see, sex, even in marriage, is bad, and leads to murder. Not even animals are spared. *Strider*, narrated by a gelding, exposes the unnaturalness of ownership, but also suggests that sexual passion addles the minds of his fellow horses. With magnificent confidence that his reader will follow him everywhere, in his late stories Tolstoy rages against the body so as to achieve for himself and his readers that embrace of the infinite that he believes will only come when one's belief in the pleasures and goodness of the finite – that is, the material – is destroyed.

In many ways, of course, Tolstoy was consistent in his beliefs throughout his life. To the extent that this is true, his later, avowedly dogmatic works and tracts on various subjects are continuations of the project of self-analysis and moral improvement initiated in the 1840s, during his university years. Behind all the twists in his ideas and behavior, there is a psychological consistency in his life from beginning to end. His genius is narrow but deep: no man has lived a more sincere life than he did, or one more dedicated to serving the needs of the individual. This consistency produced a great artist, and also a flawed thinker and activist who contributed to the tragic political history of his country. From his early youth he longed for an emotional intimacy with others that his mind could accept as truthful. His greatest work of art, *War and Peace*, is, among other things, a fantasy of such complete intimacy expressed in the marriage of Pierre and Natasha. Experience disabused him of the possibility of such a union based on feeling alone, and he spent the second part of his life trying to construct one based on reason. The more reasonable he claimed to be, however, the more isolated he became from others, including members of his own family. For the last thirty years of his life he lived as a stranger in his own house, preaching love and sowing dissension.

His theories wrought havoc abroad as well as at home. Whilst remaining absolutely true to his own individual needs, he accused the members of his class of selfishness, and imagined, along with many other Russians of his generation, that Russian peasants were different psychological beings than himself, both better and simpler. Not spoiled by "civilization," they would willingly share naturally sparse goods and limit their passions. As he strapped on his armor in one last public battle, during the Russo–Japanese War, the revolution of 1905 and its aftermath, he called for a social contract based on moderation and love of others, to be peopled by those unspoiled Russian peasants and young people whom he had conjured into existence.

All the while he was spinning his theories, however, Tolstoy did not lose touch with the wellspring of his genius in his own soul, and he continued to produce great works of art from this source. It is significant that the happiest, most lyrical moments in his later diaries are almost always solitary encounters with nature. In human interactions his passions are often on display, leaving him vulnerable to accusations of inconsistency or even hypocrisy that he is the first to level against himself. Tolstoy's contemporaries, like writers Anton Chekhov and Maxim Gorky, who witnessed his struggles to "Be Reasonable," regarded him with awe as a Titan among men. We do not share the privilege of knowing him personally, and even scaling the mountain of evidence left by Tolstoy himself and by memoirists does not give us a view of the giant himself, alive and whole. My own opinion is that Tolstoy did not intend to make sense in his old age, and therefore cannot be reconstituted according to rules of psychology or reason. In keeping with his later beliefs, he presented both himself and his fictional characters as trying to be good and rationally consistent, and rarely, if ever, succeeding at it. In this sense, in his own mind he became more like his contemporary and rival Feodor Dostoevsky, whom he once described (in a letter to Strakhov) as "all struggle." The older Tolstoy stressed that great writers are not better than other people – they do not sit on Olympus, as he put it in *So What Then Must We Do?* – on the contrary, great in vice as well as virtue, they convey their moral lessons through their struggles, as portrayed for us in their works.

NOTES

1 He said this to G. A. Rusanov in 1883. See N. N. Gusev, *Letopis' zhizni i tvorchestva L'va Nikolaevicha Tolstogo, 1828–1890* (Moscow: Gosudarstvennoe izdatel'stvo khudozhestvennoi literatury, 1958), p. 561.

2 *Ibid.*, p. 61.

3 Gusev, *Letopis' zhizni i tvorchestva L'va Nikolaevicha Tolstogo, 1891–1910* (Moscow: Gotlitizdat, 1960), p. 358.

4 *Lev Tolstoi, semidesiatye gody* (Leningrad: Sovetskii pisatel', 1960), p. 32.

5 *The Life of Tolstoy* (Oxford: Oxford University Press, 1987), vol. I, p. 59.

6 *Ibid.*, vol. I, p. 60.

7 See *The Young Tolstoy*, trans. and ed. Gary Kern (Ann Arbor, MI: Ardis, 1972).

8 Compare the 1847 philosophical fragment in which he states that the goal of philosophy is to make human beings free (*PSS* 1: 229) with another untitled fragment, probably written in 1851, in which he states that people read fiction to become virtuous, and therefore happy (*PSS* 1: 246).

9 *Detstvo Otrochestvo Iunost'* (Moscow: Izdatel'stvo "Nauka," 1978), p. 474.

10 Robert Whittaker, "Tolstoy's American Disciple: Letters to Ernest Howard Crosby, 1894–1906," *Triquarterly* 98 (Winter 1996/1997), 212.

11 *Ibid.*, 221–22.

12 One can add others, from the sour grapes of old age, to the possibility, first suggested by William James in *Varieties of Religious Experience*, that Tolstoy suffered from a depressive mental illness that made him spiritually profound but sapped his love of life.

13 The changes actually took place more gradually, and can be seen infecting *Anna Karenina*. Only in 1880, however, did Tolstoy clearly articulate his differences

with his own earlier position, and therefore decisively distanced himself from it. An added complication later on was the fact that the "new" Tolstoy was not able to fully satisfy his own artistic impulses, and had to do this on the sly, hiding not only from others, but from himself. The creation of his greatest late work, *Hadji Murat*, thus became an illicit activity.

14 See his explanation to Aylmer Maude in 1901 about the difference in this respect between himself and John Ruskin (Gusev, *Letopis'* [1960], p. 385).

15 The metaphor, discredited, recurs in the mouth of Slavophil intellectual Koznyshev in *Anna Karenina*.

I

THE THREE NOVELS

I

GARY SAUL MORSON

War and Peace

It may seem strange to say so, but only now are readers beginning to appreciate just how great a book *War and Peace* really is. Not that it took long for this work to achieve its reputation as the greatest novel ever written, but that reputation was based largely on just one of its sources of appeal, its incomparable realism. Tolstoy was able to describe to perfection the smallest details and the largest overall feeling of any sphere of life, from the confines of the nursery to the vastness of the battlefield and from the seriousness of a council of war to the unrestrained joy of a wolf hunt or a dance. And how, readers enthused, he could understand the tiniest movements of the conscious mind or the finest nuances of the soul!

And of the body, too, for no one, it was noticed, had ever quite so well described the ways in which the mind affects the body or the body the mind. Time and again Tolstoy's characters take an action not because they have decided to but because, by habit or happenstance, their bodies have "for some reason" assumed a posture that suggests it, as if the body has a mind of its own, as it does. Or a smile may appear on a character's face, "as if forgotten there," not because the character is thinking of anything happy, but because of an earlier thought he no longer remembers or a pleasant sound the character is not aware of hearing. No contingency of flesh or spirit in their ceaseless interaction escaped Tolstoy. This is realism as no one else has ever practiced it. But at the beginning of the twenty-first century, realism is no longer the supreme virtue it once was; and yet Tolstoy's reputation has, if anything, grown in recent years. Something else has been discovered in Tolstoy's masterpiece.

The philosophy of the book at first proved much less appealing than its meticulous descriptions. Those interminable inserted essays about "the historians" and "cause and effect" were felt to be naïve, boring, an embarrassment: oh, why can't those Russian geniuses be content to rank as superlative artists?[1] Why must they aspire as well to be – speak the word with heavy irony – teachers? Flaubert complained to Turgenev about the essays:

"He repeats himself! He philosophizes," as if no worse complaint against taste – and what else is there? – could be made.[2] The influential Jamesian critic Percy Lubbock complained that "he whose power of making a story *tell itself* is unsurpassed, is capable of thrusting into his book interminable chapters of comment and explanation in the manner of a controversial pamphlet."[3] It is a mark of Tolstoy's incomparable genius, Lubbock mused, that in spite of this and other major flaws, *War and Peace* is still the greatest novel ever written.

Now, a general rule for all literary critics and theorists ought to be: if your theory tells you a work must fail but it nevertheless triumphantly succeeds, then re-examine your theories.

Tolstoy the artist rises above Tolstoy the thinker: that was the consensus until recently. All that has changed, however. The views that seemed so perverse in challenging what everyone knew to be true now seem prescient, anticipating not so much where we are as where we are apparently going. That incomparable artistry, which seemed so separate from the philosophy and so much the product of raw inexplicable talent now seems to be significantly informed by those very ideas. Tolstoy's supreme realism reflected his more abstract meditations on the world, the mind, and human action. In applying these ideas to the form of the novel, to its plot and psychology, Tolstoy produced an incomparably greater verisimilitude than those with more sensible beliefs: and surely, that is some kind of proof that the ideas cannot be easily dismissed.

Pierre Bezukhov – Peter Earless – cannot hear the particular, indistinct signals of daily life by which more prudent folk govern their lives, because he is always attending to some distant call, some indistinct voice from Heaven that will answer not just this or that but all questions of importance. When Pierre hears that divine voice, or human speech that claims to speak its words, he leaps to believe, and, until disillusionment again ensues, knows how he must govern his life and how everyone else must govern theirs. So he reacts to Bazdeev, to Freemasonry, and to the Decembrist reformers, and, we surmise, would respond in the same way to any charlatan or true believer who might speak with the tones of pure conviction. When he gazes into the face of Bazdeev – a generous man of faith who, for all his absurdities, is no charlatan – Pierre is immediately convinced of everything the Mason has said or might say. The aspiring disciple assents in advance to doctrines he can barely grasp, "as children are convinced by the tone of sincerity and authority in the vibrant voice . . . at any rate, he longed with all his soul to believe, and did believe, and he experienced a joyous feeling of solace, regeneration, and return to life."[4]

"Return to life": Pierre has just emerged from a spiritual coma, which is his other defining state of soul. Until he finds the Truth, or after he has discovered that his most recent Truth is a sham, Pierre exists in a state of extreme melancholia where nothing, not even the smallest thing, is worth doing. At such moments, he tells Prince Andrei, he cannot even wash, which provokes Andrei, himself no stranger to such moods but an aristocrat to the depths of his soul, to remark tautologically: "Not wash? But that's unclean" (467; *PSS* 10: 113). No hygienic routine or aristocratic finickiness distracts Pierre from the ultimate, unanswerable questions.

> No matter what he turned his thoughts to, he always came back to these same questions, which he could neither solve nor cease asking himself. It was as if in his head the main screw that held his life together was stripped. The screw would neither go in nor come out, but went on turning in the same groove without catching, yet it was impossible to stop turning it.
>
> (424; *PSS* 10: 64–65)

If absolute certainty marks Pierre's moments of spiritual elation, total relativism serves as the philosophical expression of his despair. The innkeeper cheats me because officers thrash him; but officers thrash him because others mistreat them; and so on. No one chooses, everyone reacts, and the chain of causes is interminable. No one is responsible, there is no right or wrong, it all depends on point of view, and why worry about such questions when we face death, which would make nonsense even of the right answer, if we could somehow find it.

> I shot Dolokhov because I considered myself injured. And Louis XVI was executed because they considered him a criminal, and a year later they killed those who had killed him – also for some reason. What is bad? What is good? What should one love and what hate? What does one live for, and what am I?
>
> (424; *PSS* 10: 65)

But, as Pierre also realizes, there is no answer to these questions "except the one, illogical reply that in no way answered them, which was: 'You will die ... and find out everything – or cease asking'" (*ibid.*).

Truth for Pierre cannot be tentative, local, or merely practical. It must be as universal as mathematical logic and as certain as Descartes and Leibniz claimed their systems were. The truth about the world must be timeless, not varying with age or culture; absolute, in principle explaining everything worth knowing; theoretical, not a mere series of generalizations from experience; and perfectly clear and convincing to all who see it. As William Blake once observed, truth can never be told so as to be understood and not believed. This is what Aristotle called *episteme*, theoretical knowledge, not *phronesis*, practical wisdom; but whereas Aristotle held that life requires both, Pierre follows – in fact, existentially enacts – the dominant philosophical tradition since Descartes and Leibniz, which respects only *episteme*. David Hume famously declared that however convincing absolute theoretical arguments may seem at his desk, he finds that when he leaves his study and mixes with people, he lives like everyone else. Pierre, unlike the philosophers themselves, lives the implications of philosophy since the seventeenth century. And a key purpose of *War and Peace* is to demonstrate what is wrong with philosophy so conceived and so to revivify and reinvigorate the tradition, from Aristotle to Montaigne, that found an important place for practical wisdom. Away with the ethereal purity of ideas; back to the rough ground!

Tolstoy never ceased to mock the pretensions of intellectuals that they were, or soon would be, in possession of a key to society and history. In all such claims, which he exposed as utterly groundless, he detected the operations of vanity and the desire for power; the hope that, if it were commonly accepted that theories explain the world, then theorists would be asked to govern it. From at least Lenin on, the twentieth century has been shaped by just this sort of claim, and if Tolstoy did not foresee just how destructive the putative scientists of society would be, he showed, more cogently than anyone, the fatal fallacies that doomed their self-flattering ideas. If we have philosophies of history that attribute historical change to ideas and intellectuals, but no philosophies that ascribe such a role to shoemakers, he writes in *War and Peace*, that is only because it is intellectuals rather than shoemakers who compose philosophies and write histories. We still live in an age of hubristic theory, and one reason for Tolstoy's relevance is our increasing suspicion that those who offer to explain and thereby change the world know little about it.

Tolstoy was fascinated with the spurious but enticing rhetoric behind claims to what we now call "social science." With merciless satire and a sharp logical knife, he dissected the errors of those who – from Hegel to Buckle, as he liked to say – look only for evidence supporting their ideas and not for counter-evidence that might refute them. Peasant women do the same, and, in *War and Peace*, *Anna Karenina*, and elsewhere, Tolstoy or his heroes show how, for all their erudition, footnotes, and jargon, the professors are no more logical than peasant women. Typically, what they present as evidence is only illustration, but a theory, especially a scientific theory, must be supported by looking for what might refute it. "'For example' is no proof," as the Yiddish proverb counsels.

Still worse, if counter-evidence does appear, theorists have ways to dismiss it. Take the Hegelians and all those who believe that history is governed by an iron law (apparently, there are no clay ones) of progress:

> We have noticed a law of progress in the dukedom of Hohenzollern-Sigmaringen, which has three thousand inhabitants. We are aware that China, which has two hundred millions of inhabitants...refutes our whole theory of [a law of] progress, and we do not doubt for a minute that progress is the general law of all mankind.

China, don't you see, is a "nonhistorical" country (*PSS* 8: 333). Oh, the wonder of a philosophical term! "Progress is the general law for mankind, they say, with the sole exception of Asia, Africa, America, Australia...To say that progress is the law of humanity is as unfounded as to say that all people are blond except those with black hair" (*PSS* 8: 332–33).

In such critiques, Tolstoy meant to criticize not just Hegelianism but also any theory that attributes a direction to history. Such theories disable real thought, for they encourage people to avoid assessing whether a position is true or good by substituting an assertion that it is somehow "of the future" or "progressive." "History is on our side," "this position is to be rejected because it is backward looking": such spurious arguments were common in Tolstoy's time and, as he anticipated, would cause serious damage. They persist, in part because it is "natural and agreeable" (as Tolstoy liked to say) to believe that later is wiser, because, after all, every time I speak, it is at the latest moment of history.

Skepticism directed at all historical laws or presumed patterns forms the argument of numerous essays in *War and Peace*. In the narrative sections, we are given General Pfühl and others who believe that they possess a social science, the "science of strategy." It is crucial to recognize that Tolstoy means such a claim to stand for all self-annunciated sciences of society and history – all that already existed and all others that might appear in the future. In reading of Pfühl, we may think of Freud as well as Marx, contemporary mathematicized economics and rational choice theory no less than utilitarianism. All social science is, and ever will be, pseudo-science.

> Pfühl had his science – the theory of oblique movements deduced by him from the history of Frederick the Great's wars...In 1806 Pfühl had been one of the men responsible for the plan of the campaign that ended in [the defeats of] Jena and Auerstadt, but in the outcome of that war he failed to see the slightest evidence of the fallibility of his theory. On the contrary, to his mind it was the departures from his theory that were the sole cause of the whole disaster...
>
> (771; *PSS* 11: 48)

If his plan leads to victory, that result confirms the theory, but so does failure, because the plan was not implemented in detail – and since no plan ever could be, all results are positive.[5] This reasoning is just what Andrei's friend, the diplomat Bilibin, mocks before Austerlitz when he says that, no matter how the battle goes, the glory of Russian arms is assured, for victory earns glory and defeat will be blamed on Russia's foreign generals. The celebratory dinners after Russia's catastrophic loss prove him right.

Believing that there is either system or nothing, Pierre is a direct literary descendant of a familiar figure in satire, the mad proponent of an absolute theory, who, like Voltaire's Pangloss, Samuel Johnson's mad astronomer, or Sterne's Walter Shandy, "was systematical, and, like all systematick reasoners, ... would move both heaven and earth, and twist and torture every thing in nature to support his hypothesis."[6] Dostoevsky's underground man characterizes the Russian version of such theories as "mere logical exercises ... But man is so fond of systems and abstract deductions that he is ready to distort the truth intentionally, he is ready to deny what he can see and hear just to justify his logic."[7] Like Tolstoy, the underground man has in mind comprehensive philosophies of history and putative sciences of society.

Think of Hegel and Marx, of liberal progressivism and pseudo-Darwinian optimism, or of any other claim to possess the key to history when Pierre discovers, by a logic as mad as it is irrefutable, that Napoleon is destined to be killed by an assassin and that history's bloody instrument is Pierre himself. Pierre is impressed with a numerological interpretation of some verses in the Apocalypse, a system that assigns to French (why French?) letters numerical value, as in the Hebrew. When the words "*L'empereur Napoléon*" is arithmeticized in this way, "it appears that the sum ... equals 666 (including a five for the letter *e* dropped by elision from the le ...), and therefore Napoleon is the beast prophesied in the Apocalypse" (801; *PSS* 11: 78). This is a "therefore" that echoes through all systems at all times, supreme arbitrariness presented as perfect syllogism. One may ask whether that elided *e* would have been counted if the sum were 666 without it. By the same method it is determined that Napoleon will be killed in his forty-second year, 1812.

Like any good adept, Pierre extends the theory to make further discoveries. What will destroy Napoleon? He writes down numerous possibilities – *l'empereur Alexandre, la nation russe* – and adds them up with no success. At last it occurs to him to write "Comte Pierre Besouhoff," which also fails to total 666; but here there is room to "massage the data," as mathematical economists like to say. Transliteration from Cyrillic allows Pierre's surname to be spelled in many ways, and there are many adjectives and titles that might describe him. At last he writes "*Le russe Besouhof*," which adds up to 671. "This was only five too much, and corresponded to the *e*, the very letter elided from the article *le* before the word *empereur*. By dropping the *e*, though ungrammatically, Pierre got the answer he sought. L'russe Besouhof came to exactly 666. The discovery excited Pierre" (802; *PSS* 11: 79).

By such a method, anything can be proven; and by similar methods, anything is. What is particularly brilliant here is the way in which Pierre takes an earlier fudge – counting or not counting the elided *e* – and by applying it again, raises it to the dignity enjoyed in our day by psychoanalytic loopholes. But an explanation does not cease to be *ad hoc* because it is applied more than once; for what makes it *ad hoc* is not its singularity but its use whenever convenient. Psychologically, however, the theorist feels that he has made a "discovery," which excites him. It is an elation familiar to all systematizers.

Let us suppose for a moment that Pierre's name had totalled 666 without such effort. Why does it not occur to him to ask how many other people out of Russia's millions have names with the same total? After all, pretty much all names must total somewhere in a range of a few hundred, and so any given number must have tens of thousands of names that fit it. Has history destined them all to kill Napoleon?

It would be possible to read *War and Peace* as a catalogue of fallacies to which all would-be social sciences are subject and to interpret the work's plot as the story of those who succumb to or overcome fallacies like the following:

(a) The fallacy of "retrospection" (854; *PSS* 11: 131), which consists in treating earlier events as if they already contained the later events. The problem here is that we can easily see the potential for what did happen, but miss the potentials for numerous other outcomes that might have happened but did not. If such bias does not cloud the analyst's judgment, let him use the method to predict events subsequent not only to the pregnant past events but also to the analyst's own time.

(b) Closely related, the "stencil fallacy," according to which, as in a stencil, we examine events to see only those facts which conform to the thesis one wishes to prove (1432; *PSS* 12: 317).

(c) The fallacy of "reciprocity," which consists in singling out one event that contributed to an outcome as if it were essentially different from other events that also contributed to it.

> A good chess player who has lost a game is genuinely convinced that his failure is due to a mistake on his part, and looks for that mistake in the opening, forgetting that at each stage of the game there were similar blunders...The mistake on which he concentrates his attention has been noticed simply because

his opponent took advantage of it. How much more complex is the game of war...where it is not a question of one will manipulating inanimate objects, but of everything issuing from countless collisions of diverse wills!

(854; *PSS* 12: 131–32)

(d) The "log-hauling" fallacy. If a group of men decide to haul a log and each pulls in a different direction, they will necessarily wind up going in a direction that one of them wished; but it would be a mistake to say that they followed a plan to go that way. For they might easily have wound up going in a different direction, and then it would be said, with equal confidence, that they were following another man's plan. One must not conclude from an action that anyone planned it, even if some predicted or advocated it (1434–35; *PSS* 12: 319).

(e) Related to "reciprocity" is the fallacy of the decisive moment, which underlies almost all heavily plotted narratives. In history, there is very rarely such a moment. Kutuzov asks himself: At what point did it become necessary to abandon Moscow? Although later historians were to cite several crucial moments and decisive choices, Kutuzov knows that there was no such moment and that no particular decision was crucial. Historical and social events typically result from a mass of contingent factors, not from the sort of pregnant instant envisaged by strategists or game theorists in which a commander chooses one course of action rather than another:

A commander-in-chief is always in the midst of a series of shifting events, and consequently can never at any moment be in a position to consider the total import of the event that is occurring. Imperceptibly, moment by moment, the event is taking shape, and at every moment of this progressive, uninterrupted shaping of events, the commander-in-chief is in the centre of a most complex play of intrigues, worries, contingencies, authorities, projects, counsels, threats, deceptions, and is continually obliged to reply to a countless number of conflicting questions addressed to him.   (990; *PSS* 11: 271)

Sitting alone with Hélène, Pierre asks when it was decided that he would marry her, but there never was any such moment; rather, the outcome was shaped imperceptibly, moment by moment. And although most of us have more will power than Pierre to direct our daily lives, much of what makes us who we are could easily have been otherwise. Our situation typically results from a series of contingencies and particular decisions taken without any "total import" in mind. "Decisive moments" belong to romance, not usually to life. When had it been established that Moscow would be abandoned? "At Drissa, and at Smolensk,...and every day and hour and minute of the retreat from Borodino to Fili" (990–91; *PSS* 11: 272).

(f) The fallacy of the privileged observer. That observer is always our-selves – or people like us living in the present. Tolstoy would have appreci-ated the answer Mao is said to have made when asked to assess the French Revolution: "it's too soon to tell." Historians and other intellectuals typically judge past events as if we at last see their import; as if our standards of judg-ment are superior to all earlier ones; and as if our views will not somehow appear as odd or repulsive to later generations as those of earlier ones appear to us. And so we have the dreary spectacle, perhaps even more familiar in our time than in Tolstoy's, of professors, speaking with all the confidence and condescension that only the approbation of one's colleagues can bestow, who pass judgment on Shakespeare and Milton, Lincoln and Churchill – or, in the period described in *War and Peace*, on Kutuzov and Tsar Alexander: "All the famous people of that period, from Alexander and Napoleon to Madame de Staël, Schelling, Fichte, Chateaubriand and the rest, pass before their stern tribunal and are acquitted or condemned according to whether they promoted *progress* or *reaction*" (1351–52; *PSS* 12: 235). But why should we assume the professors have the right standards; and why should we be-lieve the historians of today rather than those of yesterday or tomorrow? Does our vanity have nothing to do with our assumption that the present moment is the superior vantage point? All such historical judgments mean is that Alexander and the others "did not have the same conception of the welfare of humanity fifty years ago as a present-day professor who from his youth has been occupied by learning, that is, with reading books, listening to lectures, and taking notes" (1352–53; *PSS* 12: 236–37).

Every one of these fallacies is committed not only by historians but also by the book's characters. When we laugh at Pierre and the generals, do we ask ourselves if we routinely commit the same errors? We are all Pfühlish enough. *War and Peace* satirizes intellectual pretensions and the pretensions of intellectuals. More than any other country, Russia has been the breeding ground of an intelligentsia – a word we get from Russian – addicted to theories of society; and Tolstoy, who despised the intelligentsia, directed his book against them and their cast of mind, wherever and whenever it might occur. Like Dostoevsky's *The Possessed* and numerous works of Chekhov, *War and Peace* belongs to the great Russian tradition of anti-ideological literature.

So concerned is Prince Andrei to live a life that is truly meaningful, and so much does he resemble Tolstoy in his capacity for icy satire and withering dismissal, that he repeatedly constructs ideals in opposition to those of the trivial people around him only to learn that those ideals, too, are trivial and false. Like his father examining Prince Ippolit, Prince Andrei always seems to be coldly observing and then saying, "you may go" (278; *PSS* 9: 275). With utter integrity, he subjects his fondest beliefs to the same merciless scrutiny.

Pride itself ensures that vanity never misleads Andrei to spare exploded beliefs rather than admit he has been wrong, because his is a species of pride above personal vanity. Reputation, admiration, and power come so easily to him that he despises them. Even if for himself alone, he desires only what comes easily to no one: wisdom.

Like the historians and the generals, Andrei at first thinks that the meaningful is the great. He admires Napoleon for having risen above low birth by sheer talent and willpower to become Emperor, and Prince Andrei dreams of leaving the petty society his wife loves to become like his hero, indeed, the conqueror of his hero. He seems a "generic refugee" from epic placed in a novelistic world, where all epic heroism is an illusion. What is truly heroic about Andrei is his utter integrity.[8]

Andrei courageously but mistakenly attributes meaning to the great events and the distant goal, whereas in *War and Peace* meaning lies in the prosaic. Thus we have the remarkable scene when Andrei, setting out to join the army in 1805, bids farewell to his sister Princess Marya. She puts a silver cross around her atheist brother's neck and he is wise enough, though smiling at her faith, to be touched by her love. He leans over and kisses her, tenderly if condescendingly, on the forehead. "Her eyes lit up with an extraordinary glow of sensibility and kindness, but he was looking not at his sister, but over her head toward the darkness of the open door" (145; *PSS* 9: 132). He looks over her head, and so misses her radiant expression; he literally overlooks the meaningful that is daily before his eyes if he only knew to attend to it.[9] Instead, he peers into the darkness of the open door, where what is vague, opaque, and unknown appear meaningful only because it is far away; and so this apparently simple physical action of the eyes catches his central error. God is here and now or He is nowhere and never.

Andrei also believes in military strategy and is at first always sketching plans for battles. Experience gradually teaches him what the two wise generals, Bagration and Kutuzov, already know: that all such thinking is nonsense. Like life, whether social or individual, battles cannot be planned, because sheer contingency predominates. Events that no one could have foreseen constantly affect everything that happens. Historians who describe battles as the implementation of rival strategies commit the various fallacies Tolstoy identifies.

When he at last encounters Pierre the night before the battle of Borodino, Andrei voices his radical skepticism of all strategy, and, implicitly, of the whole theoretical approach to life and society, as if such conclusions were a long settled matter. In part, Andrei's caustic appraisal of the generals derives from his personal disappointments, but whereas other authors might use our awareness of this psychological source to cast irony on Andrei's ideas, Tolstoy does not. Perhaps Andrei's tone could be more charitable, but he is right nonetheless.

> You talk about our position: the left flank weak, the right flank extended...
> That's all nonsense, doesn't mean a thing. But what are we facing tomorrow?
> A hundred million diverse chances, which will be decided on the instant by
> whether we run or they run, whether this man or that man is killed.
>
> (930; *PSS* 11: 208)

Life offers two kinds of situations that call for different kinds of decision-making. In a few rare cases, we face a situation of relative certainty, in which the parameters are known and the choices circumscribed; then advance planning pays off. But battles, and most of life, present situations of radical uncertainty, where the concatenating effects of multiple contingencies are incalculable. No one can anticipate the consequences of consequences of contingencies.

What is more, events are decided "on the instant"; sheer *presentness* counts. Those who see each moment as the mere derivative of earlier ones deny the significance of the present; but Tolstoy insisted that each moment contains possibilities and potentials that, even in principle, could not have been anticipated. Time is no mere unfolding. This observation, no less than an insistence on genuine contingency, separates Tolstoy and his hero not only from any particular theory, but from theory and social science *per se*. The world cannot be known in advance or from above: you have to *be there now*.

Andrei at last dismisses Pierre by saying that "before a battle one needs to get a good night's sleep" (933; *PSS* 11: 212), a lesson he has learned from Kutuzov. Seven years earlier, at the council of war before Austerlitz, when all the generals were disputing strategic plans, the commander in chief dozed, not to show contempt but because he really wanted to sleep. Just when the young Prince Andrei was about to present his plan, Kutuzov woke and called a halt to the pointless proceedings: "before a battle, there is nothing more important...than a good night's sleep" (323; *PSS* 9: 322–23). To the extent that attentiveness to the present moment matters, a good night's sleep is much more important than all the advance planning in the world.

The people who really shape battles, then, are not the generals but the line officers who are present (in both senses) and can seize unforeseen opportunities as they arise. That, indeed, is why Prince Andrei has forfeited forever his standing in court circles by choosing to serve not with the emperor but with the men, as the book's most effective soldier, Nikolai Rostov, always does. In one scene, Rostov, guided not by theory but by his experience as a soldier and a hunter, perceives that the moment offers an unanticipated opportunity. "He felt instinctively that if his hussars were to charge the French now, the latter would not be able to withstand them, but that it would have to be done at once, instantly, or it would be too late" (786; *PSS* 11: 63). No advance plan could have predicted such a moment; only unformalizable experience allows Rostov to perceive it; and attentiveness to the present allows him to take advantage of it. In a world of radical uncertainty, this is what effective action looks like.

If by the hero of a novel we mean the character who best embodies its values and lessons, then Rostov, not Andrei or Pierre, is the hero of *War and Peace*; and it testifies to Tolstoy's genius that he can make such a thoroughly ordinary, indeed mediocre, character both heroic and supremely interesting.

By the same token, the book's heroine is Princess Marya, who more than anyone can perceive the value, in fact the sanctity, of each ordinary moment. The marriage of Marya and Nikolai, more than Pierre's and Natasha's, defines the book's central point and establishes its happy ending.

If truth could be known with mathematical certainty, and if people armed with this truth could possess the power to remake the world according to it, then utopia could be achieved: this has been the guiding faith of so many thinkers, from Condorcet and the utilitarians to Lenin and Le Corbusier. Utopianism goes hand in hand with the dream of a social science. Pierre professes utopian beliefs from the book's outset, and once he accepts Freemasonry imagines he possesses the key to all social mysteries. It is in this spirit that he gives his speech to the assembled Freemasons and, when he witnesses their reaction, falls into one of his fits of despair. Interestingly enough, what depresses Pierre is the many brothers who agree with him.

> At this meeting Pierre for the first time was struck by the endless variety of men's minds, which prevents a truth from ever appearing the same to any two persons. Even those members who seemed to be on his side understood him in their own way, with stipulations and modifications he could not agree to, since what he chiefly desired was to convey his thought to others exactly as he himself understood it. (528; *PSS* 10: 175)

What sort of social mathematics, what sort of "moral Newtonianism," is possible if, unlike mathematical and astronomical propositions, social truths can never be apprehended in the same way by any two persons?[10] Agreement, as Mikhail Bakhtin liked to say, is itself a dialogic relation, since each person voices the truth from his or her own perspective and inflects it with all the unrepeatable tonalities of his or her own experience. Contingency appears essential not only to the world but even to our apprehension of it and to our most careful descriptions of it. There can be no agreed-upon certainty as, indeed, the history of religious creeds amply suggests.

By the end of the book, however, Pierre has arrived at a different, and anti-utopian, perception of the world, closely resembling the author's. Now the endless variety of men's minds provokes in him a gentle smile at the wealth of human diversity and the marvelous complexity of the world, which is all the richer for being irreducible to any system. In the book's central passage, he voices, in his own peculiar tonalities and metaphors, his version of the book's most important idea:

> ...in his captivity he had learned, not by words or reasoning, but by direct feeling, what his nurse had told him long ago: that God is here and every-where...He felt like a man who, after straining his eyes to peer into the remote distance, finds what he was seeking at his very feet. All his life he had been looking over the heads of those around him, while he had only to look before him without straining his eyes.
>
> In the past he had been unable to see the great, the unfathomable, the infinite in anything...In everything near and comprehensible he had seen only what was limited, petty, commonplace, and meaningless. He had equipped himself with a mental telescope and gazed into the distance where the petty and the commonplace that were hidden in the mists of distance had seemed to him great and infinite only because they were not clearly visible...
>
> Now, however, he had learned to see the great, the eternal, the infinite in everything, and therefore, in order to look at it, to enjoy his contemplation of it, he naturally discarded the telescope through which he had been gazing over the heads of men, and joyfully surveyed the ever-changing, eternally great, unfathomable and infinite life around him. (1320; *PSS* 12: 205–6)

The truths we seek are hidden in plain view.

To many literary critics, *War and Peace* has seemed an enigma. With its endless plot lines that go nowhere, its innumerable characters who appear only to disappear, its endless mass of disconnected and contingent events, the book seems a fabric of lost threads, a work without structure and backbone, that, by all critical rules and standards, ought to be a failure. And yet it is plainly the greatest novel ever written. How is this possible?

In an essay he wrote about the book, and in several draft prefaces, Tolstoy explains that he has deliberately avoided structure and closure, because those usual literary devices violate presentness. Where there is structure, there is no contingency, and each present moment is already weighted by the advance plan into which it must fit. But life is not like that; it is rife with contingency and loose ends are never all resolved. An author who truly aspires to realism must find an alternative to structure. Therefore, Tolstoy concludes, he is intentionally writing this book with no idea where it is going. In each separately published section he will make the most of the potentialities of each moment without worrying what future sections, should he write them at all, may contain. "I strove only so that each part of the work would have an independent interest," Tolstoy maintained. And then this draft preface contains the following remarkable words: "which would consist not in the development of events but in development [itself]" (*PSS* 13: 55). *Development itself*: contingent events, unburdened by a predetermined futurity or overall structure. The shape of *War and Peace* derives precisely from its central ideas about time. Might not its unsurpassed realism be taken as demonstration that those ideas really do describe life as we experience it?

Let us summarize.

(a) The world contains genuine contingency. Whereas other thinkers imagine that behind all the apparent mess of existence, there must be a few simple laws, the opposite is true of social life. Behind the mess is more mess, behind an incalculably large number of contingencies are incalculably more, in an ever increasing progression. If there are laws of history, they are at least as numerous as the events they would describe, and so the quest for such laws, even if they exist, is a chimera.

(b) In history and in individual lives, the most important events are not the grand but the ordinary ones in all their immediacy and multiplicity. God is here and everywhere, and what we seek is already before our eyes.

(c) Presentness matters. No mere automatic or predictable result from what came before, each present moment manifests the capacity for genuine surprise; and the "surprisingness" of the world is ineradicable. We need to attend to the inexhaustible opportunities of each moment.

(d) Taken together, these ideas suggest that, despite three centuries of modern theoretical aspiration, what we require is not just theoretical but also practical knowledge. We need wisdom, which is never formalizable. Theorists in power are either ineffective, like Pfühl, or (as we have seen in the past century), disastrous, like Lenin or Pol Pot. A putative social science or all-encompassing philosophy cannot save society but it can destroy it. If, in a Tolstoyan spirit, we reflect on the disasters of theorists in power, we may perhaps recognize that it is time to give a larger role to the prosaic, the contingent, and the timely in our thoughts.

NOTES

1 For a detailed account of the reception of *War and Peace*, see chapters 2 and 3 of Morson, *Hidden in Plain View: Narrative and Creative Potentials in "War and Peace"* (Stanford, CA: Stanford University Press, 1987).

2 Cited in a letter of Turgenev to Tolstoy, 12/24 January 1880, as cited in Morson, *Hidden in Plain View*, p. 41.

3 Percy Lubbock, *The Craft of Fiction* (New York: Viking, 1957; first published 1921), p. 35.

4 Leo Tolstoy, *War and Peace*, trans. Ann Dunnigan (New York: Signet, 1968), p. 429. Further references to the novel, occasionally modified for accuracy, are to this translation, followed by references to the Russian Jubilee edition (identified as *PSS*).

5 If the patient recovers, the therapy worked, but if he doesn't, he was not cooperating with the therapist, as the therapist, of course, anticipated. Such reasoning, in which everything can only confirm the hypothesis, is, as many have noted, the true mark of a pseudo-science.

6 Laurence Sterne, *The Life and Opinions of Tristram Shandy, Gentleman*, ed. James Aiken Work (New York: Odyssey Press, 1940), p. 53.

7 Fyodor Dostoevsky, *Notes from Underground* and "The Grand Inquisitor," the Garnett translation revised by Ralph E. Matlaw (New York: Dutton, 1960), p. 21.

8 On "generic refugees," see Gary Saul Morson, "Genre and Hero/Fathers and Sons: Intergeneric Dialogues, Generic Refugees, and the Hidden Prosaic" in Edward J. Brown, Lazar Fleishman, Gregory Freidin, and Richard Schupbach (eds.), *Literature, Culture, and Society in the Modern Age, Stanford Slavic Studies* 4, no.1 (Stanford, CA: Stanford University Press, 1991), 336–81.

9 Such "condescension" and "overlooking" (each perfectly realistic physical actions but also spiritual symbols) exemplifies what Richard F. Gustafson calls "emblematic realism" in *Leo Tolstoy, Resident and Stranger: A Study in Fiction and Theology* (Princeton: Princeton University Press, 1986).

10 The term "moral Newtonianism," which describes the aspiration to construct a social science as certain as Newton's astronomy, belongs to Elie Halévy, *The Growth of Philosophic Radicalism*, trans. Mary Morris (Boston: Beacon, 1955).

2

BARBARA LÖNNQVIST

Anna Karenina

In her diary entry for March 3, 1877, when the novel *Anna Karenina* was almost finished, Tolstoy's wife Sofya recorded her husband's words: "In order for a work to be good, one must love its main basic idea, as in *Anna Karenina* I love the idea of family [*mysl' semeinuiu*]."[1] How does this idea agree with what is generally thought to be the main theme of the novel – passionate love that transgresses all boundaries? Does Tolstoy not love Anna, this beautiful woman, so charmingly depicted when we (and Vronsky) first meet her?

> Her shining gray eyes, that looked dark from under the thick lashes, rested with friendly attention on his face, as though she were recognizing him... In that brief look Vronsky had time to notice the suppressed eagerness which played over her face, and flitted between the brilliant eyes and the faint smile that curved her red lips. It was as though her nature were brimming over with something that against her will showed itself now in the flash of her eyes, and now in her smile. (I, 18; 73; *PSS* 18: 66)[2]

Yes, the author loves her – *at this moment* when he looks at her through the eyes of Vronsky who is just about to fall in love with her. Here as in other instances Tolstoy glides into his characters, luring the reader there, too, takes his characters' point of view, but at the same time keeps his own. The character's integrity and independence and the author's view of the person are welded together so that no seams are noticeable. Speaking with A. Obolenskii in 1876, Tolstoy confesses: "I have noticed that any story makes an impression only when one cannot make out with whom the author sympathises."[3]

In a subtle, almost subtextual way, "the family idea" is introduced into the novel right in the first paragraph. Like a tolling bell the word *dom* (house, home, family) runs through the text giving a sensuous feeling of what is at stake.

> Everything was in confusion in the Oblonsky house [*dom*]. The wife had discovered that the husband was carrying on an intrigue with a French girl, who

had been a governess in their family [*dom*], and she had announced to her husband that she could not go on living in the same house [*dom*] with him. This position of affairs had now lasted three days, and not only the husband and wife themselves, but all the members of their family and the household [*dom*], were painfully conscious of it. Every person in the house [*dom*] felt that there was no sense in their living together, and that stray people brought together by chance in any inn had more in common with one another than they, the members of the family and household [*dom*] of the Oblonskys. The wife did not leave her own room, the husband had not been at home [*dom*] for three days. The children ran wild all over the house [*dom*]; the English governess quarreled with the housekeeper, and wrote to a friend asking her to look out for a new situation for her; the man-cook had walked off the day before just at dinner-time; the kitchen-maid, and the coachman had given warning.

(I, 1; 3; *PSS* 18: 3)

Stiva Oblonsky's affair with the French governess, which he himself does not take seriously, has fractured his relation with his wife Dolly, from which follows confusion and a breaking of one household bond after the other. Oblonsky's thoughtless submission to a passing infatuation has had *unforeseeable* consequences.

The epigraph to the novel is "Vengeance is mine, I shall repay." When asked what it meant, Tolstoy replied cryptically: "I chose the epigraph simply in order to explain the idea that the bad things people do have as their consequence all the bitter things, which come not from people, but from God, and that is what Anna Karenina herself experienced."[4] He meant by this that it is not in the power of human beings to foresee all consequences of their actions and therefore imagined results of an action can never be a moral guideline. Inherent in every action is an ethical implication, and so just by acting we live out a moral.

As the author of *Anna Karenina*, Tolstoy acts in accord with this comment. He does not preach or spell out any message, but moral ideas are implied, hidden, in the action itself. When contemporaries were unsure of what the writer "meant," Tolstoy explained:

> In everything, in almost everything that I have written, I was guided by the need to bring together ideas linked among themselves...But every idea expressed by itself in words loses its meaning, becomes terribly debased when it is taken alone, out of the linkage in which it is found. This linkage is based not on an idea, I think, but on something else, and to express the essence of that linkage directly by words is impossible, but it is possible indirectly, with words describing images, actions, situations.

He exhorts critics to get into the labyrinth of linkages:

We need people who would show the senselessness of the search for separate thoughts in a work of art and who would constantly guide the reader in the endless labyrinth of linkages that makes up the stuff of art, and bring him to the laws that serve as the basis for those linkages.[5]

In the nineteenth century, literature fell under the strong spell of history, facts, and photography. Every "told" event had to be measured on the procrustean bed of "could this have been?" "Realism" forced writers to go underground with what had always been the essence of art, the creation of symbols. Surplus telling became the hallmark of realism. In an essay on "realism in literature," Lydia Ginzburg speaks about "inessential features" that create "the illusion of true life."[6] Though such features or details do not have any immediate impact on the plot, they have a symbolic relation to it, created by the context in which they appear. Through them we can make our way in Tolstoy's labyrinth and participate in the symbolization process.

On her journeys all through the novel Anna carries a small bag. From being just a travel accessory, the bag gradually grows into a symbol. It also appears in Anna's dream, which strengthens its symbolic connotations. It first shows up after the fatal ball where Anna and Vronsky have fallen in love. Anna has decided suddenly to leave Moscow. While she is packing her intimate things into a tiny bag (*meshochek*), Dolly comes into the room and a discussion starts. Dolly is grateful to Anna for having patched up her marriage. But Dolly's gratitude elicits protests from Anna, who on Dolly's insistence on her goodheartedness, bursts out: "Every heart has its own *skeletons*, as the English say" (I, 28; 116; *PSS* 18: 104). Straight after that Anna confesses to Dolly that she has spoilt the ball for Dolly's sister Kitty "against my own will." During this discussion, as Anna packs, she blushes several times, and when Dolly finally says that it would be better if nothing came of Vronsky's and Kitty's courtship "if he is capable of falling in love with you in one single day," Anna turns crimson with pleasure.

When the bag appears next time it is *red* – as if Anna had hidden her flush of pleasure as well as her blush of shame in it. Now on the train to Petersburg, she takes two objects, a paper-knife and an English novel, out of the bag. Through the "cutting" knife (*razreznoi nozhik*), Anna enters the novel and soon finds herself immersed in the fictitious world. She identifies with the heroine Lady Mary, and imperceptibly in her thoughts the hero of the novel becomes *he*, Count Vronsky:

The hero of the novel had already almost achieved his English happiness, a baronetcy and an estate, and Anna was feeling a desire to go with him to the estate, when she suddenly felt that *he* ought to be ashamed, and that she was ashamed of the same thing.   (I, 29; 119; *PSS* 18: 107)

Anna's novel will later come into life when she and Vronsky live in the "English" manner on Vronsky's estate.

But the red bag continues to follow Anna and appears in decisive moments. One such moment occurs when Anna has confessed her love affair with Vronsky to her husband. Karenin leaves for town and Anna is alone at their summer villa, trying to collect herself by packing things for her own return. While she is "standing at a table in her boudoir, packing her traveling bag [*dorozhnyi meshok*]," a courier brings her a letter from Karenin that shatters all her expectations of a "change": he informs her that "our life must go on as it has done in the past" (III, 16; 347; *PSS* 18: 309).

A deeper meaning is conferred upon the bag through its appearance in Anna's dream. The reader learns about the dream when Anna relates it to Vronsky at a moment when all three – Anna, Vronsky, and Karenin – are in "a position of misery." The Karenins, husband and wife, live in the same house as complete strangers to one another. Anna sees Vronsky away from home and Karenin knows this. "Anna, on whom the position depended . . . had not the least idea what would settle the position, but she firmly believed that something would very soon turn up now" (IV, 1; 418; *PSS* 18: 372).

Anna is waiting for a "solution" without, however, taking any steps toward it. Just like her brother Stiva Oblonsky, she is hoping that "things will shape themselves," *obrazuetsia*, in the Russian expression used by Stiva's valet Matvei to comfort his master.

In Anna's case the time is most propitious for expecting a solution – she is pregnant with Vronsky's child. Tolstoy times the appearance of the dream in the novel very well. The dreaming takes place "in mid winter." Vronsky has been occupied with a foreign prince who has come to Petersburg "to enjoy to the utmost all Russian forms of amusement." Vronsky's week with the prince has a carnival flavor, as does the depiction of the prince himself as "a big glossy green Dutch cucumber." Vronsky tires of the prince but recognizes that the real reason for his discomfort is the prince's likeness to himself: "And what he saw in this mirror did not gratify his self-esteem." Although the *mirror* here is metaphorical, its appearance in the context of "mid winter" and carnival hints at the Russian festival *sviatki* around New Year, a time of ritualistic foretelling. Returning home from carouses with the prince, Vronsky finds a note from Anna, but before going to the Karenins he falls asleep and has a dream, a foreboding of what Anna will tell him: "What was it? What? What was the dreadful thing I dreamed? Yes, yes; there was a peasant-beater, a little, dirty man with a disheveled beard stooping down doing something, and all of a sudden he began saying some strange words in French" (IV, 2; 421; *PSS* 18: 374–75). Vronsky dismisses the dream ("What nonsense!") and hurries to the Karenins. There he is again confronted with it, now in Anna's version. Before telling him the dream Anna has already interpreted it: "I know it; I know for certain. I shall die; and I'm very glad I shall die, and release myself and you."

> "I dreamed that I ran into my bedroom, that I had to get something there, to find out something; you know how it is in dreams," she said, her eyes wide with horror; "and in the bedroom, in the corner stood something... And that something turned round, and I saw it was a peasant with a disheveled beard, little and dreadful. I wanted to run away, but he bent down over a bag, and was fumbling there with his hands... and he kept talking quickly, quickly in French, you know, rolling his "r's": '*il faut le battre le fer, le broyer, le pétrir...*' And in my horror I tried to wake up, and I woke up... but woke up in the dream. And I began asking myself what it meant. And Korney said to me: 'In childbirth, in childbirth you'll die, in childbirth, ma'am...' And I woke up."
> (IV, 3; 427–28; *PSS* 18: 380–81)

Anna's dream mirrors Vronsky's, a reflection of their fatal bond. But the dreams differ in important details: Vronsky's is more like a *shadow* of Anna's. His peasant plays the role of "beater" (*obkladchik*), that is, someone who rouses the game at a hunt, but does not shoot it. Metaphorically speaking, Vronsky has acted in the same way with Anna, arousing her, but not being able to bring the hunt to an end, he has not made Anna his wife.

Anna's peasant is "fumbling in a bag" – a detail lacking in Vronsky's dream. Furthermore he appears in her bedroom, and she encounters him when she goes there "to get something, to find out something" – words (*vziat', uznat'*) that suggest Eve's taking and eating the apple of good and evil. Such details hint at Anna's "night life" and the bag is linked to her traveling bag. Anna wants to run away but the man's fumbling in the bag hinders her, as if it were part of herself. Strangely for a man so unkempt and wild, he also utters some words in French. Is he a medium speaking in tongues? The valet Kornei, a simple man of the people, gives an interpretation, still part of the dream: "you'll die in childbirth." Not only Kornei's words but the bedroom context suggest childbearing and a woman's womb. And immediately after having related her dream to Vronsky, Anna feels the outcome of their liaison in the first stirrings of the child in her womb.

But what is the peasant doing and what is he saying? His French is no glossolalia and it is only interpreted as such by the dreamers. The words have meaning: "one must beat the iron, grind it, knead it." The man seems to be occupied with some creative process of forging or baking (the verb *pétrir* being used primarily in expressions like *pétrir la pâte* – "to knead the dough"). He appears as a blacksmith, who by both working the iron and baking (bread) joins a male activity to a female one. Both are symbol-laden in Russian culture: the blacksmith (*kuznets*) forges destinies, and especially marriages, which is reflected in the songs young women sing when telling their fortune at New Year's Eve. "Kneading," on the other hand, is related to childbearing in folk belief, according to which the child is "baked" in the womb. In folklore the symbolic transformation of the bride into wife is also celebrated by baking ritual "marital bread." Just like "forging," "kneading" is deeply rooted in rituals and beliefs connected with marriage and childbearing, i.e., the formation of a family.

The peasant–blacksmith in the dream springs not only out of folklore. His presence and *raison d'être* are established throughout the novel in railway stations and always close to Anna. He makes a portentous appearance when Anna, on her way back to Petersburg after the ball, leaves the carriage for some air. As she steps down on the platform, "the driving snow and the wind rushed to meet her … as though lying in wait for her." On the platform she glimpses a "bent shadow of a man gliding by at her feet, and she heard sounds of hammer upon iron." In the next instant she sees a man in a military overcoat and recognizes Vronsky. When she wonders at finding him there, he says: "You know that I have to be where you are. I can't help it" (I, 30; 122; *PSS* 18: 109). This declaration of love is sealed by a clanging of metal: "At that moment the wind, as it were, surmounting all obstacles, sent the snow flying from the carriage roofs and clanked some sheet of iron it had torn off."

The love story begun on the railway – the Russian word is *zheleznaia doroga* (iron road) – is fatefully sealed by resounding metal. Resounding metal also greets Anna's sister-in-law Dolly when she arrives at Vronsky's estate. ("The metallic clank of the whetstone against a scythe, that came to them from the cart, ceased" [VI, 17; 713; *PSS* 19: 183].) Vronsky, Anna, and their guests appear to greet her from an inspection of a new reaping-machine. At the dinner table conversation focuses on the cutting ability of the reaper. It works like "a lot of small scissors," as Anna explains, and her guest Veslovsky adds "like small penknives." The mechanics of cutting are thus underscored and joined to the metal motif. Both participate in the symbolizing of life at Vronsky's estate where machinery is a prominent feature. The linen is washed with it, and the nursery is full of modern appliances. But Dolly feels that she lives in a house of people estranged from one another. She is most appalled when she sees how distant Anna is from her little daughter, Vronsky's child. And she is outright shocked when she learns that Anna, without Vronsky's knowledge, refuses to have more children and knows how to go about it. Anna is thus cutting the lineage of Vronsky.

> [Anna] "You forget my position. How can I desire children?... Think only, what are my children to be? Ill-fated children, who will have to bear a stranger's name. For the very fact of their birth they will be forced to be ashamed of their mother, their father, their birth."
> [Dolly] "But that's just why a divorce is necessary."
> But Anna did not hear her. She longed to give utterance to all the arguments with which she had so many times convinced herself.
> [Anna] "What is reason given me for [*Zachem zhe mne dan razum*], if I am not to use it to avoid bringing unhappy beings into the world!"
>
> (VI, 23; 747; *PSS* 19: 214–15)

Dolly senses Anna's increasing isolation and understands that under a thin surface of happiness lurks an abyss of desperation. Left totally to herself after Dolly's departure, Anna devotes herself more and more to her outward appearance. She starts reading on "every subject that was of interest to Vronsky," takes part in the building of the hospital, but, as Tolstoy says, "her chief thought was still of herself – how far she was dear to Vronsky, how far she could make up to him for all he had given up" (VI, 25; 752; *PSS* 19: 219–20). Vronsky appreciates her desire "not only to please, but to serve him...but at the same time he wearied of the loving snares in which she tried to hold him fast." Vronsky is most of all concerned about the unclear status of his daughter; legally she is not in "his line," but in Karenin's. This troubles him to the extent that he even decides to confess to Dolly: "Yes, yes...She is happy in the present. But I...I am afraid of what is before us...My daughter is by law not my daughter, but Karenin's. I cannot bear this falsity!" (VI, 21; 733–34; *PSS* 19: 202).

Anna lives increasingly in the present and, having started to take opium during the birth of her daughter, becomes increasingly dependent on drugs. To feel the worth of her existence she demands Vronsky's constant presence. For his part, Vronsky, suffering from the indefinite status of their relationship, cannot live in this "make-believe world." When Oblonsky's repeated efforts to talk Karenin into a divorce fail again, a quarrel flares up between Anna and Vronsky.

> [Anna] "I said yesterday that it is absolutely nothing to me when I get, or whether I never get, a divorce...I should have liked you to care as little about it as I do."
> [Vronsky] "I care about it because I like definiteness [*iasnost'*]."
> [Anna] "Definiteness is not in the form but the love...What do you want it for?"

[Vronsky] "Oh, you know what for! for your sake and your children's in the future."
[Anna] "There won't be children in the future."
[Vronsky] "That's a great pity."   (VII, 25; 870; *PSS* 19: 326–27)

In her loneliness Anna imagines Vronsky uttering cruel words to her, forcing her back to her husband, "and she could not forgive him for them, as though he had actually said them" (VII, 26; 874; *PSS* 19: 330). Confusing reality with her own fantasies, she wants to avenge herself for imagined offences by making Vronsky feel guilty.

The night after the quarrel Anna's nightmare recurs:

> A little old man with an unkempt beard was doing something bent down over some iron, muttering meaningless French words, and she, as she always did in this nightmare (it was what made the horror of it), felt that this peasant was taking no notice of her, but was doing his horrible iron thing – over her.
>   (VII, 26; 876; *PSS* 19: 332)

A new ingredient in the dream are the words "taking no notice of her [*ne obrashchaet na nee vnimaniia*]." These same words pass through Vronsky's mind during their last quarrel:

> "You ... you will be sorry for this," she said, and went out. Frightened by the desperate expression with which these words were uttered, he jumped up and would have run after her, but on second thought he sat down and scowled, clenching his teeth ... "I've tried everything," he thought; "the only thing left is not to pay attention [*ne obrashchat' vnimaniia*]."
>   (VII, 26; 877; *PSS* 19: 333)

The words are a defence mechanism for Vronsky. But they constitute the opposite of Vronsky's words to Anna on the train ride: "I am going in order to be where you are." And Vronsky will be punished for this moment of "clenching his teeth." A terrible toothache will never leave him after Anna's death.

When Anna sets out on her last journey – with a confused idea of going to find Vronsky to "tell him all" – she again packs her little traveling bag. Driving through Moscow, she looks out of the carriage window and in her rambling thoughts she projects onto passersby and the world outside her feelings of squalor and hatred.

> "They want that dirty ice-cream, that they do know for certain," she thought, looking at two boys stopping at an ice-cream seller ... "We all want what is sweet and tasty. If not sweetmeats, then dirty ice-cream. And Kitty's the same – if not Vronsky, then Levin. And she envies me, and hates me. And we all hate each other."   (VII, 29; 885; *PSS* 19: 340)

The repulsiveness of the world around her reaches its climax at the station. It encroaches upon Anna from all sides:

> ... some young men, ugly and impudent ... Piotr, too, with his dull, animal face ... some noisy men were quiet as she passed them ... and one whispered something about her to another – something vile, no doubt. She stepped up on the high step, and sat down in a carriage by herself on a dirty seat that had been white. Trembling on the spring seat, the bag fell over on its side [*Meshok, vzdrognuv na pruzhinakh, ulegsia*] ...   (VII, 31; 890; *PSS* 19: 345)

Tolstoy uses the verb *vzdrognut'* (to tremble, quiver) when the bag meets the stained seat, thus enhancing its living status. Anna sees a lady in a modish bustle but "mentally undresses her" and is appalled by her hideousness. She rushes to the opposite window, but at that moment "a misshapen-looking peasant covered with dirt, in a cap from which his tangled hair stuck out all around, passed by the window, stooping down to the carriage wheels" (VII, 31; 890–91; *PSS* 19: 345).

Anna recognizes the peasant from her dream and moves away to the opposite door "shaking with terror." There, met by a couple entering the car, she retreats to her corner. She listens to the couple's inane remarks with growing repulsion. But it is from the woman that Anna hears the words that all of a sudden articulate a way out for her. "'That's what reason is given man for, to escape from what worries him,' said the lady in French" (VII, 31; 892; *PSS* 19: 346). These words (*Na to dan cheloveku razum, chtoby izbavit'sia ...*) resonate with Anna, and, indeed, they echo her own words to Dolly about not bringing children into the world. Now Anna herself is like that "unhappy being" she imagined freeing by not giving birth to it. And she thinks: "why not put out the light when there is nothing more to look at, when it's sickening to look at it all?"

Anna is clearly not in full control of her mind. Her thoughts of "putting out the light" mix with impressions around her: "Why did the conductor run along the footboard, why are they shrieking, those young men in that train?"

When the train pulls into the station, Anna gets out and asks for a message from Vronsky, but is informed that a carriage is waiting for Princess Sorokina and her daughter (whom Anna imagines Vronsky is about to marry). Vronsky's coachman gives Anna a note in which he repeats that he will be home later. Perhaps because of the coincidence of Sorokina's name being mentioned just before Anna receives Vronsky's note, Anna, not knowing what she is doing, starts to walk along the platform ("My God! where am I to go?") farther and farther. At that moment a freight train is coming in and Anna, already at the edge of the platform, remembers the man crushed by the train on the day she met Vronsky.

"There," she said to herself, looking into the shadow of the carriage, at the sand and the coal-dust which covered the sleepers – "there, in the very middle, and I will punish him and escape from every one and from myself."

(VII, 31; 894; PSS 19: 348)

But Tolstoy gives Anna a second chance: "the red bag which she tried to drop out of her hand delayed her, and she was too late; she missed the moment." The red bag, having followed Anna on her journey of passion, has become a symbol of her earthly, bodily existence, and only when she has freed herself of it is she ready to go. Anna hesitates once more. She feels about to plunge into water and crosses herself, as Russian children used to do before bathing. Childhood memories rush over her. But the iron wheels mesmerize her and when the space between the wheels come opposite her, she falls on her hands and knees under the carriage. At the last moment she still does not know why and what she is doing ("Where am I? What am I doing? What for?") and she begs the Lord to forgive her.

At this moment of passing over into the unknown Tolstoy again reminds the reader of the dream: "A peasant muttering something was working at the iron." Anna's fate has been forged and "the book of her life" has come to an end.

While the love story of Anna and Vronsky unfolds in symbols of iron, machinery, and artificial creation, different imagery accompanies Levin's courtship of and marriage to Kitty.

When the novel starts Levin has just come to town to propose to Kitty, the youngest sister in the Shcherbatsky family. Count Vronsky, however, has been courting her during his stay in Moscow, and young Kitty, flattered by this, thinks she is in love with him.

We are told that Levin has always loved the Shcherbatsky house, their *dom* has become his home, too, since "it was in the Shcherbatsky's house that he saw for the first time that inner life of an old, noble, cultivated and honorable family of which he had been deprived by the death of his father and mother" (I, 6; 27; *PSS* 18: 24–25). He is in love with the household, the family, but especially with its "feminine half." He has pictured the three sisters "as it were, wrapped about with a mysterious poetical veil, and he not only perceived no defects whatever in them, but under the poetical veil that shrouded them he assumed the existence of the loftiest sentiments and every possible perfection" (I, 6; 27; *PSS* 18: 25).

He arrives in Moscow on skating day for young Kitty and rushes to the rink at the Zoological Gardens. There the image of an enwrapping veil appears again: "The old curly birches of the gardens, all their twigs laden with snow, looked as though freshly decked in sacred vestments" (I, 9; 35; *PSS* 18: 31). Tolstoy's imagery keeps alive Levin's "bridal dream," but it also connects the Shcherbatsky family to Levin's estate Pokrovskoe. The meaning of *pokrov* as "veil, shroud" is at the origin of the calendar feast "Protection of the Mother of God" after which Levin's estate is named.

At the Zoological Gardens, a real place in Moscow, another image that comes to symbolize the relationship of Levin and Kitty makes its appearance. When Levin meets Kitty on the skating rink, his joy bursts out in a phrase that puts Kitty on her guard: "And I have confidence in myself when you are leaning on me" (I, 9; 38; *PSS* 18: 34). She sends him off to greet her governess and the old Frenchwoman reminds Levin of his one-time comparison of the three Shcherbatsky sisters to the three bears in the fairy tale by saying of Kitty: "*Tiny bear* [spoken in English] has grown big now." This casual remark has far-reaching consequences for the inner continuity of the novel. At this moment, however, Levin does not remember his comparison. It has flown out of his head, just as Kitty slips out of his hands in the evening when, in response to his proposal, she says "that cannot be ... forgive me."

The bear image resurfaces though, and from the fairy tale world it moves to the starry sky. Levin has gone back to his country estate and knows nothing of what has become of Kitty. Oblonsky visits him to hunt. When evening falls they are still hunting snipe. Levin looks at the starry sky, in which his love story is inscribed.

> Over his head Levin made out [*lovil*] the stars of the Great Bear and lost [*terial*] them again. The snipe had ceased flying; but Levin resolved to stay a little longer, till Venus, which he saw below a branch of the birch, should be above it, and the stars of the Great Bear should be perfectly plain. Venus had risen above the branch, and the car of the Great Bear with its shaft was now all plainly visible against the dark blue sky, yet still he waited.
>
> (II, 15; 195; *PSS* 18: 173–74)

Tiny bear Kitty has grown into the Great Bear, momentarily lost by Levin. But the love star Venus still shines "bright and silvery" above it. And when the Great Bear is in sight, Levin bursts out: "Stiva! but how is it you don't tell me whether your sister-in-law's married yet, or when she's going to be?" (II, 15; 195; *PSS* 18: 174). Only then does Levin learn about Kitty's situation and hope returns to him. His joy is represented by Tolstoy in his luck at hunting: together with Oblonsky he shoots down a snipe: " 'I've got it, Stiva!' he shouted."

The description of the Great Bear makes way for the next appearance of Kitty in Levin's life. In the passage about the stars Tolstoy repeats the words "great bear" three times and the last time he adds "*the car* of the Great Bear *with its shaft*," (emphasis added) thus underlining the outer form of the constellation. The image of the carriage with its shaft will appear again when Levin is in great distress and does not know what to do about his life. He is on his way home from the hay stack where he has spent the night, after having mown all day long.

> But a third series of ideas turned upon the question how to effect this transition from the old life to the new. And there nothing took clear shape for him. "Take a wife? Work and have to work? Leave Pokrovskoe? Buy land? Become a member of a peasant community? Marry a peasant girl? How am I to set about it?" he asked himself and could not find an answer.
>
> (III, 12; 327–28; *PSS* 18: 291)

In this mood of indecision Levin looks up at the sky, where he sees a small cloud shaped like a mother-of-pearl shell. The cloud works as a renewed, though veiled reference to Venus – the love goddess's birthplace being a shell. And following this heavenly sign is its companion, the car of the Great Bear, although now in a very earthly form.

> Shrinking from the cold, Levin walked rapidly, looking at the ground. "What's that? Some one is coming," he thought, catching the tinkle of bells, and lifting his head. Forty paces from him a carriage with four horses harnessed abreast was driving toward him... The shaft-horses were tilted against the shafts by the ruts, but the dexterous driver sitting on the box held the shaft over the ruts, so that the wheels ran on the smooth part of the road.
>
> (III, 12; 328; *PSS* 18: 292)

Tolstoy's insistence on the shaft of the carriage (*dyshlo*) – the part of a harness that "joins" everything – connects this image to the symbolic Great Bear. And as the carriage is now a real one, so is the she-bear in it.

> At the window, evidently just awake, sat a young girl... She recognized him, and her face lighted up with wondering delight.
>
> He could not be mistaken. There were no other eyes like those in the world, There was only one creature in the world that could concentrate for him all the brightness and meaning of life. It was she. It was Kitty.
>
> (III, 12; 328–29; *PSS* 18: 292)

Levin realizes that his life is connected to Kitty: " 'No,' he said to himself. 'however good that life of simplicity and toil may be, I cannot go back to it. I love her.' "

The bear motif is revived again the very day when Levin, for the second time, proposes to Kitty. Levin has arrived in Moscow from a bear hunt in the Tver-region and is visited by Oblonsky in his hotel room: "'What! you killed it?' cried Stepan Arkadevich. 'Well done! A she-bear?'"(IV, 7; 443; *PSS* 18: 395).

At the Oblonsky dinner party, bear hunting comes up again in discussion among the guests. Karenin, whose marriage has just collapsed, comments: "'I imagine great strength is needed for hunting bears.'" To which Levin joyfully responds: "'Not at all. Quite the contrary; a child can kill a bear.'" Even Kitty is drawn into the discussion: "'You have killed a bear I am told! ... Are there bears on your place?' she added, turning the charming little head to him and smiling." Levin's triumph comes a moment later when he meets Kitty alone across the card table and they find out about their mutual feelings in a strange, telepathic letter game. The successful bear hunt appears to be a prelude, a symbolic playing out of what is then acted out at the card table: the she-bear is now Levin's.

Tolstoy's intricate use of the bear image in connection with Kitty and Levin finds support in Russian folk beliefs, where bears and bearskins are related to weddings. Newly-weds were often seated on a bearskin for fecundity, and seeing a bear in a dream foretells marriage. Symbolically Levin chooses his hunting mate Chirikov as best man at his wedding. But with marriage Levin's need to hunt bears has come to end. On the day of the wedding Levin meets with his bachelor friends who try to tempt him into hunting: "'And you may say good-bye to bear-hunting for the future – your wife won't allow it!' Levin smiled. The picture of his wife not letting him go was so pleasant that he was ready to renounce the delights of looking upon bears forever" (V, 2; 521; *PSS* 19: 10).

The bear imagery then disappears from the novel until the last chapter when it returns in an unexpected form. Levin and Kitty have made their life together at Pokrovskoe, not without difficulties and quarrels, but gradually growing to understand each other. Levin has taken up a new occupation, bee-keeping (*pchelinaia okhota*, literally "bee hunting"). The bees bring back the bear, since the word for bear in Russian is a "honey-eater," *medved'*. At every free moment Levin visits his bee hives, and he is especially happy when he can "take a swarm" and create a new "honey-house." The same image of getting a swarm into a hive is used by Tolstoy to express Levin's feeling when he understands the life wisdom given to him by a peasant:

> At the peasant's words that Fokanitch lived for his soul, in truth, in God's way, undefined but significant ideas seemed to burst out [...] they thronged whirling through his head, blinding him with their light. [...] The words uttered by the peasant had acted on his soul like an electric shock, suddenly transforming

and combining into a single whole the whole swarm of disjointed, impotent, separate thoughts that incessantly occupied his mind.

(VIII, 12; 924; PSS 19: 376)

This moment of epiphany precedes a much stronger one, when a thunderstorm breaks out and Levin's wife and child are saved from under a falling oak-tree.

> Levin . . . had just caught sight of something white behind the oak-tree, when there was a sudden flash, the whole earth seemed on fire, and the vault of heaven seemed crashing overhead . . .
> "My God! my God! not on them!" he said.
> And though he thought at once how senseless was his prayer that they should not have been killed by the oak which had fallen now, he repeated it, knowing that he could do nothing better than utter this senseless prayer.

(VIII, 17; 943; PSS 19: 393–94)

It turns out that his wife, little Mitia, and the nurse are not in their usual place, under the great oak. They have taken refuge under on old lime-tree (*lipa*): "Two figures in dark dresses (they had been light summer dresses when they started out) were standing bending over something." The scene with the two women bent over the child recalls the well-known religious motif of Anne and Mary with the Christ child, and it works as a revelation for Levin. But the lime-tree (feminine in Russian as opposed to the masculine oak, *dub*) appears not only as a protectress of the family, but also as the source of honey for Levin's bees: "the working bees flew in and out with spoils . . . always in the same direction into the wood to the flowering lime-trees and back to the hives" (VIII, 14; 934; *PSS* 19: 385).

In the evening Kitty asks her husband to the nursery to witness how little Mitia has started to recognize people:

> Kitty bent down to him, he gave her a beaming smile, propped his little hands on the sponge and chirruped, making such a queer little contented sound with his lips, that Kitty and the nurse were not alone in their admiration. Levin, too, was surprised and delighted. (VIII, 18; 946; *PSS* 19: 396)

Then, in front of his breast-feeding wife (an earthly version of an icon motif of the Eastern Christian Church, "The Milk-giving Mother of God") Levin confesses that "today, after that fright during the storm, I understand how I love him."

Then Levin goes out on the terrace and gazes up at the sky. He sees the familiar stars but also "the Milky Way with its branches." It is as if little Mitia, suckling his mother's breast, had found his place in Levin's heaven.

And this happens to the sound of a rhythmical dripping from the lime-trees in the garden, the lime-trees of honey, an old source of wisdom. And Levin realizes that life need not be spectacular to be worth living:

> I shall go on in the same way, losing my temper with Ivan the coachman, falling into angry discussions, expressing my opinion tactlessly; there will be still the same wall between the holy of the holies of my soul and other people, even my wife; I shall still go on scolding her for my own terror, and being remorseful for it; I shall still be as unable to understand with my reason why I pray, and I shall still go on praying; but my life now, my whole life apart from anything that can happen to me, every minute of it is no more meaningless, as it was before, but it has the positive meaning of goodness, which I have the power to put into it. (VIII, 19; 949–50; *PSS* 19: 399)

Levin's longing for a *home* brought him to the Shcherbatsky family, but his path was tortuous before he could create his own "honey-house." His journey is like a gradual "unveiling" of life, a life formed by tradition and the experience of those before him. His love for his wife and son is thus inscribed in patterns not invented by him and therefore of a proven quality.

Levin and Kitty's love story is contrasted with Anna and Vronsky's passion, which never finds a "room of its own." Acted out in railway stations, in furnished apartments, abroad, and in the fictitious family life on Vronsky's estate, the relation is doomed to eternal insecurity. A constant focus on the feelings of the moment and Anna's cutting off past and future proves too corrosive. The passion cannot endure and its transformation never comes about.

When Tolstoy reflected on what makes up a work of art he talked about an "endless labyrinth of linkages." The aesthetic function of the linking activity lies in the creation of an integrated whole. The dimensions of a novel like *Anna Karenina* make any exhaustive mapping of possible links impossible. The bears, bags, ironwork, and stars of this essay are examples of details that form into patterns of meaning within it. Reality itself is not given and fixed once and for all – the artist joins its elements and focuses on them according to his own seeing. The reader and critic of Tolstoy's novel can only humbly follow in his footsteps, attentively stop at certain signs, and interpret, bit by bit, the landscape constructed by the artist.

NOTES

1 S. A. Tolstaia, *Dnevniki v dvukh tomakh*, vol. I, 1862–1900 (Moscow: Khudozhestvennaia literatura, 1978), p. 502.
2 The novel is quoted in Constance Garnett's translation (with some minor changes) because of its closeness to Tolstoy's text. The following edition was used:

Anna Karenina: A Novel by Count Leo Tolstoy (London: The Modern Library, 1936). In the quotes the part (Roman) and the chapter (Arabic) are indicated first, followed by the page of the English edition, and finally the volume and page of the Russian Jubilee edition noted as *PSS*.

3 Quoted from B. Eikhenbaum, *Lev Tolstoi: Semidesiatye gody* (Leningrad: Khudozhestvennaia literatura, 1974), p. 158.

4 Tolstoy's words rendered by his son-in-law M. Sukhotin in May, 1907. Quoted from Eikhenbaum, *Lev Tolstoi*, p. 158.

5 Letter to N. Strakhov, April, 1876. *PSS* 62: 269.

6 Lydia Ginzburg, *Literatura v poiskakh real'nosti* (Leningrad: Sovetskii pisatel', 1987), p. 22.

3

HUGH McLEAN

Resurrection

In June 1887, while a guest at Tolstoy's estate, Iasnaia Poliana, the eminent jurist Anatolii Koni told Tolstoy a remarkable story from his own practice. In the early 1870s, while Koni was serving as prosecutor for the St. Petersburg district court, a well-dressed young man "with a pale, expressive face and restless, burning eyes" had come to his office. He asked Koni to overrule a prison official who had refused to transmit without first reading it a letter to a female prisoner named Rozalia Oni. Rozalia Oni was a prostitute of Finnish origin. Convicted of having robbed a client of 100 roubles, she had been sentenced to four months' confinement. Without revealing his motives, the young man said that he wanted to *marry* the woman.

The young man, Koni knew, belonged to a well-known family, was well educated, and held a responsible post in the civil service. Koni tried to dissuade him, saying that Rozalia could never be happy with him, but it was to no avail. Rozalia herself had eagerly agreed to the marriage. Koni refused to expedite the wedding, however, and the advent of Lent necessitated further postponement. During this waiting period Rozalia caught the typhus endemic in Russian prisons and died. As Koni sententiously put it, "The Lord drew a curtain over her life and stopped the beating of her poor heart."

Koni lost sight of the eccentric young man, but later a female warden passed on to him the whole story as told her by Rozalia. Rozalia's father had rented a farmhouse from the young man's aunt, a rich St. Petersburg lady. Dying of cancer, he begged his landlady to take his orphaned daughter under her protection. The lady graciously agreed and after the man's death took the girl into her household. When Rozalia was sixteen, the young man, on a visit to his aunt, had seduced her. Observing signs of pregnancy, the rich lady, scandalized, had driven her from the house. Abandoned by her lover, she turned the baby over to an orphanage and after that skidded down the moral and social ladder until she ended up in a low Haymarket brothel. Some years later, by sheer chance, the young man who had first seduced her served on the jury trying her for robbery. Realizing that he had been the cause of her downfall, he was consumed with remorse and felt morally obliged to offer her marriage in recompense.

Such was the "Koni story," under which title it figured for some years in Tolstoy's diaries and correspondence. In Tolstoy this tale touched a raw nerve: the sexual guilt and revulsion that had been tormenting him all his life, but were especially acute just at this time, the late 1880s and early 1890s. These are the feelings that inspired three important works of fiction besides *Resurrection*, written in this period: *The Kreutzer Sonata*, *The Devil*, and *Father Sergius*. All these stories relate instances of sexual crimes committed by men against women – seduction, betrayal, sexually motivated murder. The "Koni story" fit these same well-formed Tolstoyan grooves.

The origin of these grooves no doubt lay deep in Tolstoy's past, perhaps his childhood. The most immediate, conscious source, however, may be parallel episodes from his own life. A few months before he died Tolstoy told his biographer, Pavel Biriukov, that in his university days at Kazan, while living in the house of his aunt Pelageia Iushkova, he had seduced a maid in the household who had later come to a bad end. The fact that in early versions of *Resurrection* the name of the hero was Iushkov (later modified to Iushkin) points to a connection in Tolstoy's mind with that epoch in his life. In her diary his wife mentions another case, a maid in the house of Tolstoy's sister Marya. "He pointed her out to me, to my deep despair and disgust," the Countess wrote on September 13, 1898. She was particularly incensed that Tolstoy attributed all these fine sentiments of repentance, recompense, and vows of sexual purity to fictional autobiographical heroes, whereas he himself had never done anything for the victims of his transgressions and remained, she added, addicted to "fleshly love."

In any case, Tolstoy was fascinated by the "Koni story," recognized its novelistic possibilities, and urged Koni to write it up. When Koni failed to do so, Tolstoy asked his friend's permission to use it himself. Koni readily agreed. So, after some preliminary turning the tale around in his mind, on December 26, 1889, Tolstoy "suddenly" began to write. Despite the initial enthusiasm, however, the gestation of *Resurrection* proved exceptionally long and tortured, not reaching a final text until ten years and more than 7,000 manuscript pages later.

The writing was carried out in three widely separated stages. Early drafts were sketched in 1889–91, during which time Tolstoy visited a court and prison in nearby Krapivna, angrily noting for later use what he saw and heard. He broke off work, however, partly because of his involvement in famine relief during 1891–92. But he also felt deep ambivalence about the whole project. Though one of the world's greatest novelists, Tolstoy had serious doubts about the morality of writing fiction at all. "Fiction is unpleasant," he wrote his son Lev in 1895. "Everything is invented and untrue." Moreover, Tolstoy had never been willing to view himself as a professional author, one whose job is to entertain people by writing stories for money. He needed a more serious purpose for his life. And now, since his religious conversion of 1879–81, this need for commitment had been greatly intensified. He had taken upon himself the most serious responsibility conceivable: to reform the world. He had set himself the colossal task of cleansing Christianity from all the malignant encrustations of the ages, including all miracles, mystery, and magic. Extracting from the somewhat garbled Gospels the true teachings of Jesus, he would show people how to live together in harmony and love.

This task was obviously far more important than writing novels. By 1890 Tolstoy had already set forth his message in a series of treatises: *A Translation and Harmony of the Four Gospels*, *An Investigation of Dogmatic Theology*, *What I Believe*, *What Then Must We Do?* and *On Life*. During 1891–93 he completed yet another, *The Kingdom of God is Within You*, spelling out how the commandment of Christ that we resist not evil (by violence), if actually carried out, would change the world. It would eliminate armies, wars, police, law courts, and indeed all governments, which rest on violence.

Tolstoy had thus given humankind the answers, but would they listen? Evidently not, or not much. Of course there were disciples, both Russian and foreign; Mohandas Gandhi became prominent among the latter. Tolstoy's personal image as a figure of exceptional moral stature was recognized all over the world. But that philistine world's interest in Tolstoy's treatises was slight, and itself mainly a by-product of his towering reputation as a novelist. By most people the treatises were written off, unread, as the eccentric concoctions of a wayward genius. They liked his novels, but were bored by his sermons.

Tolstoy took up the "Koni story" again in 1895–96. Now the novel began to branch out from its original sexual core into larger social questions, becoming more and more an outlet for the author's outrage against Russian society and indeed all "civilized" societies. He felt surrounded by, embedded in evil, and he had to strike out against it. His particular aim was to ally himself with, work for, educate, and uplift the peasantry, which still constituted the vast majority of the Russian population. The trouble was, however, that few peasants would read a big novel. He therefore found himself as before writing not for them, but for the Russian intelligentsia, a class he was coming more and more to dislike. "My writing [i.e., *Resurrection*] has become terribly complicated and I'm sick of it," he wrote on October 5, 1895, to his friend Nikolai Strakhov. "It is insignificant, vulgar, and the main thing is that I hate writing for the parasitic, good-for-nothing intelligentsia, from which there has never been anything but futility [*sueta*] and never will be." So he broke off again.

A great artist himself, Tolstoy felt obliged to explain and justify the very existence of art. What is art for? Is it moral? How can we judge it? The result of Tolstoy's grappling with these questions was another formidable treatise, *What Is Art?* (1898). Despite its fulminations against sophisticated art addressed to a small élite, in which he included his own big novels, *What Is Art?* did provide for some categories of morally acceptable art. Good art "infects" the recipient with good feelings. Thus even a big novel like *Resurrection* might be squeezed through this loophole if it instilled emotions that would impel people to carry out the moral imperatives outlined in the treatises.

So in mid-1898 Tolstoy returned to *Resurrection* for the third time, now spurred on by a new motive. The religious sect known as Doukhobors (Spirit-wrestlers) were being persecuted by the government for their refusal to pay taxes or serve in the military – exactly what Tolstoy recommended for everyone in *The Kingdom of God is Within You*. Though not directly his disciples, the Doukhobors were kindred spirits, true peasant Christians. He decided to do something he had explicitly vowed never to do again, to write for money, the funds earned to be used to pay for transporting thousands of Doukhobors to Canada, which had agreed to accept them as immigrants.

By this time Tolstoy was a world celebrity, and the prospect of a new Tolstoy novel, the first since *Anna Karenina* twenty years before, was a sensation. *Resurrection* was to be serialized in Russia before coming out in book form, and immediate translations were arranged in Europe and America. So in 1898–99 the book was finished – and greatly expanded – in a hectic rush, with new texts copied, revised, recopied by family and friends, revised again, sent to the magazine, then virtually rewritten on proofs that sometimes themselves had to be run off two or three times. Finally, on December 15, 1899, Tolstoy wrote in his diary, "Finished *Resurrection*. Not good. Not corrected. Hasty. But it's off my back and doesn't interest me any more."

The novel by this time had vastly outgrown the original dimensions of the "Koni story." The primary nucleus of sexual misbehavior and repentance had expanded into a wholesale indictment of Russian society: the luxury and callousness of the privileged classes versus the poverty and hunger of the masses; the whole cruel criminal justice system; the Orthodox church's enormous distance from true Christianity. In Soviet times some Russian commentators[1] sought to show that this larger design had been Tolstoy's intention from the beginning, that from the start he had planned a big social novel "de longue haleine" (on the grand scale), as he put it in his diary entry of September 15, 1890. The "Koni story," they claim, just happened to fit this larger scheme. This interpretation seems to me unconvincing. In the late 1880s Tolstoy may have had occasional yearnings to immerse himself in a big novel again, but in my view the "Koni story" did not grow into that novel until considerably later. One of the reasons Tolstoy gave for his difficulties with *Resurrection* was that the topic was not his own, "was not born in me." He would hardly have made that statement if he had conceived the novel from the start as a vehicle for a comprehensive social indictment.

Tolstoy aficionados will recognize that the name of the hero of *Resurrection*, Prince Dmitrii Nekhliudov, is no newcomer to Tolstoy's pages. A character with that name had been prominent in several of Tolstoy's early works. Prince Dmitrii Nekhliudov was an admired friend of Nikolenka Irteniev, the hero of *Boyhood* and *Youth*; he was the central character of three stories, *Notes of a Billiard Marker, Lucerne*, and *A Landlord's Morning* – all dating from the 1850s. This is not to say that the hero of *Resurrection* is a pure reincarnation of these earlier namesakes. But the revival of the name in *Resurrection* is surely of some, if only private, significance. Tolstoy adds the seemingly gratuitous detail that Nekhliudov's sister had once been in love with Nikolenka Irteniev, now dead. Of course only readers with excellent memories (or Tolstoy scholars), steeped in the Tolstoyan corpus, would note these linkages, but the author did.[2]

Why this particular name? Though other, more linguistically "correct" etymologies have been suggested, I read it as a thinly disguised autobiographical signal, like the Lev-in of the hero of *Anna Karenina*. In Tolstoy's mind Nekhliudov, I believe, was simply a "softened" variant of *nekhudoi*, "not thin," a synonym of *tolstyi*, "fat," of which Tolstoy is a variant.

So Dmitrii Nekhliudov is a disguised Tolstoy. But not only Lev Tolstoy. Dmitrii Tolstoy was the name of the brother closest to Lev in age, the brother who had died of tuberculosis in 1856, in a seedy hotel in Oryol, attended by an ex-prostitute named Masha whom he had bought from a brothel. With his Paphian paramour, Dmitrii Tolstoy had already served as the model for the character of Nikolai Levin in *Anna Karenina*; but the connection between a Tolstoy and a prostitute still evidently carried a creative charge for Lev Tolstoy. The "Koni story" revived it.

It should be noted that besides its "real life" connections, the theme of "rescuing" prostitutes, even by marrying them, had a long history in Russian literature. Though mocked in Gogol's *Nevsky Prospect* (1835), it was played at full sentimental volume in Nekrasov's poem *When from the Darkness of Error (Kogda iz mraka zabluzhden'ia,* 1846), which in turn is cited as an epigraph in Dostoevsky's *Notes from Underground* (1864), a work which exposes some of the pitfalls of this gratifying plot. After *Anna Karenina,* in the 1880s Vsevolod Garshin revived the theme in his *Nadezhda Nikolaevna* (1885), and Chekhov was to invoke it in *A Nervous Breakdown* (1889). It was a powerful tradition.[3]

However, the most direct real-life model for the Nekhliudov–prostitute linkage is the author himself, at a much earlier age. Though he formed no long-term bond with any prostitute, Lev Tolstoy's first experience of sexual intercourse had been with one, at the tender age of fourteen, after which he had wept, standing by the bed. We might see this as an extreme case of post-coital angst, an affliction that seems to have often troubled Tolstoy later. Sex, he felt, is always a disappointment, the pleasure brief, the aftermath sad. In *Resurrection* Nekhliudov discovers that even at its best "animal love" did not give him anything like what it promised. Despite his earlier celebration of the joys of biological fecundity in the great novels, Tolstoy by 1890 had come to the conclusion that there is no such thing as "good" sex. As the Afterword to *The Kreutzer Sonata* explains, the procreative sex of a married couple is the least offensive kind, but even that distracts people from selfless service to God and man. It is better to live together in sexless "purity," as brother and sister.[4]

The existential stance of Dmitrii Nekhliudov, as of many of Tolstoy's quasi-autobiographical heroes, is that of a young man *somehow morally superior to his environment,* who struggles to find the path of righteousness and truth despite the efforts of a vicious society to ensnare him in its net. Tolstoy himself assumed this stance in *A Confession* (1884). In spite of its flourishes of self-deprecation, *A Confession* seems remarkable for its lack of real contrition. The blame for the subject's sins is shifted to an anonymous "they," who ridicule his noble strivings and entice him with the fleshpots of carnality and greed. Similarly, in *Resurrection* Nekhliudov succumbs to the "animal" side of his nature and seduces Katiusha Maslova because "everybody" – i.e., all the well-heeled young blades of his set – does such things and is even proud of them. They, however, take their pleasures free of guilt, while Nekhliudov can only temporarily suppress his self-disgust. The source of this moral superiority is never explored.

In *A Confession* there is another figure whose youthful scrupulosity is even more pronounced than the author's: the same brother Dmitrii, who for a time, during the Kazan period, became deeply religious, punctiliously observing the fasts and attending church, including (Tolstoy adds in his *Reminiscences*) Holy Week services in a prison chapel near their aunt's house – no doubt something like the one depicted in the famous "defamiliarized" satire of the Orthodox eucharist in *Resurrection.* For this excess of piety Dmitrii's relatives, no doubt including his brother Lev, mocked him and called him

"Noah." Later Dmitrii trod the primrose path in his turn. "He suddenly began to drink, smoke, squander money, and visit brothels." His further moral development was cut short by his death, but his "purchase" of Masha seems to indicate some stirrings of conscience and sense of responsibility.

The distinction between two kinds of love, carnal and spiritual, *eros* and *agape*, had been on Tolstoy's mind for a long time. It is found in Plato's *Symposium*, a work Tolstoy singled out as having had a "great influence" on him. In *Anna Karenina* Konstantin Levin invokes the *Symposium* in his restaurant conversation with Stiva Oblonsky, the latter an unequivocal devotee of *eros* as opposed to *agape*. But the contrast of the two "loves" goes back to Tolstoy's earliest works, to the trilogy and especially *The Cossacks*, where Dmitrii Olenin veers back and forth between the two. In *Anna Karenina* Levin seemed to have found a reasonable balance of eros and agape in his married life, based on a deep spiritual bond with his wife, but with a healthy admixture of sensuality.[5] But in *Resurrection* any Tolstoyan tolerance of eros has disappeared. It was eros that led Nekhliudov to his criminal seduction of Katiusha, and it is eros that reigns in the cheap vulgarity of the whorehouse where "Liubka" Maslova had consorted with an endless succession of lust-ridden males: merchants, clerks, Armenians, Jews, Tatars, rich, poor, healthy, sick, drunk, sober, coarse, tender, military, civilian, university students, high school boys. Her life had been an erotic horror. No wonder her eventual marriage to Simonson is apparently to be at the opposite extreme: "Platonic," sexless.

In *Resurrection* Tolstoy decided to forgo strictly chronological exposition in favor of two beginnings in the middle of the action, followed by flashbacks. The situation in which we are at once immersed – after the famous introductory celebration of the power of spring *even* in the city – is a contrast of the two main characters' lives on that spring morning. The first we see is a young woman, Katerina ("Katiusha") Maslova, being escorted by soldiers from prison to the courthouse where she is to stand trial. The flashback at this point includes only the bare facts, curriculum vitae style, of the "Koni story," a "very ordinary story," Tolstoy observes: seduction, pregnancy, dismissal, downward slide into prostitution. Her crime, however, is not divulged at this point.

Very different is the morning of Prince Nekhliudov. He wakes up in a luxurious apartment. All around him are fine *things*. He wears a clean Dutch nightshirt, washes his hands, face, and "fat neck" with fragrant soap. When he dresses, everything he puts on is of the most expensive kind. Even before getting out of bed he lights himself a cigarette taken from a silver case – an act more significant than simply another attribute of his affluence. The reader will notice all through the novel how smoking as well as drinking are used to illustrate the doctrine Tolstoy had set forth in the article "Why Do People Stupefy Themselves?" (1890). The purpose of alcohol and tobacco, Tolstoy believes, is to deaden the moral sense. People smoke or drink when they are doing something that goes against their moral nature. At the beginning of the novel Nekhliudov's only visible sin is the original one of being rich (and thus, according to Tolstoy, having robbed the poor); but he is also contemplating marriage to a cultivated, well-off woman in society, before which he must break off a long adulterous love affair.

We are also given Nekhliudov's curriculum vitae. He had resigned from the military service seven years before. Since then he had devoted himself to art, only to discover (as Vronsky in *Anna Karenina* had done before him) that his talent was a minor one at best. So at present he is at loose ends and is even grateful that jury duty will give a certain fleeting purposefulness to his life.

We then move to the court, which is given a savagely satirical representation. Tolstoy had never had much use for lawyers – witness the moth-infested office of the attorney Aleksei Karenin consults concerning a possible divorce. But in *Resurrection* the hostility has become much more acute. Here Tolstoy is demonstrating his conviction that we should take literally Christ's precept, "Judge not that ye be not judged." Human beings have no right to judge and punish one another. That is God's job. "Vengeance is *mine*, saith the Lord" – this was the epigraph to *Anna Karenina*. "Let him who is without sin cast the first stone." As a plebeian juror says, "We are not saints." Criminal courts are thus by their very nature immoral institutions.

The nature of Maslova's crime has been escalated over that of Rozalia Oni. Maslova is accused not only of theft, but of murder, carried out with two accomplices. In fact, she admits to giving sleeping powders to her customer, a rich Siberian merchant, but only with the aim of putting him to sleep so that she could escape his drunken attentions. The question of intent was crucial. The jury's agreement that she had no murderous intent is inadvertently omitted from their verdict, and the judge fails to remind them of this possibility. Because of these errors Maslova receives the harsh sentence of four years at hard labor. Thus even by the criteria of Russian law there is a miscarriage of justice. There would therefore seem to be good grounds for appeal, but of course in Tolstoy the appeals process is to be treated no less satirically than the original trial. There is no justice to be had from human institutions.

Though in general he presents the courtroom and its realia through the naïve eyes of Nekhliudov, who is seeing these things for the first time (again, Tolstoy's trademark "defamiliarization"), Tolstoy has no compunctions about resorting to the god-like, "omniscient author" point of view when it suits his satirical purposes. He tells us, for example, that the presiding judge, who is supposed to represent the majesty of impartial justice, has an "open" marriage, leaving both spouses free to commit adultery *ad libitum*. The previous summer this judge had an affair with an attractive Swiss governess. This woman is just now passing through Moscow and will be waiting for him that afternoon in a hotel. Hence he is eager to conclude the proceedings with dispatch – a haste which perhaps leads him to commit the judicial error that seals Maslova's fate. Thus the law that is supposed to be so impervious to human foibles is shown to be just the opposite, caught up in the tangle of extraneous human passions. A lawyer "of genius" is admired by all because he has managed to do an old lady out of her property in favor of an unscrupulous merchant who has no right to it at all. (As the novel's god, Tolstoy knows the absolute wrongness of this decision.) There is posturing everywhere: the lawyers with their pretentious speeches, the priest who sanctimoniously administers the oath, the chief judge who so enjoys the sound of his own voice. A particular irony is that the prosecutor who so indignantly demands the severest punishment for this pernicious prostitute has himself come to court without sleep after a night on the town with friends, ending at the very brothel where Maslova had worked.

The trial is of course the scene where Nekhliudov's "resurrection" begins. The sight and recognition of Maslova force him to resurrect the suppressed memories of his relationship with her, as later he will force her to do the same.[6] Nekhliudov's memories provide motivation for a major flashback, to the time of his first visit to his aunts and his acquaintance with Katiusha. Then an earnest young man of nineteen, a reader of Herbert Spencer, and concerned about the morality of land ownership, he is also still a virgin and cannot imagine sex outside of marriage. He and Katiusha fall in love, an innocent, "pure" love, so much so that the aunts are worried that he might even take it into his head to marry this peasant. Three years later he comes again as a young officer, thoroughly corrupted by the military ethos. His "animal self" is now in command; he smokes and drinks.

Ironically, the seduction of Katiusha takes place at Easter time. The celebration in the village church of Christ's resurrection is represented with charming lyricism, as it was felt by both these young lovers, without any of the derisive satire with which the Orthodox liturgy is mocked later. The lovers are still chaste; their kiss after the ritual exchange – "Christ is risen!" "Verily He is risen!" – is rapturous but innocent. This is the zenith of their love. The seduction scene follows, symbolically accompanied by the noise of breaking ice in the river. As usual, Tolstoy is especially attuned to body language. Katiusha's lips said no, but her "whole being" said "I am all yours." The scene aroused the indignation of Countess Tolstoy, disgusted that her aged husband would propagate such salacious fantasies. "He describes the scene of the adultery of maid and officer with the relish of a gourmet eating a tasty dish," she fumed.

The memories of his callous abandonment (and payment!) of Katiusha are bitter to Nekhliudov, and he resists their emergence as long as he can. But, as Tolstoy believed, our consciences are the voice of God within us, and Nekhliudov was already a man of relatively high moral standards. He forces himself to make the ultimate commitment, not just of money and support for an appeal of her sentence, but the offer of marriage.

Though there are later some temptations to backsliding, Nekhliudov thus essentially completes his "resurrection" early in the novel. He commits himself to marry Maslova, and if she will not have him as a husband, at least to stay near her and do everything he can to make her life more endurable. His soul has been purged, and he is on the right path. Nekhliudov can then expand the scope of his benevolence beyond Maslova. An old connection with a female revolutionary named Vera Bogodukhovskaia is revived, and through her he takes on the cases of other upper-class revolutionaries along with those of mistreated common criminals he hears about from Maslova. He becomes a sort of prisoners' ombudsman, using his money and connections to alleviate the suffering caused by the tsar's system of courts and punishments.

For Maslova, however, the process of resurrection has only just begun. At their first meeting after the trial Nekhliudov perceives her as a "dead woman" in whom all natural emotions have been stifled. His appearance and support are the catalyst that initiates the revival, but it will take some time to work itself out, assisted not only by Nekhliudov, but by a series of fellow prisoners, especially the upper-class revolutionaries with whom she is allowed to associate on the journey to Siberia. Inspired by the example of the virginal Marya Shchetinina, she learns to abandon all "coquetry," all effort to exploit the power eros gives her over men. Earlier, vodka gives her the boldness to vent her anger against Nekhliudov, charging that his beneficence is nothing but an effort to use her once again, this time as a means of purifying his soul. But his moral influence is still powerful, and she soon gives up the anodynes of tobacco and alcohol.

Ultimately, both she and Nekhliudov are redeemed by agape. Putting aside their own needs and interests, they involve themselves in the problems of others, always trying to serve, to help. They thus escape from the prison of self. Life, even in a literal prison, becomes freer and richer. This is the core of Tolstoy's sermon: love thy neighbor, not *as* thyself, but *instead of* thyself.

Nekhliudov's sexual reformation is accompanied by a social and economic one, which points to one of the larger topics of *Resurrection*, the cruelty and immorality of the entire social structure. Having repudiated his own class and attained the point of view of the "patriarchal peasantry," as Lenin put it in his articles on Tolstoy cited *ad nauseam* in Soviet times, the writer tried to see the world through peasant eyes. Though serfdom had been abolished decades earlier, the peasants' poverty was as dire as ever. The problem, as they saw it, was not overpopulation, low investment, and backward agricultural methods, but the land squeeze. Their numbers increased, but their land holdings did not. Peasants saw the solution as giving them the rest of the land, the gentry's land, and Tolstoy agrees. Tolstoy's utopia was a simpler world of universal subsistence agriculture, where all would raise their own food, and there would be no exploitation and no class divisions. Cities too would disappear, because cities are nothing but places where the exploiters concentrate their power and spend the wealth extracted from the countryside.

Tolstoy does not envisage the possibility of forcible seizure of the land by an aroused peasantry – what actually happened in 1917. He wants the landowners voluntarily to surrender their ownership, as Nekhliudov had done with a small estate he had inherited from his father. He had been inspired by the American reformer Henry George (1839–97), a thinker Tolstoy greatly admired, who maintained that the root of social evil is private ownership of land. However, Nekhliudov's problem in dealing with the much larger estates he had inherited from his mother (and also from the maiden aunts) was more difficult. The peasants are at first resistant and suspicious, but they eventually come to recognize his good will and good sense. With these estates, however, Nekhliudov cannot quite go the whole distance. He is willing to rent land to the peasants on much less onerous terms and to reduce drastically his own standard of living. But he still must have money, both to live on, still in relative comfort, and to carry out his various agape-inspired enterprises. Nekhliudov never *earns* any money at all, nor does he seem to have any thought of doing so. The aristocratic mentality dies hard.

Tolstoy's picture of upper-class life is unrelentingly satirical. After the trial Nekhliudov goes to dinner at the house of his prospective fiancée, "Missi" Korchagina. The luxury is ostentatious and the young lady attractive, both physically and culturally. But Nekhliudov is now alienated, his moral energies absorbed in his thoughts about Maslova. He sees the Korchagins with changed, "defamiliarized" eyes. The father is a brute, a former governor known for his fondness for flogging and hanging criminals. The mother is an absurdly vain, self-indulgent invalid. She flatters Nekhliudov in the hope of ensnaring him as a husband for Missi, but it is too late; he has moved on.

Nekhliudov's pursuit of an appeal of Maslova's sentence takes him to St. Petersburg, the glittering imperial capital, which had long been an object of Tolstoy's dislike. Here the prince deals with a succession of the very highest officials, to whom his princely connections give him access. They are paraded before us, one after the other, like a high-class version of the parade of bribers in Gogol's *Inspector-General*. Tolstoy, via Nekhliudov, finds scarcely a redeeming feature in any of them. They are pompous and greedy, oblivious to the cruelties their offices sponsor, and in addition they are mentally vacuous. Silly fads flourish among them, such as spiritism (ouija boards) and the we-are-all-saved harangues of a sentimental German preacher. (Another evangelical, an Englishman, appears in Part III, sanctimoniously passing out Gospels to pugnacious prisoners and admonishing them to observe the nonviolent precepts of Christian morality. In a passage coming perilously close to mockery of his own cherished turn-the-other-cheek doctrine, Tolstoy has the prisoners dissolve in laughter when one of them asks the Englishman, "When he smacks me on the *second* cheek, which one do I turn then?")

Maslova's appeal of course fails, despite its obvious justification. Here the court's decision is determined not even by the usual pettifogging legal technicalities, but by rivalries and prejudices among the judges. Nowhere among all this high officialdom is there a trace of humanity or compassion. The only Petersburg character with at least a remnant of soul is Nekhliudov's old friend Selenin, whom Nekhliudov had known in his student days as a thoughtful and morally upright young man. Selenin has now, however, been disastrously corrupted by the compromises inherent in a Petersburg career.

The most famous recognizable Petersburg character in *Resurrection* is Toporov, the Chief Procurator of the Most Holy Synod, to whom Nekhliudov appeals on behalf of some sectarians who have been arrested for holding non-Orthodox prayer services. Toporov is an obvious caricature of the celebrated Konstantin Pobedonostsev, an arch-conservative who was Chief Procurator for decades. Tolstoy portrays him as a complete cynic, who without any personal belief promotes Orthodoxy as a means of brainwashing the masses. Though Toporov grants his petition (for reasons of expediency), Nekhliudov regrets even having shaken the man's hand.

In Nekhliudov eros has not yet been totally squelched; his "animal self" is still alive. He is briefly tempted by the prospect of a love affair with "Mariette," an old acquaintance now married to a high official. Mariette uses all her wiles, physical as well as psychological, but in the end Nekhliudov's newly won virtue holds out. The last straw is the perceived comparison with a vulgar prostitute who importunes him on the street. The difference between the two women, he now understands, is only a matter of class, not of substance.

With Nekhliudov back in Moscow, Tolstoy's indictment intensifies. One of the most searing representations of senseless cruelty in the penal system is the picture of the departure for Siberia of a large group of prisoners. On a day of intense summer heat the victims are lined up in the sun, counted, counted again, and finally marched through the streets of Moscow to the railway station. Several prisoners die of sunstroke or heat exhaustion; all suffer. It is one of those instances, as Nekhliudov analyzes the causes, where it is impossible to pin responsibility for the misery. Every official is just doing his job, following orders; but the result is suffering and death. Official, legal duties make people impervious to the human law written by God in their hearts, just as pavement makes a road impervious to rain.

The third part of *Resurrection* deals with the journey to Siberia of the party of prisoners to which Maslova belonged, with Nekhliudov accompanying them as closely as he can. Here Tolstoy was not writing from personal knowledge, but from accounts read or heard from those who had experienced such journeys, perhaps beginning with Dostoevsky's *Notes from a Dead House*, which had always been the Dostoevsky book Tolstoy admired most. One of his sources was the famous *Siberia and the Exile System* (1891) by the American George Kennan, who had also visited Tolstoy in 1886. The horrific account of the execution of a Pole and an adolescent Jew is based on an unpublished memoir by a witness. From these materials the power of Tolstoy's imagination and talent enabled him to create a vividly realized picture of the "great road" to Siberia, trod by so many wretched prisoners.

A major novelty in this section of the novel is the first appearance in Tolstoy's corpus of real revolutionaries. Their portraits are varied and reflect Tolstoy's marvelous capacity to perceive all human beings in their unique individuality; but they also serve as vehicles by which he can convey his judgment of them and their cause. He mostly likes them as people, though he disapproves of their methods. Through Maslova, Tolstoy recognizes that revolutionaries from the educated upper classes were almost by definition good people, because they had voluntarily sacrificed their own comfort and status for the sake of others. He also seems to acknowledge that inculcated upper-class behavior is just humanly better than the coarseness and frequent brutality of the common folk. The revolutionaries do not use foul language and are polite and considerate of one another. It is a revelation to Maslova that people can actually be kind to one another; and it plays a major part in her "resurrection."

Tolstoy is not, however, blind to the negative qualities also found among the revolutionaries. His portrait of the "famous" Novodvorov, though only lightly sketched, shows clearly the authoritarian Lenin type, vain and sure of himself, cynical in his view of revolutionary ends and means. "The masses always adore only power . . . ," he says. "The government has power – they adore it and hate us; tomorrow we will have power – they will adore us." Characteristically, he claims the support of "science" for his doctrines.

Tolstoy of course fundamentally disagreed with all the revolutionaries, soft as well as hard, on the grounds that violence only begets more violence. The assassination of Alexander II (the "event of March 1") had clearly made matters worse for everybody; the government only intensified its oppressions. Nekhliudov argues the author's theoretical case, saying of the authorities, "They too are people," when the dying tubercular Kryltsov, overflowing with rage and frustration, imagines himself empowered to drop bombs on those "human bedbugs" from a balloon. In Tolstoy's ideal solution the rich and powerful, persuaded by his treatises, will voluntarily surrender their privileges and authority; but the novel itself does not make this utopia seem likely. Nekhliudov is absolutely unique in his class; one cannot imagine the Petersburg grandees voluntarily surrendering anything.

The original "Koni story" plot – Nekhliudov's remorse and efforts to make amends to Maslova – had essentially been resolved by the end of Part I. The rest of the novel is thus almost plotless, if regarded in conventional narratological terms. The only remaining "plot" question was whether their marriage would actually take place, and if it did, what sort of a relationship it would be. An early draft had them not only marry, but escape from Siberia to London. But ultimately Tolstoy decided otherwise, thus making the structure even looser, more focused on larger social issues. After her spiritual resurrection Maslova resolutely rejects Nekhliudov's offer of marriage. Her motives are perhaps not entirely clear. Does she, as some critics maintain, still love Nekhliudov and genuinely wish only to set him free, knowing that the cultural gulf between them was too wide to be crossed? Or has she really come to love the devoted, non-erotic Simonson?

In any case, the novel seems to end rather abruptly, with Maslova, now pardoned (through Selenin's efforts), but committed to following Simonson wherever he had to go, and Nekhliudov set free to pursue his criminological interests. Though Tolstoy has had little to say about Nekhliudov's religion, he is given a religious send-off. We know only that in his youth he had been a seeker like Selenin, already free from the "superstitions of the official church," and that he believes that God has written the law of love in people's hearts. Therefore, the novel's sudden fadeout in a long series of Gospel quotations seems scarcely justified. That at any rate was the judgment of Anton

Chekhov. Though he liked the book, calling it "a remarkable work of art," he objected that "The novel has no ending... To write so much and then suddenly make a Gospel text responsible for it all smacks a bit too much of the seminary."

In its day *Resurrection* was read with excitement all over the world, argued over, condemned, and exalted. In the terrible century that has elapsed since then, Novodvorov's utopia was realized in Russia, only to create the hell of the gulag archipelago, far worse both in numbers and in cruelty than the tsarist hell described by Tolstoy. Fortunately, that Soviet hell, too, has at last faded away. Perhaps we can now take the didactic message of *Resurrection* more serenely and usefully – as a plea that human beings should allow the agape in their hearts to govern their relations with one another.

As for the novel itself, quite apart from its "message" and despite its heavy didacticism, it has retained its standing and its popularity as a major work of literary art, perhaps not quite of the same supreme stature as its two predecessors, but a book that can still immerse us, as only Tolstoy could do, in an imagined world of human beings and human life that seems as real as if it were our own.

NOTES

1 For example, Konstantin Lomunov, *Nad stranitsami "Voskreseniia"* (Moscow: Sovremennik, 1979) and Vladimir Zhdanov, *Tvorcheskaia istoriia romana L. N. Tolstogo "Voskresenie"* (Moscow: Sovetskii pisatel', 1960).
2 See Donna Orwin's thorough scrutiny of the various Nekhliudovs. "The Riddle of Prince Nexljudov," *Slavic and East European Journal* 30, no. 4 (1986), 473–86.
3 See George Siegel, "The Fallen Woman in Nineteenth-Century Russian Literature," in Horace G. Lunt, *et al.*, eds, *Harvard Slavic Studies*, V (1970), 81–108.
4 Edwina Cruise argues that the sexless love Tolstoy advocates for everyone, men and women alike, is essentially feminine, maternal. "The Ideal Woman in Tolstoi: *Resurrection,"Canadian–American Slavic Studies* 11, no. 2 (Summer 1977), 281–86.
5 See Irina Gutkin, "The Dichotomy Between Flesh and Spirit: Plato's *Symposium* in *Anna Karenina*," in Hugh McLean (ed.), *In the Shade of the Giant: Essays on Tolstoy* (Berkeley: University of California Press, 1989), pp. 84–99.
6 See Marie Semon, "Le rôle de la mémoire dans *Résurrection*," in Semon (ed.), *A propos de* Résurrection (Paris: Institut d'Etudes Slaves, 1996), pp. 15–25.

2

GENRES

4

GARY R. JAHN

Tolstoy as a writer of popular literature

In Tolstoy's time the phrase "popular literature" (*narodnaia literatura*, "literature for or of the common people") subsumed a variety of related products. It included, first, the literature of the people, especially the narrative forms of folklore: heroic songs, fairy tales, religious legends, and the like. Produced and orally perpetuated among the common people themselves, usually by quasi-professional performers, this category of popular literature assumed written or printed form only through the efforts of folklorists and other transcribers of its oral performance. Once such works became known it was not long before stylizations of them followed. These are clearly not "of the people" but imitate as closely as possible the spirit and forms of their models. Stylizations, particularly of the Russian fairy tale, are well represented in nineteenth-century Russian literature. Well-known examples are Pushkin's *Tale of the Fisherman and the Fish* (*Skazka o rybake i rybke*), V. F. Odoevskii's *Moroz Ivanovich*, S. T. Aksakov's *The Little Crimson Flower* (*Alen'kii tsvetochek*), and P. P. Ershov's *The Little Humpbacked Horse* (*Konek-gorbunok*). Tolstoy wrote many works, in particular his score or so of *Stories for the People* (*narodnye rasskazy*) which may be assigned to this category, but, as will appear below, not exclusively to it.

The life and customs of the common people were the subject of a second category of popular literature, produced by and for the educated sectors of society. From the 1760s to the 1780s various voices in Germany were raised in praise of folk literature. The collection of folklore was encouraged, and the philosopher J. G. von Herder developed the influential concept of *Volksgeist*, the idea that the essential and most significant spirit of a nation is expressed in the artistic productions of its common people. Motivated in part by the penetration into Russian intellectual life of German philosophy and particularly Herder's ideas, works in which characters and situations drawn from the life of the folk (Russian *narod*) played a featured role began to appear in Russia in the late 1820s and early 1830s. Such writing was promoted by the important Russian literary critic V. G. Belinsky and blossomed in the mid-1840s into the "Natural School," which produced such works as D. V. Grigorovich's *The Fisher Folk* (*Rybaki*) and the anthologies *The Attics of St. Petersburg* and *The Organ Grinders of St. Petersburg*. Following this precedent, literature about the people continued to be marked by the realistic style and a tone sympathetic to folk life. Famous early examples are certain of Turgenev's *Sportsman's Sketches* (*Zapiski okhotnika*) from the late 1840s. Literature about the people gained renewed support from the populist critics of the 1870s and 1880s, especially N. K. Mikhailovsky, and continued to be a powerful movement in literature even well into the twentieth century. A main tenet of Socialist Realism was that same sympathetic and realistic approach to the lives of common folk for which Belinsky called in the 1840s. Tolstoy's story of the early 1860s, *Polikushka*, is one example among many that he wrote in this category.

Tolstoy made his most distinct contribution, however, to the third category of popular literature: works created by writers from the educated classes for a popular audience. There were two main subdivisions of this "literature for the people." The more successful, purely commercial in character, had formed an identifiable part of Russian literary culture since the early eighteenth century when, because of the developing literary taste of educated society, there began to be an unmet demand for works to satisfy the relatively static taste of readers from the lower social classes. In the middle of the nineteenth century this type of literature remained what it had been at its beginnings. Song books, books on the interpretation of dreams, casual collections of folklore, and stories of romance and adventure made up the commercial inventory. Chapbooks (i.e., naïve tales of romance and adventure) like *Bova Korolevich* and *Peter of the Golden Keys* together with picaresque stories such as those attributed to Matvei Komarov, "inhabitant of the city of Moscow," continued to fascinate the popular reader. Standard titles were printed over and over again, while around this core there gathered a fairly numerous crowd of hack writers who earned their bread by producing quantities of similar works, always mindful of the cardinal rule that one should never stray far from a successful formula. The works of such now-forgotten writers as Evstigneev, Volgin, V. Suvorov, Kassirov, the brothers Pazukhin, Kuzmichev, and many others provided the staple printed diet of the popular reader in Tolstoy's time.

The second, and lesser, category of literature for the people, more idealistic in its purposes, sought to enlighten or edify the masses rather than to profit by entertaining them. Its history was much shorter than that of its commercial counterpart. Its first notable success was the journal *Village Reading* (*Sel'skoe chtenie*), published (1843–48) by V. F. Odoevskii (who dabbled also in folklore stylization) and A. P. Zablotskii-Desiatovskii.

Conducted on a high level, *Village Reading* contained contributions from such well-known writers as M. N. Zagoskin, A. F. Veltman, and V. I. Dal (who also, under the pen name "The Cossack Luganskii," contributed significantly, as a leading writer of the Natural School, to the development of literature about the common people). In the late 1850s and 1860s the magazines of A. F. Pogosskii, *Soldier Talk (Soldatskaia beseda)*, *Peasant Talk (Narodnaia beseda)*, and *Leisure and Labor (Dosug i delo)*, enjoyed some popular success. In 1854 Tolstoy himself entertained the idea of publishing a journal for soldiers to be called *The Soldier's Herald (Soldatskii vestnik)*.

In the 1870s, interest in raising the quality of the literature available to the people led to the formation of enterprises devoted solely to this goal. The most representative of these was V. N. Marakuev's *Popular Library (Narodnaia biblioteka)* founded in 1872 mainly to produce inexpensive editions of the classics of Russian and other national literatures. Most such projects failed because they lacked adequate means of distribution to rural areas. In 1884 Tolstoy and two collaborators, V. G. Chertkov and P. I. Biriukov (later Tolstoy's authorized biographer), founded the publishing house Intermediary Press (*Posrednik*), which used the distribution methods of the commercial producers of literature for the people (a combination of regional distribution centers and networks of itinerant peddlers) in the service of idealistic goals. They succeeded beyond everyone's expectations. Biriukov estimated that in the 1890s Intermediary Press distributed some 3,500,000 copies of various works per year. This must be counted one of Tolstoy's most significant contributions to popular literature.[1]

Tolstoy's interest in literature for the people is well attested. In February 1884, he wrote to Chertkov that what was then being produced was neither good, nor even useful, and some of it was actually harmful.[2] In an address to an audience at his Moscow home on February 14, 1884, he elaborated his views. Writers for profit did not satisfy the "true needs" of their readers, nor did they provide their prospective readers with works of the same quality they would demand for themselves. Even if they wanted to do this, they could not, because their own literary tradition (that of Pushkin and Gogol) was defective. Tolstoy expressed these ideas with the rhetorical heat characteristic of him at that period:

> I see only three reasons [for the failure of contemporary writing for the popular audience]: one, that the satiated wish not to feed the hungry, but to deal with them in a way profitable to themselves; second, that the satiated do not want to give that which is their own food, but give only the leftovers, which even the dogs won't eat; third, that the satiated are not in fact as full as they imagine, but only inflated, and their own food is not that good.   (*PSS* 25: 524)

Tolstoy stressed the need for artistry of an especially high order in works for the popular audience. He criticized contemporary authors for writing "for the most part in an untalented and stupid manner" and for their "naïve persuasion" that important matters of spirit and life "could be communicated by the first words and images which come to hand" (*PSS* 25: 524). He was especially hard on what he saw as the unwarranted condescension of writers and publishers to their audience. He had long believed and frequently said that the standard Russian literary language was distinctly inferior to that of the common people themselves. (His best known assertion of this belief had been in an article he had published in his own pedagogical journal, *Iasnaia Poliana*, in 1863. To the question posed by the title of the article, "Who Should Learn to Write from Whom: The Peasant Children from Us or We from the Peasant Children?," Tolstoy had answered: we from the children.) In his speech to his Moscow audience, he exempted none of the contemporary writers of literature for the people from the criticism that their works were artistic failures, but he reserved his strongest words for writers with a commercial motive. Speaking on behalf and from the viewpoint of the popular reader, Tolstoy said:

> Ladies and Gentlemen, writers of our native land, cast into our mouths mental sustenance which is worthy both of yourselves and of us; write for us, who thirst for the living literary word; save us from all of these Eruslan Lazareviches, Milord Georges [characters from popular chapbooks], and other such food from the bazaar. (*PSS* 25: 526)

As I have suggested, Tolstoy made notable contributions to each of the three major categories of popular literature. Many works throughout his long career contain minor and major characters drawn from among the people. In this he was hardly remarkable; writing "about the people" was one of the hallmarks of developing Russian Realism from its inception in the 1840s. For this reason, Tolstoy's contribution to literature about the people will not be considered further in this discussion. Much more striking was his contribution, mostly but not entirely after 1880, to the literature of folklore stylization and to writing specifically for the popular audience. Here he found a way of combining the forms associated with the literature of the people themselves with the intentions characteristic of those writing for the popular audience. To these achievements, notably his many "stories for the people" and his two popular dramas, we now turn our attention.

In February 1886, already hard at work on his own stories for the popular audience, Tolstoy wrote a letter to F. F. Tishchenko, a would-be author for the people, in which he outlined his requirements for such writing. It should be altruistic rather than produced for profit; it should communicate feelings;

and it should be written expressly for the popular audience, making no concession to the literary expectations of the educated upper classes. This letter makes it quite clear that in his own practice as a writer for the popular audience Tolstoy was guided first of all by the principle which he held to be crucial to the production of any kind of art whatever: that it be a medium for the communication of the artist's feelings. This belief was characteristic of Tolstoy throughout his career and is most fully expressed in his tractate *What is Art? (Chto takoe iskusstvo?* 1897).[3] Tolstoy demanded a simplification of language and style, specifically in comparison with the literary tradition of the recent past. Both lexical and syntactic elements foreign to Russian as spoken by common people should be avoided. The exposition should be logical, straightforward, and economical with an eye to creating the strongest possible impression within the smallest possible compass. Finally, he believed that the most suitable subject matter of works for the common people was that based upon the ethical teachings of Christ (*PSS* 63: 325–27).[4]

Tolstoy's score of stories and two plays for the popular audience amply illustrate these principles. Taken together they represent a combination, unique as far as I know, of the use and adaptation of familiar popular forms as a stylistic foundation, the overtly didactic presentation of ethically significant thematic material, and the artistic skill and power of a great literary master. In his effort to present his version of the Christian teaching in works for the common people Tolstoy re-invented the medieval ecclesiastical genre of the *exemplum*, a story told, usually as part of a homily or sermon, to illustrate a particular point of doctrine. Many of the works which he so created are exemplary also in the sense of illustrating what gems may be produced by the close study, adaptation, and application of popular and collective forms to an individual author's specific artistic purposes.

Written to exemplify certain ethical truths, the stories for the people resemble the other late works of Tolstoy, which are also, for the most part, overtly didactic. To the extent that he consciously, from an early date, sought to portray the "truth," as he understood it, in his fiction, even his early works reflect his didactic proclivities. Thus, it is not the themes or the motives of Tolstoy which ultimately set the stories for the people apart from the rest of his work, but their style, which was developed specifically and consciously as an apt and accessible medium for conveying moral concepts to the popular audience.

Critics still argue over exactly which works should be classified as stories for the people, but certainly a number of stories written in the 1880s belong to the genre.[5] Four of the more complete editions of Tolstoy's collected works contain a volume or clearly marked section of a volume designated *Stories for the People (Narodnye rasskazy).*[6] A total of some two dozen stories appeared in one or more of these editions, but only sixteen of them were included in every one.[7] Of these the most celebrated are: *What Men Live By*; *Two Old Men*; *Where Love is, There is God Also*; *How Much Land Does a Man Need*; *The Tale of Ivan the Fool*; and *The Three Hermits*.[8] In 1887 Tolstoy consented to the publication by Intermediary Press of a volume to be titled *Stories for the People*. Forbidden by censorship, the book never appeared, but its proposed contents included fifteen of the sixteen stories. To this number may doubtless be added stories written earlier, such as *God Sees the Truth, But Waits*,[9] and later, such as *Alesha Gorshok*, which share the same stylistic and thematic profile.

All of the stories are told by a third person narrator. Most commonly the narrator's voice closely resembles that of the popular characters, and his outlook is sympathetic to them. The degree of his sympathy may vary, however. Often, as in *What Men Live By*, *Two Old Men*, and *The Tale of Ivan the Fool*, the narrator identifies closely with the characters. Occasionally the narrator's stance is more objective and neutral, as in *Two Brothers and the Gold*. In no case is the voice of the narrator sarcastic, as it can often be in Tolstoy's depiction of upper-class society.

The setting of the stories may be popular and Russian, or legendary or exotic. Major characters are drawn from among the common people, most frequently the peasants. Characters from other backgrounds appear in major and sympathetic roles only when they are distanced in some way. For example, *A Grain As Big As a Hen's Egg*, in which a king has a major role, takes place in the distant past. In *Ilias*, featuring a rich landowner, the setting, vaguely Central-Asian, is far away. Supernatural characters, both angels and demons (including the Devil himself), appear in all but three of the stories.[10] By contrast, in other, non-popular, late works by Tolstoy popular characters play only supporting or comparative roles, and the supernatural is almost never present. When it is, as in *The Fruits of Enlightenment* (*Plody prosveshcheniia*, a play about the attempts of a group of occultists to contact the spirits of the dead), it is ridiculed.

Perhaps the most distinctive feature of the stories for the people is their language. The syntactic foundation of all the stories is the simple sentence, pruned of all but essential elements and frequently elliptical. Longer sentences tend to be constructed of a string of principal clauses rather than subordinate clauses grouped around a main one. Constructions have either a Biblical or a popular coloring, or both. In most of the stories, the narrative is markedly popular. The popular flavor is achieved by the consistent inversion of literary word order in the sentence (e.g., "Ne mog eshche ia poniat'..." ["not able still was I to understand..."] instead of "ia eshche ne mog poniat'..." ["I still was not able to understand..."]) and the use of popular lexical material. This material is often proverbial and sometimes from folklore, for example, the traditional opening phrase of the tale (*skazka*), "zhil-byl" (literally, "there lived-there was")[11] which appears in many of these stories. On the other hand Tolstoy often, especially in the moralizing conclusions of the stories, introduced a tone of solemnity reminiscent of Biblical language. The Bible is actually quoted in nine of the stories, either in text or as epigraph. The influence of Biblical language affects nearly all of the stories. It is clearest in the language of divine characters (the angels in *What Men Live By* and *Two Brothers and the Gold*, the heavenly voice in *Where Love is, There is God Also*), and generally whenever the narrative touches directly upon the underlying thematic sense of the work, as in the moralizing conclusion of *The Candle*.

The stories for the people, with their absence of complex metaphorical language, maximally simplified syntax, syntactic inversion, peasant words and expressions, and the use of many devices and motifs from both folklore and Scripture, have an innovative and coherent writing style. They represent a remarkable stylistic departure from Tolstoy's earlier work. Tolstoy's use of language is studied, conscious, deliberate, and directed both at the creation of a popular tonal quality and at the avoidance of his former "literary" style, with its tendency to syntactic and lexical complexity, foreignisms, and lengthy periodicity.

All the stories for the people are more or less openly didactic and may even present a moral formally, as in *The Godson*. Characters are most often developed through their actions and words. Occasionally the narrator characterizes his heroes directly, but usually he confines himself to brief physical descriptions. Very rarely, and nowhere at length, are the psychological processes of the characters described directly. This is another important distinction between the stories for the people and Tolstoy's other works, both early and late, with their frequent use of devices such as interior monologue and stream of consciousness. The reason for this is surely to be found in Tolstoy's desire to remain true to the spirit of folklore in developing his popular style. Events usually take place in simple chronological order, but they also occur, according to folk conventions, in groups of three, as in *What Men Live By*, *Where Love is, There is God Also*, *The Tale of Ivan the Fool*, and several others. Plot in these stories does not take on the complex forms with which Tolstoy experimented in such non-popular late works as *The Death of Ivan Ilich* and *Resurrection*, with their use of flashbacks and shifting points of view.

The stories for the people are united thematically by the Christian teaching as Tolstoy had come to understand it in the late 1870s and 1880s. In his long essay *What I Believe* (*V chem moia vera*; 1882) he reduced Christianity to five moral imperatives, derived from the "Sermon on the Mount" (Matthew, v–vii and parallels). Briefly stated, the five commandments are: (1) do not be angry; (2) do not lust; (3) do not swear – that is, do not, through an oath, surrender free moral choice to the will of others; (4) do not resist the evil doer with force; and (5) love all people alike. These commandments, their corollaries, and the effects of disobeying them (or, more generally, the will of God which they represent) provide a complete thematic summary of the stories for the people.

The commandment to avoid anger is prominent in *Evil Allures, But Good Endures, A Spark Neglected Burns the House*, and *Little Girls Wiser than their Elders*; its corollary, forgiveness, is the theme of *The Repentant Sinner*. The injunction against lust never appears in the stories for the people. We may surmise that Tolstoy discerned no need to preach this commandment among the people, and, judging by the frequency of the sexual theme in the non-popular late works (*Father Sergius, The Kreutzer Sonata, Resurrection*, and others), he regarded infractions of it as an essentially upper-class phenomenon. The injunction against oath-taking appears as a theme in *The Tale of Ivan the Fool* when the devil is unable to raise an army in Ivan's kingdom because the people refuse to promise allegiance. In *Two Old Men*, Elisei, the morally superior of the two characters, attaches little importance to the vow he has sworn to make a pilgrimage to the Holy Land when it conflicts with an obligation to assist others who are in need. The fourth commandment, not to resist evil with force, is the subject of *The Candle, The Tale of Ivan the Fool*, and *The Godson*. The only positive commandment, to love all people alike, is at the heart of most of the best-known stories for the people: *What Men Live By, Two Old Men, The Three Hermits*, and *Where Love is, There is God Also*.

The five remaining stories deal with the evil that comes from ignorance of or disobedience to the Christian teaching. Their theme is excess. In *How Much Land Does a Man Need*, it takes the form of greed for more land than needed; in *The Imp and the Crust*, the misuse of a bumper crop of grain to produce strong drink; in *Ilias*, the contrast between the hero's current contentedness with poverty and his former anxiety with wealth. *Two Brothers and the Gold* and *A Grain As Big As a Hen's Egg* condemn the use of money as a replacement for active human concern.

The stylistic unity of the stories for the people is the product of a number of linguistic and larger structural devices which they share. Proverbs, sayings, and other bits of popular wisdom were incorporated into the stories. As early as 1862, Tolstoy stated that he intended to write a series of brief stories, each of which was to be inspired by, and offer an explanation of, a striking popular saying (*PSS* 8: 302). Often such sayings were used as titles, for example,

Gde liubov', tam i Bog (*Where Love is, There is God Also*), *Bog pravdu vidit, da ne skoro skazhet* (*God Sees the Truth, But Waits*), *Vrazh'e lepko, a Bozh'e krepko* (*Evil Allures, But Good Endures*), and *Upustish' ogon' – ne potushish'* (*A Spark Neglected Burns the House*).

The majority of the stories rework existing popular narratives, such as those of the famous *skazitel'* ("teller of tales"), V. P. Shchegelenok, from whom Tolstoy obtained the subjects of *What Men Live By* and *Two Old Men*. Another familiar model used by Tolstoy was the *lubok* or illustrated text. Not itself a form of folklore, it was well known to the popular audience. The word *lubok* (from *lub*, the inner bark of the lime tree, or from *lubochnaia koroba*, the phrase designating the box used by peddlers to transport their goods) was known from the early seventeenth century. Essentially, the *lubok* consisted of a picture (or a series of pictures) accompanied by a printed text which might be explanatory or narrative as the case required. Many of the shorter stories for the people (for example, *Little Girls Wiser than their Elders*, *Evil Allures, But Good Endures* and *Ilias*) were modeled on the *lubok* and printed, often as separate sheets, with an accompanying picture. Finally, Tolstoy made use of folklore anthologies as sources for the stories. *The Godson*, *The Repentant Sinner*, *The Workman Emelian and the Empty Drum*, *The Three Hermits*, and *The Imp and the Crust* are all closely modeled on religious legends or fairy tales found recorded in the collections made by A. N. Afanasiev and other folklorists.

The stories contain several elements common to folk narratives and not found in Tolstoy's usual literary style. As previously mentioned, angels and demons frequently appear as do events and characters in groups of three, in distinct contrast to Tolstoy's preference in his "literary" style for comparison and contrast based upon binary groupings. There is evidence in the form of notebooks kept by Tolstoy, especially in the late 1870s, of his deliberate attempt to gather striking turns of phrase from common folk. From time to time he would conceal himself behind bushes growing by the entrance to the drive leading to the manor house at Iasnaia Poliana (his country estate). He would eavesdrop upon the conversation of those passing by along the road on foot. When he would overhear some particularly choice or juicy example of popular speech he would discreetly emerge from his hiding place, catch up with the travelers, and engage them in further conversation as they walked along together. Having thus gathered some gems of the popular lexicon or syntax he would return to his ambush and make careful notes of the discoveries he had made, not a few of which later found their way into his stories.

Finally, Tolstoy quoted freely from Scripture and adopted some mannerisms typical of the Bible and other religious literature.[12] This element is most frequently found in the epigraph (where it has a significance not unlike that of the proverbs used as titles) or at the climax of the story or, where there is a moral, in the passage where it is explained. Assuming that to the popular, Orthodox reader Biblical language would be both familiar and authoritative, Tolstoy may have used it to add weight to the moral teaching of his stories.

It may be thought unlikely that works so overtly burdened with didactic purpose and directed at so specific an audience would have much chance of being artistically memorable. In the case of many of these stories, especially the very brief ones, this prediction proves all too accurate. Yet such stories as *God Sees the Truth, But Waits, What Men Live By, Two Old Men, The Three Hermits, Where Love is, There is God Also*, and *How Much Land Does a Man Need?* possess high artistic value. They represent a masterful achievement in the creation – from heterogeneous, although related, elements – of a unified style which yet permits a modicum of flexibility and is singularly well adapted to its solemn moral purpose.

After 1880 Tolstoy produced some half dozen dramatic works of varying length. He had made some rather tentative experiments in writing plays in his earlier career, primarily in the late 1850s and the first half of the 1860s. None of these early experiments was either published or produced during Tolstoy's lifetime. It was also the fate of much of Tolstoy's later dramatic writing to remain "in the drawer," as the Russian phrase has it. Both of the plays which he wrote for the popular theatre, however, were produced, although in one case not as its author had planned.

Tolstoy's creation of the *Stories for the People* and their publication by Intermediary Press attracted the attention of persons interested in producing plays for the common people, and Tolstoy wrote two plays for them.[13] The first, called *The First Distiller (Pervyi vinokur)*, was an enlarged, dramatized version of *The Imp and the Crust*. It follows very closely the plot and style of this story for the people, which concerns the attempts of the Devil to seduce a stolid, hard-working peasant away from his life of virtue. First staged in 1886 at an open-air theatre in the factory village of Aleksandrovskoe, near St. Petersburg, it was Tolstoy's only play "for the people" actually to be performed in such a venue. Its success frightened the censorship, and further popular performances of plays by Tolstoy were banned.

Of much larger significance is Tolstoy's second popular drama, *The Power of Darkness (Vlast' t'my)*, also written in 1886. At the particular insistence of K. P. Pobedonostsev, the Procurator of the Holy Synod and an intimate adviser of Tsar Alexander III, its production was forbidden in any theatre. It was first produced only a decade later, in 1895, by various theatres, including the Maly Theatre in Moscow and the Aleksandriinskii Theatre in

St. Petersburg. The lifting of the ban on production of the play in 1895 was only partial. "Popular" theatres were still forbidden to present the work. Nonetheless, the very first performance was at the Skomorokh Theatre in Moscow, whose organizer had first besought Tolstoy to write the play a decade before. In order to make the performance possible, the Skomorokh was required to cease designating itself as a popular theatre. In 1902 the play was one of the first great successes of Konstantin Stanislavsky and the Moscow Art Theatre.

The Power of Darkness is a curious amalgam of traditional (that is, literary) dramatic forms and devices and the style of language and speech which Tolstoy developed in writing the *Stories for the People*. Organized in the manner of the well-made play of the neo-classical era, it is divided into five acts with an introductory exposition in Act I, the further development of characters and situation in Acts II and III, the catastrophe in Act IV, and the denouement in Act V. The neo-classical unity of place is carefully preserved (the entire action of the piece is set in the interior of the leading character's house)[14] and the one incident of gross violence which the play contains, the murder of an illegitimate baby, takes place off stage.

The main theme of the play is expressed by its epigraph which, as so often in the *Stories for the People*, takes the form of a folk saying: "When the claw is caught, the whole bird is lost" ("Kogotok uviaz, vsei ptichke propast'"). The play's main character, a peasant named Nikita, commits a small sin by dallying with the wife of his aged master and is, by degrees, led into the commission of one further crime after another. The action of the play is centered upon the slow moral destruction of Nikita as he sinks gradually into a morass of evil, culminating, however, in his final repentance and redemption.

The main characters are all peasants. They and their lives are depicted realistically, more unsparingly, in fact, than in any of the *Stories for the People*. It was the "dreadful" realism of the play which caused Pobedonostsev to take such a strongly censorious stand against its production in the first place. The play's realism is reminiscent of two works of the young Tolstoy (*A Landowner's Morning* and *Polikushka*) which portray the darker side of peasant life, and anticipates the harsh realism of some of Anton Chekhov's stories of peasant life, in particular his *Peasants* (*Muzhiki*). At the same time, the peasant characters symbolically represent universal types and values. Thus, Matryona, the protagonist's mother, represents evil while his father, Akim, represents good. Nikita himself is cast between his two progenitors, played upon now by the power of evil, now by the power of good. Symbolically, the play becomes the representation of the struggle between good and evil for the soul of a human being.

In contrast to the very positive representation accorded to peasant characters in general in the *Stories for the People*, *The Power of Darkness* is something of an anomaly among Tolstoy's writings for the popular audience. Not only is the power of evil much more palpably to be felt here than in the stories, but the overtly sexual themes presented in the play have no counterpart anywhere in the stories. Even so, the play was enthusiastically received by the popular audience. It remains the only dramatic work by Tolstoy to have succeeded during the writer's lifetime and to have stood the test of time to become part of the standard repertory of the Russian theatre.

The *Stories for the People* and Tolstoy's two popular dramas have a unique place in the context of "popular literature." Just as they represent a synthesis of various elements on the stylistic level, so, too, in the broader context they represent a synthesis of the various categories of popular literature. They are "of the people" in their language, their devices, and often in their sources. They are "about the people" in their emphasis on popular characters and settings and the patent tone of sympathy with the lot of the *narod*. And of course, they were "for the people," written primarily for the improvement and appreciation of what Tolstoy was convinced was the most discriminating of artistic audiences.

In the last thirty years of his life Tolstoy's activity was threefold. He was an artist, producing fictions in various genres and with various ends in view. He was also a religious thinker and publicist, developing and explaining a philosophical system that was mainly ethical in its emphasis. Finally, he was an aesthetician, elaborating a theory of universally comprehensible art which, in effect, provided the theoretical framework within which the artist and the religious thinker could cooperate. His writings for the people represent the unique confluence of these three modes of activity: the moralism of the religious thinker was presented in a manner which both pleased the artist and satisfied the requirements of the aesthetician.

NOTES

1 George Rapall Noyes, *Tolstoy* (New York: Duffield, 1918), p. 287. See also Thais Lindstrom, "From Chapbooks to Classics: The Story of the Intermediary," *American Slavic and East European Review* 2 (1957), 190–201.

2 *PSS* 85: 30. Since English translations of the stories are scattered in many different sources, all further volume–page references from Tolstoy are given in the text of the chapter and refer to the standard Russian Jubilee edition (identified as *PSS*). Providing references to English translations of Tolstoy's popular writings is problematical. While all of the stories and the two plays discussed in this chapter have appeared in English at one time or another, the most convenient volumes in which they appeared have been out of print for some time. Most good libraries, however, will have these works in English in one form or another, although it

may require some patience to discover them. There have been several versions of Tolstoy's collected works in English translation; the best of these is the *Complete Works of Tolstoy* edited by Louise and Aylmer Maude (London: Oxford University Press, 1928). There are also complete works edited by Leo Wiener (reprinted by AMS Press [New York, 1968]) and by Nathan Haskell Dole (New York: Thomas Y. Crowell and Co., 1898–1911). The most readily available edition of the *Stories for the People* in English is in a volume often included in Oxford University Press's The World's Classics series and called *Twenty-three Tales* (e.g., London: Oxford University Press, 1971). The contents of *Twenty-three Tales* have also been published electronically by the Christian Classics Ethereal Library and may be found at http://www.ccel.org/t/tolstoy/23_tales/23_tales.html. Everyman's Library published (in August, 2001) a thick volume called *Collected Shorter Fiction*, edited by Nigel Cooper with an introduction by John Bayley; and The Plough Publishing House, with permission from Oxford University Press, produced a volume in 1998 called *Walk in the Light and Twenty-Three Tales*.

3 Tolstoy's concept of the communication of feelings is more subtle than may at first appear. An explanation of Tolstoy's aesthetic views as expressed in *What is Art?* may be found in Gary R. Jahn, "The Aesthetic Theory of Leo Tolstoy's *What is Art?*," *Journal of Aesthetics and Art Criticism* 34 (1975), 261–70. See also Rimvydas Silbajoris, *Tolstoy's Aesthetics and His Art* (Columbus, Ohio: Slavica Publishers, 1991). See also ch. 12 of the present volume, "Tolstoy's aesthetics," by Caryl Emerson.

4 Tolstoy's main source for his version of Christ's ethical teaching was the "Sermon on the Mount" (especially Matthew, v-vii, and Luke, vi).

5 If all of Tolstoy's finished short stories are compared with the description offered in this chapter it appears that a complete list of Tolstoy's stories for the people would include, besides the sixteen stories discussed here, the following: *Alesha Gorshok*, *God Sees the Truth, But Waits* (*Bog pravdu vidit, da ne skoro skazhet*), *The Three Sons* (*Tri syna*), and *The Workman Emelian and the Empty Drum* (*Rabotnik Emel'ian i pustoi baraban*).

6 The following four editions were consulted in obtaining the list of stories for the people: (1) Vol. XI of the eleventh edition (1904) of Tolstoy's collected works (the titles given under the heading *Narodnye rasskazy*); (2) Vol. XVI of the first complete collected works (edited by P. I. Biriukov, *ca.* 1913), under the heading *Povesti i rasskazy dlia narodnykh izdanii* (*Tales and Stories for Popular Editions*); (3) Vol. X of *Polnoe sobranie khudozhestvennykh proizvedenii* (ed. B. Eikhenbaum and K. Khalabaev, 1930); (4) Vol. XXV of *Polnoe sobranie sochinenii* (edited by V. G. Chertkov, 1928–58) under the heading *Narodnye rasskazy*.

7 *What Men Live By* (*Chem liudi zhivy*), *Little Girls Wiser Than Their Elders* (*Devchonki umnee starikov*), *Two Brothers and the Gold* (*Dva brata i zoloto*), *Two Old Men* (*Dva starika*), *Where Love is, There is God Also* (*Gde liubov', tam i Bog*), *Ilias*, *The Repentant Sinner* (*Kaiushchiisia greshnik*), *The Imp and the Crust* (*Kak chertenok kraiushku vykupal*), *The Godson* (*Krestnik*), *How Much Land Does a Man Need?* (*Mnogo li cheloveku zemli nuzhno?*), *The Tale of Ivan the Fool*...(*Skazka ob Ivane durake*...), *The Candle* (*Svechka*), *The Three Hermits* [also known as *The Three Elders*] (*Tri startsa*), *A Spark Neglected Burns the House* (*Upustish' ogon' – ne potushish'*), *Evil Allures, But Good Endures* (*Vrazh'e lepko, a Bozh'e krepko*), and *A Grain As Big As a Hen's Egg* (*Zerno s kuriinoe iaico*).

8 The Guide to further reading at the end of this volume contains references to studies devoted to several of these stories.

9 In connection with a complete course of primary instruction (reading, writing, arithmetic, basic history, and science) which Tolstoy developed in the early 1870s, he wrote four anthologies of readings for use with the course. These he called *The Russian Books for Reading*. Most of the pieces in these anthologies are quite short, often only a paragraph or two in length. Two of the longer pieces, however, are more substantial: *God Sees the Truth, But Waits* and *The Prisoner of the Caucasus*. The first of these may be regarded as the prototype for Tolstoy's later stories for the people. For further discussion of this story see Gary R. Jahn, "A Structural Analysis of Leo Tolstoy's 'God Sees the Truth, But Waits'," *Studies in Short Fiction* 12 (1975), 261–70.

10 So different was this from Tolstoy's standard "literary" practice that he felt obliged to offer a defense of the use of the supernatural in his "popular" art. See his essay "On Truth in Art" (*O pravde v iskusstve*; 1887).

11 For example, "In a certain kingdom, in a certain land, there lived-there was a rich farmer" ("V nekotorom tsarstve, v nekotorom gosudarstve, zhil-byl bogatyi muzhik").

12 Tolstoy drew especially on *Prolog*, a medieval compendium of brief accounts of the lives and miraculous deeds of the saints, whence he also derived the subject for *Two Brothers and the Gold*.

13 Tolstoy had dealings with both M. V. Lentovskii (organizer of the Skomorokh Theatre for the common people in Moscow) and P. A. Denisenko (director of the Vasil'ev Island Theatre for Workers in St. Petersburg). *The Power of Darkness* was written to fulfill a promise made in correspondence with the latter.

14 For the Moscow Art Theatre production in 1902, Stanislavsky purchased an actual peasant house (*izba*) and had its interior set up on the stage. The actors were costumed in used (and not always very hygienic) clothing purchased at a flea market in the city.

5

RICHARD FREEBORN

The long short story in Tolstoy's fiction

The term *povest'* has a somewhat fluid meaning in Russian, as a term defining a work of fiction which can range in size between what is normally called a short story and what might also be a short novel. Tolstoy's most notable fictional works of the 1880s and 1890s fall into this category. They cannot match such masterpieces of the 1860s and 1870s as *War and Peace* and *Anna Karenina*, but they are manifestly superior to the short works of fiction designed to illustrate his religious ideas and can claim our attention more readily than his dramas or his last novel, *Resurrection*. They owe their power chiefly to the way they focus upon a single foreground figure and portray that figure's life as having meaning principally in the light of Tolstoy's ideas on death, sex, and spirituality. Apparently single-voiced and lacking the multiplicity of central figures and viewpoints of the great novels, the Tolstoyan long short story can demonstrate more directly the purpose of his art as a vehicle for infecting the reader with the author's feelings.[1]

The Death of Ivan Ilich, *The Kreutzer Sonata*, and *Father Sergius* illustrate the power of this infection in remarkable ways through depicting the experience of one individual. The psychologizing impulse in Tolstoy turns them not into tracts so much as into semi-autobiographical dramatizations of lives largely lived on false premises; and it is a falsity highlighted by one episode. Apparent authorial absence, an artful documentary objectivity, naturalistic dialogue, and a well-paced narrative drive make them models of a "moodless" *povest'* form designed as parables illustrating Tolstoyan doctrine. Inevitably an air of emotional sterility or clinical exactitude suggests withdrawal of sympathy, a literal defamiliarizing of the subject-matter, and, to that extent, a degree of alienation.

That all is traceable to Tolstoy himself and reflects his concerns can never be doubted. *The Death of Ivan Ilich* was his first major fictional work after the completion of *Anna Karenina*. It reflects something of the ambiguous love–hate relationship which had developed between his creative self, the Tolstoy who could never entirely suppress the urge to write fiction, and the moral, rational salvation-seeking self of Tolstoy, the religious thinker. It had a factual basis in the sense that it is supposed to have been based on the death of Ivan Ilich Mechnikov, former judge of the Tula Regional Court, in May 1881.[2] This led to the initial drafting of the story between late 1882 and November 1883. Simultaneously Tolstoy was completing his famous *Confession*, experiencing deep disagreements with his wife Sofya, who had become his publisher, and showing an initial interest in artistic theory.[3] His wife's need for the story, so that it could be included in volume XII of his collected works, made him complete it as a surprise for her birthday in March 1886. In it he sought to expose the falsehood that had dominated his own life and brought him close to suicide, as his *Confession* demonstrated, forcing him to confront that most awful of questions he had posed to himself: Is there any meaning in my life which would not be destroyed by my inevitably approaching death? (*A Confession*, ch. 5; *PSS* 23: 16–17).[4]

However rhetorically posed, the question infects the meaning of life in *The Death of Ivan Ilich*, as the story's structure illustrates. For it opens with the aftermath of Ivan Ilich's death when the meaning of his life is reduced to such mundane issues as the likelihood of promotion among his surviving colleagues, their unadmitted self-satisfaction at still being alive, and his widow's concern for her future in a financial sense. The distancing, even alienating description of the corpse and the funeral can be partly attributable to the viewpoint of his colleague, Petr Ivanovich, who is as unfamiliar with the protocol of such occasions as he is with the private life of the deceased. In a beautifully deadpan description of his meeting with Praskovia Fedorovna, the widow, after the funeral, he is led into the sitting-room and sits down on a pouffe with rickety springs about which his hostess had tried to warn him. She herself finds that the black lace of her mantilla becomes snagged on the carved edge of a table. He rises to help her, and the pouffe, freed of his weight, "bobbed up and bumped him," we are told.[5] She starts to unfasten her lace and he sits down again, but she fails to unfasten it and he again rises "and again the pouffe rebelled and popped up with a positive snap" (106; *PSS* 26: 65). She meanwhile takes out a cambric handkerchief and begins to weep. The pouffe, animated by the verbs, becomes an unintentionally funny and insolent witness to the solemnity of the occasion and the widow's tearful and horrified recounting of her husband's last hours. Ivan Ilich's whole story is designed to point up the self-deluding, self-aggrandizing pretentiousness of his life, which was, as the first sentence of chapter two makes clear, "the simplest, most ordinary and therefore most terrible" (109; *PSS* 26: 68) of stories. It is terrible partly because the simple, ordinary surface of his life – career, relationships, the things which fill it – seems to conceal a thinly disguised layer of satire, like the reactions of the rebellious pouffe.

Gradually this layer peels away to reveal the true horror beneath it, just as what reads initially like an extended obituary of the deceased's background at the beginning of chapter two becomes, as the story proceeds, an increasingly intimate and minutely recorded account of his dying.

The second of three sons of a privy councillor who had made a career for himself in government departments in St. Petersburg, Ivan Ilich died at the age of forty-five.[6] He had been *le phénix de la famille*, the "pride of the family," that is to say, conscientious as a student of the law, affable, lively, good-natured, and respectful of his superiors. He opened his career as a confidential clerk to a provincial governor, had several shameful, youthful flings, and advanced his career by becoming an examining magistrate in another province and then in another town. Here he met his future wife and married. He quickly realized she was a demanding, extravagant, and irascible woman and compensated for such domestic unhappiness by concentrating on his legal work. There were moments of mutual fondness between them, "islets" (*ostrovki*), as they are described, in a sea of secret hostility lasting seventeen years. By 1880, when his surviving elder daughter was already sixteen and his only son of high-school age, he reached a crisis point in his life. Apparently overlooked for promotion, he found himself at a loose end, took a holiday with his brother-in-law and resolved to improve his circumstances. By a lucky chance he suddenly found himself appointed to the position of judge in his old ministry, with a higher salary and better allowances. Temporarily reconciled with his wife, he set about arranging his new apartment in his new place of work and, in the course of instructing a workman, fell from a step ladder and injured himself.

The moment passes in the fiction with Ivan Ilich's ironically light-hearted admission to his wife that if he hadn't been something of a gymnast he might have been killed. The bruise on his left side is tender but apparently not serious. It makes him increasingly irritable and quarrelsome; and the detailed description of the material surroundings of his life underlines its pettiness while emphasizing the isolating, introspective process of his growing sickness. He consults a doctor and ironically receives the same lordly rebuttal of his concerns as he himself is accustomed to give to plaintiffs in his courtroom. All is consumed by sadness for him. Aware that his pain is increasing, that even his brother-in-law can see he is dying, as apparently his wife cannot, and more than ever skeptical of the doctors' pompous jargon about "appendicitis" (*slepaia kishka*) – Tolstoy's abhorrence of doctors was notorious – the wretched Ivan Ilich knows that the sickness is in his own life and ultimately undiagnosable in medical terms. Death haunts him like his pain; it becomes as nagging as a surrogate wife, accompanying him even to his legal work and reminding him through an album which he comes across in the sitting-room where the fall had occurred that his apparently orderly life is now done with and all he has to contemplate is "her," the feminine entity of his pain.

One single compensating relationship now offers solace. He is befriended by one of his servants, a healthy young peasant called Gerasim, whose robust acceptance of death helps the sick man to see beyond the deceit of pretending he is not dying. This friendship is most touching and profound, but it does little to diminish the air of deceit associated with the supposed benefits of his medicine or the doctors' attitudes or his wife's hypocrisy. Metaphorically, so the text insists, there may be droplets of hope for him but mostly it is a "raging sea of despair" (146; *PSS* 26: 100) and more and more pain. In a particularly heartless scene (at the end of chapter eight), his wife urges him to accompany her and their daughter, her boyfriend, and their son Vasia on a visit to the theatre to see Sarah Bernhardt.[7] Dressed for the occasion with powdered faces and bare shoulders, the ladies, especially his daughter, clearly find his illness little more than a constraint upon their own happiness and trivialize his pain with their showiness. Eventually they depart after an embarrassed silence. He is rid of their falsehood if not of his pain.

Though the reference to Sarah Bernhardt gives chronological veracity to the story, it is immediately succeeded in the fiction (ch. 9) by a deepening of the psychological portrayal of Ivan Ilich accompanied by an imagery of approaching death. He feels he is being thrust into a narrow black bag, an image as vivid and desolating as Tolstoy's dream at the end of his *Confession*. Tears of self-pity, tears of despair at the cruelty of others, at God's cruelty, and God's absence turn him toward recollections of childhood and what he supposed were the best moments of his pleasant life. What remain in retrospect are not true joys, merely the worthless, ephemeral delights of a life lived for money, duty, orderliness, whose meaning is as blank to him as the wall he stares at in his pain. He is afflicted by a duality of states of mind very similar to Anna Karenina's in her last days. In short, he is permitted none of the compensating assurances of faith which finally illumine Konstantin Levin's life.

Ivan Ilich's life has been wrong – "*ne to*" – and no priestly benediction, no opium, no medical advice can save him. Finally there are the last three days of his agony filled with unending cries of pain as he struggles against the invisible, insuperable force thrusting him ever farther down into the black bag. The tone of the narrative is steely and relentless; the imagery, while emphasizing death as claustrophobic and of course not suicidal, bizarrely recalls the death of Anna Karenina:

Suddenly some force smote him in the chest and side, making it still harder to breathe; he sank through the hole and there at the bottom was a light. It had happened to him as it sometimes happened to him in a railway carriage, when he had thought he was going forwards whereas he was actually going backwards, and all of a sudden became aware of his real direction.

(159; *PSS* 26: 223)

This insight initiates a moment of peripeteia and incipient redemption, never sufficient to halt the deathward course but giving a momentary sense of perspective, so that Ivan Ilich's death seems to him no longer fearful and becomes synonymous with light. His final spoken word is "joy!" and his final words to himself are "Death is over. It is no more" (161; *PSS* 26: 113). The selfishness of his pain has certainly been overcome, though Tolstoy's withdrawal of engagement makes ultimate judgment of Ivan Ilich as unreal and illusory as the sense of directional difference momentarily experienced through a train window. Tolstoy's objectivity both leaves the message latent and yet powerfully emphasizes the meaning of that question which he posed to himself in his *Confession* and evidently poses here in regard to the life, rather than the death, of Ivan Ilich.

Tolstoy endeavored to provide an answer in the immediately succeeding treatise *On Life* (1886–88).[8] The dualism of his thinking emerged clearly in the argument that humanity has two lives, spiritual and physical, of which the spiritual is the more important. The physical life is concerned with the well-being of the flesh and should yield to the priorities of the spiritual which, by contrast, are aimed to achieve the well-being of others. At its simplest – and when applied to Ivan Ilich's life – the message is that he lived his life for himself, largely for self-satisfaction, status, and career, and his death was a living hell, whereas his servant Gerasim, in alleviating his pain by allowing the sick man's legs to rest on his shoulders and ensuring some degree of well-being, exhibited a spiritual priority manifestly superior to the prevailing values and lifestyle of Ivan Ilich's world. That the legal milieu of his career is not described in any detail and has to be taken on trust merely sets in relief the extent to which Ivan Ilich's death can be seen as an object lesson in the poverty of a life lived without spiritual meaning.

"Remember," Tolstoy wrote at the end of his own life in *The Path of Life* (1910), "that you're not standing still, but moving, that you're not at home but on a train which is carrying you toward death" (*PSS* 45: 449).[9] Trains were instruments of fatality in Tolstoy's thinking. The fatalism surrounding Anna Karenina's destiny was manifest in the trains which both brought her into her fiction and finally destroyed her. Tolstoy's own death occurred at the wayside station of Astapovo. No work of his demonstrates more clearly than

The Kreutzer Sonata (1889) the fatalistic nature of that most "modern" of nineteenth-century phenomena, the anonymous, transient, enclosed world of the train.

The initial idea for *The Kreutzer Sonata* may date from as early as the late 1860s, between, that is to say, the conclusion of *War and Peace* and the beginning of *Anna Karenina*. It developed into the complex work we know today in approximately 1887, when the subject of wife-murder was given the context of Tolstoy's feelings on sexuality, music, and other issues of nineteenth-century life with which the story is infected. He is thought to have heard from the actor Andreev-Burlak during his visit to Iasnaia Poliana in June 1887 of a meeting with a man on a train who told of murdering his wife. If that provided the basic plot, then Tolstoy's concern with marriage, sexuality, and procreation at this time, heightened of course by poor relations with his wife, led to his writing an Afterword. As for the association with Beethoven's composition, a performance of the sonata in Tolstoy's Moscow home in the spring of 1888 served to reinforce for him a sense that music could be dangerously seductive. These and other issues were part of what appears to have been an obsession which consumed Tolstoy during the protracted composition of the story. That it finally appeared in 1891 in volume XIII of his collected works was due largely to his wife's efforts in persuading Tsar Alexander III to allow its publication after she had herself bowdlerized some elements in the text.[10]

The story is about an obsession told by an obsessive and is unusual in Tolstoy's *œuvre* for this reason. The train carriage, like the latter-day psychiatrist's couch, becomes the setting for a confession which, for Tolstoy at least, was emblematic of the pathology of the age. It was a pathology deriving from materialism, essentially escapist, unready to confront fixed norms of morality, and conditioned by that transience and lack of rootedness which characterized train travel. The story's underlying assumption is that such a state of irresponsibility would run entirely contrary to the strict injunction of the first epigraph: "But I say unto you, That whosoever looketh on a woman to lust after her hath committed adultery with her already in his heart" (Matthew, v, 28). It is an assumption emphasized, moreover, by the framing function of an observer–narrator whose anonymous and largely non-judgmental presence as a fellow traveler objectifies and sets in relief the dramatic central confession.

For all its accompanying sermonizing, the central confession is dramatic. *The Kreutzer Sonata* shows clear evidence of Tolstoy's preoccupation with the theatre – *The Power of Darkness* (1886) and *The Fruits of Enlightenment* (1890) enclose the story's composition – and the confined ambience of the train carriage has the feel of a stage set. The reader is introduced to three characters – a woman who smokes and has a worn, haggard face, her companion, a talkative man of about forty with brand new luggage, and a second man who is described in considerable detail. He is of small build, something of a loner, not old but with prematurely gray, curly hair and unusually bright eyes which match his abrupt movements in darting from object to object. Two things particularly distinguish him: his dress which, apart from an old, well-tailored overcoat with a lambskin collar and a tall lambskin hat, comprises a long *poddyovka*[11] jacket and embroidered Russian shirt, and his propensity for emitting strange sounds like a sort of throat-clearing or incipient laughter abruptly cut short.

The scene highlights the uniquely distinctive appearance and mannerism of the third traveling companion. He is Pozdnyshev, as yet anonymous, who contributes nothing to the ensuing conversation between an elderly merchant and estate manager and only becomes involved when the topic of divorce is raised by the woman's companion. The topic is discussed from several angles – the draconianly old-fashioned angle of the elderly merchant, the contemporary, liberal view of the woman's companion who turns out to be a lawyer, the woman's assertively emancipated attitude – and receives particular meaning over the question of love, which is defined as "the exclusive preference for one man or one woman above all others."[12] The anonymous gentleman's reaction is: "A preference lasting how long?" (33; *PSS* 27: 13) and this is the defining point. The fairytale "ever after" notion of love as such, whether marital or not, is ridiculed as largely the stuff of fiction. It is an argument sustained heatedly, to the dismay and shock of his audience, by a Pozdnyshev now self-confessed as the Pozdnyshev notorious for having killed his wife.

Pozdnyshev's confession can seem longwinded and wearisome in parts. The voice of Tolstoy resounds throughout and has a clear tone of special pleading to it. In personal terms, though, Pozdnyshev confesses to having been a womanizer and lecher incapable of achieving a normal relationship with a woman and particularly contemptuous of fictional romances for failing to tell the truth about sexual relations. There are no higher feelings, he insists; a man only wants a woman's body and she in turn endeavors to make herself physically attractive to him. The cynicism of such a view is elaborated into the absurdity of asserting that sex in marriage is a male-induced vice and the human race might very well come to an end since the true aims of humanity – welfare, virtue, love, universal brotherhood, the beating of swords into ploughshares – are always menaced by human passions, of which the strongest is carnal love. Pozdnyshev's own honeymoon proves a failure and precipitates not only marital conflict but a recognition of separate egoisms and disgust at love-making. Thus, his hatred of his wife, leading to a murderous jealousy, gestates over many years of marriage through his own enslavement to her physical allure, her consequent power over him and, with the arrival of children, her escape from the onus of breast-feeding on the advice of doctors. His jealousy is fueled by the arrival on the scene of the young musician Trukhachevskii to whom she obviously feels drawn. As a mature woman, sure of her sexuality, she realizes she has reached the point when she can enjoy love without child-bearing.

Pozdnyshev's description of this "rubbishy" young Trukhachevskii is vitriolic. With his moist almond eyes, smiling red lips, little greased mustache, hair shaped in the latest fashion, prominent buttocks (like a woman's or a Hottentot's), he is considered "not bad looking" (80; *PSS* 27: 49) in female eyes. More fully described than any other character, he becomes the catalyst for an obsessive jealousy now tinged with violence and a loathing especially of his demonstrably Parisian manner and dress, so opposed to the "Russian-ness" of Pozdnyshev in his *poddyovka* and Russian shirt. The drama of the confession is fueled by the increasing sense that violence is imminent, emanating, as it does, from thoughts of suicide and murder, of violent sundering of marital ties by flight to America, and exhibiting itself in such acts as throwing a paperweight or sweeping things off his desk in anger. Yet nowhere is the obsessive nature of Pozdnyshev's jealousy more obvious than in the power he ascribes to music, particularly to the first movement or "presto" of Beethoven's Kreutzer Sonata.

Music, in Pozdnyshev's judgment, is the most infectious of the arts. It is inherently obsessive. As he exclaims to his attentive listener (ch. 23) in describing his reaction to his wife's and Trukhachevskii's playing of the sonata: "Music makes me forget myself, my true condition, it carries me off into another state of being, one that isn't my own; under the influence of music I have the illusion of feeling things I don't really feel, of understanding things I don't understand, being able to do things I am not able to do" (96; *PSS* 27: 61). So strong is its obsessive, drug-like effect that music has been placed under government control in China, Pozdnyshev claims in obvious justification of his case. Yet Tolstoy has here pinpointed a flaw in human nature that poses as real a threat to morality and right conduct as the license implicit in train travel, with consequences as readily apparent in the twenty-first century as in the nineteenth. His argument presupposes that the influence of music, like that of drugs or female sexuality, is pathologically akin to an addictive compulsion or vice. In Pozdnyshev's case it incites his suspicions and his jealousy to the point of murderous rage.

In the belief that his wife's relationship with Trukhachevskii is over, he leaves for the provinces – his actual occupation, income, etc. hardly figure as items in his confession – where he receives a letter from his wife which arouses his worst suspicions. Returning home precipitately, he takes a train journey (within, of course, the train journey of his confession) and in the process redoubles his jealousy and doubts. Minutely described, the actions and thoughts accompanying his return home and confrontation with his wife constitute one of the most sustained and psychologically compelling passages in all Tolstoy's fiction. It climaxes in murder.

The act itself is a slow-motion event, described almost clinically, and the more awful for that reason. Pozdnyshev confesses to it as if he were delivering a short sermon on the art of murder, in acknowledgment of the fact that for him all existence is confined within the matrix of memory and this, the climax, is a culminating trauma. He describes cold-bloodedly how he thrust the dagger into his wife's left side, below the ribs, heard the blade momentarily encounter the resistance of the corset and then enter into the softness of her flesh. Her immediate seizure of the dagger without letting go and cutting herself in the process brought home to him the terrible realization that he was killing and had in fact killed a defenseless woman, his wife, and that – as he vaguely recalled afterward in prison – he made an instantaneous effort to withdraw the dagger in the hope of putting right what he had done and stopping it (ch. 27).

Confession can be said to be good for the soul, though one may reasonably doubt in Pozdnyshev's case whether it is ennobling, let alone capable of alleviating the torment of shame and contrition to which he is eternally condemned. The sight of his wife's corpse – "I realized that I'd killed her, that it was all my doing that from a warm, moving, living creature she'd been transformed into a cold, immobile waxen one, and that there was no way of setting this to rights, not ever, not anywhere, not by any means" (118; *PSS* 27: 77) – sets in stark relief his one final need of forgiveness. It is not exactly granted him at the story's end, for the narrator's farewell – *proshchaite* (Goodbye!) does not match the other's *prostite* (Forgive me!) (*PSS* 27: 78) – blurs the issue. The final irony for the compassionate reader is that Pozdnyshev has already received a form of forgiveness from a court of law, one supposes, in the shape of a comparatively lenient sentence.

No other work of fiction published by Tolstoy in the last twenty years of his life had quite the impact of *The Kreutzer Sonata*. In dealing with sexual issues so boldly and candidly, and in its low-key description of murder – however mitigated, if not justified, as a crime of passion – the story had the power to appall, but not exactly in the way Tolstoy seems to have anticipated. He therefore wrote an Afterword to explain his aims. With perfectly righteous but humorless logic he argued for sexual abstinence and fidelity in marriage while condemning contraception and the way contemporary society encouraged in the young both an overmastering sensuality and the pursuit of carnal love. The image of a compass based on Christian ideals of morality became the ultimate guide to right conduct in sexual matters for Tolstoy, despite the fact that his own conclusions horrified him. They were as horrifying as the diabolical temptations which faced Father Sergius in the eponymous story, never published in Tolstoy's lifetime but begun presumably shortly after the completion of *The Kreutzer Sonata* in the early 1890s, though not completed until 1898.[13]

Father Sergius chimes in with Tolstoy's major struggle at this period. He aspired to lead a spiritual life in conformity with his ideals while facing the physical temptations posed by his sexuality. He illustrated the issue in a barely disguised autobiographical long short story *The Devil* (1889). Although based on the case of a certain "Fridrikhs" who murdered a peasant girl, this work also reflects Tolstoy's own infatuation with the peasant girl Aksinia in the late 1850s. It also harks back – through the use of the hero's name, Irtenev – to the era of Tolstoy's earliest work, his autobiographical trilogy. As a study in sexual infatuation and its soul-destroying effect, it is a remarkably forceful description of Irtenev's attempts to overcome the temptation offered by the peasant girl Stepanida. Despite the solace of a loving wife and the promise of family happiness, he ends by committing suicide – or, in a variant ending, by killing Stepanida – and is thought in both cases to have acted inexplicably while the balance of his mind was disturbed.

Father Sergius explores the same issue but much more fully and at a much deeper psychological level. It opens at a period antedating the time of composition by almost half a century (relating to the beau monde world of *Two Hussars* [1856]). Such distancing does not make it a historical fiction; it gives it, rather, the perspective of a life mirroring Tolstoy's own, yet manifestly skewed to demonstrate the perils of a spiritual life from another angle. A degree of method-acting may be discerned in the particularly intimate portrayal of the hero's life – or the main incidents in it – without, however, any real loss of narratorial authority in Tolstoy's relation to his fiction. Prince Stepan Kasatskii, later known as Father Sergius, achieves a clearly focused reality, both as a person and as an emblem, in the succinct, latterday hagiography offered in this account of his life and good works.

The social meaning cannot be overlooked, nor the anti-Tsarist tone. Prince Kasatskii is depicted initially as very much a creature of the imperial court of Tsar Nicholas I. Privileged, ambitious, an adoring protégé of the emperor, he is a young officer for whom a successful military career is confidently predicted despite certain rebellious impulses in his character. Only when he discovers that his fiancée has been Nicholas I's mistress does he rebel so profoundly that he astonishes everyone by abandoning his career and becoming a monk.

His character flaw, like Tolstoy's after a fashion, is Kasatskii's determination to be perfect. He aspires to this in his life as a monk and after seven years is ordained into the priesthood and becomes known as Father Sergius. Still handsome, attractive to women and attracted by them, he is prey to a deep-seated and arrogant self-righteousness in his assessment of others. He recognizes that such pride constitutes a mockery of his spiritual aim, relinquishes all further worldly blandishments, and becomes a hermit renowned for his fasting and prayer.

The critical episode in his life begins as he approaches fifty (at much the same age as Tolstoy's crisis) when he unexpectedly finds himself assailed by the twin "enemies," as he calls them, of doubt and lust. So seductive does he find a society lady who invades his sanctuary on the pretext of drying her wet clothes that the sexual temptation becomes unbearable. It is one of those beautifully composed and profoundly startling *coups de théâtre* (ch. 5) at which Tolstoy is adept. The alternation of viewpoint between the seductress and Father Sergius achieves dramatic tension, even a degree of frisson as to his vulnerability, largely by use of dialogue and a telling descriptive emphasis on sounds and chiaroscuro. The shock comes with the hermit's deliberate self-mutilation by chopping off his finger. When she discovers what he has done in the face of her temptation she is driven by contrition into following his example and taking the veil.

For him contrition becomes more difficult. Reflecting no doubt Tolstoy's own dilemma as the cult figure he had become by the beginning of the 1890s, Father Sergius is prey to a certain vanity, beset as he is by pilgrims seeking miraculous cures. When tempted to the limit by a simple-minded merchant's daughter, he cannot resist his own sexuality, gives way to it, and is obliged to accept that his hermit's life is morally shallow. True contrition only becomes possible for him through the example of a girl from his boyhood – Pashenka, now already old and impoverished – who lives for God while imagining she lives for people. He is forced to acknowledge that, by contrast, he had lived for people on the pretext of living for God. Mendicancy and total commitment to others' needs in Siberian exile are his final purpose in life and they evidently project the unfulfilled spiritual ideal to which post-*Confession* Tolstoy might ultimately have aspired.

He did not aspire to fame, he insisted more than once, but, like his Father Sergius, he could not resist the temptation. In the case of *Master and Man* (1895) a masterpiece would have been lost had he not been tempted. "Writing, especially works of fiction, is frankly harmful to me morally," he confessed to his diary in March 1895, adding that "When I was writing *Master and Man* I succumbed to the desire for fame. And the praise and the success of it are a sure indication that it was a bad thing to do."[14] Posterity has not agreed. The short story, first conceived as a dream in September 1894, was written over the following winter and, after much re-working and quarrels with his wife over publishing rights, was published in two journals simultaneously in February 1895. Far removed from the urbanities of privilege and status of Ivan Ilich's, Pozdnyshev's or even Father Sergius's worlds, *Master and Man* springs directly out of the rural peasant environment of Tolstoy's own life and has distinct echoes of the ethos of his early *Polikushka* (1863) and his even earlier, masterly depiction of death in *Sevastopol in May* (1855).

Master and Man has been described as "the perfect type of Tolstoy's fiction."[15] It is, loosely speaking, a study in dying, like Ivan Ilich's, but illumined and clarified by deeper understanding of character and circumstance. The story occupies barely more than twelve hours in the lives of the master, Vasilii Andreich Brekhunov, and his man, Nikita. It is set in the 1870s. Just after the winter feast of St. Nicholas, on a snowy December day, Brekhunov hires Nikita to travel with him to a local landowner from whom he hopes to make a lucrative purchase. Delayed through having to participate at the feast day service, and having forced Nikita into working for half the normal pay, he sets out in a sleigh drawn by a trustworthy and intelligent horse. No sooner have they left their village than they discover that the snow storm is worse than they anticipated and they are plunged into a virtual white-out. Within a short time they have lost their way but luckily find a nearby village, leave it, return to it, set out again, and eventually become trapped by the violent storm near a gully. All Brekhunov's attempts to escape are futile and he finally returns to the sleigh, undoes his fur coat, lays down with his warm body pressed to Nikita's and falls asleep. Nikita survives the night, but his master and the horse are both frozen to death.

Brekhunov – the name implies mendacity and boasting – is a self-made, rich peasant. Tolstoy describes his thoughts, his aspirations, and his concerns with a penetrating accuracy and natural understanding. His object in life is to acquire wealth, but his specific aim in making this journey is to outsmart the town merchants who are after the same piece of property. His world is that of the peasantry, although governed in his case by such "modern" factors as time-keeping and cigarette-smoking. Brekhunov envisages himself as go-getting, on the move in life, as it were, through rather childishly enumerating his riches to himself and reveling in dreams of success. Yet his worldly ambitions are seen to be constantly frustrated by the futile circularity of his attempts to leave the village only to return to it or to leave the sleigh and Nikita in the storm and ride away only to be brought back to them. He may die much as Praskukhin died in *Sevastopol in May* by falling into everlasting unconsciousness, but he has an innocent earnestness which emerges most conspicuously in the final recognition that his warming of Nikita equates with and surmounts all his boastfulness. On the eve of death, in a finely written reprise of his life, he sees his vanity for what it is and knows he is free.

The meaning of the story is best understood through Nikita. A type of Karataev without the aphorisms, he is an amiable, unambitious peasant, henpecked by a wife engaged in a long-term affair and prone in the past to periodic bouts of drinking. Now strong-willed enough to abjure all alcohol, he has a sensible humility in the face of the inhuman violence of the storm, just as his life, for all its own storms, is lived in the present, not in future expectations like his master's. His readiness to accept things as they are is the core of the story's meaning, illustrative of the presence of the divine in life. The horse, Dappled Bay, Tolstoy's sensitive portrayal of an intelligent animal, becomes the innocent victim of Brekhunov's ambition and illustrates its dangers. Nikita, by contrast, lives within what appear to be intuitively divine limits that match and counterbalance such worldly ambition. Master and Man may not be exactly opposed to each other as satanic and divine but they brilliantly re-enact that moral balancing of character to character – Bolkonsky to Bezukhov, Anna Karenina to Konstantin Levin – so essential for an understanding of Tolstoy's greatest fiction.

Tolstoy's power to infect as a writer is demonstrated by his detailed description of the rural world, the exactitude of the dialogue, the range of thoughts and feelings evoked, and the sense of total involvement in a snowbound nature which defies all human endeavor. Out of this fierce maelstrom of wind and snow Tolstoy has created in *Master and Man* a work as near to perfection as one can imagine.

It is perfection, of course, only in a relative sense, for it highlights a major distinguishing feature of Tolstoy's approach. Other prominent exponents of the Russian long short story (or *povest'*) employed "mood" as essential to the genre. Turgenev's finest examples, bordering always on his style of novel though not identical with it, tend to be dominated by a narratorial mood of nostalgia involving regret for lost love and lost youth (e.g., *Asya* and *First Love*) and may be easily discerned as based in autobiography, no matter how great the effort of fictional concealment. There is very little method-acting principle at play in Turgenev's narratorial manner, whereas in Chekhov the narratorial mood depends often on a successful suspension of disbelief by the reader in Chekhov – the author – as a role-player. The mood of Nikolai Stepanovich in *A Dreary Story* or – in the most "Chekhovian" examples – the mood of N., the artist, in *The House with the Mezzanine*, and of Poloznev, the provincial, in *My Life*, permeate their respective stories as if, as narrator, Chekhov had method-acted himself into their lives, their personalities, their souls. Broad-brushed though such comparisons may be, they can help to identify not only, as in Chekhov's case, the anti-Tolstoyan message (particularly in *My Life*) but also the principal differences of approach to the genre of the long short story and, above all, in Tolstoy's case, the seeming abrogation of emotional engagement with the fictional central figure.

Master and Man, in its artful unpretentiousness and moral balance, illustrates the way such engagement can be objectified by a clarity of narratorial focus which simultaneously illuminates and infects. It is in consequence a monument to Tolstoy's objectivity and mastery of the genre of the long short story.

NOTES

1 The clearest concise definition of what Tolstoy considered the purpose of art is to be found in chapter five of *What is Art?* (1898) where art is said to be a human activity in which one man transmits to others feelings he has experienced so that others are infected by them.

2 N. N. Gusev, *Letopis' zhizni i tvorchestva L. N. Tolstogo 1828–90* (Moscow: Gosudarstvennoe izdatel'stvo khudozhestvennoi literatury, 1958), p. 538.

3 N. N. Gusev, *Tolstoi: materialy k biografii s 1881 po 1885 god* (Moscow: Izdatel'stvo "Nauka," 1970), pp. 140–41.

4 The reference is to the standard Russian Jubilee edition, identified as *PSS* and cited by volume and page number.

5 *Leo Tolstoy: The Death of Ivan Ilyich and Other Stories*, trans. Rosemary Edmonds (Harmondsworth: Penguin Classics, 1989, p. 106). References in the text to *The Death of Ivan Ilich* will be to pages in this edition, followed by the volume and page numbers in the Russian Jubilee edition. The translation does not adequately suggest the humanly animating quality of the verb forms used to describe the pouffe (e.g., in the first instance, *stal volnovat'sia* – "became agitated/excited"; and, in the second, *zabuntoval* – "started to rebel").

6 It has been presumed that he was born in 1837.

7 Sarah Bernhardt toured Russia in 1881–82. The son-in-law's reference to having seen her in *Adrienne Lecouvrer*, the role in the melodrama by Eugène Scribe for which Sarah Bernhardt was best known, reinforces the supposed topicality of the fiction.

8 *On Life* is a complex work accessible to various interpretations and emphases. Tolstoy's emphasis on reason as the basis of human individuality is implicit in the work, as Donna Orwin suggests in *Tolstoy's Art and Thought, 1847–1880* (Princeton, NJ: Princeton University Press, 1993), p. 194.

9 *The Path of Life*, after being banned in the Soviet Union, has only been republished extensively in Russia during the 1990s.

10 The final – ninth – authorized redaction of the text was not published until volume XXVII of the Jubilee Edition of Tolstoy's works appeared in 1936.

11 A particularly Russian form of tight-fitting jacket worn mostly by men.
12 Leo Tolstoy, *The Kreutzer Sonata and Other Stories*, trans. David McDuff (London and New York: Penguin Classics, 1986), p. 33; *PSS* 27: 13. Subsequent references in this chapter to *The Kreutzer Sonata* will be to this edition.
13 Judging by the dates appended at the end of the story, it was initially drafted over ten days in November 1889, but it was not published until 1911.
14 *Tolstoy's Diaries, Volume II 1895–1910*, ed. and trans. R. F. Christian (London: The Athlone Press, 1985), p. 402.
15 Richard F. Gustafson, *Leo Tolstoy: Resident and Stranger: A Study in Fiction and Theology* (Princeton, NJ: Princeton University Press, 1986), p. 197.

6

W. GARETH JONES

Tolstoy staged in Paris, Berlin, and London

Overshadowed by his great novels, Tolstoy's eight plays written from 1864 to 1910 have not won him a reputation as an outstanding dramatist. They are a motley collection, ranging from two farcical comedies, *An Infected Family* (1864) and *The Nihilist* (1866), that mocked the progressive intelligentsia of their time, to the two-act moral tract, *The Cause of it All* (1910), that railed against the evil of hard liquor and extolled the milk of human kindness. Two other, more substantial didactic dramas, *The Live Corpse* and *The Light Shines in the Darkness*, were worked upon in the 1900s but published only posthumously. The unpublished plays of the 1860s, however deficient their stagecraft, had anticipated a play that immediately won a place in the Russian repertoire. This was *The Fruits of Enlightenment* (1889) which, like *The Nihilist*, was designed as a romp to divert family and friends during long winter evenings on Tolstoy's country estate at Iasnaia Poliana. The play's barbs were aimed at Moscow high society, deluded by the fashion for parlor spiritualism, whose pretensions were pricked by the arrival from the provinces of a trio of peasants, desperate to buy land from their absentee landlord. Tolstoy's dramatic touch was now surer; he contrived a happy ending as the mischievous housemaid Tania tricked her master into signing over the land at a rigged spiritualist seance. After its domestic première at Iasnaia Poliana on December 30, 1889, *The Fruits of Enlightenment* was given a public performance in Tula and in 1891 it was produced in Moscow by the young Stanislavsky who was embarking on his career as a director.

Apart from their keenly observed portrayal of various strata of contemporary Russian society, these plays give no hint that Tolstoy could also have written one of the most influential dramas of nineteenth-century theatre. This was *The Power of Darkness*, written just three years before *The Fruits of Enlightenment*, yet utterly different in its conception and effect. Based on real events, it is the one play that bears the mark of Tolstoy's genius. He created a vivid gallery of primitive characters who, despite being in thrall to dark forces of sexual excess and violence, are endowed with a capacity for arousing feelings of sympathy and pity for the human condition. The main instigator of evil is Matryona, who has been compared with Lady Macbeth; however it is not the grandeur but the banality of her evil-doing that Tolstoy conveys. Matryona sees an opportunity for the advancement of her lecherous son Nikita who has an affair with Aksinia, the wife of his sickly master, and encourages Aksinia to poison her husband so that Nikita can make an advantageous match with her. Nikita then seduces Akulina, Aksinia's sixteen-year-old stepdaughter, and crushes to death the new-born baby that sprang from their union. In the final act, at Akulina's forcibly arranged marriage, Nikita, guilt-wracked and suicidal, confesses his sins before the assembled peasant community. Through the black amorality of the peasants' existence, the dim, guttering light of Nikita's conscience had not been totally extinguished. In his encounters with the drunken drop-out Mitrich some spirituality and true humanity were discernible. And the moral imperative in *The Power of Darkness* was expressed throughout the play by Akim, Nikita's father. Tolstoy, however, avoided the pitfall of turning him into a mouthpiece for Tolstoyan didacticism in his creation of an impressive but inarticulate man whose stumbling words could only grope at expressing his innate sense of moral righteousness and social justice. It is the accumulation of Akim's half-pronouncements and attempts to forestall evil-doing that builds up to the figure in the concluding scene of the forgiving father accepting Nikita's repentance and declaring God's pardon.

The play was written at a time when Tolstoy had renounced belles-lettres and had redirected his energies to propagating his ideas for moral reform. Consequently it was published in March 1887 by Intermediary Press (*Posrednik*), the publishing venture, inspired by Tolstoy and managed by his disciple Chertkov, that was dedicated to the spreading of suitable moral literature in cheap editions among the common people. By his energetic lobbying in high society, enraptured by Tolstoy's exposure of peasant life, Chertkov had managed to divert the attentions of the censorship. *The Power of Darkness* enjoyed immediate success and within a few months more than 100,000 copies had been printed in various editions. However, plans to stage the play were thwarted. Despite the approval of Tsar Alexander III who had been moved by a reading of the play on January 27, the furious intervention of Pobedonostev, Procurator of the Holy Synod, ensured that the tragedy would be banned. *The Power of Darkness* with its grim portrayal of the ugly primitivism of Russian peasant life that spawned violence, greed, and rampant sexual excess had to wait until 1895 for its first production in Russia.

Meanwhile, it had been suggested to André Antoine, whose experimental Théâtre-Libre had just been founded in Paris, that Tolstoy's play would be suitable material for his private club theatre devoted to an unorthodox repertoire and style of acting. An enthusiastic member of the Théâtre-Libre, Oscar Méténier, whose own literary forays dealt with the Parisian under-world, undertook to produce a French version in collaboration with Isaac Pavlovskii, a Russian émigré journalist. Antoine's intuition proved correct. The Théâtre-Libre's triumphant world première of *La Puissance des ténèbres* on February 10, 1888, proved to be a significant landmark for Antoine's pio-neering Théâtre-Libre and also for the French theatre in general.[1] Already Tolstoy's play was having an effect on the European theatre which its author could not have foreseen and certainly had not intended. In Paris it broke through the barrier of resistance that France had long maintained against foreign drama and opened the way for Antoine to pursue his policy of intro-ducing other contemporary Northern playwrights – Ibsen, Strindberg, and Hauptmann – to the hitherto inward-looking Parisian playgoers. What fas-cinated them was Antoine's apparent success in recreating a visual image of rural Russia with brutal realism on his stage. De Vogüé, then France's leading interpreter of Russian culture, enthused over the scenery and costumes that reflected everyday Russia without any taint of the comic-opera glitter that seemed inherent in the French theatre. Had it not been for the existence of the Théâtre-Libre, it is doubtful whether *The Power of Darkness*, adjudged by the French theatrical establishment to be utterly unsuitable to French taste, would have been produced in Paris. As the Duke of Meinigen had discov-ered when the Meinigen Company's first performance in Germany of Ibsen's *Ghosts* in 1886 was boycotted by the decent German citizenry, public taste in the Europe of the 1880s could be as rigorously opposed to harrowing naturalism as any state censorship.

In order to reform that cast of mind and circumvent the censorship, pro-gressive critics and writers in Berlin, inspired by the experience of Antoine's Théâtre-Libre, decided in 1889 to establish the Freie Bühne, whose occa-sional performances were limited to club members. In this way the Freie Bühne was able to avoid any prohibition on public performance. The Freie Bühne followed Antoine's example not only in the structure of a club thea-tre, but also by staging the banned *The Power of Darkness* as one of its first productions in January 1890, following Ibsen's *Ghosts* and Gerhart Hauptmann's *Before Sunrise*. As in Paris, the Freie Bühne's production of *The Power of Darkness*, alongside Ibsen and Hauptmann, helped to prove the dramatic qualities of Naturalist dramas known in print but deemed as unfit for staging by the theatrical establishment.

The Freie Bühne demonstrated not only Tolstoy's influence on the devel-opment of theatrical production but also on its repertoire. Hauptmann's *Before Sunrise*, as the young German writer readily admitted, owed much to the example of *The Power of Darkness*. Indeed, he went so far as to name

Tolstoy as "der große Pate," the "godfather" of his play. Members of the Freie Bühne, seeing the two productions side by side, would have recognized the similarities of their setting in provincial backwaters, their use of rural dialect (Hauptmann's exploitation of his native Silesian dialect echoed Tolstoy's reproduction of the speech of the peasants in his home district of Tula), their evocation of atmosphere, and, above all, their compassion for humanity.

The influence of the Freie Bühne's productions managed to change the attitude of the public to the new Naturalistic drama and led to a relaxation of the official censorship. News of the successful staging of *The Power of Darkness* in Paris and Berlin was immediately appreciated in Russia and undoubtedly the intellectual esteem won in the European capitals was a factor in persuading the Russian authorities by 1895 to relax their ban on Tolstoy's play. The influence of prestige was, of course, reciprocal. Tolstoy's own immense renown as writer and thinker had been harnessed by both the Théâtre-Libre and the Freie Bühne to strengthen their claims for recognition for the new theatre of naturalism.

Their insistence on stage realism in their productions of *The Power of Darkness* was repeated by the Russian theatre. When the Moscow Maly Theatre staged the play in November 1895 its designer and director were sent to Iasnaia Poliana to seek the author's advice. Tolstoy decreed that the decor should be ethnographically accurate in its depiction of a Tula district setting and his daughters helped to select examples of local peasant dress and domestic utensils to ensure authenticity. Stanislavsky went even further in his efforts to create a genuine peasant village on stage for the Moscow Art Theatre's 1902 production of the play. Not only did he and his designers spend a fortnight in the Tula district studying local buildings, customs, and rituals and collecting "costumes, shirts, sheepskin jackets, crockery and domestic utensils," but he brought back with him to Moscow an elderly couple to serve as living exemplars of peasant reality. Stanislavsky was even tempted to have the old lady play the part of Matryona. The disruptive effect of this ultra-realism on the rest of the cast in rehearsal, however, compelled him in the end to reduce her participation to a gramophone recording of her singing a folk song. Later, Stanislavsky admitted in his autobiography that the play had suffered from this excessive zeal for authenticity, "naked realism." The spiritual darkness at the heart of the play had not been expressed: "ethnography had stifled the actor and the drama itself."[2]

Initially proscribed, then misinterpreted in its homeland, *The Power of Darkness* and Tolstoy's dramatic sense continued to exert their influence abroad despite entrenched resistance. The severest proving ground in the twentieth century was the London stage. Hidebound by strict censorship and dominated by the commercial demands of an actor–manager system catering for a mass, pleasure-seeking audience, the London stage at the turn of the century remained immune to innovation. Tolstoy's drama, supported by the example of his continental promoters, was employed to loosen the censor's grip. Through adaptations and insightful versions, the Tolstoyan drama, without every being wholly assimilated, made its mark on London's theatrical experience.

With *The Power of Darkness* already well established in the Russian repertoire, Tolstoy was still an outcast from the London stage. Even at the time when the play was premièred in Paris, the censorship regime for the English stage had indeed become more rigorous. William Archer, translator and promoter of Ibsen, identified 1885 as the watershed year when censorship, hitherto mainly concerned with the propriety of political and biblical references and *risqué* adaptations from the French, was tightened in response to the increasing compulsion by playwrights to tackle social and moral problems.[3] When writing his obituary of E. F. Smyth Pigott, the "Late Censor," on March 2, 1895, Bernard Shaw used the opportunity to attack the principle of censorship. In adducing actual examples of plays stifled by the prospect of censorship, he asked the rhetorical question "Is Tolstoi's *Dominion of Darkness* likely to be produced here as it has been elsewhere?" Tolstoy was the exemplary modern dramatist ranked alongside Shakespeare and the great Greek dramatists who would not "have stood a chance with Mr Pigott."[4] One of Tolstoy's contributions to the London stage would be to represent those modern playwrights for whom the stage was a natural forum for moral and social discussion. Tolstoy's prestige as a great writer was harnessed, as it had been in Paris and Berlin, to the cause of freeing the theatre and breaking down the resistance of the official censors to such innovation.

One of the censor's justifications for his severity was that he was reflecting the conservative nature of public opinion and the general taste of playgoers.[5] There is some truth in his assertion. Even those intent on promoting avant-garde theatre were prepared, as will be seen, with the eventual London première of *The Power of Darkness*, to justify the censorship as a shield for uneducated and mixed-sex audiences.[6] The conventional West End audience was not minded to accept Tolstoy's dramas. It was only prepared to receive Tolstoy on its own terms, a Tolstoy sufficiently sanitized and neutralized to accommodate the average taste of London's playgoers.

An understanding of that taste ensured the success of a dramatized version of Tolstoy's novel *Resurrection* that ran for ninety-three performances at His Majesty's Theatre in the Spring of 1903.[7] His Majesty's, acknowledged as the handsomest theatre in London, was the creation of the greatest actor–manager of the day, Herbert Beerbohm Tree. Its vast flat stage was designed for lavish productions displaying exotic scenes for the delectation of the Edwardian audience. It was the exoticism of distant Russia that enthralled the audience for Tolstoy's *Resurrection*, a French dramatization by Henri Bataille translated into English by Michael Morton. Tree himself played the part of Nekhliudov and the betrayed peasant girl Katusha was portrayed by Lena Ashwell in two aspects. As Tree's biographer remarks, "Contemporary photographs give the two aspects of her portrayal: 'Innocence' (long braids and much peasant embroidery) and 'Corruption' (overcoat made from a blanket, headscarf and decadent cigarette hanging from the mouth)."[8] But it was the opportunity to present rich scenes with vivid costumes and pageantry that Tree seized upon and which struck the *Times* reviewer of the play (February 18, 1903: 10). "As drama," wrote the reviewer, "it lacks concentration and cumulative interest. Indeed it is rather epical than dramatic; epical in its straggling arrangements, in its time-scheme, in its chance medley of episodic personages, in its constantly changing crowds of minor people." But the audience was enraptured by the nineteenth-century Russian background which included a Moscow palace resembling a Grand Hotel of the period, singing peasants, the celebration of two "osculatory Easters" and contrasting Siberian scenes of prisons. In the view of the *Athenaeum* (February 21, 1903: 251–2) "the Easter environment furnishes much dignity to the work, and compensates for the distastefulness of some of the scenes of prison life." Memorable was a final scene where the lovers parted forever against a background lit with camp fires flickering across the snow under a canopy of golden stars. Most of the applause, noted the *Times* reviewer, was reserved for the earlier scenes with their exotic pageantry and the first Act was described in laconic and sardonic terms. "In Act I, the gallant and gorgeous Prince Dmitrii Nehludov (Mr Tree) seduces the timid little handmaiden Katusha (Miss Lena Ashwell). Preliminary hymn by Russian choir. Object lesson in Muscovite folk-lore: offering of bread and salt and exchange of Easter kisses. Everybody says 'Christ is risen' – first note of Tolstoyism."

By 1903, of course, Tolstoyism had made a profound mark on the consciousness of the English intelligentsia and Beerbohm Tree introduced it in theatrical terms. Impressed by the jury scene in *Resurrection*, the *Times* reviewer drew particular attention to the "stone-deaf juryman ... who keeps on repeating the Tolstoyan ground bass 'We are none of us immaculate; we should always forgive'." He noted that Tree had this stone-deaf juryman made up like Tolstoy himself – Tolstoy's self-dramatization of himself with patriarchal beard, peasant smock, and boots had long imprinted itself on the public mind – so that the person of Tolstoy seemed to be introduced into the dramatic action. The way that its stage version raised the novel's moral questions was found to be "deeply impressive" but the problem was that morality tended to engender second-best dramas, a tendency which in the reviewer's view was confirmed by the production of *Resurrection*. The *Illustrated London News* (February 21, 1903: 260) also regretted that the realistic novel, transformed into a romantic drama, had preserved "the very weakness of the original which is excessive didacticism." However, it concluded that "to Mr. Tree all the credit is due for the superb mounting, the pleasant musical interludes, and the thoughtful stage-management of a profoundly interesting play."

The serious, didactic strand in the adaptation of *Resurrection* was clearly exceptional enough on a London stage, devoted primarily to entertainment, to have led all its reviewers to draw particular attention to it. The *Athenaeum* was alone, however, in explaining that Tree's production of *Resurrection* belonged "to an advanced school of thought, which strikes the topmost note of social and ethical revolt" because it had benefited from the experience of Antoine's Théâtre-Libre and similar institutions in Europe. This English version of Henri Bataille's *Résurrection*, it explained, had come to London from the Odéon, "one of the great subsidized theatres of Paris." The production, therefore, should not be belittled as a travesty of Tolstoy's work to provide simply an exotic entertainment for His Majesty's. The actor–manager who had put on this play was the man of catholic interests who had not flinched from testing the public with Ibsen's *An Enemy of the People* in 1893. For those efforts to educate the taste of a conservative public Tree was praised by Bernard Shaw, who recognized "his repeated and honourable attempts to cater for people with some brains."[9] His *Resurrection* might be considered as another such honorable attempt.

To fully appreciate Tolstoy's original plays, a different sort of public was required, the kind of audiences formed by Antoine's Théâtre-Libre and Otto Brahm's Freie Bühne. In London, too, but only after a gap of sixteen years, it was a similar experimental company, the Stage Society, that first produced *The Power of Darkness*, limited to three performances at the Royalty Theatre in 1904. Its progenitor was the Independent Theatre founded in 1891 by J. T. Grein on the model of Théâtre-Libre.[10] Its small core of members, called the "Impossibilists" by Shaw, struggled on until 1897 when the Independent Theatre closed to be replaced in 1899 by the Stage Society, again dedicated to the production of new plays that were banned from public performance or not commercially viable. Its founders were Fabians convinced that the theatre could be a potent force for social change, and the Society's choice of plays in its opening years were mainly examples of social realism such as Ibsen's *The League of Youth* and Hauptmann's *The Coming of Peace*.[11]

The Stage Society's *The Power of Darkness* drew a mockingly patronizing review from the *Times* in December 1904 which imagined Voltaire's Candide being present at the performance and being particularly puzzled by the nature of the audience disposed to welcome such an outlandish play. Candide, it was suggested, in observing how London's "intellectuals" enjoyed themselves, might have been reminded of a certain *auto-da-fé* in Lisbon. "On one side of the footlights rows of thoughtful-looking gentlemen, mingled with what Mr Collins would have called 'elegant females.' On the other side a mimic representation of Russian village life – a hideous medley of swinish drunkenness and satyr-like lust and fiendish crime." So disgusting did the reviewer find the play that he felt that he should have gone into quarantine to purge himself and he imagined Pangloss explaining to Candide that

> Tolstoy is a very great man, not merely an artist of the first rank, but an important social force; that underneath the squalid horror of the play of Tolstoy's there is a profound moral lesson; and that it is the business of stage societies, with their picked audiences and their closed doors, to produce, now and then, just such plays as this one. (*Times*, December 21, 1904: 13)

The *Athenaeum* (December 24, 1904: 885–86) agreed with the *Times* that *The Power of Darkness* could only be performed in front of "a limited public in what may be regarded as a surreptitious form" despite the fact that the work was judged to be "of splendid genius and Titanic power, dramatic in the highest sense, putting to shame the accomplishment of so-called realists, and supplying in place of their prurient imaginings a large-hearted charity and a sincere desire to elevate humanity." Nevertheless a sophisticated London journal at the beginning of the twentieth century saw no incongruity in denying access to such work to the general public. The *Athenaeum* even made the extraordinary declaration that "If ever, indeed, there was a piece the stage presentment of which the Censure is justified in retarding, it is this." The truth of the relentless exposure of the rude coarseness of peasant life in Russia could be appreciated by the *élite* Stage Society audience; "before a general public, however," warned the journal, "it is as impossible as a clinical or anatomical lecture before a mixed audience of both sexes." Yet this was a play whose pictures of degraded humanity were "God-like in underlying tenderness. Shakespeare alone comes near them in magnanimity and tolerance as in fidelity."

The London stage was ruled not only by conventions of conservative propriety but also by expectations of entertaining frivolity. The general theatrical context in which the Stage Society operated was illuminated by *The Sketch's* (December 25, 1904: 378) account of *The Power of Darkness* which was yoked with a review of a typical West End society romance, *Lady Madcap*. So Tolstoy's "grim, fierce drama, hideous at times" was seen in the contrasting light of an Edwardian "pretty entertainment with gorgeous scenery, lovely dresses and galaxies of beauty aided by luscious music." The slickness of commercial productions also could not be matched by the Stage Society. The première of *The Power of Darkness* was a technical catastrophe. The leading actress fell ill during the performance and had to be replaced by an understudy who read her part. The play dragged on almost to midnight as a result, and what should have been the drama's thrilling moments "had little of their real force" according to *The Sketch*. Nevertheless, the magazine echoed the positive responses of the other critics, concluding that "despite the depressing effect of the earlier passages and somewhat brutal horror in the middle, the drama appears clearly to have a greatness that renders it deeply, strangely, and painfully interesting, and by giving it the Incorporated Stage Society has rendered another valuable service to drama." It concurred, therefore, with the *Athenaeum* which had concluded its review, however, with the rueful, "It is an experience not likely to be repeated."

The *Athenaeum* was correct in its prophecy. Even among stage societies Tolstoy's plays did not flourish.[12] *The Cause of it All* had one performance at the Court on March 28, 1912 (reviewed by *The Stage* on May 2, 1912: 16), and *The Man Who Was Dead* (*The Living Corpse*) had one matinée performance at the Court on December 6, 1912, under the direction of A. Andreev of the Theatre Royal, Belgrade. Again it was the exoticism of Russia that appealed to the *Times* reviewer (December 7, 1912: 18). The gypsy scenes and singing were full of local color and the legal proceedings were deemed to throw some light on the intricacies of the Russian legal system. Equally exotic to him was the prominence given to "Tolstoy's curious views of love and purity."

But even this well-disposed reviewer, who commented approvingly on "passages of profound insight and imaginative beauty," could not come to terms with Tolstoy's apparent disregard for the conventions of a well-made play. To English playgoers "the frank childishness of Tolstoy's machinery must seem almost comically simple." The multitude of characters was puzzling and this feature, which was a strength of his novels, rendered his plays undramatic "if drama is judged by the canons of Western Europe." The bench-marks of the well-made play were to dog critical comment on Tolstoy's plays.

Tolstoy's plays which were staged in this way in drama societies were not sufficiently influential to have ensured their transfer to the main theatres as had happened in Paris after the première of *The Power of Darkness* at the Théâtre-Libre. But much more important was the influence exerted by the play on a main provider of plays for the Stage Society, namely George Bernard Shaw.

One of Shaw's earliest plays, the one-act *The Shewing-Up of Blanco Posnet: A Sermon in Crude Melodrama*, was deliberately modeled on *The Power of Darkness*. Consequently he sent a copy to Tolstoy with a letter on February 14, 1910, stating that he had exploited the "mine of dramatic material which you were the first to open up to modern playwrights."[13] One of the features *Blanco Posnet* shared with Tolstoy's drama was the dismissal of the proprieties of polite theatre. "In form it is a very crude melodrama," wrote Shaw "which might be played in a mining camp to the roughest audience." In describing his play in this way Shaw was deliberately aligning himself with Tolstoy, who had envisaged his own play as being composed for a popular audience. Tolstoy for his part refused to accept that there was any genetic link between his play and *Blanco Posnet*. Yet the many similarities of plot and setting are evident.[14] What has obscured the kinship between the plays is the difference in the religious attitude of the two authors. Shaw disagreed with the outlook of Akim who, in Tolstoy's eyes, was the hero of his play. For Shaw, Akim is a mouthpiece of a rotten religious establishment incapable of creating a good morality. In his *Blanco Posnet*, the Akim character is recast as the despicable Elder Daniels.

Another fate that Shaw was to share with Tolstoy was the opprobrium of the censors. *The Shewing-Up of Blanco Posnet* was planned to open in May in London, but even this reflection of Tolstoy's influence did not appear on the London stage since it was refused a license.[15] Since there was no official censor for the Irish theatre, *The Shewing-Up of Blanco Posnet* would appear in Dublin's Abbey Theatre in August. Even in Dublin the Lord Lieutenant's attempts to put pressure on Lady Augusta Gregory to withdraw the play led to a furious controversy that helped to kindle international interest in the première.[16]

In its review of the occasion *The Freeman's Journal* was struck by features in Shaw's play that illustrate its debt to *The Power of Darkness*. This was a play "based on the workings of conscience in a man of rough life" in which "the language is rough and strong." The Censor might have been shocked with the irreverent tone of Posnet's attitude to God but "as heard from the rough-looking fellow on the stage, and in the uncouth surroundings of the semi-civilised village, they do not shock the ear ... The atmosphere is true; there is not the slightest incongruity either in speech or demeanour, and roughness has seldom been presented with a greater reticence. Posnet points the moral with queer, quaint eloquence."[17]

Shaw and Tolstoy became yoked in theatre critics' minds as moralists. When the question of censorship flared up again in 1912 with the appointment of Charles Brookfield, an adaptor of risqué French bedroom farces which exploited sexual innuendo, whose obnoxious farce *Dear Old Charlie* had been revived, H. W. Massingham complained bitterly in the *Nation* (March 9, 1912) that the work of sincere moralists like Shaw and Tolstoy "is turned off the English stage by the author of the worst piece now being played in London."[18]

If Tolstoy's spirit as a stage moralist had spoken through Shaw's reworking of his *Power of Darkness* in *The Shewing-Up of Blanco Posnet*, that spirit spoke again on the London stage after the First World War in Shaw's *Heartbreak House* which was subtitled "a fantasia in the Russian manner on English themes." In his preface to that play he once again acknowledged his debt to Tolstoy:

> *Heartbreak House* is not merely the name of the play which follows this preface. It is cultured, leisured Europe before the war. When the play was begun not a shot had been fired; . . . Tolstoy, in his *Fruits of Enlightenment*, had shewn us through it in his most ferociously contemptuous manner. Tolstoy did not waste any sympathy on it: it was to him the house in which Europe was stifling its soul; and he knew that our utter enervation and futilization in that overheated drawing-room atmosphere was delivering the world over to the control of ignorant and soulless cunning and energy, with the frightful consequences which have now overtaken it. Tolstoy was no pessimist: he was not disposed to leave the house standing if he could bring it down about the ears of its pretty and amiable voluptuaries; and he wielded the pickaxe with a will. He treated the case of the inmates as one of opium poisoning, to be dealt with by seizing the patients roughly and exercising them violently until they were broad awake.[19]

By 1919, the year when *Heartbreak House* was written, the pioneering work of the new theatre had changed the expectations of playgoers whose own mental outlook had been transformed by the Great War. A translation of *Zhivoi trup* (*The Living Corpse*) which had merited only one matinée performance in 1912 under the teasing title of *The Man Who Was Dead,* now had a run of 114 performances at the St. James's Theatre from September 26, 1919, to January 3, 1920, under the decidedly more austere title of *Reparation.* Never again was a Tolstoy play to enjoy such a long run.[20] The influence of the new European drama was evident in the scenery for the production, which *The Sketch* (November 12, 1919: 230) reviewer noticed were "from the designs that were used in the Art Theatre, Moscow." However, it was not the exotic décor but Tolstoy's moralistic outlook that was now judged to be the essence of the drama, *The Sketch* concluding that "Tolstoy so dominates any Tolstoyan performance that one cannot get away from him, and while one is with him all others seems worthless." Casting around for a central theme for the play, the *Times* (September 27, 1919: 3) reviewer suggested that it was the Tolstoyan view of "the soul of goodness in things evil and the stupidity of human institutions, laws, Courts of Justice, and the like in not leaving it alone."

If these two reviewers concurred on the powerful intellectual interest of the drama, they also agreed on its deficiencies as a play. Both pointed a finger at the fragmentary looseness of *Reparation*, a play that engaged the mind despite "its faults of construction and queernesses" and despite its overt preaching against all officialdom, the odd attitude to sex, and apparent sympathy for fecklessness. The *Sketch* reviewer had to admit rather ruefully that the denouement in which Fedia, the "living corpse" who has feigned suicide to free his legal wife, shoots himself to free her again, is limp. "The spell of the master weakened a little in that final tableau...and one remembered that besides knowing everything about men he was also a man."

Tolstoy's stature as a great writer remained undimmed. A leading article in the *Times Literary Supplement* on September 6, 1928, was ostensibly prompted by two volumes in Aylmer Maude's 21-volume Centenary Edition: volume XIII, *Twenty-three Tales*, and volume XVII, *Plays*. Yet it is remarkable that there is no mention of Tolstoy as a playwright; the only allusion to the volume under review was Granville-Barker's reference in his introduction to Tolstoy's commitment to truth. The *TLS's* readers had to wait until January 10, 1929, for a considered view of Tolstoy's plays.

In the meantime, on the occasion of Tolstoy's centenary, the Tolstoy Society had sponsored performances of *The Power of Darkness* and *The Fruits of Enlightenment* at the Arts Theatre Club in November. The former play was not well received since its production was considered to be weak, but the comedy, which was being mounted for the first time on a London stage, surprised the *Times's* critic who, prompted by Shaw's reading of the play as a vitriolic satire on pre-war European society, was agreeably surprised by its humor. This *Fruits of Enlightenment* proved to be no *Heartbreak House*, but a rib-tickling romp.

Despite the recognition of Tolstoy as a humorist, a half-century passed before *The Fruits of Enlightenment* graced a London stage again. However, despite all the endeavors of the National Theatre, which put all its resources into a production at the Olivier in March 1979, the play failed to find a response from its élite audience. The *Sunday Telegraph* recorded that the play "elicits only occasional laughter from the audience" while the critic of the *Daily Telegraph* "could even sympathise with the playgoer who gave it an unmistakable boo." Since then, even the National Theatre has fought shy of Tolstoy's plays and it is the tiny Orange Tree pub theater on the fringe of the London stage that has managed to revive *The Power of Darkness* to critical acclaim. Giles Gordon in the *Spectator* (March 17, 1984) found it astonishing that the play could not be presented at one of the smaller auditoria of the National Theatre, particularly since the National was in the Spring of 1984 putting on Mark Rozovsky's fashionable international success *Strider, the Story of a Horse*, "a sliver culled from a Tolstoy short story." Compared with that theatrical entertainment "*The Power of Darkness* rends the air with greatness." Michael Billington in the *Guardian* (March 6, 1984) considered that "it dwarfs any other play currently to be seen in London" while Martin Hoyle in the *Financial Times* (March 5, 1984) declared that "Tolstoy's best-known play boasts at least two scenes as spine-tinglingly tense as any in European drama in the past century." If the modern audience had been unmoved by *The Fruits of Enlightenment* in 1979, it responded keenly to *The Power of Darkness* in 1984. "For all its dramatic crudity and fundamentalist morality, this drama holds a modern-day audience as spellbound as any mystery play," noted Donald Rayfield in the *Times Literary Supplement* (April 25, 1984: 19).

In view of these positive responses, the question arises as to why Tolstoy's plays have so rarely appeared on the London stage. Rayfield's rueful acknowledgements of Tolstoy's characteristics, his "dramatic crudity" and "fundamentalist morality," have certainly been an obstacle to his acceptance by the mainstream commercial theatre. This had been the main burden of the long review of the Centenary Edition *Plays* that appeared in the *Times Literary Supplement* in 1929. The reviewer took issue with Granville-Barker's criticism of *The Light Shines in the Darkness* for its failure to fashion characters who could "get hold" of their creator and so "get hold of us," their audience. Granville-Barker's fault was that his standard of judgment, that of the contemporary "man of the theatre," was false: "criticism of Tolstoy cannot rest on a contemporary theatrical basis; every attempt to make it do so ends in disaster to the critic." Issue was also taken with those critics who patronizingly suggested that Tolstoy's drama was hampered by his moral preaching. The trouble was that the London theatre, with its "innocuous farces, crime plays and 'thrillers', which seem to have their scene in an ingenious vacuum of the spirit and to have no moral connexions at all," was barren and "an outcast from the thought of intelligent men." Yet it had to be conceded that the dramas were not always well enough made: "it may sometimes be true that they falter because his morality has been imperfectly translated into dramatic terms."

The other crucial obstacle to staging Tolstoy has been the problem of finding an authentic translation of the speech of his peasant characters. The one awkwardness of Antoine's first production had been that Tula peasants incongruously mouthed the slang of the Parisian underworld. The best that an English translator can do is to transmute Russian peasants into English rural folk who then must be endowed with an accent which inevitably fixes them to a specific region. This problem was avoided in the Orange Tree Theatre's *The Power of Darkness* by letting the actors choose their accent at will so that Matryona spoke with a Scottish accent and her stepdaughter Akulina spoke in an East London accent. The problem faced by any translator is well reflected in Michael Frayn's concluding sentence to his "A Note on Translation" for *The Fruits of Enlightenment*: "If I have managed to find a workable convention for the peasant's dialogue, I shall be forgiven in heaven for all this and more."[21] As has already been seen, the London playgoers and critics were not so forgiving. "Peasants are just *not* good box-office" was Richard Freeborn's regretful conclusion to his discussion of the production.[22] One radical way of resolving the intractable problem of transferring Tolstoy's portrayal of peasant life and peasant speech to the English theatre is by a thoroughgoing transplantation in adaptation. This is what Bernard Shaw attempted to do in setting his version of *The Power of Darkness* in the American mining-camp of *The Shewing-Up of Blanco Posnet*, although American critics were not impressed with his control of American English![23] A more recent imaginative reworking was *This Jockey Drives Late Nights* by Henry Livings, a play set in a contemporary taxi firm.[24]

In view of these impediments and the rarity of productions of his plays, is it possible to claim that Tolstoy has made any distinctive contribution to the London stage? It could not be claimed that Tolstoy, as a playwright, played a leading role in the reformation of the London stage as had Ibsen or Shaw with their dramas of social commitment, or as Chekhov did later with his dramatic statements of the human condition. He did not provide a critical turning point, as had his *The Power of Darkness* through the agency of Antoine's Théâtre-Libre, in the history of the new French theatre. Nevertheless, his influence was pervasive and profound. As we have seen, the *Athenaeum*, even through the medium of *Resurrection* in 1903, recognized how Tolstoy's influence was being mediated through the Théâtre-Libre and the French subsidized theatre, and was providing "one of the most stimulating and intellectual of modern dramas." Bernard Shaw in promoting his own plays of social commitment undoubtedly benefitted from the opportunity of being able to point to the presence of such a prestigious writer as Tolstoy in the same camp. That Tolstoy had played a significant role in the reformation of the twentieth-century stage was certainly evident in 1929 to the *Times Literary Supplement*, which argued that the interest taken by such as Granville-Barker and Shaw in his work was an indicator of "the dramatic counter-revolution which he strove to initiate." Neither of those distinguished reformers of the theatre, however, "has fully realised how complete was Tolstoy's aesthetic counter-revolution. They persist in thinking of him in terms of their own theatre." How should one think of him? The Tolstoyan counter-revolution of which the *TLS* spoke was a freeing of drama from the constricting walls of the conventional theatre and a return to the religious and philosophical dramas of the past. If that is recognized, then such plays can still, as did *The Power of Darkness* briefly at the Orange Tree, hold a modern-day audience "as spellbound as any mystery play."

NOTES

1 Neil Carruthers, "The Paris Première of Tolstoy's *Vlast' t'my (The Power of Darkness)*," *New Zealand Slavonic Journal* (1987), 81–92.

2 K. S. Stanislavskii, *Moia zhizn' v iskusstve* (Moscow: Iskusstvo, 1962), p. 318.

3 See John Russell Stephens, *The Profession of the Playwright: British Theatre 1800–1900* (Cambridge University Press, 1992), p. 181.

4 *Our Theatres in the Nineties by Bernard Shaw*, 3 vols. (London: Constable, 1932), vol. I, p. 52.

5 Stephens, *The Profession of the Playwright*, p. 182.

6 See the discussion of the 1907 censorship of Granville Barker's *Waste* in Dennis Kennedy, *Granville Barker and the Dream of Theater* (Cambridge University Press, 1985), pp. 92–93.

7 A simultaneous première of *Resurrection* was given in New York's Victoria Theatre where reviewers doubted whether such a gloomy drama, plainly produced, could prove attractive to playgoers. In the event, it ran for eleven weeks. See Gerald Bordman, *American Theatre: A Chronicle of Comedy and Drama, 1869–1914* (New York and Oxford: Oxford University Press, 1994), p. 509.

8 Madeleine Bingham, *"The Great Lover": The Life and Art of Herbert Beerbohm Tree* (London: Hamish Hamilton, 1978), p. 130.

9 Quoted in *ibid.*, p. 76.

10 Kennedy, *Granville Barker*, p. 1.

11 *Ibid.*, p. 9.

12 The experimental Theater Guild of New York discovered that American audiences were as unresponsive as London's when its attempt to produce *The Power of Darkness* in 1920 nearly bankrupted the company. See Bordman, *American Theater*, p. 121.

13 Dan H. Laurence, *Bernard Shaw: Collected Letters*, 4 vols. (London: Max Reinhardt, 1965–88), vol. II, p. 900.

14 David Matual, "Shaw's *The Shewing-Up of Blanco Posnet* and Tolstoy's *The Power of Darkness*: Dramatic Kinship and Theological Opposition," *The Shaw Review*, vol. 1 (1981), 129–39.

15 Robert Hogan and James Kilroy, "The Abbey Theatre: The Years of Synge 1905–1909," in Robert Hogan (ed.), *The Modern Irish Drama: A Documentary History*, 6 vols. (Dublin: Dolmen Press, 1978), vol. III, p. 286.

16 *Ibid.*, p. 293.

17 Quoted in *ibid.*, p. 299

18 Kennedy, *Granville Barker*, p. 94.

19 Bernard Shaw, *The Complete Prefaces of Bernard Shaw* (London: Paul Hamlyn, 1965), p. 378.

20 Under the title of *Redemption* with John Barrymore in the main role, Tolstoy's play had run for six months in New York from October 1918 although initially it had struggled to find an audience at the Plymouth Theatre. See Bordman, *American Theatre*, p. 88.
21 Lev Tolstoy, *The Fruits of Enlightenment*, trans. Michael Frayn (London: Eyre Methuen, 1979), p. xviii.
22 Richard Freeborn, "Tolstoy's 'Upstairs, Downstairs': Some Thoughts on His Comedy *The Fruits of Enlightenment*," *Journal of Russian Studies* 40 (1980), 21.
23 Matual, "Shaw's *The Shewing-Up of Blanco Posnet*," 129.
24 Henry Livings, *This Jockey Drives Late Nights: A Play from "The Power of Darkness" by Leo Tolstoy* (London: Eyre Methuen, 1972).

3
GENERAL TOPICS

7

LIZA KNAPP

The development of style and theme in Tolstoy

Most literary critics divide Tolstoy's long and productive career into three periods, with the main one stretching from 1863, just after his marriage, when he settled into writing the novel that became *War and Peace*, to 1877, when he finished *Anna Karenina*. From this perspective, the monumental novels dwarf everything else: Tolstoy's early works are seen as training for the Herculean task of writing those epics; his later works, with some exceptions, are dismissed as the suspect output of his restless old age, when Tolstoy was seeking ever new ways of using his pen to design the kingdom of God, to compose "for the people," and, in general, to give answers to impossible questions (among them, "What is Art?"; "What Then Shall We Do?"; "How Much Land Does a Man Need?"; "Why Do People Stupefy Themselves?"). Other critics who take a less literary point of view have shown greatest reverence for what Tolstoy did and wrote in his later period, after the "crisis" and "conversion" of the late 1870s, when being a humanitarian, vegetarian, wise man, moralist, and activist was more important to him than being the author of literature. The elderly Tolstoy himself tried to disavow his former selves, not just the Tolstoy who killed men in war, or the Tolstoy who committed adultery, but also the Tolstoy who composed works of literature for the educated classes in a vain desire for glory and profit. Because Tolstoy's middle and late periods attract so much attention, his early works have to a degree been undervalued and neglected. In studying these works, however, we come to see, perhaps in its purest form, what is unique about Tolstoy's writing. We see the stylistic and thematic originality that commanded the attention of his first readers, who were convinced, from the outset, that they were beholding a major new talent. And because these early works contain the quintessence of the middle and late Tolstoy, reading them enables us to see the evolution and the unity of Tolstoy's œuvre.

In terms of subject matter, Tolstoy's early works can be divided into two categories, those dealing with civilian, domestic life (including the trilogy of *Childhood, Boyhood, Youth* [1852, 1854, 1857], *A Landowner's Morning*

[1856], *Lucerne* [1857], *Three Deaths* [1858], *Family Happiness* [1859]) and those dealing with military life (including the Sevastopol sketches [1855], *The Raid* [1852], *The Woodfelling* [1855], and *The Cossacks* [1852–62]). But in his early works, as in his later epic, Tolstoy blurs and links the realms of "war" and "peace." In both his military sketches and his slices of domestic life, he seeks to redefine the role of plot – by minimizing it and creating the effect of a narrative whose flow is determined by experience and time itself. Thus, many of his works, beginning with his first unpublished attempt at fiction, "A History of Yesterday," purport to describe a period of time: *Childhood*; *A Landowner's Morning*; *Sevastopol in December*. Challenging conventional views of what constitutes an event worth narrating in fiction or in history, he explored the significance of everyday events that usually escape attention. He took pride in showing that they are "more significant, more serious" than "the facts usually printed in newspapers and histories."[1] The literary mission Tolstoy fashioned for himself was to be the author of chronicles, instead of stories where remarkable characters and cataclysmic events structure the narrative.

What is distinctive about Tolstoy's writing was obvious from the start to his early critics, who were almost prophetic in what they wrote about him. (One notable exception was Dostoevsky's private prediction after reading *Childhood* that Tolstoy, although tremendously talented, would not write much.) Contemporary reviewers, from different points on the Russian political spectrum, all focused on Tolstoy's penchant for analysis. Critics felt that Tolstoy was inappropriately applying analysis – a scientific or philosophical operation – to literature. For example, the radical Dmitrii Pisarev wrote that "nobody carries analysis further than he does."[2] The Slavophile Konstantin Aksakov commented that Tolstoy's analysis becomes "a microscope" which leads to a "a pitiless exposure of everything stirring in a man's soul."[3] The radical Nikolai Chernyshevsky wrote that "everyone who follows literature" agrees that Tolstoy has "exceptional powers of observation" and that his forte is the "delicate analysis of psychological processes."[4] Chernyshevsky noted that Tolstoy is a master of representing "the dialectics of the soul." In describing Tolstoy's technique for revealing "the very process" of inner life, Chernyshevsky also used the term "inner monologue," possibly for the first time.[5] According to Pisarev, Tolstoy was able to chart "the mysterious, unclear movements of the soul that have not reached consciousness and are not completely understood even by the person who experiences them."[6] Tolstoy was regarded as a pioneer in the exploration of the mysterious relationship between thought and language.

When Tolstoy examines not what goes on inside the human mind and soul, but rather what goes on outside, in the world a human being inhabits, his analytical method decomposes this world, dismantles it, and reduces it to its component parts.[7] Tolstoy often uses the device of *ostranenie* – "making it strange" or "defamiliarization," as the Formalist Viktor Shklovsky termed it. This technique uses a narrator who "refuses to recognize" familiar things or who "describes them as if they were seen for the first time."[8] D. S. Mirsky pointed out that *ostranenie* results when Tolstoyan analysis is pushed "to its furthest limit." Mirsky writes that

> it consists in never calling complex things by their accepted name, but always disintegrating a complex action or object into its indivisible components; in describing, not naming it. The method strips the world of the labels attached to it by habit and by social convention and gives it a 'dis-civilized' appearance, as it might have appeared to Adam on the day of creation...[9]

Because it challenges conventional modes of perception, *ostranenie* is an effective instrument of social critique, especially for "the debunking of civilization on behalf of nature."[10] It is also suited to the spiritual questioning characteristic of Tolstoy's works.

Some early critics argued that Tolstoyan analysis made mountains out of molehills, leading to excessively dreamy self-absorption and individualism, while others saw how it challenged the status quo. Aksakov voiced the opinion that Tolstoy's analysis would lead the reader to an unhealthy alienation from his fellow man and from "God's wide world, bright and full of light."[11] Tolstoy was pronounced to be "one step from nihilism," in Grigoriev's response to *Three Deaths*.[12] (In 1884, in the opening of *What I Believe*, Tolstoy himself declared that "I have lived for thirty-five years as a nihilist in the true sense of the word; that is not as a socialist and revolutionary, as this word is usually understood, but as a nihilist meaning *void of all faith*.")[13] In *Three Deaths*, Tolstoy uses the same tone and narrative techniques to describe in succession the deaths of a noblewoman, a peasant, and a tree – granting (as Grigoriev argues) more understanding to the tree than to the two human beings. It disturbed Grigoriev that Tolstoy denied to *human* life anything that would make it rise above the life of a tree. Later (1887), an English critic would lament that Tolstoy denied to the human soul "some shadow of satisfaction in the things wherein it is more noble than the world."[14] Can a human soul survive on this earth once deprived of this satisfaction?

Tolstoy's first published work, *Childhood*, is told from the point of view of its hero, Nikolai Irteniev, who describes events associated with his mother's death when he was ten. Although the voice of the adult Nikolai Irteniev is sometimes heard, most of what is narrated is from the point of view of the child who is experiencing the events. Critics have seen a childlike quality in the narrative stance of Tolstoy's subsequent works, even those that have no particular association with childhood. In *Vital Life*, V. V. Veresaev suggested that *all* of Tolstoy's works are narrated from a child's-eye view: "it is as if an attentive, all-noticing child looked at an event and described it, not according to any of the conventions, but simply the way it is – and all the habitual, hypnotising conventions are ripped off of the event so that it appears in all its naked awkwardness."[15]

In this way, Veresaev anticipated Shklovsky's discovery of the device he christened "*ostranenie*."[16] Unlike the Formalist Shklovsky, who viewed *ostranenie* merely as a device, Veresaev understood its deeper meaning. Veresaev linked this device to the child's perspective, noting that childhood, as a state of mind, was dear to Tolstoy's heart. As proof, Veresaev quotes from Tolstoy's pedagogical tract "Who Should Teach Whom to Write . . ." (1862), in which Tolstoy declares that children have an innate sense of "beauty, sinlessness, innocence and truth" and bows to the authority of Rousseau on this subject.[17]

From the age of fifteen, Tolstoy admired Rousseau. (In a famous statement, he proclaimed that Rousseau, along with the Gospels, was the major influence on his life.)[18] Tolstoy's views on childhood, education, maternal breastfeeding, language, Jesus, opera, to name a few topics, all show how much he adhered to Rousseau's critique of civilization. Tolstoy's poetics, and especially his "psychological prose," owe a great deal to Rousseau's *Confessions*,[19] and Tolstoyan *ostranenie* (often translated as "defamiliarization") may also be traced, in part, to Rousseau. Milan Markovitch noted that Tolstoy's description of opera in *War and Peace* through Natasha's eyes is "almost identical" to Rousseau's description of the opera through the eyes of Saint-Preux in *Julie*.[20] This scene, famous because Shklovsky used it as an examplar of Tolstoyan "defamiliarization," had been cited by Veresaev to illustrate Tolstoy's mode of narrating "through the deeply serious eyes of a child." In an unpublished sketch, *The Tale of How Another Girl Named Varinka Quickly Grew Up* (1857), inspired by Tolstoy's nieces and nephews going to the ballet for the first time, Tolstoy was already imitating Rousseau's faux-naïf methods of describing the opera.[21] By using a child's perspective, Tolstoy thereby lends the criticism the moral weight and authenticity Tolstoy (along with Rousseau) attributed to children. When the children find the spectacle of "a girl without drawers in a very short skirt" "lifting her leg above her head" to be "bad," the children's verdict indicts ballet and any-one who has anything to do with vile spectacles of this sort.[22]

In privileging the child's perspective, Tolstoy may also have been imitating other sources, possibly Jesus (who praises what comes "out of the mouth of babes," throwing it in the face of the scribes and Pharisees [Matthew xxi.16]), and definitely Dickens.[23] *Childhood* reproduces, in Russified and gentrified form, features of the early part of *David Copperfield*, in which David's mother dies. However, another motherless son from Dickens, Paul Dombey, may also have influenced Tolstoy. From an innocent but estranged point of view, Paul asked devastating questions of his elders, making them feel their whole world was being "threatened with annihilation."[24] At one point, Paul asks his father "What is money?" and his father in response proclaims his belief in the omnipotence of money. Paul then asks why money was not able to save his mother's life.[25] Paul Dombey's manner of inquiry, simultaneously innocent and subversive, recurs in Tolstoy's works, from *Childhood* on.

The seeming naïvety of Tolstoy's child-narrator convinced some readers that Tolstoy was interested mainly in creating nostalgic myths about happy gentry childhood and that he failed to give social problems due attention. In defense, Chernyshevsky argued that it was misguided to expect *Childhood* to address these issues, since a child lacks understanding of them.[26] Yet the salient social problems of the time – serfdom, the nobility's impoverishment, the "woman question," corporal punishment – do figure in *Childhood*, presented from the innocent, yet disarming, viewpoint of the child narrator. Thus, when Nikolai's father (whose passions are "gambling" and "women") first appears, he is engaged in an exchange with his serf steward, Yakov, over tricky financial arrangements, necessary because he has been squandering the family wealth. Tolstoy's child-narrator reports that while Yakov placidly agreed to follow his master's orders, his face seemed to say: "I am right but nevertheless have your own way!"[27] Even if Nikolai does not understand the politics of serfdom (or his father's financial dealings), his naïve perceptions subtly reveal a momentous truth about master–serf relations. Although other serfs may accept their situation, Yakov is among those who revolt, if only inwardly.

The domestic problems of the Irtenievs are reported from the same disarming childish perspective. According to the progressive critic A. M. Skabichevskii, Nikolai's mother was sent to an early grave "betrayed, humiliated and insulted" by her no-good husband.[28] Gentry mothers like Nikolai's "cry into their pillows" instead of protesting. In what is happening in the Irteniev family Skabichevskii recognizes something familiar – "a terrible family drama, one of those dramas which are so frequent in our intelligentsia milieu." He assumes that Nikolai does not notice what is going on between his parents. But Tolstoy's child-narrator *notices* everything, as Veresaev reminds us. True to Tolstoy's method, this child-narrator does not "recognize" what he is describing.

What Nikolenka naïvely reports about his family life even before his mother's death prepares the reader for subsequent Tolstoyan murkiness on the subject of "family happiness" and "happy families." Nikolai expresses love and admiration for his father, and yet his narrative provides ample evidence of his father's faults. He idealizes his mother, but in the details Nikolai so naïvely reports there is evidence that this "angelic" mother abnegated maternal responsibility by allowing her husband to be a tyrant. Indeed, his grandmother suggested that if his father were to tell his mother that "the children should be whipped as Princess Kornakova whips her children," Nikolai's mother "would agree even to that" (66; *PSS* 1: 56). Lurking beneath the myth of a happy childhood is a cautionary tale about what happens when wives and mothers meekly allow their husbands to walk all over them.

Pisarev was one of the few critics who understood that a child-narrator could be used to provoke social critique.[29] Pisarev showed that a seemingly innocuous complaint Nikolai makes about his lessons reveals that the gentry educates its young according to custom, without understanding the issues involved. Pisarev concludes that "it's disgusting the way we all take the conventions of society as a law of nature." Tolstoy himself was critical of prevailing pedagogical practices, as shown throughout the trilogy and elsewhere when Tolstoy asks subversive questions, such as "Who Should Teach Whom to Write, We, the Peasant Children, or They, Us?"

Grieving by his mother's open coffin, Nikolai intensifies his devastating observations about the conventionalized behavior of the "civilized" world, while showing his respect for the silent prayers of Natalia Savishna. Nikolai resents the expressions of sympathy from outsiders who have come to pay their respects. For these people, Nikolai's experience is summed up in one word, a label: "orphan."

> What right had they to talk about her and mourn for her? Some of them in referring to us called us *orphans*. [In Russian, the word "orphan" can be used for someone who has lost one parent.] As if we did not know without their assistance that children who have lost their mother are known as orphans! Probably (I thought) they enjoyed being the first to give us that name, just as people generally are in a hurry to call a newly-married girl 'Madame' for the first time.
>
> (95; ch. 27; *PSS* 1: 87)

Nikolai's comment about those who call him and his siblings orphans points to the arbitrariness and conventionality of language, especially the language of polite society, where, Tolstoy believes, words become labels or lies. Inspired by his own intuition, building on Rousseau's linguistic views, cheered on by Sterne's declarations about "What little knowledge is got by mere words!," Tolstoy became skeptical about language as it is conventionally used. Tolstoyan analysis aims to retrieve the meaning of words and reveal the underlying truth.

During the requiem service, a five-year-old peasant girl, brought by her mother to give a ritual kiss to the corpse, shrieks as she stares at the dead woman. Frightened, Nikolai also screams and runs out. He explains:

> Only now did I understand whence came the strong and oppressive smell which, mingling with the incense, filled the whole room; and the thought that the face that but a few days ago had been so full of beauty and tenderness, the face of the person I loved most in the world, could inspire horror, *as it were for the first time revealed the bitter truth to me and overwhelmed my soul with despair.* (96; ch. 27; *PSS* 1: 87–88; emphasis added)

Whereas others act according to custom as they kiss the stinking corpse or blithely call Nikolai an orphan, the little girl behaves in a spontaneous, uncivilized, but desperately human way. Tolstoy uses this screaming child to focus attention on the facts of death, which social convention, theological rhetoric, and the survival instinct conspire to hide.

The death of Nikolai's mother, followed by the death of Natalia Savishna, marks the end of his childhood. When the adult-narrator mourns "Oh the happy, happy, gone-forever days of childhood!," the "happiness" referred to harks back to memories of Nikolai's communion with his mother in his toddler days. Happiness was being alone with his mother, drinking milk and sugar at his high chair and gazing into her eyes, being tickled and kissed by her, and eventually being put to bed, where he would say prayers and "the love of her and the love of God in some strange fashion mingled into one feeling" (53–54; ch. 15; *PSS* 1: 44). As this passage shows, what was lost was not only maternal love but a sense of oneness with God. In *Childhood*, Tolstoy's orphaned narrator is emotionally and spiritually estranged from the world he describes, because he lives in a state of perpetual loss. An important Tolstoyan pattern emerges here. As Richard Gustafson established, the loss of his parents – especially his mother – at an early age deeply affected Tolstoy, who envisioned the search for God as a yearning for parental love, or the despair of a fledgling fallen from its nest, described in his *Confession*. In his deep old age, in his diary in 1906, Tolstoy expressed a longing for motherly love.[30] In *Childhood* and throughout Tolstoy's works, the longing for the maternal breast and for the bosom of Abraham become mingled.

To his surprise, Nikolai soon finds that life after his mother's death continues according to its former pattern. He seeks comfort in the pious stories that Natalia Savishna tells him about God needing good souls in heaven: "though [he] did not understand all she said, [he] believed every word." By listening to Natalia Savishna's stories – and eventually by telling his own story – Nikolai manages to divert himself from, but never forget, the "bitter truth" revealed to him at his mother's death. In *Boyhood* and *Youth*, Nikolai continues to live largely according to the conventions of his class. But the motherless Nikolai looks on life around him in a critical, analytical way, and is prone to see the vanity of human endeavors and the arbitrariness of human institutions. The scream of the peasant girl still echoes in his soul.

In his three sketches devoted to the siege of Sevastopol during the Crimean War (*Sevastopol in December, Sevastopol in May, Sevastopol in August, 1855*), Tolstoy uses his characteristic analysis to reveal hidden truths about the human condition. During the siege, "the angel of death" "hover[s] unceasingly."[31] The proximity of death acts as a catalyst for Tolstoyan analysis, hastening the process of dismantling the cultural constructs that order life. All that is left are the most basic human needs. In the first of these sketches (*December*), Tolstoy makes the reader a "tourist" and "voyeur" at Sevastopol.[32] Tolstoy plays on expectations as he delights in showing that the emotional and cultural baggage the reader has brought along to Sevastopol is inappropriate. The closer the visitor is brought to the site of danger, suffering, and death, the more his assumptions are shattered by an unfamiliar reality: "You will suddenly understand, and completely differently from the way you understood it before, the meaning of those sounds of shots, which you heard in the town" (91; *PSS* 4: 12). The stench of decomposing flesh and the sight of amputated limbs makes it impossible to return to the security of former conceptions about life and death.

The visitor finds that even language fails him as he faces a suffering victim: "You want to say too much, in order to express your sympathy and admiration, but you cannot find the right words and are dissatisfied with those that occur to you, and so you silently bow your head before this taciturn and unconscious grandeur and firmness of spirit" (86; *PSS* 4: 7). Language also proves inadequate for the victims themselves. When a man is wounded, he at first responds in accordance with preconceptions about suffering with "a look of premature, feigned suffering." But then his face assumes "an expression of a kind of ecstasy and lofty, unarticulated thought." At this point, the wounded man "stops the stretcher-bearers for a moment and turning to his comrades says with effort, in a trembling voice, 'Farewell/Forgive me, brothers!'" (*Prostite, brattsy!*). (This Russian expression used at parting is a form of the verb meaning "to forgive.") This man "wants to say more, something touching, but can only repeat, 'Farewell/Forgive me brothers!'" (95; *PSS* 4: 15). The dying man appears dissatisfied with his words, which are inadequate to express what he feels as he faces death. Yet here Tolstoy shows that when people leave convention behind, earthly language, for all its inadequacies, can be used in inspired ways to express a verity, here a lofty Tolstoyan truth of brotherhood and forgiveness.

In *Sevastopol in May*, Tolstoy further explores various means of defying narrative and linguistic conventions in order to use language more effectively. To describe the experience of wounded and dying men, Tolstoy uses "inner monologues," with disjointed syntax, abundant *non sequiturs*, the sensation of a multitude of thoughts and feelings compressed into a brief time.[33] The inner monologues of Tolstoy's Sevastopol heroes articulate thoughts not otherwise expressed by language. In these inner monologues, as in his later works, Tolstoy in the final moments reveals that the monologue has an ultimate addressee: God.

In *Sevastopol in August, 1855*, the narrator addresses God directly, saying "Thou alone hast heard and knowest the simple yet burning and desperate prayers of ignorance, of confused repentance, prayers for bodily health and for spiritual enlightenment, that have risen to Thee from this dreadful place of death..." (172; *PSS* 4: 90). Tolstoy's narrator has just made us privy to what he claims God alone knows. He hints at what is special about his narrative method: it involves playing God. Tolstoy carries divine omniscience beyond the limits of convention by delving into human souls and revealing in words thoughts that normally are not articulated.

Tolstoy's narrator, thus, sometimes looks at human affairs through the eyes of a child and sometimes through the eyes of an omniscient God. Different as they are, both points of view reveal the vanity of human endeavors. In *Sevastopol in May*, Tolstoy's narrator adopts another point of view, that of Solomon of Ecclesiastes, when he dismisses everything around him as "Vanity! vanity! vanity!" The narrator focuses on the current Russian obsession with social standing, which, he notes, manifests itself even at Sevastopol. Everybody wants to be aristocratic, he complains, "despite the fact that death hangs over the head of each *aristocrat* and *non-aristocrat*" (101; *PSS* 4: 23–24). In expressing dismay at how in these circumstances people can be concerned with something so ridiculous, the narrator makes a point dramatized elsewhere in Tolstoy's works. For example, Andrei in *War and Peace* and the hero of *The Death of Ivan Ilich* realize on their deathbeds that they have pursued things that appear absurd in the face of death.

Tolstoy also uses this narrative technique to reveal the absurdity of war, which the soldiers suppress and the officers ignore. At one point, two officers, gazing up at the starry sky, realize that they have grown so used to the "spectacle" of the fighting at Sevastopol that they no longer distinguish between stars and bombs: "one gets so used to them" (110; *PSS* 4: 32). (Also confused about stars and bombs is a little girl who tells her mother "Look at the stars! Look how they're rolling! [. . .] What is it a sign of, mother?" But for this child and her mother, the bombs are no mere spectacle, they are

the work of the "fiend" and they will destroy their home [112; *PSS* 4: 34].)
Before this particular night is over, one of the cocky officers will be exposed
more directly to bombs exploding and will be temporarily shaken from the
complacency that allowed him dreamily to equate stars and bombs. Yet, by
the next day, he returns to boasting about his "bravery" the night before and
to renewed vainglorious dreams of medals and stars decorating his chest.

After this violent fighting, there is a cease-fire during which "crowds of
people have poured out from Sevastopol and the French camp to see the
sight, and with eager and friendly curiosity draw near to one another."
The "sight" they have come to see is the "heaps of mangled corpses." We
are also told that "the air is filled with the smell of decaying flesh" (134;
PSS 4: 56). But the enemy French and Russians exchange remarks, light each
other's pipes, and enjoy their camaraderie.

Suddenly, the narrator declares "enough" of this scene and introduces a
child's "defamiliarizing" point of view. "Let us look instead at this ten-year-
old boy. . . ." (136; *PSS* 4: 58). This boy walks by the piles of corpses, holding
up to his nose the bouquet of blue flowers he gathered in order to "escape the
stench of the corpses." The boy approaches a body without a head, pokes at
it, and, horrified, screams and runs away. Whereas the adult soldiers accept
the "reality" of war, registering its tragedy only in conventional ways (by
making remarks about bravery, for example), this boy responds with genuine
horror.

Tolstoy's narrator wants to know why "these people – Christians profess-
ing the one great law of love and self-sacrifice – once they have seen what
they have done, do not immediately fall repentant on their knees before Him
who has given them life and placed in the soul of each the fear of death and
a love of the good and the beautiful?" (137, *PSS* 4: 59).[34] Why, he asks, "do
they not embrace like brothers with tears of joy and gladness?" Instead, they
will start the killing all over again: "No! The white rags are hidden away, the
engines of death and suffering are sounding again, innocent blood is flowing
again, and the air is filled with moans and curses."

Why, indeed, do they start killing again, instead of "embracing like brothers"? Tolstoy was to ask this question throughout the rest of his life, inspiring
advocates of non-violent resistance, including Gandhi. Tolstoyan pacifism
has its seeds here, where Tolstoy makes the boy, and the reader, pay attention to the corpses, to the sight, smell, and feel of them, and where Tolstoy
points to the basic contradiction between the brotherly love that the soldiers
at Sevastopol profess – and perhaps even feel in their hearts – and the killing
that they practice.

Tolstoy claimed to have learned from Stendhal how to depict war "the way
it actually is." In *The Charterhouse of Parma*, Stendhal describes the Battle

of Waterloo from the point of view of Fabrice, a novice soldier, who looks around understanding "nothing at all," and soon finds all his preconceptions about the glory of war shattered. Tolstoy had read Stendhal before he himself faced fire, but his subsequent experience at Sevastopol proved to him that Stendhal was right: the violence of war makes no sense to the participants. Like Stendhal, Tolstoy used very detailed psychological analysis and narrated combat scenes from the point of view of a participant "who understands nothing."[35] Inspired by Stendhal, Tolstoy, in his Sevastopol sketches and throughout *War and Peace*, depicted war from a perspective that not only "makes it strange," but also makes it obscene, a crime against humanity and against God. Tolstoy's early descriptions of war in his fiction are as much his legacy to pacifism as his later overt statements on war and non-violent resistance.

At the end of *Sevastopol in May*, Tolstoy's narrator immediately professes second thoughts about the disturbing questions he has just raised about war. "There, I have said what I wished to say this time. But I am seized by an oppressive doubt. Perhaps I ought to have left it unsaid. What I have said perhaps belongs to that class of cruel truths that lie unconsciously hidden in the soul of each man and should not be uttered lest they become harmful, as the dregs in a bottle must not be disturbed for fear of spoiling the wine...." (137; *PSS* 4: 59). Here Tolstoy seems to point out the dangers of his own method and, prophetically, the eventual crises in his own life. Is he calling a halt to Tolstoyan analysis? Through his devastating "defamiliarizing," "estranged" analysis he penetrates to cruel truths about life that are ordinarily hidden deep in the soul. But revealing these cruel truths in plain language can make life lonely and miserable, or make it impossible to live, as Tolstoy himself came to know only too well.

In the work known as *Lucerne*, the first-person narrator, Nekhliudov, usually seen as an alter ego of Tolstoy, reveals more "cruel truths." Vacationing among British tourists in Switzerland, Nekhliudov becomes convinced of the hypocrisy of both the Swiss (with their republic and doctrine of equality) and the British (with their "civilized" empire and their colonial campaigns to "better" the human race). This happens when he witnesses their cruelty to a singer who performs and begs outside the resort hotel. The English tourists fail to give the singer money; Nekhliudov chases after the musician to invite him back to the hotel dining room, where he treats him, not to "*vin ordinaire*," but to a bottle of the "best champagne." When the Swiss hotel workers and the British tourists fail to accept Nekhliudov's guest as the equal of the other customers, Nekhliudov becomes outraged and takes it upon himself to let the Swiss know that theirs is a "scurvy republic." Furious with the British tourists, he wishes himself back at Sevastopol because he "would gladly have rushed into an English trench to hack and slash at them."[36]

In the midst of his harangue about Swiss complacency and British colonialism, imperialism, and class prejudice, Nekhliudov points to contradictions between the brotherly love people profess in their official, institutional lives and the selfish, hateful way they behave in daily life.

> Why do these developed, humane people, who collectively are capable of any honorable and humane action, have no human, cordial inclination to perform a kindly personal action? Why do these people – who in their parliaments, meetings, and societies are warmly concerned about the condition of the celibate Chinese in India, about propagating Christianity and education in Africa, about the establishment of societies for the betterment of the whole human race – not find in their souls the simple elemental feeling of human sympathy? [...] Can it be that the spread of the sensible and selfish association of men called civilization, destroys and contradicts the need for instinctive, loving association? (441–42; *PSS* 5: 23–24)

Tolstoy devoted much of his life to pointing out these contradictions in so-called civilized life and trying to remedy them. The roots of his later radical Christian activism can be found in his early works. He would later write fiction and treatises on social problems arguing for a literal implementation of the precepts of the Sermon on the Mount. In *Lucerne*, we see the Tolstoyan impulse to take ordinary time and turn it into Judgment Day, an impulse that would come to fruition in later tracts such as *What Then Shall We Do?*[37]

Having raised devastating questions about the barbarism of civilization, Nekhliudov suddenly questions his own less than compassionate behavior and his attempt to play God. He ends up bowing to divine wisdom, but without stifling his protest fully. At the end of *Lucerne*, we again have a familiar Tolstoyan pattern emerging.

In his early works, Tolstoy reveals the bitter truths that he felt were kept under veil in life as in literature: death stinks (*Childhood*); war is murder (*Sevastopol in May*); beggars in the street are our brothers (*Lucerne*); art corrupts and seduces (*The Tale of Varinka*); words often lack truth (all of the above). Driven by his penchant for analysis and for penetrating the "dialectics of the soul," Tolstoy dredged up these "cruel truths that lie unconsciously hidden in the soul of each man" (*Sevastopol in May*). Tolstoy was aware of the danger in what he was doing. And he even wondered whether these truths simply "should not be uttered lest they become harmful." In the early works, Tolstoy would suggest possible antidotes to these truths, to be found in peasant spirituality, in intellectualized appeals to divine harmony, or in oblivion, for example.

In *Memoirs of a Madman* (1883), which describes in veiled form Tolstoy's "crises," the narrator speaks of his despair as follows:

> I realized that something new had entered my soul and *poisoned* my former life. [...] The whole day I had been fighting my depression and had mastered it, but it had left its terrible *dregs* [osadok] in my soul as if some misfortune had befallen me, and I could forget it only for a short time. There *it remained at the bottom of my soul* and had me in its power.   (Emphasis added.)[38]

Here Tolstoy reuses images from his early works to describe the bitter truths better left undisturbed: they are *dregs* [osadok], at the bottom of the soul, that poison life. Evidence abounds in Tolstoy's works to show that the crises narrated in his later works occurred when the "bitter," "cruel," and toxic truths, dredged up by analysis in his early works, took over and left him wondering why he should even live.

Where are these truths in the novels of Tolstoy's heyday? The common wisdom is that Tolstoy was able to keep these truths under control as he wrote *War and Peace* and *Anna Karenina*. The former, especially, is often seen as a celebration of life, particularly of Russian life. Tolstoy's own account in his *Confession* suggests that he was able to surmount or ignore these truths for a period: "the new conditions of happy family life completely diverted me from all search for the general meaning of life." Yet the more we keep in mind Tolstoy's early works, the more we are likely to discern in *War and Peace* and *Anna Karenina* the "bitter" and "cruel" truths that threaten to render life meaningless, even for the positive heroes and heroines. Tolstoyan happiness in the major novels, as elsewhere, is prey to what Virginia Woolf called the "scorpion" in Tolstoy's works. Even as she praises Tolstoy for his depiction of "life," she warns us that one can never feel safe in Tolstoyan life, for all its beauty:

> There is always at the centre of all the brilliant and flashing petals of the flower this scorpion, "Why live?" There is always at the centre of the book some Olenin [the hero of *The Cossacks*], or Pierre [the hero of *War and Peace*], or Levin [the hero of *Anna Karenina*] who gathers into himself all experience, turns the world round between his fingers, and never ceases to ask, even as he enjoys it, what is the meaning of it, and what should be our aims.[39]

Tolstoy entered the literary scene with a poetics that was, if not fully formed, then certainly well articulated. From the beginning, Tolstoy analyzed, defamiliarized, inspected the bottom of the soul, reproduced inner monologue, exposed bitter truths, looked at the world through the eyes of a motherless child. These devices he continued to use throughout his life. They exposed the frailty of the human condition. They revealed the arbitrariness, even falseness, of human institutions, the insignificance of life, the inevitability of man's mortality, and they led to a nihilism. But, at the same time, they produced a yearning for God. The Tolstoyan search for God comes out of his "nihilism," a nihilism that left him with an abyss that only faith could fill. Tolstoy's writings, from the early works on, express this tension, even as they seek to alleviate it.

NOTES

1 *Lucerne*, trans. Louise Maude and Aylmer Maude, in Leo Tolstoy, *Collected Shorter Fiction*, 2 vols., trans. Aylmer Maude, Louise Maude, and Nigel J. Cooper (New York: Alfred A. Knopf, 2001), vol. I, p. 441. Rewriting history becomes a major concern of *War and Peace*.

2 D. I. Pisarev, "Tri smerti. Rasskaz grafa L. N. Tolstogo," in *L. N. Tolstoi v russkoi kritike* (Moscow: Khud. lit., 1952), pp. 132–33.

3 In A. V. Knowles (ed.), *Tolstoy: The Critical Heritage* (London: Routledge and Kegan Paul, 1978), pp. 63–64.

4 "Detstvo i otrochestvo. Voennye rasskazy," in *Tolstoi v kritike*, p. 91.

5 *Ibid.*, pp. 97, 93, 96.

6 Pisarev, "Tri smerti," p. 133.

7 D. S. Mirsky, *A History of Russian Literature: From its Beginnings to 1900*, ed. Francis J. Whitfield (New York: Vintage, 1958), p. 263.

8 Shklovsky's phrase, quoted in: Victor Erlich, *Russian Formalism: History and Doctrine*, 3rd edn. (New Haven, CT: Yale University Press, 1981), p. 177.

9 Mirsky, *A History of Russian Literature*, p. 263.

10 Erlich, *Russian Formalism*, p. 177.

11 In Knowles, *Tolstoy*, p. 64.

12 A. A. Grigoriev, in Knowles, *Tolstoy*, p. 72. See Donna Tussing Orwin, *Tolstoy's Art and Thought, 1847–1880* (Princeton, NJ: Princeton University Press, 1993), p. 6.

13 *PSS* 23: 304. Hereafter this standard Russian Jubilee edition is cited in the text.

14 Julia Wedgwood, "Count Leo Tolstoi," *The Contemporary Review* 52 (1887), 251.

15 V. V. Veresaev, *Zhivaia zhizn'*, vol. I (Moscow: I. N. Kushnerev, 1911), p. 116.

16 V. V. Vinogradov, "O iazyke Tolstogo (50–60-e gody)," *Literaturnoe nasledstvo*, vol. XXXV–XXXVI: *L. N. Tolstoi* (Moscow: AN SSSR, 1939), p. 168.

17 Veresaev, *Zhivaia zhizn'*, p. 113.

18 Orwin, *Tolstoy's Art and Thought*, pp. 36–49.

19 Lydia Ginzburg, *On Psychological Prose*, ed. and trans. Judson Rosengrant (Princeton, NJ: Princeton University Press, 1991).

20 Milan L. Markovitch, *Jean-Jacques Rousseau et Tolstoï* (Paris: Honoré Champion, 1928), pp. 304–5.

21 *Ibid.*, p. 305, n. 2.

22 *PSS* 5: 225. This simple sketch anticipates Tolstoy's later arguments in *The Kreutzer Sonata* and *What is Art?* about the pernicious nature of the art enjoyed by the educated classes.

23 Gareth Williams, *Tolstoy's Childhood* (London: Bristol Classical Press, 1995), pp. 84–86.

24 F. R. Leavis and Q. D. Leavis, *Dickens the Novelist*, 1970 (New Brunswick, NJ: Rutgers University Press, 1979), p. 18.

25 *Ibid.*, pp. 17–18.

26 Chernyshevsky, "*Detstvo i otrochestvo*," p. 102.

27 Leo Tolstoy, *Childhood, Boyhood, Youth*, trans. Rosemary Edmonds (London: Penguin, 1964), p. 20; *PSS* 1: 10. Hereafter, references to this translation and the *PSS* are given in parentheses after the citation.

28 Skabichevskii, *Sochineniia*, vol. I (St. Petersburg: Novosti, 1890), p. 615.

29 D. I. Pisarev, "Promakhi nezreloi mysli," in *Tolstoi v kritike*, pp. 151–55.

30 Richard E. Gustafson, *Leo Tolstoy, Resident and Stranger: A Study in Fiction and Theology* (Princeton, NJ: Princeton University Press, 1986), pp. 12–15.

31 Leo Tolstoy, *Sevastopol in May*, in *Collected Shorter Fiction*, vol. I, p. 97; *PSS* 4: 18. Hereafter, for *Sevastopol in May*, *Sevastopol in December*, and *Sevastopol in August, 1854*, references to this translation, followed by references to the *PSS*, will be given in parentheses after the quoted passage. The translations have been modified in some cases.

32 Gary Saul Morson, "The Reader as Voyeur: Tolstoi and the Poetics of Didactic Fiction," in Michael R. Katz (ed.), *Tolstoy's Short Fiction* (New York and London: W. W. Norton & Co., 1991), pp. 380–81.

33 Gleb Struve argued that Tolstoy invented the technique and that Chernyshevsky was the first to use the term: "*Monologue intérieur*: The Origins of the Formula and the First Statements of Its Possibilities," *PMLA* 69 (1954), 1, 101–11.

34 Tolstoy returns to the same question in his *Confession*.

35 Boris Eikhenbaum, *The Young Tolstoi*, trans. Gary Kern (Ann Arbor, MI: Ardis, 1972), pp. 78–82.

36 Leo Tolstoy, *Lucerne*, in *Short Stories*, pp. 324–25; *PSS* 5: 19. Hereafter, references to this translation and the *PSS* are given in parentheses after the citation.

37 This formulation derives from a remark made by S. N. Bulgakov about "What Then Shall We Do," in "Prostota i oproshchenie," *O religii L'va Tolstogo. Sbornik statei* (Moscow, 1912; repr. Paris: YMCA, 1978), p. 114.

38 Tolstoy, *Memoirs of a Madman*, in *Collected Shorter Fiction*, vol. I, p. 787; *PSS* 26: 470.

39 Virginia Woolf, *The Common Reader*, intro. and ed. Andrew McNeillie (New York: Harcourt, Brace & Co., 1925; repr. 1984), p. 182.

8

ANDREW WACHTEL

History and autobiography in Tolstoy

At the end of *Sevastopol in May*, Tolstoy makes a famous claim, central to his fiction and startling in its simplicity and boldness: "The hero of my tale, whom I love with all the strength of my soul, whom I have attempted to depict in all of his beauty, and who was, is and will always be sublime, is the truth."[1] In notes to *War and Peace* a decade or so later, he wrote: "I was afraid that the necessity to describe the significant figures of 1812 would force me to be governed by historical documents rather than the truth."[2] But what did Tolstoy mean by "truth" in works of fiction which have, since Aristotle, been understood to describe not what is but what might be?

Given that both works contain this Tolstoyan truth, it makes sense to search for it in their intersection. At first, this approach may seem unpromising, however. *Sevastopol in May*, a feuilleton, focuses on the day-to-day life of a few "randomly chosen" soldiers during a short period of time in an enclosed space. *War and Peace*, set entirely in the past, sprawls over multiple characters and huge chunks of time and space. In other ways, however, *Sevastopol Sketches* and *War and Peace* are quite similar. Both are constructed of "real" material taken from life (and especially from Tolstoy's biography), while that same material is fitted into a context that disguises its provenance. Tolstoy was in Sevastopol. Although the characters in the story are fictional, the reader, knowing Tolstoy was there and guessing that he speaks through the traditional "flâneur" narrator of a sketch, may suspect that the fictional characters are thinly disguised acquaintances of the author. The *Sketches* exist on the liminal boundary of reportage and fiction. *War and Peace* was extensively based on family history, and it lies on the border of fiction, history, and the philosophy of history: it is "not a novel, still less a poem, still less an historical chronicle" (*PSS* 16: 7).

The two imperatives that govern Tolstoy's writing in the first three decades of his creative activity are: a desire for specificity (which he identifies with such non-fictional genres as autobiography, reportage, and history), and a striving for universality (that is, a need to disguise the presence of specifying material through various strategies of generalization). The finished literary work is meant to achieve balance between the two, a balance that Tolstoy defines as "truth."[3] These imperatives tended to conflict: too much specificity could cut into generalization and vice versa. And the picture is even more complex because it appears to have been undergirded by a psychological quirk. Specificity was generally autobiographical for Tolstoy: hence the conflict of specific and general often took the form of a simultaneous attempt to reveal and conceal himself. Tolstoy's basic technique (in multiple variations) to achieve truth is intergeneric dialogue, through the more or less simultaneous deployment of multiple monologic voice positions (that is, genres). As opposed to the dialogic voices described by Bakhtin, the separate Tolstoyan voices do not recognize each other. Dialogue is created by readers confronted by the coexistence of seemingly mutually exclusive genres in the same work or on the same theme.[4] This creates what one might call an inter-work – a work that exists only in the reader's mind, created by the overlap between multiple, generically exclusive voices (or texts) on the same theme.

The tendency to combine personal with general in an ambiguous generic package was present from the beginning of Tolstoy's career. *Childhood* (1852) is a pseudo-autobiography that imitates autobiography in all respects but one: its author and narrator are not the same person. For both author and reader this means that the text is to be treated as fiction, read and judged by a set of criteria different from those applied to non-fiction. At the same time, readers may forget they are reading fiction and fall into the reading conventions of autobiography. For later readers, identification of author and narrator is further encouraged (if, as in the case of Tolstoy, the author has become well known) because the pseudo-autobiography often sticks quite closely to the facts of its author's life. The pseudo-autobiography affords the novelist an unusual opportunity. He can use material from his own life in a form that has traditionally engendered an illusion of truth in readers. Yet, he is not bound by truth and is able to create the kind of fictional world characteristic for the novel.

Indeed, Tolstoy used so much material taken from his own life in *Childhood* that his sister, not knowing the author's identity when she first read it, was convinced that it could only be by one of her brothers.[5] Yet it also contains completely fictional scenes and characters. Readers, of course, could be counted on to identify the first-person narrator with the author, but the fact that the narrator was named Nikolai Irteniev while the author signed the work L. N. militated against such an identification. The final text exhibits a delicate equipoise between the autobiographical and the fictional.

That this equipoise was of crucial importance to the young author can be seen in his reaction to the editorial changes Nikolai Nekrasov made when publishing *Childhood*, in particular the fact that Nekrasov changed the title to *The Story of My Childhood*. Tolstoy was enraged by this and dashed off a letter (never actually mailed) in which he complained; "The very title *The Story of My Childhood* contradicts the sense of the work. Who cares about *my* childhood?" (*PSS* 1: 332). The complaint is, perhaps, illogical, since a reader who believed that the narrator wrote the whole work could just as easily be expected to think that he had written the title. Nevertheless, Tolstoy's distress is telling; he connected the word "my" in the title to the author and not to the narrator, indicating his fear that the illusion he had carefully created might be lost.

There was one major drawback to Tolstoy's pseudo-autobiography; although he himself could perceive the dialogic interplay of the autobiographical and the fictional in *Childhood*, readers could not. Now that we possess an almost full edition of Tolstoy's writings as well as commentaries by contemporaries, it is often (though by no means always) possible to ascertain which aspects of the "Trilogy" are autobiographical. But there is no way to figure out when Tolstoy is describing his own life and when not, because the division of voice positions in the text does not correspond to the split between fiction and autobiography. Although the narrative is multi-voiced and multi-perspectival, the lack of a discernible break at the autobiography/fiction border prevents dialogue across the fiction/non-fiction boundary. Instead, Tolstoy achieves a type of internal dialogue (actually trialogue, for there are three separate voices present) by placing each voice at a unique spatio-temporal distance from the events it describes.

An example of what I mean would be the description of the behavior of Natalia Savishna after Irteniev's mother's death, as recalled by the three narrators:

> At the time I was amazed at the change from touching emotion, with which she spoke to me, to grumbling and trivial calculation. [The child's voice is speaking here: it does not analyze or seek to explain, but merely to present what happened. Of course the words "at the time" show that there is a sense of lost time.] Thinking about it later, I understood that despite what was happening in her soul she still had enough spirit left to take care of her work [. . .] Grief had affected her so strongly that she did not find it necessary to hide the fact that she could take care of other things: she wouldn't have even understood how such a thought could arise. [Here we are in the presence of the adult-narrator's voice which looks back on the raw material of the child's perception, interprets it, and sometimes even tries to "correct" the child's impression.]
>
> Vanity is the feeling most incompatible with true grief but, at the same time, the feeling is so deeply imbedded in human nature that it is very rare that even the strongest grief can drive it out. Vanity in grief is manifested in the desire

to seem either afflicted or unhappy or firm. [This is the absolute voice of the all-seeing author, which extrapolates a general truth about mankind from the story of Natalia Savishna and the child's reaction to it.][6]

(*Childhood*, ch. 28, *PSS* 1: 91)

Each narrator sees the same event but is interested in a different aspect of it. Not superseding or contradicting each other, the three voices, taken together, make a whole. Although the reader of *Childhood* must be aware of frequently shifting narrative perspectives, those shifts do not disturb the overall harmony of the text. Dialogue is there to be perceived, but we tend not to perceive it; instead, we slide easily from one perspective to another, generally unaware of having done so. We also have no sense of what is fictional and what not. What pleased Tolstoy in his first-published works would have been the technique of multi-voiced narrative presentation. The trick, however, was to find a way to use this to partially reveal the truth about dialogue rather than to conceal it completely. For, already in the 1850s, Tolstoy feared his own power to make the fictional seem real, and worried that this ability would make his work convincing but not "true." For all this, he did not abandon the attempt to use belletristic writing to uncover himself (both for his own benefit and for that of his readers), nor did he give up completely the multi-voiced narrative techniques. Rather, as he matured, he constantly recombined these with newer inventions.

In *War and Peace* Tolstoy tries again to balance specificity and universality in order to tell the truth. The narrative material has shifted from the personal to the historical, but the novel is linked to the trilogy through *The Sevastopol Sketches* which again present material taken directly from Tolstoy's own experience. Although the autobiographical material now has general historical significance, for Tolstoy there is no difference *in principle* between a historical and nonhistorical subject. In the struggle to achieve "truth" it does not matter what sort of factual material – autobiographical recollections, war reportage, historical fact – occupies the "specific" pole of the equation. This was even more the case because there was always a substantial "Tolstoyan" substratum in the "specific" material.

In *War and Peace* Tolstoy recycled his multi-voiced presentation from the pseudo-autobiographical *Childhood* but now he connected each voice to a clear generic viewpoint. As a result, the principles of intergeneric dialogue become apparent to the reader as well as to the author. Tolstoy was aware of the potential incompatibility of the various voices in his work. Discussing the novelist's and historian's perspectives in notes to *War and Peace* he said: "When describing a historical epoch the artist and the historian have two entirely different objects. Just as the historian would be wrong if he attempted

to present a historical figure in all his entirety, in all his complicated connections to all aspects of life, so an artist would not be doing his duty if he
presented that figure in all of his historical significance" (*PSS* 13: 57). Truth
demanded both of these perspectives, and the complicated narrative form of
War and Peace was devised precisely to present both in a single work. What
is more, the reader had to perceive their juxtaposition, even their conflict –
precisely what Tolstoy had avoided in *Childhood*.

The following chart shows the characteristics of the three narrative voices
in *War and Peace*:

	Fictional	Historical	Metahistorical (authorial)
Genre	novel	history	philosophy of history
Time	now	then	eternal
Place	here, inside	there, outside	Archimedean point, high above
Trope	metonym	rhetorical question	metaphor
Person	first person singular	first person plural	impersonal/universal

In the course of the novel, Tolstoy quite frequently juxtaposes narrative
voices, openly showing the same event from multiple, even conflicting perspectives. The seamlessness that characterized the narration of *Childhood* is
thereby lost, but this mode of presentation preserves the separate perspectives of historian and novelist. Instead of a blurring together we get two
sharp images – a double exposure, as it were. Thus, for example, Tolstoy
begins his description of the battle of Borodino firmly in the voice of his
historical narrator. Book 3, part 2, chapter 19 opens: "On the 24th was the
battle at the Shevardino redoubt; on the 25th not a shot was fired from one
side or the other; on the 26th the Battle of Borodino was fought" (*PSS* 11:
184). The rest of the chapter consists of a fairly straightforward presentation
of "facts" by the historical narrator and some general commentary on these
facts in the absolute voice. The tone is clearly polemical; Tolstoy strongly
disagrees with other historians, and the assumption is that on the level of
generality that interests the historian, the truth can be discovered. Phrases
like "what happened, obviously, was this" make this apparent (*PSS* 11: 187).

The historian's position is outside and a bit above events, after them in time. Nowhere is this made more obvious than in Tolstoy's inclusion of a map of the battlefield in chapter 19. Its very existence convinces us that the position of the historical narrator vis-à-vis the fictional is that of dialogic opposition. For what the chapters that follow in the fictional voice seem designed to show is precisely the impossibility of a position anything like the one provided in chapter 19. The contrast is starkest when we juxtapose the map with Pierre's observations:

> Everything Pierre saw to his right and left was so indefinite, that neither the right or left side of the field completely satisfied his preconceptions. Wherever he looked he could see no field of battle as he had expected to see, but rather fields, dells, troops, woods, smoking camp-fires, villages, mounds, and creeks. No matter how hard he tried, Pierre could not make out a military position in the living landscape. He could not even distinguish between our troops and the enemy's. (*PSS* 11: 194)

The perspectives of chapters 19 and 20 could not be further apart. No mental operation will allow us to combine these pictures into one, and that is the point. Fictional and historical narration present different perspectives and different truths – equal, perhaps, but separate, and presented here in dialogical contrast.

As Tolstoy discovered when reading the early reviews of the first part of his book, readers seemed unable to grasp what he was doing. The metahistorical (authorial) voice, actively suppressed in the earlier sections of the work, was introduced primarily to highlight problems that receive more subtle and complicated treatment on other narrative levels and in the inter-generic dialogue between them.[7] Thus, such problems as free will and necessity, and the role of the "great man," are all afforded complex dialogic treatment in the historical and fictional narration. Were they not mentioned so obviously on the metahistorical level, the reader might fail to notice them.

At the same time, although we have separated the three narrative voices of *War and Peace* for analytic purposes, they do not actually live in their own narrative worlds in the text. No matter how monologic or monolithic one of them may seem at a given moment, it is always in actual or potential dialogue with the others. Despite the seemingly dominating presence of one or another of the voices at certain points, in the novel as a whole no voice is primary. The work succeeds precisely because of the lines of tension that this interaction engenders. If Tolstoy's philosopher of history believes that individuals are unimportant for the historical process while his fictional narrator is concerned only with individuals, this is not muddled thinking, nor does a recognition of this contradiction lead to a "deconstruction" of *War and*

Peace. Rather it points to the fact that fiction and the philosophy of history are not the same thing, that each has its own narrative stance. Within the structure of the book their coexistence leads to mutual understanding rather than mutual annihilation. Any voice taken individually leads to a narrative dead end, but taken together they lead to a productive narrative equilibrium.

These interpenetrating voices produce a book that, like the earlier "Trilogy," although in a different way, cannot be understood by employing one set of interpretive conventions. It is truly, as Tolstoy put it, "not a novel, still less a poem, still less an historical chronicle," just as the "Trilogy" is neither autobiography nor first-person fiction. As with the "Trilogy," however, Tolstoy's multifaceted presentation of truth in *War and Peace* still did not completely satisfy him. In notes for the epilogue, he divided his readers into three groups. His favorites were "artistic readers," who do not need the metahistorical meditations: "without meditating, they will read between the lines and perceive everything that I wrote in the meditations, and that I would not have written had all readers been like them. In the presence of such readers I blame myself for having disfigured my book by inserting the meditations"(*PSS* 15: 241). By the time he had finished his book, Tolstoy was worried that compromises to make it understandable had vitiated its artistic integrity. In 1873, he published an edition of the novel in which the metahistorical comments were removed from the main text and placed in an Afterword. Ultimately, *War and Peace* pleased him no more than had the trilogy. Both required compromises to soften the seeming narrative incoherence that intergeneric dialogue produced. The problem, as Tolstoy might have come to see it, was that, although a powerful technique, intergeneric dialogue poses serious interpretive obstacles for readers. They tend simply to ignore its implications, or, when these are too obvious to be ignored, to complain about them.

It is in the context of Tolstoy's striving to strike a balance between the specific and the universal, and his perceived failure to do so successfully in his work of the 1850s and 1860s, that we should examine *Anna Karenina* and *A Confession*. At first glance, it seems strange to couple *Anna Karenina*, generally believed to be Tolstoy's best-behaved fictional work, and intergeneric dialogue. *Anna Karenina* is indeed far more conventionally structured than the "loose and baggy" *War and Peace*. The stories of Kitty and Levin, Anna and Vronsky are presented, for the most part, by an unobtrusive third-person narrator; true, the Tolstoyan "absolute" voice is present now and again, but much more infrequently than in *War and Peace*, and the voice of a non-fictional historical narrator is completely absent. But *Anna Karenina* can only be seen as conventional if we do not recognize *A Confession*, written in 1879 and published abroad in 1881, as its partial intergeneric twin.

Tolstoy himself sets up this comparison. In *A Confession* he not only describes himself undergoing the same crisis that had stricken his main fictional hero in the novel, he employs almost the identical language.

> And Levin, a happy husband and a healthy man, was several times so close to suicide that he hid a rope so as not to hang himself and was afraid to go out with his gun lest he shoot himself.   (*Anna Karenina*, 8, ch. 9; *PSS* 19: 371)

> And so at that time, I, a happy man, removed a rope from the room where I spent each evening alone while undressing so as not to hang myself on the bar between the armoires, and I stopped going out hunting with my gun so as not be tempted by this overly easy way of relieving myself of my life.
> (*A Confession*, ch. 4; *PSS* 23: 12)

This doubling practically forces us to identify fictional character with autobiographical narrator. To do so, however, is to fly in the face of all the rules of reading that teach us to beware of identifying characters and authors, as well as genre expectations that lead us to classify autobiography and fiction in distinct compartments.

At the same time, the story Tolstoy tells about Levin and the one he tells about himself do not entirely overlap: specifically, the ending of *Anna Karenina* is far more optimistic than that of *A Confession*, a divergence that problematizes identification of fictional character and author. In *Anna Karenina* the doubts that were to lead Tolstoy first to despair and then to radical religious conversion are resolved through family happiness. In *A Confession*, they are resolved through religious awakening. This does not mean that *A Confession*, as autobiography, is meant to supersede *Anna Karenina*. Although as an essay that purports not to be a work of fiction it asks to be read using different genre conventions, *A Confession* is no less an experiment than is *Anna Karenina*. Both stand in a mediated relationship to Tolstoy's life, and both can be seen as attempts by Tolstoy to comprehend the riddle of his own existence.

It is not clear whether the Tolstoy of *A Confession* is more or less like the author than is Levin. The genre conventions of autobiography do suggest a closer relationship between character and author than do those of the novel. Perhaps the author wanted to be more like "Tolstoy" than like Levin and wrote *A Confession* to convince the outside world and, most importantly, himself that this was so. More likely still, the two works reflect different sides of his personality. In this case, the truth would be available only if one were to know both sides, one illuminated by novelistic, the other by autobiographical means. Having given up his attempts to combine multiple genres in a single text, Tolstoy may have tried a new type of intergeneric dialogue. He tells the same story twice – though not all of it is the same even in the sections that overlap, a fact that further confuses the relationship between the two works. He never mentions *Anna Karenina* in *A Confession*: each version is secure in its own genre and is, evidently, totally unaware of its double. The dialogue between them is created by the reader, who only recognizes their ambiguous relation when reading them in tandem.[8]

The most recent critic to comment extensively on the relationship of *Anna Karenina* to *A Confession* was George Steiner. In his view, the ending of the novel seems arbitrary; "there could well be a book IX in *Anna Karenina*, recounting Vronsky's search for martial expiation or the beginnings of Levin's new life. Indeed, *A Confession*, on which Tolstoy began to work in the fall of 1878, takes up precisely where *Anna Karenina* ends. Or would it be more accurate to say, where it breaks off?"[9] In Steiner's view, therefore, *A Confession* may be a kind of sequel to Tolstoy's novel.

Two important facts make Steiner's thesis problematic. The first was noted earlier: *Anna Karenina* and *A Confession* are written in two genres that make very different truth claims. The implied autobiographical pact between reader and writer at least theoretically obligates the author to tell the truth about himself. Fictional texts do not require this; indeed, one of the elementary rules of reading fiction is to avoid identifying fictional narrators and authors. The situation is further complicated by the temporal relationship between the two works. We have not succession, but overlap, and in a number of places *A Confession* covers the same material as the novel. *A Confession* begins with Tolstoy's recollection of a childhood incident, while *Anna Karenina* begins with an already adult Levin, so in some sense *A Confession* can be said both to precede and to antecede *Anna Karenina*. Perhaps it might be better to call the two works "equels" – that is, parallel and in a sense competing texts that illuminate the same situation from multiple points of view.

Before beginning our own analysis of the relationship between these two works, it is necessary to review a few facts. From his earliest youth, Tolstoy analyzed and tried to reform himself. In his fiction such characters as Nikolai Irteniev in *Childhood*, *Boyhood*, and *Youth*, Olenin in *The Cossacks*, and Pierre Bezukhov in *War and Peace* do the same. While writing *Anna Karenina*, Tolstoy was struck by a deeper and longer-lasting spiritual crisis, which forms the basis both for the descriptions of Levin in book eight of *Anna Karenina*, and of "Tolstoy" in chapters four through twelve of *A Confession*. In real chronology, Tolstoy first experienced his great crisis in life, then wrote about it in fictional form, and finally rewrote it in autobiography. As regards a solution, however, the chronology is different: Tolstoy himself never succeeded in finding a stable solution, Levin does find one at the close of *Anna Karenina*, while "Tolstoy" in *A Confession* contradicts Levin's solution and proposes a different one. The acceptance of the latter as a kind of "ninth book" of the former therefore entails a severe perspectival shift. Having forced us to see the partial identity between Levin and himself, Tolstoy challenges us to treat fictional and autobiographical texts as completely on a par. We must begin to read *Anna Karenina* more like autobiography than we would probably wish to or *A Confession* more like a fictional text than it purports to be.

Of course, it could still be argued that the two have nothing to do with each other: Tolstoy did not wish us to use fiction to interpret autobiography or vice versa. In this view, using *A Confession* to interpret *Anna Karenina* would be as illegitimate as using Tolstoy's letters or diaries. There is, however, a crucial difference: Tolstoy invites such an interpretive strategy. Publication is a public act; Tolstoy chose to insert the passage that doubles *Anna Karenina* knowing full well that it might be recognized. Although Tolstoy may have suspected that his diaries and letters would some day be published, there is a significant difference between contradicting oneself in print and merely allowing for posthumous publication.[10]

It is possible to see the partial identity between Levin and Tolstoy as a radical trick to achieve the goals of realism. If Levin's tortured search for philosophical equilibrium may seem unconvincing in the novel, the autobiography "guarantees" that it was genuine, and retrospectively makes the novel more believable. The famous hay-mowing scene may seem unrealistic, because Levin's epiphany in the fields is not presented through careful psychological analysis but rather as revelation. If, however, we believe that Levin is Tolstoy, it is hard to reject this revelation, because it actually "happened."

And it is not merely the "doubled" scenes that seem more real. Once we have come to accept the specific identity between the Levin of book 8 and the "Tolstoy" of the beginning of *A Confession* it becomes tempting to imagine that the Levin of, say, book 1 is also a hypostasis of the author, and, even more interestingly, to expect that if they shared part of their adult life then Levin and Tolstoy must have shared a childhood as well. The penumbra of the novel broadens to include all that novel readers always want but never get: "but what happened before the novel started?" "Did they really live happily ever after?" What is more, this trick of identity makes all the other scenes more convincing, because once we are sure that Levin is a "real person" it becomes easier to believe in the reality of the novel's other characters. After all, Levin (Tolstoy) spent an evening at Anna and Vronsky's apartment. So she, too, might have been a real person, not merely a fictional character acting in a world that looks vaguely like ours.

The identification of Levin with Tolstoy inevitably colors our reading of the novel's ending. Gary Saul Morson has discussed the ending of *War and Peace* as an example of the "poetics of the 'unfinalizable' continuum."[11] *Anna Karenina* read alone appears to work similarly. The story of Anna is, of course, finished, but those of Vronsky, Karenin, and the minor characters remain open. When we read *Anna Karenina* in tandem with *A Confession*, however, the novel's openendedness is diminished. We know (or think we know) that Levin and Tolstoy are "the same person" and this fact gives us some specific answers as to what happens after the ending. For one thing, it is hard to believe that Levin and Kitty continued to lead their blissful life after the end of the novel, because we know that family happiness was only one step on Tolstoy's path, a step that would ultimately prove false.

This knowledge can change our entire interpretation of the novel. If *Anna Karenina* ends after book 8, we have to do with a symmetrical novel based on the opposition of the positive "prosaic" love of Levin and Kitty, and the negative "romantic" love of Anna and Vronsky. The stark contrast between Anna's death and Levin's optimistic hymn to life makes this interpretation hard to resist. If, however, as Tolstoy claims in *A Confession*, prosaic love ultimately produces no greater happiness than does its romantic counterpart, then it is difficult to make this interpretation stick. All of the major characters are deluded.

From the point of view of *A Confession*, the novel's famous opening line no longer seems to describe anything – there are and can be no happy families, because only the deluded can be happy in family life, and while other people may be able to sustain this delusion, Levin/Tolstoy clearly will not. Levin's family happiness is as illusory and temporary as was Anna's during her Italian trip; the difference is that he has not yet realized it. Instead of two diametrically opposed lines, one leading to death and destruction, the other to happiness, we see the structure of the novel as descending spirals, one of which has hit bottom before the other.

At the same time, intergeneric dialogue is not a unidirectional phenomenon. We do not merely read the novel differently because of the autobiography. We understand Tolstoy's attempts to make sense of his own life in textual form differently because of the existence of the fictional Levin. Just as it is impossible to dismiss entirely Tolstoy from Levin's biography, it is impossible to banish Levin from Tolstoy's.

As was the case with Tolstoy's original audience and as is usually so today (since most people are likely to have read *Anna Karenina* before turning to Tolstoy's less well-known works), readers of the passage in *A Confession* have a sense of *déjà lu*, a vague recollection that they have heard this before. Having recalled the relevant passages in *Anna Karenina*, they cannot help but notice differences as well as similarities. While both works end optimistically, Levin's anchor, which consists of family life and useful agricultural work, is presented at the end of *A Confession* as having been merely a stage on the way to the new, religious optimism. While Levin shares much of Tolstoy's angst, he is in many respects more "autopsychological" than autobiographical – the phrase is Lydia Ginzburg's – or at least he is not identical to Tolstoy.[12] He is not a writer, for example, or not a writer of fiction at any rate.

The existence of two hypostases of the author eventually produces in the reader a feeling akin to double vision; that is, a disorienting blurriness which has the effect not of bringing Tolstoy into focus through the melding of two separate perspectives, but rather of distancing the real Tolstoy from us. The first motivation for this might well be literary, and related to genre. The obvious immediate model for Tolstoy's work is *The Confessions* of Jean-Jacques Rousseau. There is, however, something quite problematic in comparing Tolstoy's *Confession* to Rousseau's. From the first lines, the latter insists on his own originality: "I have resolved on an enterprise which has no precedent and which, once complete, will never have an imitator . . . I dare believe that I am like no one else. If I am no better, I am at least different."[13] Tolstoy, on the other hand, insists, time and again, that individuality is at the root of his problems. Whenever he thinks he is special or different he despairs, but when he thinks like "everybody else," he is saved. In this respect, the tenor of Tolstoy's autobiography is far more like Augustine's than Rousseau's. For, like Augustine, Tolstoy wishes to merge himself into something larger, outside the self. After Rousseau it is hard to see a confessional text as anything other than a document celebrating the author's individuality. If individuality is the very problem to be overcome, a means must be found to allow the author to be not just himself but a model or a symbol of Everyman. The blurred perspective provided by *Anna Karenina*, I would suggest, does just this. Instead of focusing on Tolstoy and reading his problems as his alone, we are now confronted with two beings who have basically the same problems, and this helps us to ignore the unique and personal and to recognize the universal.

The existence of the novel, we may hypothesize, provided the possibility of avoiding an overly close identification of the author with the "Tolstoy" of *A Confession*. After all, if readers recognize that actions ascribed to the autobiographical narrator were first tried out in fiction, they will be less inclined to believe that narrator, whose discourse is inevitably infected with a taint of the fictional. It appears, then, that what we have in the *Anna Karenina/ A Confession* dialogue is a new attempt on the part of Tolstoy to write about himself and to conceal the fact that he was doing so simultaneously. On the surface, it is now possible to see where Tolstoy is writing about himself and where he is not, at least in the fictional text, for we now have an "authentic" autobiography against which to check Levin's actions. However, hard as he might try to avoid the problems posed by the psychological need for a doubled self vision, Tolstoy cannot succeed in banishing them even with his new dialogic method. For although we can now "know" the difference between truth and fiction in the novel, we lose our certainty that there is truth in the autobiography.

It seems likely, for example, that the optimistic ending Tolstoy provided for Levin in the novel was a form of wish fulfillment. Through Levin, he hoped to exorcise the demons that were tormenting him. It appears from *A Confession* that this strategy failed. Yet, there is no reason to trust *A Confession* either. It, too, was merely an experiment in self-presentation, and its optimistic ending may be no more or less true than the novel's. Breaking the fictional/non-fictional dialogue across two works seems to have muddied the issue of truth, rather than clarified it.

We must recall, in addition, that the overlapping events recounted in the two literary works under consideration occurred, for the most part, before both of them were written. That is, *Anna Karenina* represents an initial response and *A Confession*, which comes later, can be seen as a dialogic modification. Tolstoy may have been using his novel to explore possible solutions to his own life problems. The literary work is not a mirror of the author's life but is, instead, a substitute life in which Tolstoy can try out solutions to his own crisis.

The post-conversion Tolstoy never returned to intergeneric dialogue in anything like the systematic ways in which he had employed it earlier. What is significantly different in the writing of the later period is the attenuation of the specific pole. Only rarely in Tolstoy's later work do we find a strongly autobiographical character. Instead, he provides autopsychological figures; that is to say, characters who think and behave the way Tolstoy would or would have liked to in a given situation. Perhaps the only major exception in the later work is the character of Nikolai Ivanovich Saryntsev in *The Light Shines in the Darkness*. The pain Saryntsev feels because of the insoluble collision between his old and new life seems to mirror Tolstoy's situation. This is particularly true because it derives not from weakness of the will or fear of the loss of creature comforts, but from a recognition of how much suffering his renunciations cause those whom he loves.

The Light Shines in the Darkness remains unfinished, and an exception to the rule in Tolstoy's later oeuvre. In general, the post-conversion Tolstoy found untenable the delicate mix of *dichtung* and *wahrheit* that was the central characteristic of his earlier work. This can be seen most strikingly in a short biographical sketch he produced at the urging of disciple Pavel Biriukov:

> In order not to repeat myself in the depiction of childhood I reread what I had written under that title and regretted that I had written it: it is so bad, so literary, so insincerely written. It could not have been otherwise, first of all because my idea was to write the story not of my childhood but of that of my friends and so the result was a clumsy mix of their childhood and mine.
>
> (*PSS* 34: 348)

It may well be, as J. M. Coetzee has asserted, that while "all of Tolstoy's writing, fictional and nonfictional, is concerned with *truth*; in the late writings the concern with truth overrides all other concerns."[14] But the truth of the later works is not identical to that in *Sevastopol in May* or in *War and Peace, Anna Karenina,* and *A Confession.*

NOTES

1 *PSS* 4: 59. Further references to the works of Tolstoy will be in the text by page and volume number from this standard Russian Jubilee edition. For the convenience of Anglophone readers, I also provide chapter and part numbers where appropriate. Unless otherwise indicated, translations are my own.

2 From the notebooks for *War and Peace*, in *PSS* 13: 53.

3 It is this balance, by the way, that makes Tolstoy the consummate Russian realist, between the poles of Turgenev's generalizing attempts "to extract from human characters their essences" (Ivan Turgenev, *Polnoe sobranie pisem* [Moscow 1961–68], II, 77) and the quiddity of Dostoevsky's "realism in a higher sense" (the term is used in Dostoevsky's notebooks; see N. N. Strakhov, *Biografiia, pisma i zametki iz zapisnoi knigi F. M. Dostoevskogo* [St. Petersburg, 1883], p. 373). For a slightly different interpretation of this phenomenon, see Boris Eikhenbaum, *The Young Tolstoi*, ed. and trans. Gary Kern (Ann Arbor, MI: Ardis), p. 93.

4 For a fuller explication of intergeneric dialogue and its use in Russian literature, see Andrew Wachtel, *An Obsession with History: Russian Writers Confront the Past* (Stanford, CA: Stanford University Press, 1994), pp. 9–13 and *passim*.

5 Aylmer Maude, *The Life of Tolstoy*, 2 vols. (Oxford: Oxford University Press, 1987), vol. I, p. 84.

6 A diary entry for March 20, 1852, indicates just how close the voice I call the author's in the trilogy could be to Tolstoy's own: "Vanity is an incomprehensible passion [. . .] it is a kind of moral disease like leprosy – it does not just destroy one part, but maims the whole – little by little, unnoticed, it sneaks in and then it develops throughout the organism" (*PSS* 46: 94).

7 For a discussion of Tolstoy's suppression of the metahistorical voice in the first sections of *War and Peace*, see Kathryn B. Feuer, *Tolstoy and the Genesis of "War and Peace,"* eds. Robin Feuer Miller and Donna Tussing Orwin (Ithaca, NY: Cornell University Press, 1996), pp. 123–24.

8 Although this type of strategy for generating intergeneric dialogue had never, to my knowledge, been used in autobiographically oriented texts, it had been employed on historical material by Pushkin, whose 1834 *History of Pugachev* "doubles" his 1836 novel *The Captain's Daughter*. For an analysis of this phenomenon, see Wachtel, *Obsession with History*, ch. 3.

9 Steiner, *Tolstoy or Dostoevsky* (New York: Knopf, 1971), p. 105.

10 Thus, I refrain from considering the dialogic implications of the story *Notes of a Madman* which describes the same crisis treated in *Anna Karenina* and *A Confession* precisely because Tolstoy never published the work. That experiment was, it would seem, primarily for himself, and thus readers were not meant to compare it with the two published works, at least not in the same way.

11 Gary Saul Morson, *Hidden in Plain View: Narrative and Creative Potentials in "War and Peace"* (Stanford: Stanford University Press, 1987), p. 162.

12 Lydia Ginzburg uses this term but does not define it in *On Psychological Prose*, ed. and trans. Judson Rosengrant (Princeton, NJ: Princeton University Press, 1991), p. 198.

13 Jean-Jacques Rousseau, *Les Confessions* in *Oeuvres complètes* (Paris: Gallimard, 1959), vol. I, p. 1 (translation mine).

14 J. M. Coetzee, "Confession and Double Thoughts: Tolstoy, Rousseau, Dostoevsky," *Comparative Literature* 37 no. 3 (Summer 1985), 206.

9

EDWINA CRUISE

Women, sexuality, and the family in Tolstoy

In Tolstoy's artistic pursuit of the meaning of human life, femaleness plays a crucial, if not always enviable, role. Especially in the first half of his writing career Tolstoy created female characters who often embodied the potent and volatile emotions aroused by love. Studied both as individuals and as a chronological aggregate, these heroines rehearse and refine over time a quest to find and put into practice the elusive concept of "true love." This search almost invariably assumes transgression.

A major impediment to a full reading of Tolstoy's fiction, especially to his writing on women, centers on a tendency to equate his art and his life, that is to say, to interpret his art as a barely disguised annotation to his personal beliefs. According to one such view, Tolstoy's contempt for women's liberation (called in nineteenth-century Russia "the women question") finds fictional expression in his ideally virtuous mothers – most conspicuously Natasha in *War and Peace* and Kitty in *Anna Karenina* – whose preoccupation with their children satisfies all needs and desires and exhausts all creative potential. Following this line of thinking, Anna Karenina – despite any sympathetic traits she may possess – is condemned because she subverts her biologically determined maternal role and destroys the sanctity of her family. For this violation of natural law, she must die.

On the threshold of fame Tolstoy developed a reputation for orneriness, or, to put it more charitably, he revealed what was to become a defining feature of his life and art: an inherent antipathy toward popular theories and accepted authorities, especially if they were endorsed by members of his own class. In 1855, for example, he locked horns with the editors of *The Contemporary* (Russia's leading literary magazine, which first encouraged Tolstoy's talent) during a dinner given in his honor. In advance of the dinner he had been advised by an older acquaintance (the now forgotten, but then influential novelist D. V. Grigorovich) to abstain from attacking the immensely popular George Sand, whom, in the absence of a distinguished Russian candidate, the literary intelligentsia had adopted as an icon of sexual liberation and women's rights.[1] When the celebration was in full swing, the conversation turned to Sand's latest book. Predictably, Tolstoy created a scene, suggesting that if the heroines of her novels existed in real life, they should be carted around Petersburg on a pillory wagon for the edification of the citizenry. It did not help the situation that among the dinner guests whom Tolstoy addressed were N. A. Nekrasov, his mistress A. Ia. Panaeva, and her husband I. I. Panaev, all three advocates of women's emancipation and well-settled into the socially provocative nature of their *ménage à trois*.

His bluntness on the subject of women became a Tolstoy trademark. There is no shortage of evidence in the ninety-volume edition of Tolstoy's works to persuade even the most dispassionate reader that he espoused a tightly corseted view of appropriate roles for women. Just one example: in an oft-quoted private letter of 1886, prompted by a liberal newspaper's attack on his conservative views on women, Tolstoy wrote that in contrast to the many roles that a man could play in life, a woman had only three charges: "to bear, feed and raise as many children as possible." If she betrayed two of these three responsibilities, she was "negative" and "pernicious."[2] When Tolstoy edited his remarks for publication a few months later he removed the veiled attack against contraception ("as many children as possible") and softened the negative characterization of a non-compliant woman from "pernicious" to "morally inferior to a man" (*PSS* 25: 413–14). Twenty-two years later Tolstoy included a slightly edited version of this essay, now titled "Women," in his well-known series of inspirational texts, *Cycle of Reading*.

Since Tolstoy's death surely the most intelligent defense of Tolstoy against charges of misogyny has been offered by Amy Mandelker. She uses texts written after *Anna Karenina* to affirm complex shifts in Tolstoy's thinking.[3] Indeed, in later life Tolstoy addressed the enormous inequities between time-endorsed roles for women and men with the same passion that characterized male feminists in America almost a century later: "I thought about my churlish and egotistical attitude to my wife...I gave her all the hard work, the so-called women's work to do and went out hunting myself" (*PSS* 52: 143; quoted in Mandelker, *Framing Anna Karenina*, p. 23).

Without characterizing Tolstoy's views as either "for" or "against" women – for that often raises more questions than it answers and says less about Tolstoy and more about the bias of his critics – it is fair to say that *in his essays*, even though he acknowledged the high price a woman had to pay, Tolstoy consistently regarded the mothering role as the most worthy human calling. Tolstoy's views on women, sexuality, and the family expressed *in his fiction*, however, fundamentally changed over time. There is an oft-told story that during the writing of *Anna Karenina* he emerged from his study shaking his head in bewilderment at what Anna had done that day (interestingly almost the same story is told about Flaubert and Emma Bovary). Tolstoy surely did not cast off his convictions when he sat down to creative work, but neither was he fettered by them. As his own characters repeatedly attest, furthermore, moments of certainty, when life seems unwaveringly "clear and simple," are often threatened by their inherently destabilizing potential. In other words, to draw on Isaiah Berlin's dichotomous characterization of Tolstoy, the wily fox is always threatening the single-minded hedgehog. It is in this context that we propose to study Tolstoy's female characters from the early novella *Family Happiness* (1859) to his last novel, *Resurrection* (1899). Over this forty-year period, Tolstoy charts a female quest that overcomes the entrenched barriers of gender conventions. As with the male quest for truth and meaning in life, the female odyssey pursues a moving target. Each moment of understanding contains within it the seeds of a new conflict and, therefore, the stimulus for a course correction to the journey. Nowhere is this more explicitly revealed than in Tolstoy's first major work devoted to the female quest, *Family Happiness*.

Family Happiness is based on Tolstoy's bizarre, mostly epistolary, courtship of Valeriia Arsenieva, a young woman for whose brother Tolstoy had been appointed guardian. His correspondence to her suggests that, while he was toying with the idea of marrying her, he was also exploiting the opportunity to critique popular attitudes toward romantic love and marriage. The letters often assume the tone of a lecture, alternately condescending and reverent:

> Please go for a *walk* every day ... wear a corset and put on your stockings yourself...   (*PSS* 60: 98)

> A great deal that concerns me you shall never understand; but on the other hand I shall never reach that pinnacle of love that you may reach...
>   (*PSS* 60: 115)

> Besides the fact that the vocation of a woman is to be a wife, her major vocation is to be a mother, and to be a *mother* and not simply a *child-bearer* – do you understand the difference? – development is necessary.   (*PSS* 60: 122)

If Tolstoy was in love with Arsenieva, it was not so much with her personally, as with the idea of creating a model wife and mother. His admonitions to her to eschew the frivolous pleasures of their social class may have fallen on deaf ears, but the exercise of composing a virtuous life was surely more for his own benefit than for hers. His sermons on virtue read like an antidote to commonly accepted rituals and mores of his social class. In any case, Tolstoy was affronted when Arsenieva made a successful entrée into high society and their relationship soon foundered. She was not interested in the rather constrained behavior that Tolstoy would have her embrace.

The failed Pygmalion relationship to Arsenieva provided Tolstoy with rich material for his subsequent exploration of women and sexuality in *Family Happiness*, the story of the marriage of an older, worldly man to a provincial young woman. A significant feature of the novella is that it is written in the first person, by the heroine. The Russian text, with its feminine-ending verb forms, morphologically reinforces Tolstoy's boldly female point of view. Writing retrospectively from what we eventually discover is her position as a devoted mother, Masha takes us through her life, occasionally commenting on, but mostly narrating events as a participant in the action. For much of that time she is at the mercy of an unexamined adherence to models of behavior offered by the romantic fiction of her time.

Awaiting the visit of Sergei, the cheerful family guardian twice her age, Masha imagines that her future husband will be quite different, a man of contemporary style: "thin, pale, and sad" (*PSS* 5: 68).[4] Expecting the traditional greeting from men of her class, she is surprised that Sergei does not kiss her hand. Nor, later, does he allow her to play more than one movement of Beethoven's Moonlight Sonata, coolly commenting "you don't play that right" (*GSW* 7; *PSS* 5: 70). From this inauspicious beginning, so much at odds with her romanticized projections, Masha falls under Sergei's influence. In an excess of affected simplicity, she shapes her life around what she thinks he would have her become: "the only certain happiness in life is to live for others" (*GSW* 16; *PSS* 5: 80). She quite believes that only "a trifling effort" is required "to abstain from sin" (*GSW* 27–28; *PSS* 5: 90).

The sober voice of the older narrator breaks the bubble of young Masha's poeticized self-deception: "I was surprised at my own quickness in guessing what was good and worthy of love, when I certainly did not know then what was good and worthy of love.... All my thoughts and feelings of that time were not really mine: they were his thoughts and feelings" (*GSW* 15; *PSS* 5: 79). But that is retrospective wisdom. Masha enters marriage wholly believing the prosaic lessons she has learned by rote from Sergei: "I have always desired just that quiet domestic life and prized it" (*GSW* 38; *PSS* 5: 101).

The adopted sentiments that lead Masha into marriage soon collapse under the pressures of her inexperienced heart. She reverts to romantic fantasies:

> I wanted feeling to be the guide of life, and not life to guide feeling. If only I could go with him to the edge of a precipice and say 'One step, and I shall fall over – one movement and I shall be lost!' then, pale with fear, he would catch me in his strong arms and hold me over the edge till my blood froze, and then carry me off whither he pleased. (*GSW* 49; *PSS* 5: 111)

She finds a cure for the stagnation of domesticity in the hurly-burly of society, basking in her position of its first lady. Only when she is deposed by a younger and prettier woman does she realize that the power-giving adoration of society is ephemeral, and not, as she had thought, "the real thing" (*GSW* 54; *PSS* 5: 116). One more disillusionment awaits her. In the appropriately romantic setting of a ruined castle near the fashionable resort of Baden, she is assaulted by a "storm of feeling" aroused by an Italian marquis, a convenient emblem of predatory and selfish desire (*GSW* 68; *PSS* 5: 131). Only the interruption of a female companion saves her from "the abyss of forbidden delights" and from her imagination's melodrama of "sin and shame" (*GSW* 69; *PSS* 5: 132).

Masha's excursion into society, initially a playground for desire, becomes a battlefield for self-identification; she must lose before she can win. Having experienced the frightening loss of control that accompanies sexual desire, she retreats to the protective security of husband and life in the country. Back in the same music room, with the same scent of lilac and the same sound of nightingales, she plays again the Moonlight Sonata, the emotionally naïve prelude to her relationship with Sergei. This is no simple *de capo aria*, for Tolstoy's characters in quest are always in transition and cannot walk through the same river twice. Aware of life's false paths as she could not have been when she last played Beethoven, Masha prays in anguish to God "to teach [her] what to do and how to live now" (*GSW* 74; *PSS* 5: 136). (With almost the same words Natasha Rostova will pray for guidance after her mock "fall."[5] [*PSS* 11: 73]) The platitudes of her indulgent husband are small comfort: "All of us, and especially you women, must have personal experience of all the nonsense of life" (*GSW* 79; *PSS* 5: 141). Behaving "not [as] a lover, but an old friend," Sergei explains to his wife that "the excitement of searching is over for us; our quest is done" (*GSW* 80; *PSS* 5: 142). And in that instant, Masha directs her unfulfilled passion to her infant child, pressing him to her breast and thinking "Mine, mine, mine!" (*GSW* 81; *PSS* 5: 143).

If by this final image Masha intends to convey a harmonious resolution to her story, she is betrayed by an odd sense of discord. Her narrative neither prepares for nor adequately explains the sudden transformation into a devoted mother. Until this moment, she has ignored her children; the infant she now holds has been mentioned only in passing, and only as an implied cause of ill health. Furthermore, her husband, from whom Masha deliberately conceals her swaddled baby, seems irrelevant both to the birth of her children and to her future life. Even more discordant, affirmation of closure for this now apparently happy family is undercut by issues of control. The treachery inherent in the specious promise of romantic love may have been exposed, but the image of ferociously possessive mother love that replaces it does not bode well for the domestic tranquillity that is supposed to replace it. The maternal passion expressed in Masha's grip on her child leaves no room for any meaningful union between wife and husband.

Regrettably, the monumental quests of Prince Andrei and Pierre Bezukhov in *War and Peace* (1863–69) find no equivalent among the roles cast for female characters. Women have no place on the battlefield, nor are they permitted in the halls of political power, except as visual adornment for the men who decide the fate of nations. Their combative spirit is confined to the drawing room and the bedroom. Marya Dmitrievna, the battle ax known in society as *le terrible dragon*, affectionately calls Natasha a "Cossack" for her fearless and unladylike behavior (*WP* 52, 56; *PSS* 9: 73, 78). The venerable salon hostess Anna Pavlovna, "in the excited condition of a commander on a battlefield," expertly maneuvers Pierre to within striking distance of Hélène's bewitching smile (*WP* 178; *PSS* 9: 248). Princess Lisa, in advanced pregnancy, nonetheless prepares for visitors "like an old war horse that hears the sound of the trumpet" (*WP* 197; *PSS* 9: 275). With a few significant exceptions, women's wars are conducted on the domestic front.

Tolstoy's fictional universe rarely admits women to the greatest battle of human life: death. Natasha and Kitty after her react to the inevitability of death with the grace and intuition that are inherent to their sex. They may puff pillows to ease physical pain and keep vigil over the dying, but these good women are not bogged down by abstract questions of life and death. In exchange for "missing out" on what, it can be argued, are fundamental issues to any sentient being, Tolstoy's virtuous women are privileged in their profoundly satisfying role as mothers and in their secure and uniquely female way of knowing the world.

In Natasha, his most affecting and detailed portrait of a young girl's challenging course to adulthood, Tolstoy presents the most persuasive argument for the nobility and complexity of a woman's successful quest for true love in motherhood. The inflexible and non-developing women who surround her – Liza, Hélène, and Sonia (but not, as will become clear below, Princess Marya) – illuminate the limitations of the kinds of love through which she passes.

Liza, the charming but frivolous child bride, lacks the stamina to be a mother. She is trapped in the captivating innocence which first drew Prince Andrew to her. Her light gait and tripping tongue are inadequate to the weighty responsibilities of bearing and raising a child. And yet, as portrayed by the young Natasha, the artlessness of childhood belongs to the most precious moments of family happiness. Nestled in the bosom of the Rostov tribe, a family of eccentric Dickensian charm, and blissfully ignorant of the struggles ahead, Natasha captures hearts with her enthusiastic and untested curiosity about life's potential. As readers we may know that childhood cannot last, but Tolstoy invites us to join in her world and to reminisce nostalgically about that most perfect time of life.[6]

Vestiges of childhood remain even as Natasha becomes betrothed. The narrator casts doubt on the validity of her feelings when she professes her love for Andrew: "'You know that from the very first day [I met you] I have loved you,' she said, firmly persuaded that she was speaking the truth" (*WP* 422; *PSS* 10: 226). Before Natasha can speak knowledgeably about love, however, she must visit Tolstoy's Opera of Eden and fall prey to that garden's plumply naked serpent, Hélène, an "over the top" Mae West of voluptuous excess, but without the latter's playfulness. It is left to brother Anatole to play Lothario to Natasha's maiden almost gone astray, but credit for the power behind the seduction surely belongs to Hélène. From the moment she fixes her gaze on this most self-confident and beautiful of society's women, Natasha is, without being aware of it, drawn in by Hélène's sexual aura: "She's a woman one could easily fall in love with" (*WP* 498; *PSS* 10: 323). Even as she struggles against the opera's artificial atmosphere (in one of the novel's most celebrated passages), by the end of Act One, and before she has met Anatole, she is already in a state of powerless intoxication and quite ready to "to lean over to Hélène and tickle her" (*WP* 499; *PSS* 10: 325). While both Kuragins conspire to break down Natasha's vestigial defenses, it is Hélène who gains entry to her young protégé's dressing room, there to admire Natasha's beauty while she is in a state of undress.

In the character of Hélène Tolstoy gathers a rich harvest of sexuality's dangerous yield: self-gratification, incest, adultery, abortion, and, most important, the corrupting power that sexual expression awards its practitioners. What is missing in Hélène, of course – aside from her inability to love anyone but herself – is a sense of teasing lightheartedness about erotic desire. Natasha seems to mimic some of that solemnity. Throughout the Kuragin incident Natasha earnestly assumes that she and Anatole will consummate their troika ride down lover's lane at the altar. She can justify her physical attraction to him only as long as he is an eligible suitor. Natasha's sexual horse must always be harnessed to a nuptial carriage: where there is love, there must be marriage. Like almost all virtuous female characters – except Anna – she may imagine, but is never obliged to test, her erotic potential outside of wedlock.

Nonetheless, Natasha escapes the Kuragin snare endowed with the proverbial knowledge of good and evil and a moral strength that not even the best-intentioned child could intuit. But there is no proportion to the curative she imposes on herself. In the period of stern self-denial and atonement that follows, the only actions that she allows herself – to shelter and transport the wounded soldiers, to nurse Andrew and attend his passing, and to take command of the family after Petia's death – are all directed toward others. At this point in her life, as the war literally enters her family's home, Natasha's behavior parallels Sonia's conspicuous dedication to the Rostovs. Unlike Natasha's impassioned altruism, however, there is calculation in Sonia's sacrifices; she accumulates good deeds as if she were using the installment plan to buy her wedding bells. Her release of Nikolai from his pledge, only *after* Natasha and Prince Andrei have been reunited, exposes the shrewdness of Sonia's reckoning. Seemingly at opposite ends of the moral spectrum, Sonia and Hélène have in common their predisposition for self-serving behavior. While Hélène's scheming is ultimately punished by premature death, Sonia is sentenced to live out her days on the margins of the family happiness she has so craved.

Unlike Sonia, Natasha is incapable of calculating shrewdness in hopes of a deferred reward. Fidelity to the past (such as the love Sonia will always feel for Nikolai) is also contrary to Natasha's deeply pragmatic nature. Thus, a resurrected instinct for love, after a hardly decent period of mourning for the deaths of Andrei and Petia, brings Natasha to the threshold of marriage. Moments after she has seen Pierre, "something hidden and unknown to herself, but irrepressible, aw[akens] in Natasha's soul" (*WP* 995; *PSS* 12: 230). Recognizing in her future husband the same "moral bath" (*WP* 990; *PSS* 12: 223) that has washed over her, Natasha is now prepared to fulfill her destiny. Here ends Natasha's journey.

When we next see Natasha, this elaborate prelude to marriage has borne prodigious fruit. Seven years and four children later, she is shockingly unrecognizable: "Her soul was not visible at all. All that struck the eye was a strong, handsome, and fertile woman" (*WP*, Epilogue, 1020; *PSS* 12: 266). Only her own mother is not surprised by this transformation; she can intuit the vital continuity between Natasha the child, who first appeared in the novel clutching a baby doll at her side and bossing her elders at table, and Natasha the overzealous mother and domineering wife. The three generations of Natashas in the epilogue – the old Countess, Pierre's wife, and Princess Marya's child – give concrete definition to the genetic patent for female virtue, enviable for its clarity and conviction, but regrettable for what it denies. Nonetheless, in Natasha's control over her husband and her devotion to him, and in her devotion to her children, expressed most vividly in the way she clutches at her youngest child Petia, she has achieved an enviable state of happiness. Restless with yearning when Pierre is gone, she finds consolation in her child: "That creature [Petia] said: 'You are angry, you are jealous, you would like to pay him out, you are afraid – but here I am! And I am he...'

and that was unanswerable. It was more than true" (*WP* 1024; *PSS* 12: 271). Natasha has achieved a whole and complete love in which the roles of wife and mother are indivisible and interchangeable.

Princess Marya, the other happy wife and mother described in the epilogue, replicates significant moments in Natasha's journey to motherhood: an encounter with Anatole that arouses hopes of "earthly love" (as she so prudishly describes her erotic dreams); a period of self-sacrifice when she believes that serving others is the only vocation available to her; and her (not entirely sanguine) acceptance that she "love[s] her father and her little nephew more than God" (*WP* 429; *PSS* 10: 236). Like Natasha, Princess Marya is guilty of excess in her marriage, but it is of a completely different order. Where Natasha seems fulfilled when she waves diapers in the air to prove that her darling infant is restored to health, Marya's spiritual strivings carry her beyond motherhood and cast a shadow on her marriage. Her husband reverently but fearfully senses her superior intellect and her exalted spiritual capacities. "Countess Mary's soul always strove toward the infinite, the eternal, and the absolute, and could therefore never be at peace. A stern expression of the lofty, secret suffering of a soul burdened by the body appeared in her face" (*WP* 1038; *PSS* 12: 290).

Marya is unique among Tolstoy's female characters; her spiritual aspirations propel her into a realm of cerebration otherwise reserved for male characters. Nikolai may prefigure Levin's zealous dedication to farming in *Anna Karenina*, but it is his wife who best models the spiritual distress that will mark Levin after his marriage. Marya's deeply reflective nature, so characteristic of the Bolkonsky men, may complicate her life as a mother, but she has access to fundamental questions of life and death. Among women, only Anna Karenina explores these issues more viscerally.

In the first epilogue to *War and Peace* "the woman question" is tersely inserted into the final portrait of Natasha, "but these topics were not merely uninteresting to Natasha, she positively did not understand them" (*WP* 1021; *PSS* 12: 268). The Pandora's box of women's rights and relations between husband and wife is opened wide in *Anna Karenina* (1872–77), in many respects an encyclopedia of changing attitudes toward women in Russian society of the 1870s. The epigrammatic opening to the novel, surely the most often quoted lines from any of Tolstoy's works, suggests that happy families do not provide worthwhile material for the novelist. The same may be said of the female characters who bear the weight of ideal virtue: to the extent that they replicate each other, they are devoid of interest. Consider, for example, the similarities between Natasha and Kitty after they have rejected a sincere offer of marriage and been forced to realize the deceit in the men whom they have desired. The operative concept here is desire, although neither young woman has the knowledge to identify that feeling. Treated by doctors (amoral agents of society's march to divide the flesh from the spirit), who cannot recognize spiritual malaise, Kitty and Natasha nonetheless recover. Once they have purged themselves of desire, they acquire an impenetrable armor of virtue. In the process, however, they become straw women, having gained perfect self-control by cutting themselves off from the full experience of emotion inherent in human nature. Their short journey accomplished, they become petrified statues on a pedestal of single-minded and implausibly idealized mother love. True, Kitty sets off amorous sparks and a feisty temper early in marriage, but she soon settles comfortably into the maternal nest sketched by Natasha in the first epilogue of *War and Peace*, oblivious to its resemblance to a straitjacket.

A much more plausible candidate for admiration in *Anna Karenina* is Dolly, who, as Marina Ledkovsky has observed, "represents the ideal of womanhood"; she is "the keeper of the family principle" who embodies the "capacity for selfless love and self-sacrifice."[7] Dolly, Tolstoy's most realistically depicted woman, may be the standard bearer for female virtue, but she pays a heavy price for her loving nature. For all and forever the generous friend, Dolly makes a point of visiting Anna on Vronsky's country estate. On her journey there, in the leisure of unaccustomed solitude, she reflects on her life, on the death of her last born, and the dulling travail of her fifteen-year marriage. "And all that for what?" she asks herself, "so much torment, so much work...A whole life ruined" (*PSS* 19: 181–82).[8] She characterizes herself as a prisoner temporarily released "from a world that is killing [her] with cares" (*AK* 608; *PSS* 19: 182). Reflecting on Anna's love affair, she finds comfort in imagining "an almost identical love affair of her own" (*AK* 609; *PSS* 19: 183). Softened by these reveries, Dolly arrives at her destination predisposed to approve of Anna's new family and new life. But when her theoretical approval is tested by Anna's disclosure that she uses contraception, even though that is "the very thing she had dreamed of that morning on her way there," Dolly visibly shrinks from the proposition that sexual relations have pleasure as their sole aim (*AK* 637; *PSS* 19: 214).

While Dolly may embody the domestic values of the novel, she does not accept that responsibility lightly. But she does accept it: she will not condemn Anna, but neither will she permit herself to cross the line into Anna's terrain. She may chafe under the restrictions of her life, she may fantasize about liberation from her rôles as wife and mother, but the dissociation of sexual intercourse from procreation represents for her too great a transgression of the natural order of things, of the way that life is supposed to be. Cutting short her visit to Anna, Dolly will return to and remain in an asymmetric marriage, loving Stiva, but not being loved by him in return. Her husband will continue to cheat on her with impunity, but she will no longer fantasize about a different or better life.

It is not possible to be sanguine about Dolly's future. Her tenuous relationship to Stiva and her depressive anger more realistically capture the downside of the marriage contract than the overly schematic intellectual and spiritual barriers that divide Levin from an unsuspecting Kitty. To keep her children safe she will make the best of her deeply flawed marriage. The emotional pain of that tight-fitting paradigm of virtuous motherhood ennobles her commitment to family.

It is left to Anna, then, Tolstoy's most brilliant and most complex heroine, to do battle against the rigid distinctions between male and female experience, between the push of the spirit and the pull of the flesh. Anna is the première example of a woman in quest, neither an antipode to desexualized motherhood, nor an erotic cartoon like Hélène, but a woman at war with herself. That Anna is in conflict is apparent from her very first appearance in the novel. Her future lover recognizes Anna's erotic potential the moment he sets eyes on her:

> Vronsky had time to notice the restrained animation that played over her face and fluttered between her shining eyes and the barely noticeable smile that curved her red lips. It was as if a surplus of something so overflowed her being that it expressed itself beyond her will ... She deliberately extinguished the light in her eyes, but it shone against her will in a barely noticeable smile.
>
> (*AK* 61; *PSS* 18: 66).[9]

In her marriage Anna finds no release for the sexual energy that lies so close to her surface. She is inured, perhaps unconsciously, to the inappropriateness of expressing that vitality in her relationship to her husband; meeting him at the station on her return from Moscow she shuts it down (*AK* 106; *PSS* 18: 112–13). Nor does she find release in mothering. Despite her exaggerated search for the maternal joys that save Dolly from unadulterated despair, Anna is, even before her affair with Vronsky, erratic in her attitude toward Seryozha. He, too, can be a drag on her spirit, "produc[ing] in Anna a feeling akin to disappointment" (*AK* 107; *PSS* 18: 114). Ultimately, at least not in terms of society's judgment, neither the fact of Anna's affair with Vronsky nor her inconstancy as a mother are especially crucial issues. The central – indeed, the only – issue for these powerful arbiters of respectability is not *what* Anna does, but *how* she does it.

There are among Anna's friends women who can carry on their extramarital relationships with careless *joie de vivre*, immune to feelings of guilt or society's censure, if only because they acknowledge no wrongdoing. On the pretext of speaking about another woman's affair, Betsy Tverskaia (Vronsky's first cousin) advises Anna on the etiquette of adultery: "You see, one and the same thing can be looked at tragically and be made into a torment, or can be looked at simply and even gaily. Perhaps you're inclined to look at things too tragically" (*AK* 298; *PSS* 18: 315). Indeed, Anna's passion for Vronsky and her struggle to suppress that passion take their relationship out of the realm of casual pleasure, easily gained and painlessly relinquished or exchanged. That fact alone distinguishes her from her brother, to whom she is unjustly compared. Stiva's shameless abuse of his marital vows is just that – without shame or guilt. Anna, by contrast, is both troubled by the choices she has so much trouble making and anguished by the deceptions they require. Anna cannot adopt the fatuous deceptions of Princess Betsy's demi-monde society. As Princess Miagkaia, a woman of blunt common sense, explains it: "[Anna] did no more than what everybody, except me, does but keeps hidden. She didn't want to deceive and she did splendidly" (*AK* 731; *PSS* 19: 309).

A measure of Anna's struggle is contained in her attempt to unite her heart's desires to the demands of conscience defined by her marital bond. She achieves a sense of wholeness about her life only in dreams – a realm of imagination beyond her or anyone's control – by projecting the dividedness she feels onto Vronsky and Karenin. In this happy and impossible resolution to her conflicts, she is wife to *both* Alexeis, and they are content to share her. Only in her "deathbed" scene – and it is crucial to our understanding of the situation that, despite the atmosphere of an elaborately staged melodrama, all present, including Anna, are quite convinced that she will die – does she choose to exorcize what she regards as the sinful part of herself, her awakened body. Perhaps Anna is not making a choice, but fearfully acceding to the moral dictates of church and society, begging forgiveness at the eleventh hour for the transgressions that have allowed her to taste life's fullness. In her feverish delirium she addresses her husband with a disarming emotional intensity, transferring the doubling that she has ascribed to Karenin and Vronsky onto herself: "I'm the same... But there is another woman in me, I'm afraid of her – she fell in love with that man, and I wanted to hate you and couldn't forget the other who was there before. The one who is not me. Now I'm real, I'm whole" (*AK* 412; *PSS* 18: 434). These lines, in which Anna alternately speaks of herself as "she" and as "I" may reflect the dividedness that she feels, but the statement "Now I'm real, I'm whole" suggests that she believes she has achieved a unity of her body and her soul. Whatever Anna means to say, she is clear about her desire for forgiveness. It is one of the few moments in the novel when she states emphatically what is on her mind. An agitated and imperious Anna commands Karenin: "Give him [Vronsky] your hand. Forgive him," after which she is ready to die (*AK* 413; *PSS* 18: 435). Only her apparently final words, in which she simultaneously appeals to God and cries for morphine suggest that she is not entirely free of her evasive fantasy of doubling and dividing. Her soul calls to God, while her body cries for physical comfort.

Whatever she may be feeling, the reactions of Vronsky and Karenin smack of a momentary exchange of rôles, rather than a genuine concurrence with the feeble logic of Anna's vision of harmony and wholeness. Karenin is emotionally laid bare by the rapture of the moment; he experiences a tearful epiphany of ecstatic Christian love for his wife, the new-born child that he will accept as his own, and even for his enemy Vronsky. Vronsky, for his part, acknowledges that he has been defeated by Karenin and he envies the honor and dignity that his rival has denied him. Vronsky feels for the first and only time in his relationship to Anna a sense of shame and unpardonable guilt. Peculiar to both men is that in their powerful and powerfully self-centered reactions, they think about Anna's situation only as it affects themselves.

In any case, Anna's timely and gracefully orchestrated exit is not to be. The men in her life shortly revert to character, thereby destroying any hope of compromise. When her life is no longer in danger, Anna once again responds to the strongest push, in this case Vronsky's passionate embrace. Later, when she cannot find fulfillment in that relationship, she will be pulled back to hearth and home by thoughts of her adoring son. These opposed and competing attractions of lover versus son, and of the rich erotic potential of her body's yearnings versus a mother's sacrifices of self for children and family are mutually exclusive. Therein lies her tragedy. Hers is a spiritual struggle without the possibility of resolution.

But who or what is responsible for the situation in which Anna is trapped? Should we view Anna's suicide as a decisive assertion of self-control over her life? Or is Anna a victim, done in by the men to whom she has aligned herself, to a husband who cannot imagine his wife as a sexual being, to a lover who cannot imagine the depths of her suffering? Is Anna a heroine for her valiant quest to resist the pressure of public opinion and live to her full potential? Is society justified in limiting Anna's freedom of action? Is Anna accountable for her choices and therefore guilty of selfish excess? . . . Such questions replicate the conflicts that Anna herself experiences; they do not lend themselves to simple "Yes" or "No" answers. Such questions also reveal a great deal about the experience of reading *Anna Karenina*. Unlike *War and Peace*, which slowly unfolds its diverse, but interconnected and mutually reinforcing wholesome messages about the human condition, *Anna Karenina* equivocates, destabilizes, and denies a sense of security or certainty. Anna models that destabilization and as readers continue to puzzle over issues of personal freedom and family responsibility, she will forever be caught in the conflict.

Anna Karenina has prompted generations of readers to propose, dispose, and continually revise and reinvent the nature of female experience. The novel embodies Tolstoy's most sustained inquiry into the irresistible power and destructive potential of sexual desire, female *or* male. After it the erotic conflict that characterizes Anna's quest is passed on to men, but Tolstoy never again writes about human sexuality with such complexity or dramatic power. Furthermore, female characters after Anna are most often reduced to emblematic vessels of desire and their journeys become increasingly schematic. In *The Kreutzer Sonata* (1889), for example, sexuality takes on the character of addiction. The raving Pozdnyshev murders his wife – the guilty vessel – to quell his sexual conflicts, but whatever he thinks he may have achieved, he has failed to conquer his flesh. He will spend the rest of his days riding the rails in search of an audience so that he may restage and relive his dramatic story. In the two endings to the unfinished *The Devil*, also written in 1889, the adulterous hero Irtenev alternately hauls himself out of the sexual abyss by (1) killing himself in an excess of guilt for betraying his wife and giving in to his animal passion, or by (2) killing the guilt-free, lusty peasant woman who fires his desire. More important for the female quest, the moral authority previously bestowed on virtuous mothers no longer applies. Irtenev's innocent and unsuspecting wife may be without sin, but like her namesake in *War and Peace*, sickly Liza, prone to complications in pregnancy and unable to nurse her child, is no model for motherhood or the power of family love. It is only in *Resurrection*, with its wholesale rejection of sexuality, that women and men together can achieve a harmonious relationship with each other and with themselves.

In *Resurrection* (1899) Tolstoy resoundingly denies the former idyll of family happiness and the virtues of motherhood he so insistently affirmed in earlier novels. The "true love" that *Resurrection* celebrates is celibate. It liberates women from the nuclear family and liberates both women and men from the inevitable corruption of relationships with a sexual component. Once the Gordian knot has been boldly cut, once eros has been exorcized from love, the angst of the female quest won't even make it to moot court. The love sanctioned in *Resurrection* is neither whole nor complete, but it does vitiate the destructive power of sex. The former prostitute Katiusha embodies that generous quality of love. Like Masha, Natasha, and Kitty before her she has been seduced by the power of erotic love; unlike them, she has been obliged to live with the consequences. Like Anna she has endured the social penalties of unsanctioned love. But unlike Anna, Katiusha's experiences as a prostitute have exposed her to the hypocritical underbelly of sexual desire and she has been its degraded and helpless victim.

In the introduction to this chapter we spoke of "a female quest that overcomes entrenched barriers of gender conventions." Anna tries, but dies in that quest. Katiusha succeeds, but takes that quest to an absurd extreme. Under the influence of the utopian vision that guides her fellow convicts, Katiusha willingly embraces celibacy, thereby freeing herself from the destructive influence of predatory male desire, but the baby and the husband and the family all get thrown out with the bath water. It is an implausible solution to an insoluble problem.

NOTES

1 D. V. Grigorovich, "Literaturnye vospominaniia," *L. Tolstoi v vospominaniiakh sovremennikov* (Moscow: G.I.Kh.L., 1960), p. 174.
2 *PSS* 85: 347–48. Subsequent references from this standard Russian Jubilee edition will be cited in the text by volume and page numbers.
3 Amy Mandelker, *Framing Anna Karenina: Tolstoy, the Woman Question, and the Victorian Novel* (Columbus, OH: Ohio State University Press, 1993), pp. 15–33.
4 Leo Tolstoy, *Great Short Works of Leo Tolstoy*, trans. Louise and Aylmer Maude (New York: Perennial Library, 1967), p. 4. Subsequent quotations from this edition will be cited in the text as *GSW*.
5 Leo Tolstoy, *War and Peace*, trans. Louise and Aylmer Maude, ed. George Gibian, 2d ed. (New York: W. W. Norton, 1996), p. 587. Subsequent quotations from this edition will be cited in the text as *WP*.
6 See George Clay, "Balancing Immediacy with Overview," *Tolstoy's Phoenix: From Method to Meaning in War and Peace* (Evanston, IL: Northwestern University Press, 1988), pp. 7–19.
7 Marina Ledkovsky, "Dolly Oblonskaia as a Structural Device in Anna Karenina," *Canadian-American Slavic Studies* 12, No. 4 (Winter 1978), 543–48.
8 Leo Tolstoy, *Anna Karenina*, trans. Richard Pevear and Larissa Volokhonsky (New York: Viking Penguin, 2001), p. 607. Subsequent quotations from this edition will be cited in the text as *AK*.
9 This passage is deftly analyzed by Donna Tussing Orwin in *Tolstoy's Art and Thought 1847–1880* (Princeton, NJ: Princeton University Press, 1993), p. 183.

10

GEORGE R. CLAY

Tolstoy in the twentieth century

War and Peace and *Anna Karenina* were written more than 130 years ago and, to quote Lionel Trilling, since the end of the nineteenth century "literary production has been enormously brilliant and enormously relevant."[1] Relevant, that is, to the era of Einstein, Freud, the Russian Revolution, two world wars, the Great Depression, the Holocaust, the atomic bomb, Vietnam, the Cold War, movies, television, and our current electronic sea change. This era has produced the often overwhelming fiction of such writers as Proust, Joyce, Mann, Woolf, Kafka, Hemingway, Faulkner, Bowen, Welty, and Porter: writers who, between 1900 and 1950, achieved the "psychologizing" of the novel, its powerful adoption of interior monologue and other stream-of-consciousness techniques. Where, then, does Tolstoy fit into this Modernist web?

He is right at the center of it. For instance, what has been called the "deathbed monologue" – in such twentieth-century fiction as Thomas Mann's *Death in Venice* (1912), Marcel Proust's *Time Regained* (1927), Dorothy Richardson's *Pilgrimage* (1931), Ernest Hemingway's "The Snows of Kilimanjaro" (1936), Katherine Ann Porter's *Pale Horse, Pale Rider* (1939), Hermann Broch's *The Death of Virgil* (1945), Samuel Beckett's *Malone Dies* (1951), Carlos Fuentes's *The Death of Artemio Cruz* (1962), D. M. Thomas's *The White Hotel* (1981) – such monologues can be traced as far back as the death of Praskukhin in *Sevastapol in May* as well as to the severely wounded Prince Andrei's stream-of-consciousness in *War and Peace* (816–17; *PSS* 11: 385–88), Anna's last ride in *Anna Karenina* (684–689; *PSS* 19: 336–43), and of course *The Death of Ivan Ilich*. If we consider near-sleep to be the "living" counterpart of near-death, we could add to this list Nikolai Rostov's guard duty the night before Austerlitz (230–33; *PSS* 9: 322–23),[2] when, time and again, he nearly drops off to sleep on horseback as his interior monologue segues into stream-of-consciousness. And probably the most famous modernist near-sleep monologue reminiscent of those in Tolstoy's fiction is Molly Bloom's soliloquy at the end of James Joyce's *Ulysses* (1919–22).

While he was experimenting with stream-of-consciousness as early as his quickly abandoned "A History of Yesterday" (1852), and also *Childhood, Boyhood, Youth* (1857), Tolstoy was not the first to use such psychologizing devices. As has often been pointed out, to one extent or another all creative writers try to render aspects of their characters' inner lives. For examples of monologue long before Tolstoy, turn to Lawrence Sterne's *Tristram Shandy* (1759–67), Daniel Defoe's *Robinson Crusoe* (1719), or to *Hamlet* (performed 1600–01). But Tolstoy's monologues are not, or not entirely, internalized dialogues: characters talking to themselves, as Hamlet does – verbalizing ideas already formed in the character's mind, and clearly addressed to the reader or audience. In his most daring attempts, Tolstoy tries to convey the psychic process itself: the spontaneous, chaotic, rapidly spinning or uncannily slowed-down interchange of feelings and thoughts as they unfold into surprising new feelings, or perhaps into fleeting memories which double back on themselves, blending the real with dreamlike fusions of past, present, and future.

Here is an example from the chapter including Nikolai's guard duty before Austerlitz:

> *Rostov lifted his head that had sunk almost to his horse's mane and pulled up beside the hussar. He was succumbing to irresistible, youthful, childish drowsiness.* "But what was I thinking? I mustn't forget. How shall I speak to the Emperor? No, that's not it – that's tomorrow. Oh yes! Natasha . . . sabretache . . . saber them . . . Whom? The hussars with mustaches . . . I thought about him too, just opposite Guryev's house . . . Old Guryev . . . Oh, but Denisov's a fine fellow. But that's all nonsense. The chief thing is that the Emperor is here. How he looked at me and wished to say something, but dared not . . . No, it was I who dared not. But that's nonsense, the chief thing is not to forget the important thing I was thinking of. Yes, Na-tasha, sabretache, oh, yes, yes! That's right!" *And his head once more sank to his horse's neck.*
>
> (231; italics added; *PSS* 9: 322–23)

Here is a wide awake, daytime example from *Anna Karenina*. Anna is being driven in a "comfortable calèche, which rocked gently on its elastic springs," to confide in and ask advice from her sister-in-law, Dolly Oblonskaia:

> *She began reading the signboards.* "'Office and Stores . . . Dental Surgeon . . .' Yes, I will tell Dolly everything. She is not fond of Vronsky. It will be humiliating and painful, but I will tell her everything. She is fond of me and I will follow her advice. I won't submit to him; I won't let him educate me . . . 'Filippov, Bakery . . .' It is said they send dough to Petersburg. The Moscow water is so good. Oh, and the wells in Mytischi, and the pancakes!"

And she remembered, when she was seventeen, she visited the Troitsa monastery
with her aunt.   (684–85; italics added; *PSS* 19: 336–37)

The italicized sentences show us Tolstoy the omniscient nineteenth-century novelist, guiding the reader, using logical concepts understood by everybody: consensual language. But in the rest of each passage, Tolstoy intermittently employs techniques later adopted by Joyce, Virginia Woolf, and all the interior monologists that followed them. Thus while Tolstoy is a prime Realist, when the occasion requires it he applies Modernist stream-of-consciousness techniques. The main one (pre-dating Freud's discussion of it) is free association: "The hussars with mustaches...I thought about him too, just opposite Guryev's house...Old Guryev...Oh, but Denisov's a fine fellow"; "'Filippov, Bakery'...it is said they send their dough to Petersburg. The Moscow water is so good. Oh, and the wells in Mytischi, and the pancakes!" Another device – words whose sounds breed other words, which evolve into ideas: "Natasha...sabretache...saber them...Whom? The hussars with mustaches."

Like Tolstoy, Joyce veers from the real to the surreal. Here are Leopold Bloom's mental meanderings as he thinks about his wife's lover, Blazes Boylan:

> Mr. Bloom reviewed the nails of his left hand, then those of his right hand. The nails, yes. Is there anything more in him that they she sees? Fascination. Worst man in Dublin. That keeps him alive. They sometimes feel what a person is. Instinct. But a type like that. My nails. I am just looking at them: well pared. And after: thinking alone. Body gets a bit softy. I would notice that from remembering. What causes that I suppose the skin can't contract quickly enough when the flesh falls off. But the shape is there. The shape is there still. Shoulders. Hips. Plump. Night of the dance dressing. Shift stuck between the cheeks behind.[3]

While Tolstoy was not the first European writer to use interior monologue, he may well have been the first to use it so often, and so purposefully; not until Joyce did any writer match his virtually Modernist sophistication. In this respect, it is interesting to compare Tolstoy with two important premodernists: Henry James and Marcel Proust.

James, for example in *The Ambassadors* (1903), is a step closer to Modernism than Tolstoy in one respect, and well behind him in another. He is closer in that, like Joyce and Woolf, he uses the viewpoint of a single character, his protagonist Lambert Strether, for the entire novel, thus shifting the dramatic center from outside, where Tolstoy pretty much kept it, to inside, reducing the visible author to a relatively (though not entirely) indirect role. James is standing, as it were, just behind his protagonist's left shoulder, selecting who and what he will be exposed to, notice, learn from . . . and in what order. But he is not as Modernist as Tolstoy in that interior mono- logue at the pre-speech level was not even remotely within James's creative consideration. As Richard Blackmur noted, "Looseness of any description, whether of conception or of execution, he hated contemptuously."[4] "There is nothing," James said, "so deplorable as a work of art with a *leak* in its interest."[5]

Even Proust's awesome mental gyrations are not as close to Joyce's interior monologue as Tolstoy's are. In his *Remembrance of Things Past* (1913–27) he uses a single viewpoint (his own) but, unlike either Joyce or Tolstoy, he makes no attempt to convey the psyche *qua* psyche. He is only interested in the memory capacity of consciousness – its ability to bring back the past in such a way as to show us a disintegrating Parisian society. Still, he introduces us to one of the most basic Modernist achievements, preceding even Joyce in what has been called the "musicalization" of the novel: its exchange of a forward-marching story line for a back-and-forth thematic development.

Nevertheless, it is not until Joyce that a Tolstoyan level of interior mono- logue is achieved, then surpassed. And whether or not he was consciously influenced by his predecessor, we know how much Joyce admired Tolstoy: relished "their common interest in the minutiae of life" and in "the myster- ies of conscious and unconscious life." Joyce felt that Tolstoy was "second in magnitude [. . .] only to such major luminaries as Ibsen, Dante and Shakespeare." Indeed Joyce once claimed that Tolstoy's *How Much Land Does a Man Need?* is "the greatest story that the literature of the world knows."[6]

As others have pointed out, the difference between Tolstoy's and Joyce's stream-of-consciousness is not one of kind but of degree. Such passages as the two quoted above, from *War and Peace* and *Anna Karenina*, repre- sent samples of interior monologue embedded within the realistic narrative framework of each novel – most often before death or sleep or, if awake, in a state of crisis. In Joyce's work, interior monologue is sustained throughout two very long novels – *Ulysses* (1918–22) and *Finnegans Wake* (1928–39) – with the least possible authorial intervention.

When stream-of-consciousness is used so extensively, the novelist faces problems which Tolstoy could never have imagined. Put simply, the chal- lenge for Joyce was to render the free-flowing, utterly private (therefore incoherent to an outsider) nature of his character's psyche, but to do so in ways allowing the reader to arrive somewhere that makes sense. As Derek Attridge put it, Joyce had, gradually, to provide "judiciously organized nuggets of information that will create an onward drive toward revelation and resolution."[7] Such "nuggets" were not needed by Tolstoy, who used stream-of-consciousness intermittently; and the same is true, for the same reason, of Mann, Woolf (except in *The Waves*), and much of Faulkner. After Joyce and Woolf, pre-speech monologue slowly worked its way back to where it had been under Tolstoy: used occasionally – and with great skill by, for example, Elizabeth Bowen and Katherine Ann Porter.

With unbelievable ingenuity, Joyce devised techniques that could lend meaning (enough meaning) to his inherently meaningless novels, giving the reader reference points, like rocks in a mountain stream, within the free flow of his character's psyche. One of his principal devices is Aristotelian: the unities of time, place, and cast. *Ulysses* takes place over eighteen hours, in one city, with three characters; *Finnegans Wake*, also in one city, is rendered through the dreaming psyche of a single character during one night. Another Joycean device is the *leitmotif*: filling his novel, almost musically, with recurring images, words, symbols, and phrases that relate to a particular idea, or perhaps to a theme running through the entire novel, such as (in *Ulysses*) Stephen Dedalus's remorse over the way he behaved at his mother's deathbed. Joyce also tells us such homely details as the songs his characters sing and how much they pay for whatever they buy. Perhaps the most important anti-confusion device of all, as the title *Ulysses* makes clear, is Joyce's Homeric prototype, the *Odyssey*. Bloom is Ulysses, Stephen Dedalus is his son, Telemachus, and Molly Bloom is Penelope. Everything Bloom does, throughout this June day and night in Dublin, is related in some way to one adventure or another in Homer's *Odyssey*... often as not, turning it into burlesque.

Joyce's rationalizing techniques and devices allow readers to keep returning, despite his "Jabberwocky" streams-of-consciousness (Edmund Wilson's nonsensical term, from Lewis Carroll's *Through the Looking Glass*), to fairly reliable focal points. And they also allow Joyce to plunge, as Wilson says, to "a level below particularized language [...] in the region whence all languages arise and where impulses to all acts have their origin."[8] In short, Joyce has, with *Ulysses* and *Finnegans Wake*, altered the previously assumed connections between language and narrative, language and the reader, language and the world... as well as altering the relationship between the ordinary and the heroic, making each stand for the other. And in achieving these fundamental shifts Joyce, of course, departs radically from Tolstoy's reliable, omniscient narrator, consensual language, altogether stable world where values and identity are taken for granted. Yet despite the immense differences between these two writers' approaches to reality, *Ulysses* and *War and Peace* have a surprising number of basic aspects in common – so many, and so important, one can't help feeling that Joyce may have learned

considerably more from Tolstoy than his nineteenth-century interior monologue techniques.

To begin with, each writer rebelled against the conventional novel of his
day. Tolstoy deliberately discarded traditional elements of the "well-made"
European novel with its dovetailed, tongue-and-grooved plot developing inevitably toward some sad or happy ending: Elizabeth and Darcy's marriage in
Pride and Prejudice, Emma's death in *Madame Bovary*. In such novels, time
is predominantly psychological. The hero or heroine's destiny determines
the rate at which time passes because all scenes postulate an end that will
resolve some problem posed at the beginning and which, at the climax, will
reveal the protagonists' comic or tragic fate. But Tolstoyan time (like nature's)
doesn't run out; it runs on. His novel is seemingly plotless and open-ended,
with neither a causal progression nor a clear climax. Like *War and Peace*,
Joyce's novel is also open-ended; since there is no climax for it to lead to, his
time is Tolstoyan – running on, not out. Is it not possible that Tolstoy's highly
structured lack of structure was, among many other sources, an important
part of Joyce's quarry? I say "structured lack of structure" because each
writer's departure from convention required an even more rigorous organiz-
ing conception than is needed by novels of narrower scope; and in both cases
their masterpieces were given exactly that, in the form of a complex cyclical
structure.

Tolstoy's two major themes in *War and Peace* – the War of 1812, and
what critics have called "the march of generations" – show us that God's
(or Nature's) cyclical design is *death-and-resurrection*: the symbiotic relationship between life and death and all their surrogates, including not only
war and peace but such presumed opposites as good and evil, tears and
laughter, right and wrong, sun and shade, selfishness and unselfishness, the
finite and the infinite, joy and sorrow, ecstasy and despair. Tolstoy was convinced that such reciprocal opposites, surrogates for Life and Death, are
symbiotic: that one could not exist without the other, for each presupposes
the other. Symbolically speaking, there is no death without resurrection and
each resurrection is followed by the next death, ad infinitum.

This phoenix design is dramatized by Napoleon's eastward invasion, starting in 1805 and ending seven years later with the Battle of Borodino, the
burning of Moscow, and the disastrous French retreat. Russia "died" with
the burning of its ancient capital and was resurrected as the French drew back
in deathly flight from the northern winter. As for Tolstoy's second story, the
march of generations, its phoenix cycle is obvious: like every generation, his
protagonists rise as their parents die off, then gradually decline as the children begin, in turn, their natural succession. Tolstoy starts his novel in 1805

with Natasha, just thirteen, snatching her first kiss, and ends it with Prince Andrei's son Nikolenka, at fourteen, having dreams of glory – a cyclical orbit from puberty to puberty.

Thus with admirable economy the historical phoenix pattern of the invaded Russian people's fall and rise is enacted within the biological phoenix cycle of the defending generation's rise and fall. This is the juxtaposed, twice-repeated death-and-resurrection design within which Tolstoy fits his characters' interactions. And through those interactions he renders endless variations of the same overall phoenix pattern as he puts each of his five protagonists through a series of mock deaths and resurrections, intricately interwoven with the war and with the process of growing older. Each death (physical or spiritual, real or symbolic) leads to a rebirth bearing seeds of the next death, which in turn is transformed into another regeneration, forming chains of phoenix replications so subtly interlinked and overlapping that they are beyond human conception. By dramatizing its replications, Tolstoy is rendering his cyclical conception of what governs the life, not just of five protagonists or even just of his numerous subsidiary characters, but of everyone, everywhere, at any time.[9]

To convince us that this phoenix design is the law of life, Tolstoy needs to create a whole world around his five protagonists, a sample large enough to constitute a cross-section of humanity and its typical concerns. In its staggering totality, his cross-section provides a truly panoramic outlook, consisting of perspectives and values reflecting not only multifarious personality types but social positions ranging from the peasants Karataev and Dron, to Count Ilia Rostov's manager Dmitrii, to the cheerfully déclassé "Uncle," through the Tushins, Denisovs, Rostovs, Bolkonskys, right on up the scale to Tsar Alexander. All phases of military life are represented, headquarters to front line, generals to footsoldiers. Views on religion range from Princess Marya's unquestioning faith and drenching spirituality to her father's irritated atheism. Parent-to-child relationships range from those of old Count Bezukhov to those of Countess Rostova, with many in between. Kinds of love, or of lust, and kinds of hate or hostility, are enormously varied, as are friendships, ambition, courage, greed, enjoyment.

In *Ulysses*, the counterpart to Tolstoy's cross-section of humanity is Joyce's Dublin which, through the multiplex consciousness of his three protagonists, becomes a symbolic day–night condensation of all possible human responses. Like the *Odyssey* (though in microcosm), it is epochal; and the epoch form is, by definition, cyclical. Its universality implies repetition, rendering what all humanity experiences over and over again: the Joycean/Homeric adventure after adventure, eventually leading home.

As for *Finnegans Wake*, it begins in the middle of a sentence which becomes the last half of the book's last sentence, conveying the novel's circular, hence timeless nature. Moreover, Joyce structured it around the cyclical theory of Giambattista Vico's *New Science* (1725, 1744), which posits four endlessly repeated eras: the Divine Age, followed by the Heroic Age, which leads to the Human Age, finally coming around to the time of *Ricorso* or Rebirth, after which there is a God-like clap of thunder and the four-part cycle begins again. Each of the novel's four sections represents one of these Viconian quarters. And following Vico, Joyce (like Tolstoy with his phoenix cycles) believed that while all comic or happy-ending eras will sooner or later become tragic, the reverse is just as true: everyone who has experienced mock death will be resurrected.

We have mentioned the crucial Homeric element in *Ulysses*. *Wake* also has not a Homeric but an ancient Irish mythic element that parallels the death-and-resurrection design of *War and Peace*. Finnegan – infamous hod-carrier from the old Irish ballad, "Finnegan's Wake" – falls off a ladder and dies; then, in the ballad, some kindly fellow spills whiskey on his lips and brings him back to life. *Wake* opens at the very end of this mythic age, which is where it also closes: a circular, Viconian loop.

Since both of Joyce's big novels are cyclical, therefore timeless, neither has what we think of as a climax. And there is no suspense, for suspense is what leads, through causal progress, to a novel's climax. And, as already discussed, the same lack of suspense applies to *War and Peace*. We are not encouraged to wonder anxiously whether Prince Andrei will survive his wounds at Austerlitz; whether Pierre will be killed in his duel with Dolokhov, or by Davout's firing squad; whether Princess Marya will escape capture by the French. Instead of suspense, in both *Ulysses* and *War and Peace* there are what Henry James called "shocks of recognition." Such shocks (sudden, unexpected realizations) are what hold the reader's attention in the absence of curiosity about what will happen next. As one critic put it, while reading *War and Peace* "we are not concerned with the causes or consequences of the scene; we are concerned with the immediacy, the pure present time, of the fictive experience."[10] And such "immediacy" applies more than fully to *Ulysses*. As Samuel Beckett tells us, Joyce's writing "is not *about* something; *it is that something*."[11]

Joyce and Tolstoy have the same goal: to capture reality, unveil the universal. But of course each one does it in his own highly effective way. Tolstoy was determined to present his characters' interactions in all their humdrum complexity, at a level where truth is least avoidable – the level of involuntary thoughts, habitual gestures, surprised and secret feelings. Here are two almost random examples. In the first, sixteen-year-old Nikolai is home on his first army furlough:

> His brother and sisters struggled for places nearest to him and disputed with one another who should bring his tea, handkerchief, and pipe.
>
> Rostov was very happy in the love they showed him; but the first moment of meeting had been so beatific that his present joy seemed insufficient, and he kept expecting more, more and yet more. (259; *PSS* 10: 6)

When Natasha was engaged to the absent Prince Andrei, she and her father called on the Bolkonskys for the first time. They were met by Princess Marya, who tried to be gracious but felt, and seemed, less than friendly. Sensing her father's discomfort, Natasha blushed, "grew still angrier at having blushed, and looked at [Princess Marya] with a bold and defiant expression which said that she was not afraid of anybody" (494; *PSS* 10: 318).

Nikolai "expecting more, more and yet more"; Natasha following her blush of embarrassment with a look of defiance... these are universal interactions, shocks of recognition that show us ways we have all felt at one time or another. Tolstoy assumes that there is a common reservoir of everyday responses to which we have access through our own personal experiences, and he would lead us there by way of shared associations – so many of them that we almost enter into collaboration with the author as a universal language is formed, based on our agreement with his behavioral insights. And Joyce's insights into the mind's pre-conscious life (or lives) seem just as timelessly real, as universal, on an entirely different level. Rather than through collaboration, he involves us by giving us unbelievably subtle clues with which to try to "solve" his intricate puzzles within puzzles within puzzles.

"Influence" is perhaps too presumptuous a word to use when considering Tolstoy's effect upon Joyce. But it is not claiming too much to suggest that, since Joyce so greatly admired Tolstoy's fiction, Joyce's own fiction might have been enriched by those Tolstoyan devices and techniques, approaches and goals, that must particularly have appealed to him: the open-ended, cyclical structure and meaning of *War and Peace*, combined with its infinite detail – Tolstoy's microscopic focus combined with his universal overview; his cross-section of humanity; his Naturalism, with truth as its goal; his comprehensiveness; his staggering variety of viewpoints; the way he provides the reader with so many different approaches to life that it is virtually impossible for any one set of values to dominate; his unending immediacy, taking the place of suspense; his epochal outlook.

I have spent so much time comparing aspects of *War and Peace* to *Ulysses* because Joyce's influence throughout our era is pervasive. In Derek Attridge's words:

Such was the impact of his [Joyce's] literary revolution that few later novelists of importance in any of the world's languages have escaped his aftershock, even when they attempt to avoid Joycean paradigms and procedures [...] Even those who have read very few novels encounter the effects of Joyce's revolution every week, if not every day, in TV and video, film, popular music, and advertising, all of which are marked as modern genres by the use of Joycean techniques of parody and pastiche, self-referentiality, fragmentation of word and image, *open ended narrative*, and *multiple point of view*. [Also:] *the unprecedented explicitness with which he introduces the trivial details of ordinary life* [italics added].[12]

The italicized phrases might just as well have been describing *War and Peace*. To the extent that Tolstoy's fiction enriched Joyce's, Tolstoy's imprint is on the twentieth-century world which Joyce so deeply affected.

Tolstoy's influence on this past century's writers goes well beyond his effect on Joyce's novels. In Thomas Mann's opinion, "the pure narrative power of his work is unequaled." In 1939, referring to *Anna Karenina*, Mann wrote: "It is the Homeric element, I mean, the story going on and on, art and nature at once, naive, magnificent, material, objective, immortally healthy, immortally realistic! All this was strong in Tolstoy, stronger than in any other creator of epic art."[13] No doubt these Tolstoyan qualities were in Mann's mind while writing *Buddenbrooks*. And, as mentioned earlier, the end of *Death in Venice* is reminiscent of Tolstoy's deathbed monologues.

In his recent biography, *Marcel Proust: A Life*, Jean-Yves Tadie tells us Tolstoy was "one of his [Proust's] favorite writers"; that he was definitely influenced by *The Death of Ivan Ilich*; that he had read *Anna Karenina* more than once; and that he "gives a Tolstoyan inflection to certain passages in *Les Plaisirs et les Jours*."[14]

Virginia Woolf was awed by the width and breadth of *War and Peace*: "There is hardly any subject of human experience [she wrote] that is left out of [it]."[15] But what might have affected her own writing was something quite different: the way Tolstoy rendered his characters' growing awareness – their gradually acquired intuitive sense of God's integrative design, His phoenix pattern. "Woolf," says Robert Humphrey, "believed that the important thing in human life is the individual's search for meaning and identification, and her characters are fulfilled when they are ready to receive that vision." Thus, like Tolstoy, she writes about her characters' "preparation for the final insight." As he does, she conveys "a special sense of immanent vision," especially in *Mrs. Dalloway* (1925) and *To the Lighthouse* (1927).[16]

Tolstoy's epic qualities, which Woolf and Mann so greatly admired, had a forceful effect on such fellow-Russian writers as Isaak Babel (*Odessa Tales*,

1916), Mikhail Sholokov (*And Quiet Flows the Don*, 1934), Boris Pasternak (*Dr. Zhivago*, 1956), and Alexandr Solzhenitsyn (*The Gulag Archipelago*, 1973). In America, John Dos Passos also reaches for a Tolstoyan epic effect (*U.S.A.*, 1930–36).

As for Ernest Hemingway, his primary interests, according to Hugh McLean, were in Tolstoy's treatment of hunting and of war. "*War and Peace*" Hemingway said, "is the best book I know"; Tolstoy "is more formidable than any other writer except Shakespeare." Besides *War and Peace*, McLean tells us, Hemingway owned two copies of *Anna Karenina*, and a volume containing *The Cossacks* and *Sevastopol Sketches*. In the 1,000-page volume of literary selections, called *Men at War*, which Hemingway was editing in 1942, he included three excerpts from *War and Peace*: "Bagration's Rear-Guard Action," "Borodino," and "The People's War" (partisan warfare behind the French lines, ending with the death of Petia at Shamshevo). "The account of Bagration's rearguard action," he wrote in his Introduction, "is the finest and best understood relation of such an action that I have ever read and it gives an understanding, by presenting things on a small enough scale to be completely understood, of what battle is that no one has ever bettered."

In that same Introduction, says McLean, Rostov's bragging to Boris and Berg about the cavalry charge at Schön Grabern reminded Hemingway of the journalists' and historians' flag-waving treatment of the First World War – a war that was "the most colossal, murderous, mismanaged butchery that has ever taken place on earth."[17] So *War and Peace* taught him to stick to what actually happened, in or out of war; to record in the simplest language what his characters said and did, felt, and thought – the pure details that would come together in such a way that they would speak for themselves, and in doing so would imply more, and more vividly, than the ingenious but explicit tying-up of the conventional story's loose ends. His goal (not unlike Tolstoy's) was to show those literally indefinable feelings that hover between the characters in his often very short, reverberating stories, such as *Hills Like White Elephants*, and *A Clean, Well-Lighted Place*.

Not only did Proust, Mann, Joyce, Woolf, and Hemingway revere Tolstoy, but throughout the twentieth century authors and critics considered him one of the greatest novelists of all time. Early in the 1920s Percy Lubbock (despite considering *War and Peace* formless) called him "the supreme genius among novelists."[18] Toward mid-century, E. M. Forster insisted that *War and Peace* was "the greatest novel ever written." So, in the same words, did John Galsworthy and Hugh Walpole.[19] Referring to *Anna Karenina*, Lionel Trilling wrote: "There are moments in literature which do not yield the secret of their power to any study of language [...] times when the literary critic can do nothing more than point."[20]

In 1942 Simon and Schuster brought out its special edition of *War and Peace*, with a foreword by Clifton Fadiman which points out the analogy between Napoleon's Russian Campaign of 1805 and 1812, as described by Tolstoy, and Hitler's then-ongoing Russian campaign. In February 1942, writes Fadiman, "the *London Sunday Graphics* printed a cartoon showing Hitler and Göring saluting an army of men and planes all moving eastward. Hitler is saying, 'Do you ever get that feeling that all this has happened before, Hermann?' Behind the pair rises the ghost of Napoleon."[21] This edition became an instant best seller in America. In Russia, during the siege of Stalingrad (when most of that city's population, cut off from almost all supplies, was starving), more than a million copies of *War and Peace* were sold.

After the Second World War ended, after the Holocaust, then the atomic bomb with its powers of instantaneous global destruction, post-modernist writers like Samuel Beckett, far from bowing in Tolstoy's direction, seemed almost catatonic. In 1941 Beckett had joined the French underground and, nearly caught by the Nazis, went into hiding in 1942. Not surprisingly, in 1949, talking with the abstract painter George Duthuit, Beckett said, "there is nothing to express, nothing with which to express, nothing from which to express, no power to express, no desire to express, together with the obligation to express."[22] In 1952 he fulfilled that obligation with one of the world's great *tours de force*: *Waiting For Godot* – a two-act play in which, as someone said, "nothing happens, twice." Nothing except that, in brilliantly dramatizing the human predicament, he shows hopeful hopelessness in comic relief.

By the early 1950s, not only literature but all the arts seemed (on their frontiers, at any rate) to be in a state of shock. We had arrived at the age of non-paintings and random music, as well as the unpoem, the looseleaf novel which the reader could rearrange, the play that doesn't play. Artists like Robert Rauschenberg, Jasper Johns, Oyvind Fahlstrom, and Jean Tinguely largely rejected the whole idea of conception-execution and substituted for this the goal of incorporating reality without initiating it: of pushing beyond self-expression to the point where, said Rauschenberg, "the artist becomes just another kind of material in the picture, working in collaboration with the other materials."[23] Thus his white paintings, the picture being whatever shadows it reflects from passersby, clouds, and so forth. And thus, in music, John Cage's Silent Piece where a pianist sits motionless before the keyboard while the audience provides a "concert" of scraping chairs and clearing throats. These works try to eliminate the human element, to promote objects and random sounds to the rank of subjects created by the audience, to deliver a Thing in all its Thingness. We had arrived at post-modernism, with a vengeance.

"The highest purpose," said John Cage, "is to have no purpose at all."[24] This dictum quite accurately describes the goal as well as the overall effect of much post-modernist fiction: novels and short stories from 1950 until yesterday, written by the likes not only of Beckett but of Alain Robbe Grillet, Nathalie Saurraute, Marguerite Duras, Thomas Pynchon, John Barth, Donald Barthelme, and Jorge Luis Borges, as well as younger writers such as David Foster Wallace and Mark Z. Danielewski.

According to the perceptive *New York Times* book reviewer Michika Kakutani, these novelists "attempt to capture the chaos and cacophony of the world through whatever means come to hand." She says *Infinite Jest* (1997), a 1,079-page novel by David Foster Wallace, not only lifts "bits and pieces" from the likes of Pynchon, Barth, and Barthelme, but employs "jokes, soliloquies, run-on footnotes, and proliferating series of subplots"; also "demented little riffs on everything from feral hamsters to tongue scrapers to Lemon Pledge as a sunscreen." And Mark Danielewski's *House of Leaves* (1997) "bristles with lists of photographers and girls, interpolated passages of gibberish, and [. . .] asides about architecture and construction," while scattering throughout "poems, screenplay excerpts, playful typography, assorted appendices, and a succession of stories within stories . . ." Such novelists, in Kakutani's opinion, are "the most exciting writers at work today . . . [cerebral, yet] hot-wired to the gritty world around them, rendering it with uncommon spontaneity and vigor." They "have been influenced not only by their literary precursors, but also by television, the Internet and movies," all of which have "helped them to push the elliptical, modernist formulation of their predecessors to another level [post-modernism]."[25] In effect, these writers are surfing our culture.

Why, bombarded by such explosive evidence of the non-Tolstoyan world we now live in, do we still read and re-read Tolstoy's two great novels? Granted, he lacks what Henry James called "the imagination of disaster." "To many of us," wrote Trilling, "the world today has the look of a Dostoevsky novel, every moment of it crisis, every detail of it the projection of exacerbated sensibility and blind, wounded will."[26] To repeat Kakutani, we live in an aura of "chaos and cacophony." Nevertheless, there is still a strong undertow of truth to Gertrude Stein's observations, in her book about Picasso:

People really do not change from one generation to another, as far back as we know history people are about the same as they were, they have had the same needs, the same desires, the same virtues and the same qualities, the same defects, indeed nothing changes from one generation to another except the things seen and the things seen make that generation, that is to say nothing changes in people from one generation to another except the way of seeing and being seen.[27]

In *Ulysses*, Molly Bloom's soliloquy amazes and enthralls us. We are hypnotized by Joyce's insights; but we never feel that we are collaborating with him, or with Kafka, with Faulkner, or with Flannery O'Connor. Often we don't even know what they mean to convey until afterward; sometimes not even then. So we are overwhelmed by the depth and subtlety of such writers; with their experimental thrust. But perhaps what we also need, after so many *tours de force*, is not to go on being challenged to solve yet one more psychological detective story. Perhaps we need to share the characters' responses – what Tolstoy allows us to do with such empathy that we are able, as Trilling said, to "live" his novels.

Thomas Mann agreed: "[T]o read him again," Mann said, "is to find one's way home, safe from every danger of affectation and morbid trifling; home to originality and health, to everything within us that is fundamental and sane."[28] Maybe this is why, in his mid-eighties, William Maxwell – novelist, short-story writer, long-time fiction editor of *The New Yorker* – said that his only regret at the prospect of dying was that he would no longer be able to keep reading *War and Peace*.[29]

In this chapter I have, for reasons of space, concentrated on *War and Peace*; yet what Lionel Trilling has to say about Tolstoy's paradoxical relevance to our times applies just as directly to *Anna Karenina*:

> [I]t is a striking fact that, although many writers have been able to tell us of the pain of life, virtually no writer has been able to tell us of pain in terms of life's possible joy, and although many have represented the attenuation or distortion of human relationships, scarcely any have been able to make actual what the normalities of relationships are. But in Tolstoi the family is an actuality; parenthood is real and not a symbolic condition; the affections truly exist and may be spoken of without embarrassment and as matters of interest; love waxes and wanes, is tender or quarrelsome, but is always something more than a metaphor; the biological continuity is a fact, not as in James Joyce's touchingly schematic affirmations, but simply and inescapably. It is, we may say, by the very reason of the low pitch of his imagination of disaster that Tolstoi serves us, for he reminds us of what life in its normal actuality is.[30]

By "eavesdropping" on the thoughts and feelings of his many characters in *War and Peace*, Tolstoy forms for us a common pool of insights about human behavior – a pool to which we add our matching memories, thus making the particulars of this novel both private and universal. The overall effect is to drench us in what one critic has called "abnormal normality."[31] We are swept along by Tolstoy's "genius for the ordinary," and find ourselves responding to his characters' "smiles, the pressure of their hands," just as they themselves do.[32] Indeed they seem to be acting on our behalf. We "lose [...] the sense of distance between us and the characters; not because we are transplanted to their age, because they are transplanted to ours."[33] We feel that we are escaping not from but *into* the real world: a world where Nikolai cannot understand why the French would want to kill anyone so likable as himself; where Natasha, at the Grand Ball, would resent being danced with by a member of her own family; where Princess Marya wakes up hoping, to her horror, that her father has died during the night.

NOTES

1 Lionel Trilling, *The Opposing Self* (New York: Viking Press, 1955), p. 71.

2 References to *War and Peace* are to the Norton edition, trans. Louise and Aylmer Maude (New York: W. W. Norton & Co., 1966, 1996); to *Anna Karenina*, to the Norton edition, trans. Louise and Aylmer Maude (New York: W. W. Norton & Co., 1970, 1995). References to both novels also include volume and page numbers of the standard Russian Jubilee edition (*PSS*).

3 James Joyce, *Ulysses* (New York: Random House, 1961), p. 92.

4 Henry James, *The Art of the Novel*, intro. Richard Blackmur (New York: Charles Scribner & Sons, 1947), p. xvi.

5 *Ibid.*, pp. 307–8.

6 Neil Cornwell, *James Joyce and the Russians* (Basingstoke: Macmillan, 1992), p. 28.

7 Derek Attridge (ed.), *The Cambridge Companion to James Joyce* (Cambridge University Press, 1990), p. 8.

8 Edmund Wilson, *Axel's Castle* (New York: Charles Scribner & Sons, 1959), p. 205.

9 George R. Clay, *Tolstoy's Phoenix: From Method to Meaning in "War and Peace"* (Evanston, IL: Northwestern University Press, 1998). Here, and elsewhere, passages are quoted or paraphrased from chapters 2, 3, 10, and 11.

10 Richard Freeborn, *The Rise of the Russian Novel* (Cambridge University Press, 1973), p. 21.

11 Joseph Wood Krutch, *Five Masters: A Study in the Mutations of the Novel* (Bloomington, IN: Indiana University Press, 1959), p. 301.

12 *The Cambridge Companion to James Joyce*, p. 1.

13 Mann, *Essays of Three Decades,* trans. H. T. Lowe-Porter (New York: Alfred A. Knopf, 1947), p. 177.

14 Jean-Yves Tadie, *Marcel Proust: A Life* (New York: Viking/Penguin, 2000), pp. 178, 196–97, 219 (n.).

15 Leo Tolstoy, *War and Peace* (New York: Simon and Schuster, 1942), introductory opinion pages, unnumbered.

16 Robert Humphrey, *Stream of Consciousness in the Modern Novel* (Berkeley, CA: University of California Press, 1954), p. 13.

17 Hugh McLean, "Hemingway and Tolstoy: A Pugilistic Encounter," *Tolstoy Studies Journal* 11 (1999), 20–24.

18 Percy Lubbock, *The Craft of Fiction* (New York: Peter Smith, 1947), p. 24.

19 Leo Tolstoy, *War and Peace* (New York: Simon and Schuster, 1942), introductory opinion pages, unnumbered.

20 *The Opposing Self*, pp. 72–3.

21 Leo Tolstoy, *War and Peace* (New York: Simon and Schuster, 1942), p. xxxix.

22 Mark Schorer, "Technique as Discovery," in William Van O'Connor (ed.), *Forms of Modern Fiction* (Bloomington, IN: Indiana University Press, 1961), p. 24.

23 Calvin Tomkins, "Moving Out" (New York: *The New Yorker* February 29, 1964), p. 61.

24 *Ibid.*, p.66.

25 Michiko Kakutani, "New Wave of Writers Reinvents Literature," *The New York Times* (April 22, 2000), p. B 9.

26 *The Opposing Self*, p. 71.

27 Gertrude Stein, *Picasso* (London: B. T. Batsford, 1938), p. 10.

28 Thomas Mann, *Essays of Three Decades*, p. 177.

29 *Publisher's Weekly*, 3 April 1995, vol. 242, no. 4, p. 11 (1).

30 *The Opposing Self*, p. 171.

31 Leo Tolstoy, *War and Peace* (New York: Simon and Schuster, 1942), p. xxviii.

32 Malcolm Jones, "Problems of Communication in *Anna Karenina*" in Malcolm Jones (ed.), *New Essays on Tolstoy* (Cambridge University Press, 1997), p. 89.

33 Dmitri Merejhkowski, *Tolstoi as Man and Artist* (New York: G. P. Putnam's Sons, 1902), p. 192.

11

DONNA TUSSING ORWIN

Courage in Tolstoy

"... why doesn't [Tolstoy] think, instead of taking everything by bravery,
charging as if he were at Sevastopol?"[1]

In a review of *War and Peace*, N. N. Strakhov, the critic who was later
to become one of Tolstoy's closest friends, wrote that the novel was about
"the idea of the heroic life."[2] An essential ingredient of heroism is courage,
which was a cardinal virtue for Tolstoy. A war hero himself, he first became
known to the general public as the author of war stories about the siege
of Sevastopol, at which he fought. (His earlier works had been signed with
initials.) As the epigraph to this chapter suggests, his contemporaries perceived him, for better or for worse, as obsessed with courage. These qualities
are apparent as well to those who only know him through his writings: an ad-
miring Ernest Hemingway, for instance, saw him as a fighter without equal.[3]
The purpose of this essay is to explore what Tolstoy meant by courage, and
why it was so important to him.

Not surprisingly, from the time Tolstoy arrived in the Caucasus at the
age of twenty-two in 1851 and joined the army in 1852, he began a struggle to define what courage is. The war stories that he wrote in this period
were anti-romantic, and most of what passes for courage in them stands
revealed as mere show.[4] In the early war stories and *War and Peace*, Tolstoy,
sometimes sympathetically and often sarcastically, illustrates how men, inwardly trembling, outwardly strut their courage on the battlefield to win
medals and fame. While debunking romantic heroism, however, he strove
to replace it with "true" courage. The narrator of his first war story, *The
Raid* (1852), finds this in the behavior of the modest Captain Khlopov
(ch. 10). Dissatisfied with this effort, Tolstoy returns obsessively to the
theme.

In defining courage Tolstoy drew on Plato, whose dialogues he read while
in the Caucasus in the French translations of Victor Cousin. In the earliest
surviving fragment related to *The Raid* ("Courage is the science.... [*PSS* 3:
238–39]), he discussed a definition of courage evidently drawn from Plato's
work devoted to the subject, the *Laches*.[5] As an inquiry into a particular virtue, the published story resembles a Platonic dialogue, and, like the

Laches, it provides two different definitions of courage. In the first place, the narrator asks Captain Khlopov what courage is, and then compares his answer to one of Plato's.

> "*A man is brave when he behaves as he should,*" he said, having thought a little. I recalled that Plato defines bravery as *the knowledge of what one needs and needs not to fear* . . . [The two definitions are similar, but Khlopov's is superior] because he would have said that a brave man is he who *fears* only *what he should* and not *what he need not fear.*

The distinction between the two definitions is a moral one: the second one implies that for the brave man, duty – what one *should* do – overrides what is truly fearful. (The distinction is clearer in the Russian, where the word *nuzhno*, with more of a connotation of necessity, is juxtaposed to *sleduet*, which connotes obligation.) As the narrator goes on to explain:

> in every danger there is a choice, and a choice made under the influence, for instance, of a feeling of duty is bravery, while the choice made under the influence of a low feeling is cowardice; therefore it's impossible to call a person brave who risks his life from vanity, or from curiosity or from rapacity, and on the contrary, it's impossible to call a person a coward who under the influence of an honorable feeling of family obligation or simply conviction removes himself from harm's way. (*PSS* 3: 16–17)

Khlopov regards this elaboration suspiciously, as "philosophizing." For him (as for Laches), real courage can be demonstrated only in action, not in discussion. Later, the narrator observes Khlopov in battle and judges him truly courageous because "he was *just the same as I always observed him to be*" (*PSS* 3: 37). This definition supplements the narrator's first one, because, following Plato in the *Laches*, Tolstoy observed that courage required a mixture of "true knowledge" and "steadfastness." The Greek for steadfastness is *karteria*, *la constance* in Cousin's translation. In a diary discussion of Platonic virtue (*PSS* 46: 241) and many times subsequently, Tolstoy used the Russian word *sila*, "strength" or "force," to express the quality of steadfastness required to do the right thing despite temptation (say, to impress others) or justifiable fear.

On the one hand, then, true courage requires knowledge, both of what is fearful, and also of when we should stand and fight. On the other, the real test of courage on the battlefield begins only when a man recognizes that he may be killed at any moment, and despite this "endures." In the early war stories all characters, whether or not they admit it, feel fear under fire. The few exceptions include the incorrigibly foolhardy (the unit commander who perishes in chapter eleven of the second Sevastopol sketch), the superstitious (Melnikov in the third Sevastopol sketch), and the naive. In *The Raid*, the young officer Alanin dies because he does not heed the advice of the combat-seasoned Khlopov to retreat rather than attack. If courage were merely recognition of his vulnerability such as the unfortunate Alanin acquires too late, the realities of war would make cowards of us all. But Khlopov, though wise, is no coward.

In "Courage is the science..." (that first draft of *The Raid*), Tolstoy explains why a soldier might risk his life. First, following Plato, whom he credits, he argues that, wisely or not, we fear certain things more than death. A soldier, for example, may advance in battle because he fears the whip; an officer – because he fears the reputation of coward. Neither man, inasmuch as he acts from fear, is more courageous than the horse who braves bullets because he fears the spur. In addition to these negative incentives, men at war may be seduced by such passions as "the desire to distinguish themselves, to slake their malice, hatred [or]...rapacity" to overcome their fear of death. Therefore, "it's not always that one fear overwhelms another (although usually this is so), but [some other] feeling may overwhelm fear" (*PSS* 3: 238–39).

As Tolstoy himself had learned, and illustrated many times in his fiction, even if feelings may be influenced by true or false knowledge, courage on the battlefield depends not on what you know, but on how you feel. Captain Khlopov can do what he knows is right because he has the steadfastness to act courageously. This quality is related to the natural spiritedness that propels a youth like Alanin. To understand it, one must look at what Tolstoy in *The Woodcutting* first identified as the "desperate" type of soldier (ch. 2). Antonov, the example of such a man in this story, is related, through the Kozeltsov brothers in *Sevastopol in August, 1855*, to Denisov in *War and Peace*. All such characters, whatever their social status, are leaders by temperament, musicians, gifted speakers – in the case of Denisov, a poet – and all of them like to fight and carouse. Their spiritedness is related to physical vitality, and therefore they are solid specimens with bushy mustaches and sinewy arms. There is something of this type in every human being; hence even cowards like Vlang in *Sevastopol in August, 1855* can blossom into heroes in desperate situations (ch. 26). In *The Woodcutting*, the "humble" soldier Zhdanov loves Antonov's singing because it expresses a love of life undiminished in him despite his grasp of life's tragic limitations. Spiritedness therefore can never be utterly extinguished until death. It is the source of the "noble spark" of heroism that, according to Tolstoy in *Sevastopol in August, 1855*, burns "at the bottom of [every] soul" (ch. 17). Defined as "steadfastness," courage for Tolstoy is the natural resistance of the spirited human individual to "fearful" things, the most formidable of which is death.

Anger and shame, feelings aroused when a soldier is physically threatened or humiliated, ignite the "spark" of heroism. (Of course these secondary passions, to be legitimate, must be aroused by the right, not the wrong stimuli.) Soldiers ordered to retreat from the bastions at the end of *Sevastopol in August* are said to feel first confusion, then both fear and "a [mixed] feeling resembling repentance, shame and irritable anger" (*raskaianie, styd i zloba*). A similar sense of injury and desire for revenge animates the soldiers in *War and Peace* once the French invade Russia. In an appropriately spirited mood, "with venomous irony," and "excited," Prince Andrei explains to Pierre on the eve of the battle of Borodino that "the relative strength of bodies of troops can never be known to anyone," because strength depends, not on numbers, tactics, or position, but "on the feeling [of anger] that is in me and in him" (689; *PSS* 11: 208).[6]

Tolstoy highlights the unifying value of courage underlying what he calls the "spirit" (*dukh*) of an army, which, however, it must be remembered, originates in the individual. And despite Tolstoy's debunking of leadership, he shows in *War and Peace* that *esprit de corps* coalesces around leaders all of whom, even the elderly Kutuzov, communicate their own spiritedness to the troops. Of the various psychological reasons given for courage in the leader, the most powerful ones are anger and shame. Shame is most often expressed in the form of a prohibition. When Zhilin, the officer hero of the story *The Prisoner of the Caucasus* (1872), refuses to abandon his exhausted companion, he twice repeats "it's not right to leave a comrade behind." Tolstoy's most noble characters, Prince Andrei, whose very name comes from *andrea*, the Greek word for manliness, and the Chechen warrior Hadji Murat (in the posthumously published unfinished long story of the same name), act courageously out of shame at doing otherwise. Relating his life story to the Russian adjutant Loris-Melnikov, Hadji Murat says simply that, having run away once to save his life, he never did so again.

> Hadji Murat stopped, his sunburnt face flushed deeply, and his eyes went bloodshot. "I felt fear, and I ran away." "Is that so?" said Loris-Melnikov. "I thought that you had never been afraid of anything." "Afterwards I never was; from that time on I would always recall this shame, and when I would remember it, I would never fear anything." (ch. 11)

At Austerlitz, Prince Andrei responds to the appeal for help from Kutuzov with "tears of shame and anger" (243; *PSS* 9: 340). Later, at Borodino, even as Andrei stares at the smoking shell which in a second will explode and maim him, even as he inwardly declares "I cannot, I do not wish to die," at the same time he hesitates, "remembers that people were looking at him," and shouts aloud to his adjutant, who has flung himself on the ground: "It's shameful, sir" (722–34; *PSS* 11: 254). Andrei's concern for his reputation – the "desire to distinguish oneself" mentioned in "Courage is the science" – is not in his case ignoble. In the natural leader, what is mere vanity in lesser men takes the form of desiring not only to appear, but to be, best. He feels shame when he does not live up to standards of conduct worthy of the best men.

In "Courage is a science," in place of Plato's negative definition, Tolstoy proposes a new one, namely, that "courage is the ability of a human being to suppress the feeling of fear in favor of a higher feeling." This definition both accounts for courageous behavior in the person who knows what is truly fearful and adds a very important qualification, that the feeling that motivates the courageous man must be "higher" than fear of death. This is necessary, Tolstoy explains, because otherwise courage would not be a virtue. So a naturally spirited man can be evil or good, depending on his "egotism" or his "self-abnegation" ("Courage is the science . . ." [*PSS* 3: 239]). Antonov, the good "desperate" type in *The Woodcutting*, "fought and brawled not so much for his own satisfaction, as in support of all soldiery, of which he felt himself the representative."

The ranking of feelings as "higher" and "lower" is a form of knowledge, but – essential for Tolstoy – it is practical, not theoretical knowledge. Tolstoy's new definition is reflected in the narrator's correction of Plato in *The Raid*. When Captain Khlopov says that a brave man *behaves as he should*, he means that in certain circumstances, a brave man, fully aware of *what it is necessary to fear* (Tolstoy's rendering of the Platonic formulation), will suppress his fear in order to do right. In *The Woodcutting*, the battle-hardened Zhdanov comes to the assistance of Velenchuk, whose critical wound arouses in his comrades a natural revulsion arising from fear for their own safety (ch. 7). In another relevant example, the quite ordinary Captain Mikhailov (from *Sevastopol in May*), who dreams of a medal and yet repeatedly struggles with fear, returns to check on a wounded, possibly dead officer because he feels that it is his *duty* to do so (ch. 13).

While Mikhailov heeds the voice of duty reluctantly, other more spirited characters do so gladly. In *Sevastopol in August*, the elder Kozeltsov dies happy because "he had fulfilled his duty well [and] for the first time in his entire service he had acted as well as he could have, and there was nothing for which he could reproach himself" (ch. 25). In the case of Prince Andrei, both educated and thoughtful, honor takes precedence over both piety and duty as the principle that can overcome fear of death. For all the apparent differences, however, both duty and honor are enforced in the individual by a sense of shame that only vicious or bestial men lack. There is a tension between the two sides of courage. As steadfastness, it originates as self-defense which blurs the distinction between egotism and "self-abnegation."

Honor, too, is a personal, not a social goal. Hadji Murat and Prince Andrei both understand that no honorable man can permit himself to be cowardly. The man of honor is first concerned with his own worthiness, and only then, because honor demands it, with the good of the community. In his search for confirmation of himself as an individual, Andrei's political ambitions gradually give way to more personal goals.

Tolstoy minimizes the dark side of courage. Already in *The Raid* "rapacity" (*al'chnost'*) is declared by the narrator an illegitimate reason for it. Young Alanin is not angry but innocent and, strange to say, without bloodlust. He is horrified when he thinks, mistakenly, that soldiers are about to kill a child. Like Petia Rostov in *War and Peace*, he expects neither to die nor to kill others. In *The Cossacks* (1863), Lukashka listens to Olenin's reasons why he should not kill Chechens but refuses to internalize them. When such a character survives his initiation into the realities of war, we see him revising his attitude in response to them. The old cossack Eroshka condemns killing men. In *War and Peace* Nikolai Rostov loses his appetite for war once he has confronted the possibility of his own death and has looked into the utterly human eyes of his supposed enemy. The ferocity that others might associate with natural spiritedness is for Tolstoy a secondary phenomenon, brought on by the presence of danger. Natural spiritedness, itself innocent and healthy, curdles into evil when, instead of learning the sobering truth of human limitations from death, the spirited man occupies himself with futile efforts at self-aggrandisement in order to overcome it.

Tolstoy insists that courage rightly understood is a virtue, based on moral knowledge, and he therefore as much as possible distances it from its ugly relatives, whose kinship to it he nonetheless, for the sake of truthfulness, acknowledges. Surprisingly in fact, given his later pacifism and anti-militarism, not a single man of true courage in all his fiction, early or late, commits an atrocity. Although Prince Andrei declares himself ready to massacre Frenchmen wherever he finds them, he does not do this. There are characters whose seemingly courageous behavior is fueled by selfish and even evil intentions. Dolokhov in *War and Peace* is the most developed example in Tolstoy of egotistical courage. Dolokhov's vicious aggressiveness in battle notwithstanding, the "pale-greenish tint" of his face during the partisan raid in which Petia Rostov dies suggests fear.[7] Tolstoy seems to imply that an unregenerate egotist like Dolokhov, whose primary motivation is lust for power, ultimately cannot rank any good greater than the preservation of his own life. As we learn after Dolokhov's injury in the duel with Pierre, he has never grown up and still basks narcissistically in the uncritical spotlight of his mother's and sister's adoration. The second half of courage, a need for true knowledge, comes into play as the spirited youth, chastened by contact with necessity, seeks for a principle that will trump fear of death. Dolokhov has iron nerves because he never gets beyond the youthful sense of invincibleness. The fleeting moments of the partisan raid pass without making any lasting impression on him. In another episode, at the millpond in book 3, Dolokhov disperses a crowd trying to cross a narrow dam by beckoning men out onto the thin ice of the pond. Some forty of them drown in the ensuing break-up of the ice. Dolokhov disappears from the scene altogether, and one can assume that he has stepped back and crossed safely to the other side by the dam. What seems like an act of desperate courage on his part is a ploy, perhaps unselfconscious, to save himself at the expense of others. We cannot be sure of this, of course, because here as elsewhere we have no direct access to Dolokhov's inner life. This is appropriate, because Dolokhov, having never critically examined himself let alone acknowledged his own mortality, does not connect with others.

Dolokhov represents the frightening combination of charisma, ferocity, and cruelty that Tolstoy observed in certain warlike men. A more sympathetically portrayed ferocious man in *War and Peace* is the peasant partisan Tikhon Shcherbatyi, whose preferred weapon is an ax, and who takes no prisoners. The other partisans treat Shcherbatyi as a comic character, and his ferocity is more understandable than Dolokhov's, because it is based on anger rather than aggressiveness. Shcherbatyi, like Gamzalo in *Hadji Murat* and other angry Chechen characters, depicts excesses of justifiable rage. Men like Dolokhov and Shcherbatyi function in the comprehensive account of courage in *War and Peace* as scapegoats who display the dark qualities of courage and therefore leave heroic characters like Andrei or Nikolai Rostov unblemished by these.

The representation of courage, false and true, is one of the building blocks from which *War and Peace* is constructed. Central to this account is the story of Nikolai Rostov's baptism of fire during the skirmish at the Enns bridge in book 2 (117–28; *PSS* 9: 174–80). Nikolai's first battle stands for every soldier's first experience of war: no one seems to notice his reactions because "everyone knew the sensation that the cadet under fire for the first time had experienced." As the hussars are fired upon, all of them, with "faces so alike yet so different," hold their breath, stand up in their stirrups, sink back down into their saddles. "Every face, from Denisov's to that of a bugler, showed one common expression of conflict, irritation, and excitement." Rostov alone has "a clear, bright expression" as he looks around for approval of his bravery under fire. Even he, however, "despite himself," displays "something new and stern ... around the mouth."

On some level Nikolai already suspects "what it is necessary to fear." Nonetheless, he goes through a number of stages before he acknowledges that death is the real enemy. He begins by fearing the disapproval of others. During the first stage of his initiation, he is preoccupied with an imagined duel with his colonel, whom he suspects of testing his courage, and whom he regards as his "enemy." A little later, the imagined contest with the colonel continues as he orders Nikolai's squadron to return to the bridge under fire. "'There, it's just as I thought,' said Rostov to himself. 'He wishes to test me!' His heart contracted and the blood rushed to his face. 'Let him see whether I am a coward!' he thought."

When, at the colonel's command, the squadron dismounts, the fear of being separated from his comrades replaces Nikolai's fear of dishonoring himself.

> Rostov no longer looked at the colonel, he had no time. He was afraid of falling behind the hussars, so much afraid that his heart stood still. His hand trembled as he gave his horse into an orderly's charge, and he felt the blood rush to his heart with a thud.

Nikolai's focus shifts. He runs, he is "brave," "trying only to be ahead of the others," not because of his fear of the colonel, but because he fears not being part of the group. He no longer acts as an individual. This realization of his dependency on others is a crucial one in the moral education of the soldier.

Once at the bridge, Nikolai has returned to the duel with his imaginary enemy, the colonel, when someone next to him falls wounded. Now at last Rostov grasps the situation, and his untested courage, uncertainly supported by imagination and vanity, dissolves. In its place, "the fear of death and of the stretchers, and love of the sun and of life, all merged into one feeling of sickening agitation." Afterward Rostov counts himself a coward. In fact, however, everyone, including Denisov, and the colonel himself, who sets to bragging at the end of the chapter, has felt the way he does.

A few days later, during the Battle of Schön Grabern, Rostov is under fire again (160–63; *PSS* 9: 227–29). His colonel and an infantry general engage in a battle of "courage" like the one that Rostov had imagined earlier between himself and the colonel. They are like "two fighting cocks preparing for battle, each vainly trying to detect signs of cowardice in the other." Without a detailed explanation now, because we understand this particular element of the psychology of war from the earlier scene, Tolstoy shifts from this mock contest to the fact that the French have cut off the hussars from behind, and they "had to attack in order to cut a way through for themselves." Once again Rostov imagines himself a hero. "'Oh, how I will slash him!' thought Rostov, gripping the hilt of his saber." But then his horse, hit, goes down, his arm is trapped under the horse, he is wounded, and he experiences the full terror of war. The reverse of what he has previously imagined happens: running "with the feeling of a hare fleeing from the hounds," he is not the hunter, but the hunted. A wounded, thoroughly dispirited Rostov closes the final chapter of book 2. Simple soldiers and line officers, sitting around a fire, comfort him.

So who in the first battles of the novel is truly courageous? It is Denisov, in the first place, whose demeanor once in battle changes only to reflect heightened excitement. Denisov knows the true enemy, cowardice, and, in a telling example, he challenges death in full knowledge of its arbitrary power. When the colonel at Enns bridge chastises Denisov for running unnecessary risks, he responds that "every bullet has a name on it" (126; *PSS* 9: 177). Perhaps rashly, Denisov believes that he cannot control his fate on the battlefield, and this fatalism, which he shares with Homeric heros, liberates him to behave bravely.[8]

The courageous man who receives the most extended treatment in the first battle of the novel is Captain Tushin, the artillery officer who comes to Nikolai's aid after his wounding. The story of Captain Tushin functions within the larger narrative as a lesson for Prince Andrei in heroism.[9] As Andrei sets off for Schön Grabern from Brünn to "save the army," the diplomat Bilibin declares (in French) "My dear fellow, you are a hero!" (142; *PSS* 9: 199). At the council after the battle, Andrei claims that "we owe today's success chiefly to the action of that battery and the heroic steadfastness of Captain Tushin and his company" (172; *PSS* 9: 241).

We view Tushin first through Andrei's eyes, as a figure of slight ridicule (149; *PSS* 9: 209–10). Not a good parade soldier, he feels embarrassed and guilty around higher officers. Then, just before the battle, Andrei overhears a conversation in a bunker. Tushin and two others are discussing, not careers or promotions, not even courage, but death and what comes after it (153; *PSS* 9: 215–16). This conversation, precisely the right one for the place, is interrupted by the beginning of the battle. A cannonball lands near the bunker, and Tolstoy allows himself a Homeric image to describe the awesome impression it makes: "the ground seemed to groan at the terrible impact." Next we see Tushin after consultation with his sergeant-major deciding on the spot to fire on the village of Schön Grabern. General Bagration, rather than objecting, pretends that this was his intention. We see the battle shaping up and being decided by men like Tushin, with Bagration allowing his officers to respond to facts on the ground.

Eventually Tushin, maintaining his position, holds the whole French army at bay (165–67; *PSS* 9: 231–35). Excited but composed, he inspires his men, who take their cues from him. In this expanded treatment of the good field officer, Tolstoy suggests how such a man might stay calm on the battlefield.

Vulnerable, outside the bunker, his "home," Tushin resists death even to the point of creating fantasies in which he is a giant throwing cannonballs at the enemy, or the enemy guns are pipes puffing smoke. When he awakes from his trance, he feels like weeping. His tears both reflect and release the incredible emotional tension generated by his effort to "endure" in the face of death. Like Captain Khlopov, Tushin does "what he should" even though he knows most definitely "what it is necessary to fear." In a significant departure from Mikhailov (in *Sevastopol in May*), moreover, he does so, as we know from the conversation in the bunker, without a firm belief in an afterlife. He acts simply out of duty, without expectation of reward.

Hadji Murat is an example of a man who dies "like a hero" (*molodtsom*; ch. 24), seeming not to struggle at all with fear. He is thoughtful, but his thoughts are all practical and therefore, as Tolstoy portrays him at the end of his life, there is no disharmony between thought and action in him. Once he decides that he must somehow rescue his family, he moves decisively to do this. When during the final siege he realizes that he might die, "his soul suddenly [becomes] serious" as he accepts this eventuality (ch. 25). He puts duty above self-preservation or even glory. Unlike Andrei before Austerlitz, he chooses not to sacrifice his family to his hopes for glory if he stays with the Russians. Like Denisov, he believes in fate – "Allah's will" – as he tells Butler (ch. 20), and this frees him to act courageously without worrying about future consequences. Like Prince Andrei, as he is dying he fixes his mind's eye upon something grander "that was beginning and had begun in him." As courage is the battle against death, however, so Hadji Murat's body continues to fight.

If the greatest act of courage is to die well, then all of us are eventually called upon to be courageous. Socrates' death as depicted in Plato's dialogue the *Phaedo* was Tolstoy's model for the good death: in his early works, the deaths of Natalia Savishna in *Childhood*, of the humble soldier Velenchuk in *The Woodfelling*, and of the peasant in *Three Deaths* are all Socratic in their calmness and acceptance. These characters die well in large part because they have lived right. All of them come from a peasant milieu that emphasizes community over the individual, and this cultural orientation makes death psychologically easier for them. Other, non-peasant characters in Tolstoy's fiction have to change in order to face death well. Such a man is the judge Ivan Ilich, whose terrifying death is as random as any on the battlefield.

Chapter 6 of *The Death of Ivan Ilich* (1886), which begins with the line "Ivan Ilich knew that he was dying," openly makes the connection to war. The pleasant existence led heretofore by Ivan Ilich has depended on his ability to ignore his own mortality. Now death forces itself to the center of his consciousness just as it does to the soldier in wartime. Ivan Ilich himself compares the event that may have triggered his illness – a fall from a ladder while decorating a new apartment – to a "military assault in which I lost my life." As the chapter ends, he lies on his couch like a downed soldier, mortally wounded, face to face with *it*.

Ivan Ilich must now live on for several chapters fully aware of his impending death, and his psychological adjustment to that fact resembles the reaction of simple soldiers to the "knowledge of what is to be truly feared." Like them, he becomes aware of his personal vulnerability and therefore of his need for others. It is in chapter seven that the peasant Gerasim begins to help him. In chapter eight his progress toward death moves beyond his need for Gerasim to a solitary confrontation with the enemy. In preparation for this, "he dismissed Gerasim and stretched out his legs." This second action mimics a dying man's final gesture – indeed the story ends with the traditional formula "he stretched himself out, and died" – and it is meant to convey that Ivan Ilich tries to imagine his death. In chapter nine he begins to distance himself from his body. Listening more intently to the voice of his soul than to his pain, he begins to doubt the worth of his earlier life.

In place of his cardinal principles of respectability and pleasure, Ivan Ilich comes to value pity, at first of Gerasim toward himself, and then, at the end, of himself toward his son and others. In his dream after Borodino, Pierre also connects a distancing from bodily concerns with an increased concern for others (749–51; *PSS* 11: 92–94). The starting point of Pierre's meditation has been his relief at the cessation of his own fear at the end of the battle, and his observation that during it the soldiers, unlike him, "were steady and calm all the time, to the end." He wishes that he could "enter communal life entirely, to be imbued with what makes them what they are. But how [can I] cast off all the superfluous, devilish burden of my outer man?" The courage to face death in battle and an acceptance of communal life in both war and peace have a common psychological origin in the "true knowledge" of the inescapability of death. Like the soldiers whom Pierre so admired, Ivan Ilich switches from an egotistic to a communal point of view and is rewarded by the cessation of his spiritual torment. Totally helpless, dragged toward physical annihilation, Ivan Ilich discovers that while he can do nothing to prevent it, he can still help others.

For ordinary men like Tushin, Nikolai Rostov, or Ivan Ilich, virtue requires a moderate life for oneself and kindness to others. In the extreme case described in *Master and Man*, however, active love leads the hero, Vasilii Brekhunov, to sacrifice his life to save his servant Nikita. Unlike Ivan Ilich, Brekhunov is a seeker after fame and the love of others, which at the outset he wrongly imagines that he has procured. In the course of a fatal battle (with a blizzard), he, like Ivan Ilich, must come to terms with death. He first abandons Nikita in an effort to save himself. Yet when he returns accidentally to his cart, he lies down upon Nikita and warms him through the night at the cost of his own life. His point of view shifts from an individual to a communal one.

> [...] it seems to him that he is Nikita and Nikita is him, that his life is not in him himself, but in Nikita [...] "Nikita lives, and that means so do I," he says triumphantly to himself [...] And he remembers about the money, the shop, the house, the purchases, the sales and the Mironov millions; it is hard for him to understand why this person called Vasilii Brekhunov occupied himself with what occupied him.   (ch. 9)

Brought to a standstill by the blizzard, Brekhunov does not just give up; he responds with a resolute act that deprives death of its sting. His active concentration on the task at hand, reflected in the narrative by a switch to the present tense, signals his escape from fear of death, always a future event for individual consciousness. He has separated himself from "this person called Vasilii Brekhunov" and identifies himself with his manservant, who will live on after him, at least for a little while. Brekhunov's sacrifice, calculated with the same verve employed earlier to increase his assets, is courageous in the way Tolstoy defined courage back in 1852, in "Courage is the science...," as "the ability of the soul to be carried away by a higher feeling to the point of forgetting fear of death" (*PSS* 3: 239).

In chapter 8 of *What I Believe* (1882–84), Tolstoy argues that the acquisition of material goods and even glory are attempts, bound to fail, to avoid death, and he calls upon people to instead take up "an activity that will not be destroyed by inevitable death." The activity he has in mind is communal and in extreme circumstances even self-sacrificing, and the question arises as to why this activity, unlike others, should be spared from death. After all, in the case of *Master and Man*, Nikita is saved by Brekhunov only to die himself a few years later. The answer resides in Tolstoy's religious beliefs, which are based on ethics rather than dogma. Unlike the ancient Stoics, whom he admired, or for that matter twentieth-century Existentialists, Tolstoy did not regard life as humanly incomprehensible. It does make sense, but not to our minds. Eternal clarifying truths are accessible only through certain feelings, among them a sense of duty and self-sacrifice. So ethics replaces dogma or theology as the only real proof of the existence of God in Tolstoyan religion. When we act out of duty or self-sacrifice, we are responding to the eternal truths within us, and to this extent, temporarily and through our subjectivity, escaping death.

For Tolstoy, religion rather than philosophy is the source of the true wisdom necessary for courage. Not reason or knowledge, but religious feeling or instinct guides us in choosing a higher over a lower feeling ("Courage is the science..." [*PSS* 3: 239]). To this extent, courage has nothing to do with knowledge understood as the power to reason. As Captain Mikhailov, quaking, makes his way back to check up on his missing comrade, he fingers the saint's image hanging round his neck. Contrary to the contention of Guskov, the main character in *Caucasian Notes: The Demoted Officer* (1856), Tolstoy observed that education and intelligence make it harder, not easier to be courageous. Captain Mikhailov, in contrast to the adjutants who despise him, has a low brow and a "dullness of mental abilities." According to the narrator of *The Raid*, a Russian soldier like Captain Khlopov does not verbalize his courageous feelings (as a Frenchman might do) for fear of weakening them (ch. 10). A critically wounded soldier explains in *Sevastopol in December* (1855) how to cope on the battlefield: "The most important thing...is *not to think a lot*; if you don't think, you'll be all right. Everything happens because you think."

Like anger and shame, piety reinforces the sense of duty, and in Christianity at least, piety includes belief in an afterlife. In *The Woodcutting*, one example of many, Velenchuk dies courageously because his "simple faith in a future heavenly life could [not] waver at the decisive moment." In descriptions of death, especially of heroes, Tolstoy seems to promise, if not immortality, freedom from limitations imposed by material existence. For the dying Prince Andrei, death is "liberation from the force that had previously bound him and [a feeling of] strange lightness"; Hadji Murat turns his attention to "something grander" than his present life; Vasilii Brekhunov, as his body slowly freezes, also experiences death as freedom. *The Death of Ivan Ilich*, *Master and Man*, and *Hadji Murat* all end with references to an afterlife the existence of which cannot be refuted even if it cannot be proved.

Belief in an afterlife would seem to undercut courage by rendering it superfluous, because death itself is understood as only an illusion or even a passage to a better life. Rather than facing death, the pious Christian (or Muslim) denies its reality and therefore has no need for courage at all. It's true that the dying often seem more like saints than warriors in Tolstoy, as if something transcendental were comforting them for the loss of life. As a psychologist, Tolstoy assumed that people find it difficult to do necessary or right things that are not obviously in their self-interest; and as a moralist he welcomed encouragement from any source, including traditional religion, to right action. He envied men like Hadji Murat whose piety made them more resolute than he, as a modern man and a thinker, felt himself to be. He himself, however, never claimed to have achieved the level of certainty about an afterlife that he ascribes to some of his characters. Less certain and saintly than them, he was called upon to be more courageous, because his instincts for the good were not supported by his milieu. He had to live right and die well without any outside certainty that there was any universal sanction for this. His only compass was his own conscience and the strength of will to abide by its dictates.

It is no accident that these two ingredients correspond respectively to the wisdom and strength of which courage is composed: for Tolstoy, right living and heroism were synonymous. He tried to demonstrate this in his writings, but as he grew older, he seems to have decided that he would have to model it in life in order to convince people that it was true. His reputation as a hero only grew over time. It depended not only upon heroic feats in various arenas, but also, especially later in his life, on his own determination to make himself an example of upright conduct, a Christian warrior for the good. One can easily ascribe this ambition to incorrigible hubris, but it is also a reflection of his religious and philosophical beliefs, according to which individuals rather than institutions introduce transcendental truths into the world and nourish them. Tolstoy may have modeled his own activity partly on the English essayist Thomas Carlyle's notion of the hero. He read at least parts of Carlyle's *On Heroes* in the 1850s, and was a great admirer of Carlyle in later life.[10]

Tolstoyan heroism is anti-romantic because it is in the service of the good of the community rather than the individual. At the same time, and paradoxically, in its emphasis on authenticity rather than rationality as the source of ultimate truths it is individualist in the extreme. Whereas in Plato as Tolstoy presents him in *The Raid*, knowledge understood as reason is necessary to moderate excesses inherent in courage, for Tolstoy both parts of courage – steadfastness and the knowledge of where to direct it – are grounded in sentiment, and human reason acts to weaken, not strengthen it. The wise man listens to his heart, not his head, and his heart will always tell him to do the right thing. Courage then becomes the "strength" necessary to stay the course in the face of external and internal resistance or temptation. To live entirely authentically, bowing neither to received opinion nor to threats from man or nature, was the heroic and humanly impossible task Tolstoy set himself in old age, and it is doubtful whether any other person has tried harder than he to succeed at it.

NOTES

1 Alexander Herzen, in a letter to Turgenev after having met Tolstoy in London in February 1861. Quoted in N. N. Gusev, *Letopis' zhizni i tvorchestva L'va Nikolaevicha Tolstogo, 1828–1890* (Moscow: Gosudarstvennoe izdatel'stvo khudozhestvennoi literatury, 1958), p. 25. Unless otherwise indicated, all translations from the Russian are mine.

2 N. Strakhov, *Kriticheskie stat'i ob I. S. Turgenev i L. N. Tolstom (1862–1885)*, vol. I, 4th ed., 1901 (repr. The Hague and Paris: Mouton, 1968), p. 196.

3 Hugh McLean, "Hemingway and Tolstoy: A Pugilistic Encounter," *Tolstoy Studies Journal* 11 (1999), 20.

4 Boris Eikhenbaum, *The Young Tolstoi*, trans. Gary Kern (Ann Arbor, MI: Ardis, 1972), ch. 3.

5 Both the *Laches* and the *Phaedo*, mentioned below, are named after participants in the respective dialogues.

6 Page references to *War and Peace* are to the Norton Critical edition of the novel (New York: W. W. Norton, 1996). They are followed by volume and page references to the standard Russian Jubilee edition (*PSS*). I use the Maude translation from the Norton edition, but change it wherever necessary to stress a point.

7 John Bayley, *Tolstoy and the Novel* (New York: Viking Compass Press, 1966), pp. 175–76.

8 The Russian proverb, of which Denisov quotes only the second half, is *Pulia dura, a vinovatogo naidet*, "A bullet may be a fool, but it will find the guilty party." Compare this to Eroshka's advice to Olenin in *The Cossacks* to avoid crowds on the battlefield.

9 Thanks to Edwina Cruise for pointing this out to me.

10 On the subject see Donna Orwin, "Tolstoy and Patriotism," *Lev Tolstoy and the Concept of Brotherhood*, eds. Andrei Donskov and John Woodsworth (Ottawa: Legas, 1996), pp. 63–70.

12

CARYL EMERSON

Tolstoy's aesthetics

Among the many definitions and defenses of art produced by the world's great practicing artists, Tolstoy's is surely one of the most peculiar. It is curiously selfless. In fact, so far is Tolstoy from using such a forum to defend his own practice that in his most programmatic statement on aesthetics, the 1897 treatise *What is Art?*, he consigns his own acclaimed masterworks to the category of bad art. The company, to be sure, is superb: Shakespeare, Dante, much of Pushkin, and almost all of Beethoven and Wagner are also so classified. Tolstoy's eccentric and provocative judgments on individual world-class artists cannot be judged, however, apart from his larger vision of art's place in the human world. That worldview can be (and by many, has been) rejected, but my purpose in the present discussion is to examine it from within and on its own terms. For there is a surprising toughness, subtlety, and integrity to many components of this vision, which Tolstoy's categorical tone often masks.

Tolstoy's aesthetic convictions naturally evolved during his long, well-documented life, and the degree of their continuity across his crisis watershed of the early 1880s remains a matter of debate. His letters and diaries over half a century record hundreds of instances of excellent practical criticism and intuitive judgments that fit under no theoretical rubric. In the 1850s, defining himself against the new generation of materialist civic critics, Tolstoy briefly endorsed the idea of art as an autonomous medium that serves the artist's own inner strivings. His own views began to take stable form, however, only during his radical pedagogical experiments with peasant children at Iasnaia Poliana in the early 1860s. From that point on, a growing sense that human experience must be a unity, and that human relations must unify, led Tolstoy to cleanse and categorize his aesthetic views.

By his own admittance, Tolstoy worked over *What is Art?* for fifteen years. Near the beginning of that work, during the winter of 1883, he received an inflammatory letter from his close friend Nikolai Strakhov on the subject of Dostoevsky, who had died two years before (Strakhov knew both men well, although the two titans were not acquainted with each other). In his cautious response, Tolstoy applied a metaphor to the great literary figures of his generation that sheds some light on the quest to come. He confided to Strakhov that he preferred calm, measured writers like Ivan Turgenev over Fyodor Dostoevsky because the former was a "horse without a flaw," a horse who will "get you where you are going," whereas Dostoevsky, for all his largeness of heart, can stumble, can even "land you in a ditch" – and such writers have less staying power; and "one cannot set on a pedestal for the edification of posterity a man who was all struggle."[1] This letter to Strakhov is a helpful bridge to *What is Art?* Great and true art, for the mature Tolstoy, must not stumble. It may of course show signs of conflict, grief, disappointment, failure, but it must not endorse a radical multi-directionality – that is, it cannot posit as its endpoint an evil or impossible paradox (that would be "getting nowhere"), no matter how swift, interesting, or well-crafted the journey. If a work of art portrays struggle, it must show us a way out. The responsibility of art to "get us there," and where in fact that final place is, are among the most ancient concerns of moral philosophy. Tolstoy belongs with those philosophers who do not believe that art can be explained by a poetics. It is, rather, an indispensable part of organic life, in Tolstoy's literal understanding of that phrase: it has life-bearing functions, whose proper metabolic activity is essential to the health of each individual organism and to the health of the social body as a whole. Art, Tolstoy writes, is the "spiritual organ of human life, and it cannot be destroyed."[2]

Tolstoy does not waste time on rhetorical questions. His concrete answer to the question *What is Art?* is found in chapter five of that treatise.

> To call up in oneself a feeling once experienced and, having called it up in oneself, to transmit it by means of movements, lines, colors, sounds, images expressed in words, so that others experience the same feeling – in this consists the activity of art. Art is that human activity which consists in one person's consciously transmitting to others, by certain external signs, the feelings he has experienced, and in others being infected by those feelings and experiencing them.
>
> (5: 39–40; *PSS* 30: 65)

Let us look carefully at this sequence of psychological events.

The epidemiological resonances of "infection" and "infectiousness" (*zarazhenie, zarazitel'nost'*) are of course deliberate – for in Tolstoy's view, every important truth had to prove itself on the individual body. But we should not dismiss the metaphor as mere sensationalism. Impulsiveness and restraint are in fact well balanced in it. Art begins with a personal experience so strong that we feel the need to confirm it, to call it up and fix it "in signs." This need creates the material grounds for sharing the experience with another person. Such sharing is almost involuntary, like radiation or an "electric spark" (16: 131; *PSS* 30: 158); one "catches" art from a person who "has" it. In Tolstoy's model, communication (or communion: the Russian term *obshchenie* can mean both) is a consonance, a filament linking like to like. But this duplication, although rapid and involuntary like every contagion, is no plague; it is not out of control. It has been consciously structured. Tolstoy's favorite examples are intonation in musical performance, where the artist or performer must find "those infinitely small moments of which the work of art is composed," and easel painting, where touching up a "little bit" can suddenly bring the whole canvas to life (12: 99; *PSS* 30: 128). For all its instantaneous effects on the receiving end, then, every successful work of art must be painstakingly fine-tuned, bit by bit. Infection is a craft.

Tolstoy then introduces further distinctions. Works of art are judged according to two axes, true versus counterfeit and good versus bad. Along the true/counterfeit axis, the standard of success is simply communicative: art is true if it infects. This replication of emotion in the recipient must be immediate and unmediated; its happy result is to make us experience an event of life more deeply, without having to analyze it or struggle with it. In fact, the highest compliment Tolstoy believed we could pay to a work of art was to feel that we had created it ourselves, out of our own inner necessity; there are no longer any boundaries between our own self and the artist or between our self and all fellow selves exposed to the same artwork. (By the same token, Tolstoy could cavalierly reject whole genres as divisive and inauthentic if he personally was not moved by a feeling of effortless co-creation.) Again revealing his deep suspicion of the Romantic period, Tolstoy implicitly rejects any cult of the individual artist – for the true artist is a conduit and an enabler, not an isolated or misunderstood genius. In Tolstoy's view, there are only three legitimate criteria by which the success of art is measured: the degree of particularity or definitiveness of the feeling transmitted (*osobennost' chuvstva*), its clarity (*iasnost'*), and the sincerity (*iskrennost'*) of the artist.

When these conditions are not met, we have "counterfeit art" (*poddel'noe iskusstvo*). It relies on four devices (ch. 11; *PSS* 30: 112–18). The first is "borrowing" (*zaimstvovanie*), which for Tolstoy means taking poetic subjects secondhand from other artworks. Artists borrow when they do not have (or are afraid to trust) emotional experiences of their own; they are turned into borrowers by the baleful influence of professional art schools and art criticism, both of which invent, and then impose, artistic norms and canons that can only deform individual talent. To copy prior artworks in a passive or mechanical way is always bad. But also bad is to copy life in a passive way – and this is Tolstoy's second counterfeit technique, "imitativeness" (*podrazhatel'nost'*). To imitate means to describe in photographic detail all the particulars of a given scene, without concern for their spiritual or transfiguring aspect. (It was this practice that Tolstoy so intensely disliked in his contemporaries of the Naturalist school.) Too much physical detail in a line of narrative – which Tolstoy correlates with excessive harmonic complexity in a line of music – becomes an obstacle to the conveyance of a feeling and thus to successful infection (apparently Tolstoy envisions both processes, verbal narrative and musical line, unfolding in time toward "cadence" in the manner of a simple diatonic melody). In a bold aside that anticipates the famous opening thesis of Erich Auerbach's *Mimesis*, Tolstoy suggests that "what is called realism" often does not clarify our vision but in fact encumbers and narrows it – and thus might "better be called artistic provincialism" (16: 134; *PSS* 30: 162).[3]

A third device of counterfeiters is a "striving for special or striking effects" (*porazitel'nost'*). Tolstoy's complaint here is complex. On one level, he means horror stories and other overheated, sensational plots, which "do not convey any feeling but only affect the nerves" (11: 89; *PSS* 30: 117). This argument is compromised somewhat by Tolstoy's own personal disaffection for many Romantic genres and by his extreme hypersensitivity to erotic themes in art, aggravated by his insistence that the chronically overfed, physically underworked upper-class consumers of art are motivated by lustful appetites alone. (A recurrent motif in *What is Art?* is the "erotic mania" of all Western – especially French – literature, and the fact that "sensuality . . . constitutes the chief subject of all works of art in modern times" [9: 62; *PSS* 30: 88].) At another level, Tolstoy's disapproval of "striking effects" is part of his larger understanding of the ethical relation between sublime or exceptional acts and everyday habitual ones. Our moral growth, Tolstoy came to believe, is actually impeded by a fixation on "crisis ethics," that is, on the big exciting crime – murder, rape, armed robbery – which we will probably never have the chance nor the desire to commit and thus can contemplate without anxiety. Necessary instead are a cultivation of the practical virtues. No discussion of my theoretical right to kill, say, an evil pawnbroker could matter as much as the constant, tiny self-disciplinings I bring to daily temptations (equivalent to fine tunings in music and the "little bits" of painterly adjustment on a canvas). Have I the right to kill an innocent animal for my plate? Tell an innocent lie? The modest, arduous steps needed to address those questions and realize those quotidian virtues can only be dulled by a bombardment with "special, striking effects." By invalidating those effects, Tolstoy, with his usual audacity, would redefine what we mean by "plot interest" in a work of art.

The fourth and final telltale device of counterfeit art is closely related to "striking effects," but it is arguably even more difficult to avoid. This is the baffling sin of *zanimatel'nost'*, variously translated as "distraction," "diversion," or "entertainment," but in fact not carrying in Russian the overtones of triviality that we detect in those English equivalents. Its root meaning is simply the ability to arouse and occupy our interest, which Tolstoy then glosses as "intellectual interest added to the work of art" (11: 87; *PSS* 30: 115). This animus against "ideas" in art, preached with great stubbornness by the indefatigable autodidact Tolstoy, is justified by three arguments. First, we find an artwork "interesting" when it "provokes unsatisfied curiosity" or is "not entirely comprehensible" to us; in either case, we apply mental effort to it and "find a certain pleasure in the guessing process" (11: 90; *PSS* 30: 118). All this ratiocination interferes with infection. Second, having to guess about the meaning of an artwork (as one must do while reading, for example, one of Dostoevsky's "novels of ideas") will inevitably end up dividing rather than uniting its audience. And third, people who are trained to understand Wagner or to interpret a French Symbolist poem (that is, who have been taught how to guess them out) will feel no sympathy toward those who are not so trained. Thus, Tolstoy concludes, the workings of art must be distinguished from mental activity, for the latter requires "preparation and a certain sequence of learning" (10: 81; *PSS* 30: 109) – always discriminatory and always tending to favor those groups already profoundly favored in all societies: the rich, the tutored, the clever, and the quick. "The business of art," Tolstoy insists, "consists precisely in making understandable and accessible that which might be incomprehensible and inaccessible in the form of reasoning" (10: 81; *PSS* 30: 109).

This exile of specialized training and intellectual prowess from the realm of authentic art provides a transition to Tolstoy's second set of subcategories. It follows from the above definition that a true artist can experience, fix in signs, and infect others with a whole range of feelings, sophisticated as well as trivial, noble as well as ignoble. "The stronger the infection, the better the art is as art, regardless of its content – that is, independently of the worth of the feelings it conveys" (15: 121; *PSS* 30: 149). Hence an additional, morally-informed axis of judgment is necessary with regard to content: good versus bad (*khoroshee/durnoe*). Tolstoy calls the authentic, good art of our time – non-denominationally, of course, and stripping the term of any institutional associations – "Christian art." It can be of two sorts: religious, reflecting an ethical ideal endorsed by a certain people in a given historical time or place, or universal, accessible at all times to everyone in all cultures, without exception (16: 131–32; *PSS* 30: 159–60).

It is instructive here to note the two works of his own – and there are only two – that he exempts from the category of bad art (16: 197–98; *PSS* 30: 163 fn. 1). First is the brief tale *God Sees the Truth, but Waits*, assigned to religious art because its understanding of crime, punishment, justice, and penance reflects the morality of our Judeo–Christian European culture. Second is *Prisoner of the Caucasus*, written in the dry sparse style of a folktale, describing the capture, imprisonment, and successful escape of a Russian officer from the Chechen enemy (universal art, because it transmits courage, natural compassion, pain, fear of death, and relief at release from death). Unfortunately, the actual psychology of "religious" and "universal" narratives receives little analysis from Tolstoy – who, consistent with his own criteria, rests his case on immediate subjective impressions. But it might be helpful to speculate on one of Tolstoy's positive examples, provided in contrast to Wagner's *Ring of the Niebelung* (discredited at great length in chapter thirteen) and to a stage performance of Shakespeare's counterfeit work *Hamlet*. The positive example Tolstoy provides is folk theatre among a "savage people," the nomadic tribe of the Voguls in north-central Siberia (14: 119; *PSS* 30: 147). Spectators gather in a small yurt – a circular tent made of animal skins – to watch the dramatization of a familiar scene, the tracking and killing of a reindeer and her calf. A hunter moves in on the animals, attacks them with arrows, and as they lick their wounds and the hunter reloads his bow, the audience sighs and weeps. This, Tolstoy concludes, is "a true work of art." Why?

The Vogul drama – efficient, lean, taken direct from life, transparent in plot – is clearly not counterfeit. But there is an additional reason, I believe, why this performance qualifies in Tolstoy's eyes as good ("Christian") art, art that infects in a morally correct direction. The Voguls, a hunting and gathering people of the northern Urals, earn their livelihood by killing reindeer. In their daily working lives, they cannot afford to recoil from this killing. It would be easier for them, of course, if they could justify this violent activity by automatizing it, or by persuading themselves that deer were somehow so different from human beings that killing them was not murder. But for this very reason, in order to forestall such comfortable psychological accommodation and to allow the heart to feel anguish, is the drama necessary in their culture. Two human hunters dressed up in deerskins become the prey; a third human hunter strikes them down. This plot presents the essential components of the culture's most indispensable activity from a displaced ("Christian," compassionate) point of view. So powerful is the clash of these two legitimate perspectives that even Leo Tolstoy, distant in every respect from the culture and plight of the Voguls, is moved to tears.

It should be noted that the catharsis Tolstoy describes in this deer-slaying drama is not the utilitarian emotion that Aristotle celebrates at the close of Greek tragedy. Measured against the terror and pity experienced by this Siberian tribe, the intricate plot resolutions in ancient drama would strike Tolstoy as superstition, their emotional release gratuitous and artificed. Among the Voguls in that yurt there is no philosophy, no frivolous gods to appease, no complex kinship relations to avenge. There are only daily patterns of physical survival. Which is to say, there is only nature, with its mandate that we partake in (and answer for) the unity of the natural world. And for Tolstoy, as Donna Orwin astutely notes, Nature was a stern and sovereign force, strictly defined: it is "conscience in human beings and necessity in the outside world."[4]

True/counterfeit and good/bad: these two axes of judgment must be applied to every human product that claims to be art. Tolstoy was aware of the difficulties involved in making aesthetic discriminations, especially for social classes whose tastes had been perverted. "False works" can superficially appear to be better constructed, more interesting and worthy than true ones (14: 114; *PSS* 30: 143). While authentic (that is, contagious) bad art will always be around and inevitably will infect us, we should strive wherever possible to create conditions for the right sorts of infection to occur.

We now turn to the problems that people have had with this definition of art – which were immediate. Most obviously, *What is Art?* does not address in any detail the rigors of the craft or the perfections of the artifact. It concentrates almost entirely on the action and effects of art, thereby defining art not by what it is but by what it does, or should do. This approach in itself is in no way objectionable or new. Of the four major rubrics under which the aesthetic impulse has been investigated – art as imitation (Plato, Aristotle), art as actualization (Hegel, Schopenhauer, Croce), art as play (Schiller, Spencer), and art as an expression of emotion – Tolstoy would fit reasonably well into the fourth. Even his sweepingly denunciatory tone was almost mainstream. Russian social thought in the second half of the nineteenth century was full of social critics who condemned the art of their day as immoral or trivial and who censured artists for their self-indulgence. Why, then, was Tolstoy's theory of art so scandalous?

In part it was the spectacle of a great writer turning against himself. In part it was because Tolstoy condemned far more, and far more damningly, than the nihilists. Readers who are irritated by his authoritarian stance and tone in this tract often find unpersuasive the didactic intonations in the great fictional works from this period: *The Death of Ivan Ilich*, *Master and Man*, *Resurrection*. A singular definition of a complex human activity comes at high cost. If the idea of aesthetic "infection" is correct, would it not thin out the emotional field? Can mere replication of an emotion give rise to enough of those rich, differentiated relations and alternative worlds that are among art's most precious contributions to life? What role (if any) is played by the individualized creative response? Tolstoy's concept of communication and transmission is oddly one-way. Does not an artist intuitively listen to (and create for) a specific audience, taking its needs and desires into consideration? More basically still, what does it mean to transmit a feeling to another person, with intent to infect? Feelings, after all, arise from private inner experience. Can we ever know whether the feelings aroused in the infectee are identical to the feelings in the heart of the artist? Anger in a primary creator might produce horror in us (or, for that matter, mirth); what caused anguish for the artist might arouse our disgust. And finally, can emotions be confidently separated from thoughts? Certainly great works of art – and especially verbal art – are an inspired mix of both ideas and feelings.

Tolstoy would not be surprised by these objections. But he would argue that ideas and feelings are indeed separable, if not in their substance then at least in the treatment we accord them. Ideas, after all, can be disputed and manipulated: they exist objectively. By the time we register a feeling, however, it is already an accomplished fact. Such time compression, which allows for no maturation or refinement of the relevant emotion, is significant. The Russian word *iskrennost'* (sincerity), Tolstoy's central requirement for authentic art, is built off *iskra*, a "spark": that which flashes momentarily and either catches fire or dies. The artistic effect either takes, or fails to take.

More challenging is the complaint that the infection thesis, if correct, impoverishes both art and its recipients by limiting our vocabulary and pre-determining our response. Here Tolstoy would urge us to consider carefully what precisely he intends by the flowing-together, or unity, of artist and audience in a work of art. In this he has an able ally in Richard Gustafson, who, in his study of Tolstoyan "ways to know," distinguishes between the kindred states of ecstasy, intoxication, and infection.[5] All three states are un-apologetically self-centered (for Tolstoy, never a reproach). But while the first two can be inspirational, elevating, self-revelatory, only infection functions as an art. And peculiar to art, Gustafson writes, is that it "connects, but it is not coercive. Art does not force you into a position not your own ... art leads you into your own position" (371).[6]

Unification, then, is not homogenization. Just as *iskrennost'* is explained by *iskra*, so is the *osobennost'* (the "particularity" or definitiveness) of the artist explained by the Russian root *osob-*, the individualizing principle, that quality which makes each of us what we uniquely are. The unity between people brought about by the spark of infection does not result in our amal-gamation, loss of identity, or even necessarily in our casual agreement; such unity is measured, above all, by an increase in mutual tolerance and love. Art destroys separation – but emphasizes individuality. What is more, infection by art is not some irreversible chemical fusion that takes place between two bodies once and for all. People are unified (and love is released) in exceptional moments. Although our organisms must be susceptible and receptive in a general way, of course, as with any infection we are not susceptible in the same way each time, nor for the same length of time. "Since each person is unlike all others," Tolstoy writes, "one person's feeling will be [felt as] particular for every other person, and the more particular the feeling is – the more deeply the artist has dipped into his own nature – the more heartfelt and sincere it will be" (15: 122; *PSS* 30: 150). What is more, nothing in this transaction is foisted upon the receiver. Although Tolstoy would very much like to see violence eliminated from the world and "only art can do that" (20: 166; *PSS* 30: 194), the true artist need not be an altruist. The artist hardly notices the receiver. Of Tolstoy's three criteria for ideally infectious art, two of them (particularity and sincerity) stress precisely the selfishly individualizing, not the homogenizing, aspects of the artistic effect. "Sincerity" has nothing to do with a moral imperative to ennoble the world according to some showcase virtue. It is present only when the artist is infected by his own artistic production. The primary value that is "caught" by the receiver is sincerity. To be sure, Tolstoy – unlike his compatriot Dostoevsky – would consider it peculiar if a large number of people independently reacted with vulgar guffaws to a scene intended by its author to be tragic. But he would appreciate first of all the strength and spontaneity of their response. An acute individuality is essential to both sides, if the infection dynamic is to work.

Let us now turn to another and more awkward set of problems. Harmony, unity, and love are the prime values that art should serve. But Tolstoy's own attitude toward the human subject is weighed down with wrath and disgust. Belligerently, he reduces even modest quests for pleasure and self-affirmation to a crude hedonism. Art, we are told, should help rid the world of intolerance and violence, but art that is "bad" (non-Christian) "not only should not be encouraged, but should be banished, rejected and despised as art that does not unite but divides people" (16: 136; *PSS* 30: 164). In the current corrupt state of affairs, "any reasonable and moral person would again decide the question the way it was decided by Plato for his Republic" (17: 146; *PSS* 30: 175). If we resist such "reasonable" moral decisions, Tolstoy invokes what are now recognized as Marxian or Freudian modes of defense. We cannot be free in our judgments, since our way of life has instilled in us a false consciousness: "if it seems there is no religious consciousness in society" it is because we have repressed an awareness of it, "we do not want to see it . . . because it exposes our life" (16: 124; *PSS* 30: 152).

This deep pessimism about the human material currently present, its hopeless and unredeemable habits, is combined in Tolstoy with a radiant faith in the purity of humanity to come. The paradox here is complex. Tolstoy clamored loudly against historical progress. In his 1862 essay "Progress and the Definition of Education," he polemicized against Hegelianism and its "very singular mental hocus-pocus called the historical view."[7] All theories based on a self-propelled "progress toward universal well-being" are discredited out of hand. In *What is Art?*, however, he writes without irony that "the evolution of feelings proceeds through art – [and] feelings that are lower, less kindly and less necessary for the good of humanity will be squeezed out by feelings that are kinder and more necessary" (16: 123; *PSS* 30: 151).

These apparent inconsistencies in Tolstoy's vision can be explained only at their beloved source, the worldview of Jean-Jacques Rousseau. As Thomas Barran advises in his illuminating comparison of "Rousseau's Political Vision and Tolstoy's *What is Art?*," Tolstoyan aesthetics must be approached as a politics – in the broad sense of philosophical anthropology, a meditation on what men live by.[8] Art will find its proper place only after life has been arranged so that people live by the right things. Thus Tolstoy can despise the developmental "historical view" and yet still posit a utopia up ahead, because, like Rousseau, he is convinced that humanity's task is not to move forward but to move back. Rectify the social error, and the Tolstoyan ideal of unity – which of course feels oppressive imposed upon our present multiplicity – must reveal itself as Rousseau's general will, the timeless standard.

These aspects of Rousseau's worldview (our natural goodness, the high worth of spontaneity, authenticity defined as a bypassing of the mental processes) help us to resolve another dilemma. Tolstoy himself was an indefatigable craftsman. Yet there is a curious effortlessness in his accounts of the production and reception of art. At times it seems to happen "by itself," without prior training or noticeable stress. In a probing essay, Gary Saul Morson discusses this issue in the larger context of "Work and the Authentic Life in Tolstoy."[9] Tolstoy was fascinated by daily work, and appalled that so many nineteenth-century novels ignored it (in favor of plots built around inheritance, crime, or carnal love). But what is work? It is obviously not tourism, seduction, military life, or the routines of high society. But it is also not merely strenuous activity, bureaucratic fussiness, or fulfilment of duties. For Tolstoy, "the right sort of work must be grounded in the essential things of life," Morson speculates. "It must seem so necessary as to be almost inevitable ... More than that, it must involve our whole self ... Finally, such work must be authentic, performed without pretense."[10] Placed within a Rousseauean perspective, this explicit parallel between art and work (not the familiar parallel between art and play) can help us to understand Tolstoy's dismissal of the entire historical aspect of art as a developing guild conscious-ness. Although Tolstoy does hold that Christian views on art are an important historical advance over pagan ones, there is no hint in his treatise that art it-self has a legitimate history, that it requires special languages, an institutional base with apprenticeships and hierarchies, or a critical apparatus.

Quite the contrary. Art schools and lessons not only squander money but cripple children physically and morally, requiring from them long hours of "playing scales, twisting their limbs, singing solfeggios" and – sooner or later – sketching lewd naked models. "Pseudo-artistic books spread depravity," as does regular contact with concerts, exhibitions, and galleries. The quest for professionalism so perverts young practitioners that "they lose all ability to produce genuine art" (17: 140; *PSS* 30: 169). Tolstoy insists that unperverted groups – "simple people and children" – immediately sense the wrongness of upper-class art. Greatness, to the unperverted mind, can only be a reward for physical strength (bestowed on a military hero) or moral strength (bestowed on an ascetic or saint). How, Tolstoy asks, can any hon-est simple person understand a monument to Pushkin, that "man of light morals," who wrote indecent verses and died trying to murder another man in a duel (17: 142–43; *PSS* 30: 171)?

This portion of Tolstoy's argument, when not dismissed as outright crank-ishness, has provoked spirited debate. Some peasants love Pushkin's verses. It is simply not true that a life of manual labor and authentic work has cleansed the Russian folk, any more than the rest of us, from violence, lazi-ness, stupidity, or craving for strong drink. And although a great primary artist like Tolstoy might believe that the secrets of creativity cannot be shared and should not be discussed in print, he should not conflate the private cre-ation of art with the public performance of it. How could so competent a pianist as Tolstoy not see the need for repetition and rehearsal? What is more, this father of thirteen children must have known that young people crave repetition and delimitation, and that at any age, deep psychological satis-faction can be had from ritualized activity. And yet, from Natasha Rostova at the opera in *War and Peace* to the clumsy parodies of Wagner in *What is Art?*, Tolstoy rejects conventionality in the art of the upper classes while not rejecting – or polemically not noticing – the high degree of conventionality in folk singing and folk art. Can these objections be met?

Probably only in part. But we might note certain refinements in Tolstoy's apparently brutal stance. For him, as for Rousseau, "spontaneity" did not mean arbitrariness or formless dionysian release; the discipline and tuning-up occurred within. Of course preliminary work happens (think of Mozart or Musorgsky with their impeccable manuscripts), but it should not be pa-raded for show. In her discussion of Tolstoy's attitude toward conventionality

in art, N. F. Filippova makes the sensible argument that Tolstoy indeed resisted fixed genres and schools as civilized forms of coercion, but his view
of aesthetic activity never endorsed unfettered free play.[11] In fact, she argues, one could hardly imagine an artist more possessed (on his own behalf,
and on behalf of his best-loved fictional characters) with *kak nado*, "how
precisely a thing is supposed to be done." It was Tolstoy's keen sense of pre-
cision and appropriateness that led him to oppose any mixing of the arts (as
in opera), any deforming of language to highlight a predetermined structure
(as in poetry or in Shakespeare's puns), and any abstraction – or distraction –
of an artistic medium from its singular expressive task.

"The artist of the future will live the ordinary life of a human being, earning
his living by some kind of labor" (19: 153; *PSS* 30: 182). By this renunciation
of professionalism, Tolstoy envisions more than just amateur art, and more
than a guarantee that talent will continue to develop outside exclusive caste
systems of wealth and privilege. He would mandate actual poverty for the
artist. "Giving artists security in their material needs is the most harmful
condition for artistic productivity," he writes, "because it releases the artist
from the condition proper to all men of struggling with nature to support his
own and other people's lives, and thereby deprives him of the occasion and
the possibility of experiencing the most important feelings proper to human
beings" (19: 153; *PSS* 30: 182). Again we recall the Voguls huddled in that
yurt, confronting in their art the most excruciating moments of their struggle
to survive. Again, authentic nature is understood as "conscience in human
beings and necessity in the outside world." And presiding over this utopian
vision is wealthy Count Leo Tolstoy, hopelessly endowed with too much
security, too many gifts, too many appetites, too many children, too many
words, trying vainly for the last thirty years of his life to cut a hole in this
pattern of life and escape. "So what then should we do, Lev Nikolaevich?
Really just give up writing?" asked Aleksandr Zhirkevich, military lawyer
and would-be poet, in December 1890. "Of course, give it up!" Tolstoy
answered. "That's what I say to all beginners. That's my usual advice. Now's
not the time to write . . ."[12]

In closing, let me suggest how we might come to terms with Tolstoy's paradoxical answers to *What is Art?* While his ideas do challenge mainstream
Western aesthetics, they are not wholly outside it. A sober analysis of the
art-as-infection thesis reveals that Tolstoy is not against differentiation, not
against individualized response, not opposed to artists perfecting their form,
and not in denial against the darkness of human nature (true art can be evil
while being authentic). Tolstoy's views on art have been undervalued in part
because they have been misclassified. No one would consider his treatise a

descriptive aesthetics of the artistic product. But it should also not be reduced entirely to an ethics. Tolstoy's aesthetics is closer to a psychology. What interests him are the psychological effects of producing and receiving art.

This is psychology in a special sense, however. It is of a different order than William James's celebrated portrait of the post-*Confession* Tolstoy as a "sick soul," published while Tolstoy was still alive (1902),[13] and bears no relation to the more recent attempts to psychoanalyze Tolstoy and his creations according to Freudian constructs. As provocative as those studies can be, the feeling remains that it is not for us to interrogate and reduce to system the inexhaustible creative energy of Leo Tolstoy. What is seemly to investigate, in my view, is how Tolstoy strove to stimulate a sense of artistic productivity and receptivity in others. In one of his abandoned drafts from the mid-1890s entitled "About what is and is not art, and when art is an important matter and when a trivial one," Tolstoy called the moment of self-elucidation (when the artist is infected and driven to articulate a feeling so as to share it) the moment of spiritual creativity (*dukhovnoe tvorchestvo*).[14] This moment begins within the self, out of nothing; it feels absolutely new. It is confirmed as infection spreads, and culminates in a community of artistically attuned persons, each raised to a higher level of awareness. There are parallels between the genesis of an artistic fact and the more general anti-entropic emergence of life itself: an organized set of relations enters into dynamic motion, becomes self-regulating, responsive to the environment, and able to rejuvenate new wholes from parts. Such analogies might indeed be of only peripheral relevance to a formalist or a neoplatonic theory of art. But they fit quite comfortably within the mid-twentieth-century American school of humanistic psychology, several of whose members have looked closely at the creative process and considered how to enhance it.

Erich Fromm's work on creative attitudes,[15] for example, or Abraham Maslow's studies of the peak experience, all bear comparison with *What is Art?* Maslow in particular discusses moments of "self-actualizing creativeness" in terms that Tolstoy would consider profoundly aesthetic.[16] During a peak experience, which shares certain traits with Tolstoyan infection, Maslow detects a kindred dual movement of the psyche toward unification with others while defining its uniqueness as a self: the soul becomes more whole, unified, ego-transcending, and self-forgetful precisely as it becomes more idiosyncratic.[17] Art is an efficient condenser of this paradoxical movement. The focus for these researchers, as for Tolstoy, is always on the psychological dynamics of the experience, not its product.

Tolstoy, of course, would not stop at "self-actualizing creativity" – the modest and merely private therapies of the American school. At the end of *What is Art?* Tolstoy asserts, perhaps with intonations of despair, that "everything, short of violence and punishment, that makes it possible for people to live together at present . . . all of it has been brought about by art" (20: 166; *PSS* 30: 194). Which is to say: aesthetics is indeed a type of politics. But more can be asked of it. Politics ties down and exhausts; successful art realizes a unity out of our natural variety, and comes with a sense of creation for free. As in Christ's most difficult parables, the selfish and recalcitrant participant reaps as many benefits as the most virtuously altruistic. Art must make us that offer, for we will agree to abandon our vices for nothing less. Tolstoy was a shrewd and unsentimental man. He surely felt that only the miraculous economy of art could hope to win over our flawed minds and bodies, turning brotherhood and love, that impossible ideal, into a "habitual feeling, an instinct for everyone" (20: 166; *PSS* 30: 195). Who would not wish to be drawn into its life-sustaining circle?

NOTES

1 Tolstoy to N. N. Strakhov, December 5 1883, in *Tolstoy's Letters*, ed. and trans. R. F. Christian Volume II: 1880–1910 (New York: Scribner, 1978), pp. 363–64. *PSS* 63: 142 (Nov. 30?–Dec. 1? 1883, Moscow).

2 Leo Tolstoy, *What is Art?*, trans. Richard Pevear and Larissa Volokhonsky (New York: Penguin Books, 1995), ch. 18, p. 148. Reference will be made to this edition, with translation adjusted where necessary toward greater literalness. Further chapter and page references will be given in the text, followed by references to volume and page numbers in the standard Russian Jubilee edition (*PSS*).

3 In the first chapter of his *Mimesis*, "Odysseus's Scar," Auerbach remarks on the detailed, fully illuminated richness of Homeric epic versus the nakedness of Old-Testament scenes and language. He suggests that the latter gains in "realness" and permanence to the extent that it is emptied of illustrative background – one way that Biblical narrative approaches the sublime. See Erich Auerbach, *Mimesis*, trans. Willard R. Trask (Princeton, NJ: Princeton University Press, 1953), pp. 3–23.

4 Donna Tussing Orwin, "The Return to Nature: Tolstoyan Echoes in *The Idiot*," in *The Russian Review*, 58 (January 1999), 87–102, esp. 91.

5 Richard F. Gustafson, *Leo Tolstoy: Resident and Stranger* (Princeton, NJ: Princeton University Press, 1986), Part two ("States of Human Awareness"), ch. 7, "Intoxicated Consciousness," pp. 338–402, esp. pp. 370–72.

6 *Ibid.*, p. 371.

7 "Progress and the Definition of Education" (1862), in *Tolstoy on Education*, trans. Leo Wiener (Chicago: University of Chicago Press, 1967), pp. 152–90, esp. p. 153. *PSS* 8: 325–55, esp. 326.

8 Thomas Barran, "Rousseau's Political Vision and Tolstoy's *What is Art?*," *Tolstoy Studies Journal* 5 (1992), 1–12.

9 Gary Saul Morson, "Work and the Authentic Life in Tolstoy," *Tolstoy Studies Journal* 9 (1997), 36–48.

10 *Ibid.*, p. 36.

11 N. F. Filippova, "Voprosy uslovnosti iskusstva v ponimanii Tolstogo," *Iasnopolianskii sbornik* (Tula: Tul'skoe Knizhnoe izdatel'stvo, 1972), pp. 187–98, esp. p. 187.

12 A. V. Zhirkevich (1857–1927), "Vstrechi s Tolstym," entry for December 20, 1890, in *L. N. Tolstoi v vospominaniiakh sovremennikov v dvukh tomakh* (Moscow: KhudLit, 1978), vol. II, p. 11.

13 William James, *The Varieties of Religious Experience* (first publ. 1902), ch. 6 and 7, "The Sick Soul."

14 "O tom, chto est' i chto ne est' iskusstvo, i o tom, kogda iskusstvo est' delo vazhnoe i kogda ono est' delo pustoe" (1895–97), in *PSS* 30: 442–54, esp. 447. In this earlier variant, Tolstoy's three criteria for true art are different: it must be full of significant content (*soderzhatel'nyi*), beautiful (*prekrasnyi*), and heartfelt (*zadushevnyi*). The absolute exile of the beautiful from Tolstoy's aesthetics, and its replacement with clarity, was a late development.

15 See Fromm's essay "The Creative Attitude" in Harold H. Anderson (ed.), *Creativity and its Cultivation* (New York: Harper & Brothers, 1959), pp. 44–54; also Erich Fromm, *Man for Himself: An Inquiry into the Psychology of Ethics* (New York: Holt, Rinehart and Winston, 1947), Part three, on the "productive orientation" as a character type, esp. pp. 82–98.

16 Abraham H. Maslow, "Creativity in Self-Actualizing People," ch. 7 in Anderson (ed.), *Creativity and its Cultivation*, pp. 83–95, esp. pp. 89–90.

17 Abraham H. Maslow, *Religions, Values, and Peak-Experiences* (New York: Penguin, 1970), p. 67.

GUIDE TO FURTHER READING

Most of the secondary works in this bibliography are in English, with only a few key Russian texts included. They have been selected by the editor with the help of individual bibliographies submitted by contributors. Many of the books contain highly interesting essays that are not listed separately, and also extensive bibliographies.

The publisher has used its best endeavors to ensure that URLs for external websites referred to in this book are correct and active at the time of going to press. However, the publisher has no responsibility for the websites and can make no guarantee that a site will remain live or that the content is or will remain appropriate.

Collected works

Polnoe sobranie sochinenii. 90 vols. Moscow: Gosudarstvennoe izdatel'stvo "Khudozhestvennaia literatura", 1928–58. This is the standard edition of Tolstoy's works in Russian. In addition to works and some drafts, it contains thirteen volumes of diaries and forty-one volumes of letters. A 120-volume new Russian edition is underway, but will take many years to complete.

The Centenary Edition of Tolstoy. Translated by Louise and Aylmer Maude. 21 vols. London: Oxford University Press, 1929–37.

Complete Works of Count Tolstoy. Translated by Leo Wiener. 24 vols. 1905. Reprinted New York: AMS Press Inc., 1968.

Tolstoy's Letters. Selected, edited, and translated by R. F. Christian. 2 vols. London: Athlone Press, 1978.

Tolstoy's Diaries. Edited and translated by R. F. Christian. 2 vols. London: Athlone Press, and New York: Scribner Press, 1985.

Bibliography

Egan, David R., and Melinda A. Egan, eds. *Leo Tolstoy: An Annotated Bibliography of English Language Sources to 1978.* Netuchen, New Jersey and London: Scarecrow Press, 1979.

Sendich, Munir. "Tolstoj's *War and Peace* in English: A Bibliography of Criticism (1879–1985)." *Russian Literature Triquarterly* 41, nos. 138–39 (1987), 219–79.

Sorokin, Boris. *Tolstoy in Prerevolutionary Criticism.* Miami, Ohio: Ohio State University Press, 1979.

Terry, G. M. "Tolstoy Studies in Great Britain: A Bibliographical Survey." In *New Essays on Tolstoy*, edited by Malcolm Jones, pp. 223–50. Cambridge: Cambridge University Press, 1978.

Wreath, P. J. and A. I. "Leo Tolstoy: A Bibliography of Criticism in English, from the Late Nineteenth Century through 1979." *Canadian–American Slavic Studies* 14 (1980), 466–512.

Journals and special issues on Tolstoy

Tolstoy Studies Journal. 1988–present. In addition to many articles, the journal, published annually, contains an annotated bibliography. For the contents of *TSJ*, see its website at www.utoronto.ca/tolstoy/.

The Russian Review (April 1960).

Canadian–American Slavic Studies 12 (1978).

Russian Literature 40.4 (November 1996).

Biography

Citati, Pietro. *Tolstoy.* Translated from Italian by Raymond Rosenthal. New York: Schocken Books, 1986.

Gorky, Maxim. *Reminiscences of Lev Nikolaevich Tolstoy.* Translated by S. S. Koteliansky and Leonard Woolf. New York: B. W. Huebsch, 1921.

Maude, Aylmer. *The Life of Tolstoy.* 2 vols. in 1. Oxford: Oxford University Press, 1987.

Rolland, Roman. *Tolstoy.* Translated from French by Bernard Miall. New York: E. P. Dutton and Co., 1911.

Shklovsky, Victor. *Lev Tolstoy.* Moscow: Progress Publishers, 1978.

Simmons, E. J. *Leo Tolstoy.* New York: Vintage, 1960.

Troyat, Henri. *Tolstoy.* Translation from the French. London, 1960.

Wilson, A. N. *Tolstoy.* London: Penguin, and New York: W. W. Norton and Co., 1988.

Critical studies

Bayley, John. *Tolstoy and the Novel.* New York: The Viking Press, 1966.

Benson, Ruth Crego. *Women in Tolstoy: The Ideal and the Erotic.* Urbana, Illinois: University of Illinois Press, 1973.

Berlin, Isaiah. *The Hedgehog and the Fox: An Essay on Tolstoy's View of History.* 1953. Reprinted New York: Simon and Schuster, 1970.

Bilinkis, Ia. *O tvorchestve L. N. Tolstogo: Ocherki.* Leningrad: Sovetskii pisatel', 1959.

Bloom, Harold, ed. *Leo Tolstoy: Modern Critical Views.* New York: Chelsea House Publishers, 1986.

Bunin, Ivan. *The Liberation of Tolstoy: A Tale of Two Writers.* Edited, translated, and with an introduction by Thomas Gaiton Marullo and Vladimir T. Khmelkov. Evanston, Illinois: Northwestern University Press, 2001.

Cain, T. G. S. *Tolstoy*. London: Paul Elek, 1977.

Christian, R. F. *Tolstoy: A Critical Introduction*. Cambridge: Cambridge University Press, 1969.

Coetzee, J. M. "Confession and Double Thought: Tolstoy, Rousseau, Dostoevsky." *Comparative Literature* 37.3 (Summer 1985), 193–232.

Donskov, Andrew, ed. *Lev Tolstoy and the Concept of Brotherhood*. Ottawa: Legas, 1996.

Eikhenbaum, Boris. *Tolstoy in the Seventies*. Translated by Albert Kaspin. Ann Arbor, Michigan: Ardis, 1982.

———. *Tolstoy in the Sixties*. Translated by Duffield White. Ann Arbor, Michigan: Ardis, 1982.

Emerson, Caryl. "The Tolstoy Connection in Bakhtin." *PMLA* 100 (January 1985), 68–80.

Feuer, Kathryn. "Solzhenitsyn and the Legacy of Tolstoy." In *Aleksandr Solzhenitsyn: Critical Essays and Documentary Materials*, eds. John B. Dunlop, Richard Hough, and Alexis Klimoff, pp. 129–46. Belmont, Massachusetts: Nordland, 1973.

Galagan, G. Ia. *L. N. Tolstoi: Khudozhestvenno-eticheskie iskaniia*. Leningrad: Izdatel'stvo "Nauka", 1981.

Gerigk, Horst-Jürgen. *Die Russen in Amerika: Dostojewskij, Tolstoj, Turgenjew und Tschechow in ihrer Bedeutung für die Literatur der USA*. Hürtgenwald: G. Pressler, 1995.

Gifford, Henry. *Leo Tolstoy: A Critical Anthology*. Harmondsworth: Penguin, 1971.

Ginzburg, Lydia. *On Psychological Prose*. Translated and edited by Judson Rosengrant. Princeton, New Jersey: Princeton University Press, 1991.

Greenwood, E. B. *Tolstoy: The Comprehensive Vision*. London: J. M. Dent and Sons Ltd., 1975.

Gustafson, Richard F. *Leo Tolstoy: Resident and Stranger; A Study in Fiction and Theology*. Princeton, New Jersey: Princeton University Press, 1986.

Hamburger, K. *Leo Tolstoi: Gestalt und Problem*. Bern: A. Franke, 1950.

Jones, Malcolm. *New Essays on Tolstoy*. Cambridge: Cambridge University Press, 1978.

Jones, W. Gareth, ed. *Tolstoi and Britain*. Washington, D. C.: Berg Publishers, 1995.

Katz, Michael R., ed. *Tolstoy's Short Fiction*. New York and London: W. W. Norton & Co., 1991.

Knowles, A. V., ed. *Tolstoy: The Critical Heritage*. London and Boston: Routledge and Kegan Paul Ltd., 1978.

Kupreianova, E. N. *Estetika L. N. Tolstogo*. Moscow and Leningrad: Izdatel'stvo "Nauka", 1966.

Lednicki, Waclaw. *Tolstoy Between War and Peace*. Reprinted The Hague: Mouton and Co., 1965.

Mann, Thomas. "Goethe and Tolstoy." In *Thomas Mann: Essays of Three Decades*. Translated from the German by H. T. Lowe-Porter, pp. 93–175. New York: Alfred A. Knopf, 1947. [Also contains an essay on *Anna Karenina*.]

Markovitch, Milan I. *Jean-Jacques Rousseau et Tolstoi*. Paris, 1928.

Matlaw Ralph, ed. *Tolstoy: A Collection of Critical Essays*. Englewood Cliffs, New Jersey: Prentice-Hall, 1967. [This anthology includes essays not available elsewhere.]

Maude, Aylmer. *Tolstoy and His Problems: Essays*. 2nd edn. New York: Haskell House, 1974.

McLean, Hugh, ed. *In the Shadow of the Giant: Essays on Tolstoy*. Vol. XIII, California Slavic Studies. Berkeley: University of California Press, 1989.

Merezhkovsky, D. S. *Tolstoi as Man and Artist. With an Essay on Dostoevski*. London: Archibald Constable, 1902. Reprinted St. Clair Shores, Michigan: Scholarly Press, 1970.

Morson, Gary Saul. *Narrative and Freedom: The Shadows of Time*. New Haven, Connecticut: Yale University Press, 1994. [Contains discussions of both *War and Peace* and *Anna Karenina*.]

_____ . "Tolstoy's Absolute Language." *Critical Inquiry* 7, no. 4 (Summer 1981), 667–87.

Noyes, G. R. *Tolstoy*. New York: Duffield, 1918.

_____ . *Oreligii L'va Tolstoyo: Sbornik Statei* 1912. Reprinted Paris: YMCA Press, 1976.

Orwin, Donna Tussing. *Tolstoy's Art and Thought, 1847–1880*. Princeton, New Jersey: Princeton University Press, 1993.

Price, Martin. "Tolstoy and the Forms of Life." In *Forms of Life: Character and Moral Imagination in the Novel*, pp. 176–203. New Haven, Connecticut: Yale University Press, 1983.

Rancour-Laferriere, D. *Tolstoy on the Couch: Misogyny, Masochism and the Absent Mother*. New York: New York University Press, 1998.

Rowe, William W. *Leo Tolstoy*. Boston: Twayne Publishers, 1986.

Rzhevsky, Nicholas. *Russian Literature and Ideology: Hertzen, Dostoevsky, Leontiev, Tolstoy, Fadeyev*. Urbana, Illinois: University of Illinois Press, 1993.

Sampson, R. V. *Tolstoy: The Discovery of Peace*. London: Heinemann, 1973.

Sankovitch, Natasha. *Creating and Recovering Experience: Repetition in Tolstoy*. Stanford, California: Stanford University Press, 1998.

Shestov, Leo. *Dostoevsky, Tolstoy and Nietzsche*. Athens, Ohio: Ohio University Press, 1969.

Silbajoris, Rimvydas. *Tolstoy's Aesthetics and His Art*. Columbus, Ohio: Slavica Publishers, 1990, 1991.

Spence, G. W. *Tolstoy the Ascetic*. London and Edinburgh: Oliver and Boyd, 1967.

Steiner, George. *Tolstoy or Dostoevsky: An Essay in the Old Criticism*. 2nd edn. New Haven, Connecticut: Yale University Press, 1996.

Wasiolek, Edward. *Tolstoy's Major Fiction*. Chicago: University of Chicago Press, 1978.

_____ , ed. *Critical Essays on Tolstoy*. Boston: G. K. Hall and Co., 1986.

Williams, Gareth. *Tolstoy's Childhood*. London: Bristol Classical Press, 1995.

Early works

Dieckmann, Eberhard. *Erzählformen in Frühwerk L. N. Tolstojs, 1851–1857*. Berlin: Academie-Verlag, 1969.

Eikhenbaum, Boris. *The Young Tolstoi*. Translated and edited by Gary Kern. Ann Arbor, Michigan: Ardis, 1972.

Jackson, Robert Louis. "The Archetypal Journey: Aesthetic and Ethical Imperatives in the Art of Tolstoj: *The Cossacks*." *Russian Literature* 11.4 (1982), 389–410.

Jones, W. Gareth. "The Nature of the Communication between Author and Reader in Tolstoy's *Childhood.*" *Slavic and East European Journal* 55 (1977), 506–16.

Wachtel, Andrew Baruch. *The Battle for Childhood: Creation of a Russian Myth.* Stanford, California: Stanford University Press, 1990.

Zweers, Alexander. *Grown-up Narrator and Childlike Hero: An Analysis of the Literary Devices Employed in Tolstoy's Trilogy, "Childhood," "Boyhood," and "Youth."* The Hague: Mouton, 1971.

Critical studies of War and Peace

Bocharov, S. *Roman L. Tolstogo "Voina i mir."* Moscow: Gosudarstvennoe izdatel' stvo khudozhestvennoi literatury, 1863.

Carden, Patricia. "Career in *War and Peace.*" *Ulbandus Review* 2, no. 2 (Fall 1982), 23–37.

_____ . "The Recuperative Powers of Memory: Tolstoy's *War and Peace.*" In *The Russian Novel from Pushkin to Pasternak*, edited by John Garrard, pp. 81–102. New Haven, Connecticut: Yale University Press, 1983.

Christian, R. F. *Tolstoy's "War and Peace."* Oxford: Clarendon Press, 1962.

Clay, George R. *Tolstoy's Phoenix: From Method to Meaning in* War and Peace. Evanston, Illinois: Northwestern University Press, 1998.

Feuer, Kathryn. *The Genesis of War and Peace.* Edited by Robin Feuer Miller and Donna Tussing Orwin. Ithaca, New York: Cornell University Press, 1996.

Jackson, Robert Louis. "Pierre and Dolokhov at the Barrier. The Lesson of the Duel." *Scando-Slavica* 39 (1993), 52–61.

_____ . "The Second Birth of Pierre Bezukhov." *Canadian-American Slavic Studies* 12, no. 4 (Winter 1978), 535–42.

Lehrman, E. H. *A Guide to the Russian Texts of Tolstoy's "War and Peace."* Ann Arbor, Michigan: Ardis, 1980.

Leontiev, Konstantin. "The Novels of Count L. Tolstoy: Analysis, Style, and Atmosphere." 1890. Reprinted in *Essays in Russian Literature. The Conservative View: Leontien, Rosanov, Shestov*, pp. 225–356. Athens, Ohio: Ohio University Press, 1968.

Morson, Gary Saul. *Hidden in Plain View: Narrative and Creative Potentials in "War and Peace".* Stanford, California: Stanford University Press, 1987.

Rancour-Laferriere, Daniel. *Tolstoy's Pierre Bezukhov. A Psychoanalytical Study.* London: Bristol Classical Press, 1993.

Shklovsky, Viktor. *Material i stil' v romane "Voina i mir" L'va Tolstogo.* 1928. Reprinted The Hague: Mouton, 1970.

Sloane, David. "The Poetry in *War and Peace.*" *Slavic and East European Journal* 40 (Spring 1996), 63–84.

Wachtel, Andrew Baruch. "*War and Peace*: Intergeneric Dialogue in One Text." In *An Obsession with History: Russian Writers Confront the Past*, pp. 88–122. Stanford, California: Stanford University Press, 1994.

Critical studies of Anna Karenina

Arnold, Matthew. "Count Leo Tolstoy." In *Essays in Criticism*, 2nd ser. London, 1888.

Babaev, E. *"Anna Karenina" L. N. Tolstogo.* Moscow: Khudozhestvennaia literatura, 1978.

Blackmur, R. P. "*Anna Karenina*: The Dialectic of Incarnation." *Kenyon Review* 12 (1950), 433: 56.

Feuer, Kathryn B. "Stiva." In *Russian Literature and American Critics*, edited by Kenneth Brostrom, pp. 347–57. Ann Arbor, Michigan: University of Michigan Press, 1984.

Jackson, Robert Louis. "Chance and Design in *Anna Karenina*." In *The Disciplines of Criticism: Essays in Literary Theory, Interpretation and History*, edited by Peter Demetz, Thomas Greene, and Lowry Nelson, Jr., pp. 315–29. New Haven, Connecticut: Yale University Press, 1968.

_____ . "On the Ambivalent Beginning of *Anna Karenina*." In *Semiotic Analysis of Literary Texts*, edited by E. De Haard, T. Langerak, and W. G. Weststeijn. Amsterdam: Elsevier, 1990, pp. 345–53.

Leavis, F. R. *"Anna Karenina."* *Critical Quarterly* 2 (1965–66), 5–27.

Mandelker, Amy. *Framing Anna Karenina: Tolstoy, the Woman Question and the Victorian Novel.* Columbus, Ohio: Ohio State University Press, 1993.

_____ . "The Woman with a Shadow: Fables of Demon and Psyche in *Anna Karenina*." *Novel* (Fall 1990), 48–68.

Turner, C. J. G. *A Karenina Companion.* Waterloo, Ontario: Wilfred Laurier University Press, 1993.

Critical studies of Resurrection

Cruise, Edwina Jannie. "The Ideal Woman in Tolstoi: *Resurrection*." *Canadian-American Slavic Studies* 11, no. 2 (Summer 1977), 281–86.

Nivat, Georges. "L'Effacement de Nekhlioudov (Remarques sur *Résurrection*)." In *Tolstoi Aujourd'hui, Colloque International Tolstoi* (Paris: Institut d'Etudes Slaves, 1980), pp. 193–98.

Orwin, Donna Tussing. "The Riddle of Prince Nexljudov," *Slavic and East European Journal* 30, no. 4 (1986), 473–86.

Semon, Marie, ed. *A propos de "Résurrection."* Paris: Institut d'Etudes Slaves, 1996.

Zirin, Mary. "Prince Dmitrii Nekhlyudov: A Synthetic Portrait." *Russian Literature Triquarterly*, no. 17 (1982), 85–101.

Late works

Dayananda, Y. J. "The Death of Ivan Ilych: A Psychological Study on Death and Dying." *Literature and Psychology* 22 (1972), 191–98.

Halperin, Irving. "The Structural Integrity of *The Death of Ivan Il'ic*." *Slavic and East European Journal* 5 (1961), 334–40.

Hirshberg, W. R. 'Tolstoy's *The Death of Ivan Ilich*." *Explicator* 28, Item 26 (1969).

Jahn, Gary R. *The Death of Ivan Ilich: An Interpretation.* New York: Twayne Publishers, 1993.

_____ . "L. N. Tolstoj's Narodnye rasskazy." *Russian Language Journal* vol. 31, no. 109 (1977), 67–78.

_____ . "L. N. Tolstoj's Vision of the Power of Death and 'How Much Land Does a Man Need?'." *Slavic and East European Journal* 22 (1978), 442–53.

_____ . "A Structural Analysis of Leo Tolstoy's *God Sees the Truth, But Waits.*" *Studies in Short Fiction* 12 (1975), 261–70.

_____ . "Tolstoj and Folklore: The Case of 'Chem ljudi zhivy'." *Russian Language Journal* 44.147–49 (1990), 135–50.

Lindstrom, Thais. "From Chapbooks to Classics: The Story of the Intermediary." *American Slavic and East European Review* 2 (1957), 190–201.

_____ . *The Death of Ivan Ilych: A Critical Companion.* Evanston, Illinois: Northwestern University Press, 1999.

_____ . "The Role of the Ending in Lev Tolstoi's *The Death of Ivan Il'ich.*" *Canadian Slavonic Papers* 24, no. 3 (September 1982), 229–38.

Möller, Peter Ulf. *Postlude to The Kreutzer Sonata: Tolstoi and the Debate on Sexual Morality in Russian Literature in the 1890s.* Translated by John Kendal. Leiden, New York, Copenhagen, and Cologne: E. J. Brill, 1988.

Olney, James. "Experience, Metaphor, and Meaning: *The Death of Ivan Ilych,*" *Journal of Aesthetics and Art Criticism* 31 (1972), 101–14.

Orwin, Donna Tussing. "Nature and the Narrator in *Hadji-Murad.*" *Russian Literature* 28 (1990), 125–44.

Shestov, Leo. "The Last Judgement: Tolstoy's Last Works," In *Job's Balances: On the Sources of the Eternal Truths*, pp. 83–138. 1935. Reprinted Athens, Ohio: Ohio University Press, 1975.

Turner, C. J. W. "The Language of Fiction: Word Clusters in Tolstoy's *The Death of Ivan Ilyich.*" *Modern Language Review* 65 (1970), 116–21.

Wasiolek, Edward. "Tolstoy's *The Death of Ivan Ilych* and Jamesian Fictional Imperatives." *Modern Fiction Studies* 6 (1960), 314–24.

INDEX TO TOLSTOY'S WORKS AND CHARACTERS